CROWS AND JAYS

CROWS AND JAYS

Steve Madge and Hilary Burn

Princeton University Press
Princeton, New Jersey

This paperback edition first published 1999

Copyright © 1994 Steve Madge and Hilary Burn

Published in the United States, Canada, and the Philippine Islands by
Princeton University Press, 41 William Street, Princeton, New Jersey 08540

In the United Kingdom and European Union, published by Christopher Helm,
an imprint of A & C Black Ltd., 37 Soho Square, London W1D 3QZ

Library of Congress Catalog Card Number 00-112184

ISBN 0-691-08883-7

This book has been composed in Optima

www.birds.princeton.edu

Printed in Hong Kong through Colorcraft Ltd.

10 9 8 7 6 5 4 3 2 1

CONTENTS

Systematic list of genera, subgenera and species of the *Corvini*

INTRODUCTION

Crows have fascinated man for a very long time; their black plumage, supreme avian intelligence, longevity and melancholy voices have involved some of the more familiar species in folklore, mythology and the supernatural. The most widespread of all corvids, the Raven (Northern Raven) with its ominous, deep croaking voice, and 'black cross' silhouette, is a prime example.

In Norse mythology the god Odin had two sacred ravens, Huginn and Munnin ('Thought' and 'Memory'), who flew about the world during the day and returned to their master in the evening to tell all that they had observed. In other parts of western Europe the raven has been considered a bird of ill omen, possibly linked in no small part to the raids of Viking invaders. In the Celtic Welsh, Cornish, and Breton languages, the raven is known as 'Bran', which was also the name of a Celtic warrior god who was accompanied by a raven. The raven became a symbol of death, particularly heroic death on the battlefield, in Celtic and other legends. In Cornwall tradition has it that both the raven and the chough (Red-billed) hold the spirit of the legendary King Arthur and that misfortune will befall those who harm them. It was a raven that left Noah's Ark to seek dry land but returned, not to the Ark, but to feed on the drowned corpses nearby; for this it was transformed from a white bird into a black one and its song reduced to a guttural croak. There are many other raven legends from around the northern hemisphere, from Siberia to North America, from Greek mythology to the present day. Even in the late 20th century ravens are held at the Tower of London, in the belief that when the last ravens leave the tower, the tower will fall.

Mystique also surrounds other species, from folk rhymes associated with numbers of magpies to tales of jackdaws stealing rings and in India, stories of the House Crow being immortal. However, these birds are far from immortal, although their super-abundance at many coastal towns in the Middle East and East Africa is testimony to their great success as colonisers and makes immortality seem quite plausible. The future of the House Crow, possibly the only bird species totally dependant upon man for its existence, is safe but no less than 22 of the other 121 world corvids are endangered on an international scale. It is these species that might well become legendary in the not too distant future, in some cases before we know very much about them and their requirements. Even a number of widespread species are decreasing in parts of their world range (e.g. Red-billed Chough).

The great majority of crows, jays and magpies are resident, territorial species. This has given rise to a remarkable degree of endemism through geographical isolation, particularly in the tropics of Central America, northern South America, south-east Asia and the islands of the East Indies. These species are dependant upon man for their future survival merely through his restraint in forest destruction and over-grazing by domestic animals. Such habitat degradation not only fragments the ranges of rare, specialised species, but allows more successful congeners to expand into their ranges and compete with them.

It is true that this fascinating family of birds is not the most popular with birdwatchers, and even many keen field workers tend to dismiss them as uninteresting, preferring to concentrate on the subtleties of waders, gulls, raptors, pipits and warblers. However, what better challenge to the travelling birder could there be than to move from island to island in the East Indies and the Philippines, armed with a tape recorder and notebook, and attempt to sort out the relationships between the variety of crows that inhabit these islands? Most published contributions have so far been based on surveys of museum material, and these have produced conflicting opinions on the precise relationships of these island forms. Only detailed behavioural and vocal studies will resolve these taxonomic problems, as was so admirably carried out in the 1970s with the Australian crows and ravens.

Despite man's long association with corvids, chiefly in regarding them as pests to be controlled or as birds of ill omen, much remains to be discovered about many species. Derek Goodwin's superb monograph *Crows of the World*, first published in 1976, brought the whole group into focus for the birding public to admire; his work drew our attention to gaps in our knowledge and even nearly 20 years later many of the gaps still exist. These have also been emphasised in our book, which we hope will further stimulate interest and fascination for these remarkable birds.

Our researches have been fairly comprehensive but with such a plethora of journals, we will have overlooked some important published information. The author would be grateful to learn of errors for correction, or overlooked papers and updated information for inclusion in future editions. Please address any correspondence to the publishers.

ACKNOWLEDGEMENTS

A work of this nature relies heavily on previously published material. We therefore would like to thank all corvid specialists whose papers and books appear in the Bibliography. We are particularly indebted to Derek Goodwin, whose monograph *Crows of the World* was a source both of reference and inspiration. We also thank him for commenting on parts of the text.

For the loan of specimens and allowing access to their collections we are indebted to the Zoology Department at Liverpool Museum and the British Museum (Natural History) at Tring; at Liverpool special thanks go to Tony Parker and at Tring to Michael Walters and Peter Colston for making this possible. John Meek of The Tropical Bird Gardens at Rode allowed access to their collection of living birds and helped with various enquiries. Hadoram Shirihai willingly gave copies of the corvid texts from his forthcoming *Birds of Israel*.

Many others supported us in answering our queries, reading sections of text and in obtaining obscure reference materials:-

Norman Arlott, John Ash, Mark Van Beirs, Darrell Clegg, Tzidipzhap Dorzhiev (Novosibirsk State University, Buryat Branch, Ulan Ude), Chris Doughty, Tim Fisher, Orlando Garrido (Academia de Ciencias de Cuba, Havana), Mary LeCroy (American Museum of Natural History, New York), Sara McMahon (Plymouth University), David Mead, Rich Meyer (Operation Chough Project), Alex Randall, Craig Robson, Ian Rowley (CSIRO, Australia), Richard Schofield, Dave Showler, Steve Smith and Tim Webber (Florida Museum of Natural History). Particular thanks go to Craig Robson and Steve Smith for access to their sound recordings of oriental species.

Special thanks to Marc Dando for handling the technical side of producing the maps and getting the text transferred to a compatible format; to Nigel Redman and Iain Robertson for reading through the text and to Christopher Helm for overseeing the entire project. Not least we extend our gratitude to our families; Hilary to Dave and Steve to Penny, Bryony and Elysia. Without their support this project would have been longer in fruition.

CONSERVATION

Our knowledge of the world's birds has increased dramatically in recent decades; previously undescribed populations and even species are being discovered almost annually. This is partly due to the number of new field guides being published which has permitted easier access to information on birds of relatively obscure parts of the world. World travel has become relatively easy and field skills have developed to a remarkable degree. Many more people than ever before now have a chance of contributing to our knowledge of little known or rare species. Conversely, rare species have greater threats to their continued survival than ever before. Habitat destruction, especially through excessive forest clearance, damming of major river systems, cultivation of natural grasslands, irrigation of deserts, overgrazing by domestic animals and pollution, is fragmenting the ranges of many birds to dangerously low levels.

We can all help to improve this situation by supporting wildlife conservation organisations and also by making personal field records and tape-recordings of little known species more widely available. The following organisations in particular would benefit from this kind of support.

Field observations
ORIENTAL BIRD CLUB
c/o The Lodge, Sandy, Bedforshire SG19 2DL, UK.

NEOTROPICAL BIRD CLUB
c/o The Lodge, Sandy, Bedforshire SG19 2DL, UK.

These two organisations are involved in promoting the study and conservation of birds in regions containing some of the most vulnerable corvid species. Both welcome field observations from amateur birdwatchers.

Sound Recordings
BRITISH LIBRARY OF WILDLIFE SOUNDS (BLOWS)
The National Sound Archive, 29 Exhibition Road, London SW7 2AS, UK.

LIBRARY OF NATURAL SOUNDS (LNS)
Cornell Laboratory of Ornithology, 159 Sapsucker Woods Road, Ithaca, New York 14850, USA.

These two major organisations have extensive archival collections of worldwide bird sounds. As some 1800 species still remain to be sound-recorded, new, properly-documented, material of little-known species is welcome.

Endangered and threatened species
BIRDLIFE INTERNATIONAL (formerly ICBP)
Wellbrook Court, Girton Road, Cambridge CB3 0NA, UK.

An influential worldwide organisation specialising in bird conservation, which is responsible for many important publications and surveys, including the Bird Red Data books.

BirdLife International list 22 species of corvid as globally endangered or threatened (see Collar and Andrew 1988). Observations concerning these species would be welcomed by them at the address given above:-
Beautiful Jay *Cyanolyca pulchra* : Colombia and Ecuador.
Dwarf Jay *Cyanolyca nana* : Mexico.

White-throated Jay *Cyanolyca mirabilis* : Mexico.
Azure Jay *Cyanocorax caeruleus* : Brazil and Argentina.
Tufted Jay *Cyanocorax dickeyi* : Mexico.
Sichuan Jay *Perisoreus internigrans* : China.
Lidth's Jay *Garrulus lidthi* : Japan.
Ceylon Magpie *Urocissa ornata* : Sri Lanka.
White-winged Magpie *Urocissa whiteheadi* : China, Laos, Vietnam.
Ratchet-tailed Treepie *Temnurus temnurus* : China, Vietnam, Thailand.
Collared Treepie *Dedrocitta frontalis* : India to Vietnam.
Andaman Treepie *Dendrocitta bayleyi* : Andaman islands (India).
White-bellied Treepie *Dendrocitta leucogastra* : India.
Hooded Treepie *Crypsirina cucullata* : Burma.
Stresemann's Bush-Crow *Zavattariornis stresemanni* : Ethiopia.
Pleske's Ground-Jay *Podoces pleskei* : Iran.
Banggai Crow *Corvus unicolor* : Indonesia.
Flores Crow *Corvus florensis* : Indonesia.
Mariana Crow *Corvus kubaryi* : Marianas islands, Western Pacific.
Hawaiian Crow *Corvus hawaiiensis* : Hawaii.
Palm Crow *Corvus palmarum* : Cuba, Haiti and Dominican Republic.
White-necked Crow *Corvus leucognaphalus* : Haiti and Dominican Republic.

RELATIONSHIPS AND ORIGINS

Until recently the species treated in this work constituted a well defined family, the *Corvidae*, and were considered amongst the most advanced in evolutionary terms of all bird families. However, recent research into avian genetics in the USA has resulted in a monumental reclassification of the world's birds (Sibley and Ahlquist 1990 and Sibley and Monroe 1990) which has turned the long accepted sequences inside out and divided and lumped former bird families.

This reclassification is controversial and has had a mixed reception. Are such monumental changes in the sequences of standard ornithological literature necessary? Only the future will show how well this innovative classification will stand the test of time and further research. Luckily the treatment of the corvids has escaped major revision, only the precise limits of the family *Corvidae* have been expanded.

Under this new classification, which is still regarded as controversial, the family *Corvidae* has been expanded to encompass a vast assemblage of almost 650 passerine species and now includes birds as diverse as the Birds-of-Paradise, Cuckoo-shrikes, Minivets, Paradise Flycatchers, Jewel-babblers, Quail-thrushes, Orioles, Bush-shrikes, Sittellas, Drongos and many more. To simplify matters this huge family has been divided into Subfamilies and these have been further subdivided into Tribes; species included in the former family *Corvidae* are now relegated to the Tribe *Corvini* within the Subfamily *Corvinae* of the family *Corvidae*.

Subfamily *Corvinae* (297 species, 56 genera)

Tribe *Corvini*
Crows, Jays and allies (113 species, 25 genera).

Tribe *Paradisaeini*
Birds-of-paradise (45 species, 17 genera).

Tribe *Artamini*
Butcherbirds, Currawongs and Wood-swallows (24 species, 6 genera).

Tribe *Oriolini*
Old World Orioles, Cuckoo-shrikes and Minivets (111 species, 8 genera).

Characters of the *Corvini*
Members of the *Corvini* have certain characteristics that unite them; not all of these are unique to the group but they are shared by the majority of corvids.

Structure
The most obvious feature of the group is the tuft of nasal bristles extending forwards over the base of the upper mandible to conceal or partially conceal the rounded nostril opening. At the base of the bill in the loral and gape region are finer, more hair-like, rictal bristles. The bill itself, although variable in shape, is generally stout or slim, relatively long and the culmen curves to a slightly overlapping tip. Corvids have very strong feet, especially the toes and claws and their tarsi are strongly scaled at the front, but smooth at the rear. Primaries and tail feathers are relatively stiff, especially the primaries of *Corvus* species and related genera.

Plumage
Despite tremendous variation in colouration and patterning, no corvids show heavy streaking or vermiculations on the body plumage; many, however, have complex markings on their wings and tail and some nutcrackers have very extensive white spotting on their body plumage. Plumage colouration varies little between the sexes and with age, although in the short-lived juvenile plumage stage the colouration is invariably drabber than in adults and the feathers softer in texture. Unlike many groups of passerines the juvenile plumage is unspotted; an

apparent exception is the primitive Crested Jay which does show vestigial spotting, especially on the wings.

Behaviour

Certain behavioural traits are shared by nearly all corvids. Vocally they typically utter harsh, squawks, croaks or screeching calls, but, despite this, many corvids have a remarkably varied vocabulary. Their display behaviour is complex and plays an important role in mate selection and pair-bonding; indeed many of the larger species are believed to pair for life. Nests are relatively bulky and are constructed chiefly of twigs with a softly-lined interior cup by both sexes. Both parents share the duties of feeding the young, although only the female incubates the eggs and broods the nestlings (there are very few proven exceptions to this). The male feeds the female at the nest and both sexes feed the young. Food is not carried to the nest in the mandibles as in most other passerines; food items are either carried in the throat or in a small pouch within the chin (the sublingual pouch). Large food items and nuts are held by the foot and stabbed at or torn with the bill and most of the genera are known to store or hide surplus food items. All corvids are single-brooded, and with very few exceptions, lay mottled eggs. The great majority are resident, or locally dispersive, although northern populations of some Northern Hemisphere species are quite highly migratory.

Variation and Origins of the *Corvini*

The *Corvini* are amongst the most varied of all passerine 'families', especially in size, and in this respect can be compared more with some of the non-passerine groups such as the woodpeckers or pigeons and doves. The two extremes are the diminutive Hume's Ground-Jay of Tibet, only 19 cm in length and weighing a meagre 45 grams and the Thick-billed Raven of Ethiopia, marginally the largest of all passerines (followed closely by some races of the Northern Raven) which is 64 cm long and weighs approximately 1500 grams.

Between these two extremes, speciation has produced a tremendous variety of corvids, especially in the tropics of Central and South America and in south-east Asia. Tropical Africa is remarkably poor by comparison although an interesting parallel is shown by a quite unrelated family, the *Picidae* (woodpeckers). However Africa does contain two of the most aberrant of all corvids, each in a monotypic genus. The table below lists the number of endemic corvid species in each of the the main faunal regions and the genera chiefly confined to these regions:-

Australasian	Oriental	Neotropical	Afrotropical	Palearctic	Nearctic
9	27	36	6	18	9
	Platylophus	*Cyanolyca*	*Ptilosomus*	*Cyanopica*	*Gymnorhinus*
	Platysmurus	*Cynocorax*	*Zavattariornis*	*Podoces*	
	Urocissa	*Psilorhinus*		*Pseudopodoces*	
	Cissa	*Calocitta*		*Pyrrhocorax*	
	Dendrocitta				
	Crypsirina				
	Temnurus				

The high number of endemic genera in the Oriental region suggests that ancestral corvids originated in that region, radiating out during a northwards expansion into the adjacent Palearctic and across the land-bridge between Siberia and North America eventually to reach the tropics of Central and South America. However, the fact that two very primitive corvids exist in Africa suggests that some forms must have been evolving there a very long time ago, but why there are no tropical forest corvids in Africa is a mystery. It is also notable that there are no endemic Australasian genera, no naturally occurring corvids at all on New Zealand (the Rook has been introduced) and very few on the most far-flung of the the Pacific islands (just the Hawaiian and Mariana Crows).

FORMAT OF THE BOOK

This book has been divided into two major sections; the colour plates, together with the maps and brief caption texts and the species accounts in systematic order. Both sections are cross-referenced after the species headings.

The plates
The colour plates depict the main plumage stages and extremes of racial variation for each species. On the facing caption pages are short texts to highlight useful identification features alongside world distribution maps. These captions are brief in the case of island endemics where no confusion species share their ranges. Groups of similar species from each region have generally been depicted together for comparison; this has not always been possible and some strange combinations occur on the few plates which contain monotypic genera or aberrant species. Figures are to scale within each plate, genus or group of genera. Corvids show little plumage variation between the sexes although males are typically a little larger than females. Juveniles have only been shown if they differ substantially from adults, although a few individuals of each major genus have been included; this plumage stage is quickly replaced in corvids and is only worn for a few weeks after fledging, during which time juveniles remain chiefly in the company of their parents. Flying figures have been included for those species with distinctive wing or tail patterns to clarify the extent of these markings which may not be apparent on the perched individual (e.g. American Jays and Ground-Jays) or simply to show differences in wing and tail shape (e.g. in some crows).

The maps
All species have distribution maps showing main breeding and non-breeding ranges. Maps should be read with a degree of caution as the chances of locating a species within a mapped range depends upon habitat availability and population density. The current known range of rarer species which have contracted their ranges is shown. The maps should be used in conjunction with the more detailed information given in the main text under the Distribution, Habitat and Status sections.

Map colours:-
Green: Areas where birds may be expected throughout the year.
Yellow: Regular breeding areas, but birds are normally only present in the breeding season. Although the majority of corvids are largely sedentary by nature, northern populations of several species are strongly migratory.
Blue: Areas where birds occur, but do not breed, either in winter or during seasonal dispersal. Areas where migrants can be expected to occur on passage or as vagrants are not shown.

The systematic section
The species accounts follow a specific format, the conventions of which are summarised below:-

Sequence: Opinions on the classification sequence and number of genera of corvids differ considerably. The sequence and naming of genera in this work follow the recent revision of the classification of all birds by Sibley and Monroe (1990). In general this treatment is quite controversial but the corvid sequence is remarkably similar to that suggested in Peters (1962), which was also adopted by Voous (1977).

Names: Selecting English names for a work of worldwide coverage creates special problems. For example there are birds known as 'Black Magpie' in Africa and in tropical Asia; both are very different species in their own monotypic genera. Common names also often differ in various parts of the English-speaking world. In recent years attempts have been made, with varying degrees of success, to standardise them.
The names used in this work have been compiled from the most recent regional reference sources: the RAOU list (1978) for Australasia, the AOU checklist (1983) for North and Central America, Ridgely and

Tudor (1989) for South America, Britton (1980) and Maclean (1985) for Africa, White and Bruce (1986) for Wallacea and King *et al* (1975) and Sibley and Monroe (1990) for tropical Asia.

The Oriental region was the most problematic. At present the Oriental Bird Club recommends using the names employed by Sibley and Monroe in their publications pending publication of their own checklist. Therefore the Sibley and Monroe names have been followed rather than the more traditional names of Indian and older Asian literature.

The author is not entirely happy with the modern attempts to standardise English names by placing adjectives before well-established common names 'to avoid confusion'. For example, European field-guides have simply used Chough and Alpine Chough for many decades without any apparent confusion. However, as this trend seems to be inevitable species such as Jackdaw, Jay, Nutcracker, Chough and Raven are here called Western Jackdaw, Eurasian Jay, Spotted Nutcracker, Red-billed Chough and Northern Raven.

Certain controversial taxa which are probably well on their way towards speciation, have been given separate accounts after the main species entry. Thus we have Hooded and Mesopotamian Crows after Carrion Crow; such forms are indicated by the specific part of the scientific name being placed in parentheses, e.g. *Corvus (corone) cornix* for Hooded Crow.

Alternative names: Alternative English names used in other works are given after the main heading to ease cross-referencing to other literature.

Identification: This section summarises the major features of a species to enable a rapid identification. Ageing and sexing criteria are not mentioned here unless relevant to distinguishing the species from other similar ones. In the case of very distinctive species this section may be brief, but is considerably expanded when discussing difficult groups.

Description: A relatively detailed descrip-tion of a fully adult bird is given here. The descriptions are not necessarily feather-by-feather, which would become too unwieldy to be of much use in the field, but summarise the basic patterns and colours of the plumage and bare parts (bill, irides and legs). This section expands on the specific highlights given under Identification. The terms used in the plumage descriptions are shown on page xx. Where wing formulae have been compared, the primaries have been numbered ascendantly, i.e. the short outermost primary is the first.

Sex/Age: Ageing and sexing features are discussed here. The terminology of plum-age stages and moults varies, the British system is followed in this work. See 'Topog-raphy and plumages' for clarification of terms used in this section.

Measurements: Measurements can often be useful when comparing similar birds in the field; such subtleties as relative leg and bill lengths may be judged by comparing measurements. All measurements in this section are given in millimetres.

Wing length is measured from the carpal joint to the tip of the longest primary on the folded wing, with the ruler placed under the folded wing.

Tail length is from the root of the tail (concealed by the tail coverts) to the tip of the longest tail feather.

The tarsus measurement is taken from the centre of the 'knee' to the base of the middle toe.

Bills have been measured from the tip of the upper mandible to the base of the culmen where the bill joins the skull (con-cealed by the feathers of the forecrown).

Weights are also summarised and are given in grams, but with such large birds weights can vary tremendously according to season. Weights are possibly of limited use in a book of this nature, but can give an idea of the bulk of a bird in comparison with another similar species.

It should be remembered that all meas-urements and weights refer to adult birds. Juveniles and even first winter birds are often smaller and less bulky than adults. Weights have been taken from various literature sources, but especially Dunning (1993).

Where a species has more than one subspecies, only the measurements applicable to the nominate race (or the race described in the text) are given under this section, but, where relevant, others are given under Geographical Variation.

Geographical Variation: A species with a wide or fragmented distribution may vary, sometimes quite significantly, over its overall range. In many cases such variation can be quite marginal and involve only subtle colouration or mensural features. Those populations with relatively constant and definable differences are separated into recognisable subspecies or races. Those subspecies generally recognised by modern authorities are listed in this section, together with a brief summary of each form's range and their differences.

A few subspecies are so different as to be clearly separable in the field. Some of these forms in the future may prove be to full species in their own right. In these cases, this has been mentioned and a few very well marked forms have even been given separate treatment following the main species account.

The term *nominate race* is used for the first named of a group of races, e.g. the nominate race of Northern Raven is *Corvus corax corax*. The third name is the subspecies or racial name and in the nominate race is always the same as the species name. All subsequently described subspecies have a different third name, so that race *tingitanus* would be fully termed *Corvus corax tingitanus* or abbreviated to *C. c. tingitanus*. Those species with no accepted racial differences are referred to as 'monotypic'.

Voice: Most corvids have a remarkably varied vocabulary, but many of these calls are only given in display or near the nest, and are not often heard in the field. The advertising calls and general contact and alarm calls, which are the sounds likely to be heard in the field during casual encounters with the birds, are discussed here. Voice is particularly important when separating sympatric black crows, but care should be taken over which type of call is being uttered.

The major pitfall of course is in writing meaningful transcriptions of such sounds, which is very much a personal matter. Users of this book might translate or transcribe several calls in a manner quite different from the author's.

Habits: In a work of this nature, space does not allow a full discussion of the complex behavioural displays of corvids, which are only of limited use for identification purposes. An exception is the Australian crows and ravens where certain display features are extremely helpful in separating these similar species. Those wishing to read more about the displays and posturing of corvids are recommended to consult Goodwin (1986) and Coombs (1978) where very readable accounts are given for many species. Foraging, flocking and roosting habits are often helpful for identification purpose and have been included in our guide under this section.

Breeding: A summary of the nesting habits, and known egg-laying seasons are given. These are often useful when comparing similar species, especially the black crows.

Habitat: The type of habitat in which the bird is most likely to be encountered.

Distribution: This section details precise ranges and expands on the brief information conveyed by the maps.

Status: The overall abundance of each species is discussed here including estimates of regional numbers if known. The decline of the rarer species and the pressures on them are also summarised here.

References: The works cited are the most useful literature sources referred to during the compilation of the species accounts. These may be consulted by anyone wishing to undertake further reading on a particular species. Details of the references will be found in the Bibliography on page 184.

TOPOGRAPHY AND PLUMAGES

When consulting the descriptions a number of technical terms will be encountered. These have been kept to a minimum and generally follow the system adopted and recommended by the journal British Birds. The figure below shows the definitions of the feather tracts and structural parts mentioned in the text.

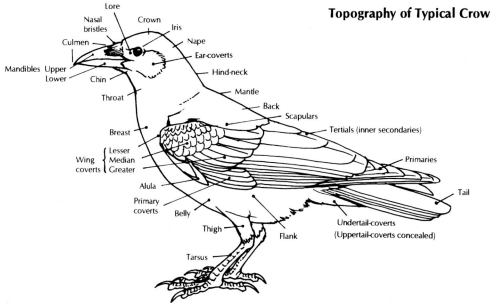

Topography of Typical Crow

Plumage sequences

Understanding the basic significance of plumage sequences is a useful tool towards reaching correct identification. Most corvids are remarkably constant in plumage colouration and there is little variation due to age or sex. Of course there are several exceptions, e.g. Daurian Jackdaw and Grey Crow.

For ease of reference, a comparison of the American (Humphrey and Parkes 1959) and the British (British Birds 1985) systems is outlined below. The majority of corvids attain an adult-like plumage quite quickly and have only one annual moult. Therefore these terms rarely appear in the book.

British	American
Juvenile	Juvenal
First winter	First basic
First summer	First alternate
Adult breeding	Definitive alternate

The following summary of plumage progression, provides a background to understanding moult sequences in this group. With such a complex group there is some variation in these generalisations, but such differences are given in the main text entries where relevant.

Nestling

Nestling corvids are of the altricial or nidicolous type, i.e. they are naked, blind and helpless when first hatched. Some species rapidly acquire a sparse covering of nestling down after hatching. The most striking feature of nestlings is the gape, typically scarlet or pink in most corvids, with pink or yellow gape flanges. Within a few days feather tracts of stubble-like growth appear on the body and wings, pushing out the nestling down (if present) which may show at the feather tips. This is the start of the growth of the juvenile plumage.

Juvenile
The juvenile plumage is the first covering of feathers, and is weaker, softer and looser in texture and duller in colouration than subsequent plumages. The primaries are also slightly shorter and more narrowly pointed than in older birds. The legs are more fleshy in texture, less stiff and 'dry' than those of adults. The underwing-coverts show areas of bare skin and the bill may be incompletely grown for the first few weeks of fledging. The upper mandible is pale, often pinkish-red on the inside, and the irides are duller in colouration than in adults. After a few weeks the juvenile head and body feathers are gradually lost as stronger, brighter adult-like feathers come through.

First winter
Generally acquired a few weeks after fledging through a gradual head and body moult. This includes some wing-coverts, but the juvenile flight and tail feathers are retained until the second moult. At this stage the plumage resembles that of the adult in most corvids, except for the presence of the duller retained wing and tail feathers. The pinkish or pale interior of the upper mandible persists into the first year of life in many species, especially *Corvus*, and is often a useful age clue when handling birds (in black-billed adult corvids the inside of the upper mandible is black). The colour of the iris is generally duller than in older birds, the colour gradually changing over the first three to twelve months of life.

First summer
By the spring of the second calendar year the difference in age of many corvids is apparent as first-year birds show browner abraded flight and tail feathers. By contrast adults will have moulted into fresh plumage during the previous autumn and have these feathers distinctly cleaner and showing no contrast with the rest of the wings and body. First summer birds undergo a gradual complete moult through the summer and early autumn and cannot be separated from adults by the autumn.

Subsequent moults
The majority of corvids have a gradual, complete moult once a year, unlike many other passerines, especially the migratory species which moult twice a year. Although the major part of the moult takes place after the completion of the breeding cycle, it begins quite early, especially in northern species which might be in active moult whilst they are still feeding young.

Aberrant plumages
From time to time birds may be encountered which do not seem to fit anything in the book. Birds with heavy feather wear and, at times of moult, with markedly patchy plumage patterning can appear distinctly peculiar. With such birds the all important size and structural features compared to other nearby individuals should provide the correct answer.

This is particularly true of the green magpies which may become bluish or turquoise, instead of the typical emerald green, colouration; the significance of this in the wild is unclear but wild 'blue' green magpies do occur and of course this is well known in captive birds and in museum skins, where green magpies fade to blue.

Other strange birds might be the result of a genetic aberration. Birds with white feathering would indicate partial albinism. A true albino is extremely rare and can only be deemed as such if it is completely white with pinkish bare parts. Others may show extensively blackish plumage, known as melanism, or have their entire plumage colouration pale and diluted giving a washed-out appearance, known as leucism.

GLOSSARY

Throughout the book the number of technical or unfamiliar terms have been intentionally kept to a minimum. Clarification of the terminology encountered in bird descriptions will be found under 'Topography and Plumages'.

Aberrant: Abnormal general reference to a species differing strikingly from the others of a group or of abnormally plumaged individuals.
Afrotropical: Faunal region of sub-Saharan Africa. Formerly called the Ethiopian region.
Allopatric: Where two or more similar forms exist, replacing each other geographically without overlapping. Compare **Sympatric**.
Arboreal: Living in trees.

Cloud forest: Neotropical mountain forest, frequently shrouded in clouds, damp and mossy with trees festooned with lichens, bromeliads etc.
Conspecific: Of the same species.

Elfin forest: Higher parts of cloud forest at limits of tree line, the trees stunted, gnarled and twisted.
Endemic: Exclusively confined to a defined area.

Holarctic: Faunal region of northern hemisphere north of the tropics, combining the Palearctic and Nearctic regions.

Immature: Not adult; term used to describe a variety of plumage stages following juvenile. Often includes juvenile stage if precise age not known; **sub-adult** sometimes used for later stages.

Juvenile: The first feathered plumage stage attained prior to fledging; this plumage only lasts for a few weeks.

Monotypic: The sole member of a classification grouping.

Nearctic: North American faunal region.
Neotropical: Central and South American faunal region.
Nominate race: The first named race of a species, typified by its scientific name being the same as the specific name.

Palearctic: Faunal region of Europe, North Africa and Asia, north of the tropics. Often divided into eastern and western sectors for convenience, the division being roughly the Ural Mountains.

Relict distribution: A distribution pattern that is relatively large but consists of isolated, well spaced pockets indicating that these may have been joined in former times.

Sub-adult: See **immature**.
Sub-lingual pouch: A small area of expandable skin at the chin, which distends when birds are carrying food.
Sundas: The islands off south-east Asia, which are part of the Oriental faunal region. May be divided into **Greater Sundas** (Borneo, Sumatra, Java and Bali) and **Lesser Sundas** smaller islands to the south-east).
Superspecies: A group of two or more closely related species that replace each other geographically. May be regarded by extremists as either full species or races of one species.

Sympatric: Where breeding ranges of similar forms overlap. Compare **Allopatric.**

Taiga: Northern forest belt of Scandinavia and Asia.
Taxon: A named form; in discussion can refer to either a defined species or subspecies.
Taxonomy: The study of classification and naming of life forms.

Wallacea: Faunal region comprising the eastern Indonesian islands of Salawesi, the Moluccas and Lesser Sundas, situated between the Australasian region and the Oriental region, but with its own distinct fauna.

PLATES 1-30

PLATE 1: North American Jays

1 Blue Jay *Cyanocitta cristata*

Text page 67

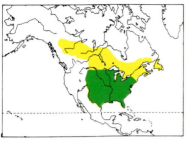

Familiar jay of woodland, parks and yards. The only North American jay with white markings in wings and tail. Races similar with cline towards smallest birds in Florida.

1a. adult
1b. juvenile: duller and greyer, less white in wings and tail.

2 Steller's Jay *Cyanocitta stelleri*

Text page 69

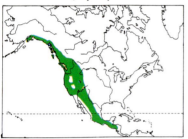

Coniferous and broad-leaved woodland and forests, chiefly in mountains. Dark, crested appearance coupled with barred blue wings and tail diagnostic but much racial variation (see text), northern birds blackest and with most developed crest, whereas Central American forms are very blue overall and have short crests; some racial extremes shown.

2a. adult nominate race (Alaska south to Oregon).
2b. juvenile nominate race: wings and tail greyer, crest shorter.
2c. adult race *carlotta* (Queen Charlotte Islands, Canada): largest and darkest form.
2d. adult race *suavis* (Nicaragua): very blue overall (typical of Central American forms), this is the smallest and shortest crested race.
2e. juvenile race *suavis*: duller and greyer than adult.

3 Pinyon Jay *Gymnorhinus cyanocephalus*

Text page 66

Dry pine and juniper woodland. Stocky, long-billed, short-tailed and almost uniform dull blue appearance diagnostic in range. Highly sociable, often in large flocks which fly in closely-bunched groups.

3a. adult
3b. juvenile: greyer than adult.

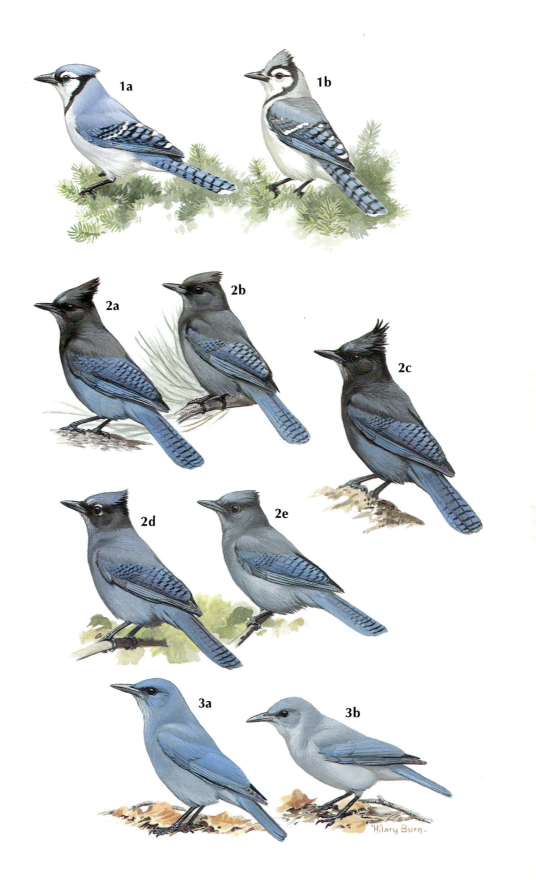

1a

1b

2a

2b

2c

2d

2e

3a

3b

Hilary Burn

PLATE 2: Aphelocoma Jays (see also plate 8)

1 Scrub Jay *Aphelocoma coerulescens*   **Text page 70**

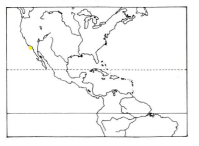

Scrubby and lightly wooded country. Bluish hood, wings and tail contrast with dull brown mantle and white throat (compare Grey-breasted Jay). Studies indicate considerable behavioural and vocal differences between the isolated populations; splitting into at least three species is an option favoured by some authorities (see text), as indicated below.

A. (c). insularis   Santa Cruz Jay
Endemic to Santa Cruz island, California. The largest and most richly-coloured form.
1a. adult.

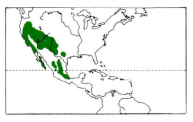

A. (c). californica   Scrub Jay
Complex of mainland western USA and Mexican races (see text).
1b. adult race *californica* (California): typical of northern races.
1c. adult race *remota* (southern Mexico): typical of southernmost races, being pale overall and with a weak breast band.
1d. adult race *woodhouseii* (south-central USA): typical of interior USA races; paler and weaker-billed than *californica*, with less contrast between hood and mantle and between breast band and lower underparts

A. coerulescens   Florida Jay
Endemic to Florida. Slightly smaller and longer-tailed than *californica* group and with whiter forehead and supercilium.
1e. adult
1f. juvenile (typical of the genus): blue areas of plumage washed grey-brown.

2 Grey-breasted Jay *Aphelocoma ultramarina*   **Text page 72**

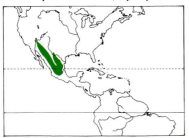

Montane woodland, chiefly mixed oaks and pines. Almost uniform bluish-grey above and greyish-white below, lacking contrasting brownish mantle and white throat of Scrub Jay. Several similar races (see text), two examples given.

2a. adult nominate race (southern Mexico): a dark race.
2b. adult race *arizonae* (north-west Mexico and adjacent USA): a pale race.
2c. juvenile race *arizonae*: duller and greyer than adult, some races have yellowish or flesh bills when young, gradually darkening.

4

1a

1b

1c

1d

1f

1e

2a

2b

2c

Hilary Burn

PLATE 3: Andean Cyanolyca Jays

Relatively slim dark bluish jays of humid forests in the northern Andes. Specific determination difficult in the field, but altitude and range aid identification; there is overlap between some species.

1 Black-collared Jay *Cyanoluca armillata*   **Text page 74**

Chiefly west Venezuela, rarer through Colombia to north Ecuador. 1800-3000 m, humid forest and edges. Deep blue with black tail underside, mask and narrow collar and paler crown. Meets Turqouise Jay (which see). Three races (two shown), other is race *meridana* (north-west Venezuela) which is darker, more purplish, blue than nominate.

1a. adult nominate race (east Colombia and south-west Venezuela).
1b. juvenile nominate race: duller and greyer overall (typical of genus).
1c. adult race *quindiuna* (rare, south Colombia and Ecuador): slghtly larger, bill stouter, head and throat darker mauve and wings and tail tinged greenish.

2 Turquoise Jay *Cyanoluca turcosa*   **Text page 75**

Ecuador, also extreme north Peru and south Colombia. 1500-3000 m, humid forest borders and secondary forest. Slightly shorter-tailed than overlapping *quindiuna* Black-collared, but throat and especially crown much paler (latter almost whitish) and greener-blue overall. Adult shown.

3 White-collared Jay *Cyanoluca viridicyana*   **Text page 75**

Peru and Bolivia. 2000-3000 m, humid forest. Resembles Black-collared but greener-blue and with diagnostic narrow white collar, however does not overlap with any similar jay. Three races (two shown), other is race *cyanolaema* (south-east Peru) which is somewhat intermediate.

3a. adult nominate race (north-west Bolivia).
3b. adult race *joylaea* (north and central Peru): less white on forehead, deeper, brighter, almost purplish, blue overall, more contrast between throat and mask and narrower white collar.

4 Beautiful Jay *Cyanoluca pulchra*   **Text page 76**

Pacific slope of Andes in Colombia and north Ecuador. Rare and little known. 900-1800 m, humid forest. Forages lower in canopy than other jays, note difference in altitudinal range. Violet blue with black mask and very pale, almost whitish, crown, lacks breast band. Adult shown.

Hilary Burn

PLATE 4: Central American Jays

Relatively small, dark bluish jays of humid mountain forests; only Azure-hooded is widespread, the others having very restricted ranges.

1 Azure-hooded Jay *Cyanoluca cucullata*　　　　　Text page 76

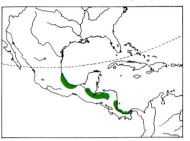

Humid forest, 800-2100 m. Dark blue with sky-blue crown, bordered narrowly with white. Compare other jays on this plate. Four similar races, two shown, others intermediate (see text). Juvenile duller, with less white on crown.

1a. adult nominate race (Costa Rica and west Panama).
1b. adult race *mitrata* (Mexico to Guatemala): black forecrown extends further back, white border to crown more extensive at sides.

2 Black-throated Jay *Cyanoluca pumilo*　　　　　Text page 77

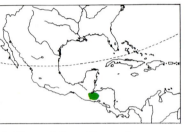

South-east Mexico to Honduras. Cloud forest, 1800-3000 m. Often forages in shrubbery. Small dark blue jay with indistinct white border to crown sides, not curving down behind ear coverts as in larger, brighter-crowned Azure-hooded with which it overlaps.

2a. adult.
2b. juvenile: duller and greyer, lacks white line at crown sides.

3 Dwarf Jay *Cyanoluca nana*　　　　　Text page 77

A small, rare, jay restricted to the Puebla/Oaxaca/Veracruz border area in southern Mexico. Above 1500 m, pine-oak forest. Very pale throat contrasts with black mask and blue crown; weak pale blue stripe along crown sides, bordering ear-coverts often apparent. Compare White-throated. Adult shown.

4 White-throated Jay *Cyanoluca mirabilis*　　　　　Text page 78

Another rare jay with a very limited range in the Guerrero/Oaxaca border in southern Mexico. Up to 3500 m, pine-oak forest. Striking white throat, joined by white supercilia contrasts with black crown and mask. Compare Dwarf Jay. Adult shown.

5 Silvery-throated Jay *Cyanoluca argentigula*　　　　　Text page 78

Costa Rica and west Panama. 2000-3200 m, oak forest. Smaller than Azure-hooded and with blackish crown and stunning white (race *albior* of central Costa Rica) or grey (nominate race of south Costa Rica/Panama) throat. Adult race *albior* shown. Juvenile duller overall.

PLATE 5: Cissilopha Jays

Subgenus of large Central American jays all with black head and underparts and blue upperparts and tail. Social behaviour and voice differs between the species (see text). Bare part colouration changes with age over first two to five years of life (see text). Identification eased by range.

1 Bushy-crested Jay *Cyanocorax melanocyaneus*   Text page 79

Guatemala to Nicaragua. 800-2450 m, open forest. Replaced by Yucatan Jay from coastal lowland Guatemala westwards; adults differ in having bluish lower underparts (rarely wholly blackish below), yellow (not dark) iris and black (not yellowish) legs. Juvenile greyer on head and underparts and has yellow bill and dark iris. Two races.

1a. adult nominate race (Guatemala).
1b. adult, black-bellied morph, race *chavezi* (Honduras and Nicaragua): darker, less greenish, blue above with underparts richer mauve-blue; some all black below (as shown).

2 San Blas Jay *Cyanocorax sanblasianus*   Text page 80

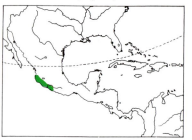

Pacific Mexico (Nayarit to Guerrero). Scrubby woodland. Range virtually meets Purplish-backed; adult San Blas is smaller, bluer (less purplish-blue) above. Full adult has black bill, yellowish iris and dull yellowish legs. Two similar races, nominate shown, race *nelsoni* (central coastal Guerrero) differs slightly in voice and age process (see below).

2a. adult nominate race (south Nayarit to extreme west Guerrero).
2b. juvenile: duller overall, first-year birds have small frontal crest (up to second-year in race nelsoni), bill of first year *nelsoni* with extensive pale areas, wholly black in nominate by this age.

3 Yucatan Jay *Cyanocorax yucatanicus*   Text page 81

Yucatan region to Belize. Scrubby lowlands, up to only 100 m (separated from Bushy-crested by range and habitat in Guatemala). Differs from Bushy-crested in having wholly black underparts, yellow legs and dark iris when adult. White juvenile distinctive. Two similar races, nominate shown.

3a. adult.
3b. juvenile: white head and underparts; resembles adult after first moult, but has bill and eye-ring yellow and tail feathers tipped whitish.

4 Purplish-backed Jay *Cyanocorax beecheii*   Text page 82

Pacific Mexico (south Sonora to Nayarit). Dry scrub to 500 m. Range possibly meets San Blas in Nayarit but Purplish-backed is larger, more purplish-blue above and has brighter yellow legs.

4a. adult.
4b. juvenile: duller overall, with yellow bill; first-year birds resemble adult but bill yellow and iris dark until well into second year.

1 Curl-crested Jay *Cyanocorax cristatellus* **Text page 84**

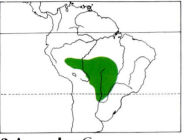

Central Brazil. Wooded grassland. Wholly black hood, stiff-standing crest and dark iris prevent confusion with overlapping White-naped and Plush-crested (plate 7) which have similar tail and underpart patterns, but prefer denser forest. Juvenile duller with shorter crest. Adult shown.

2 Purplish Jay *Cyanocorax cyanomelas* **Text page 84**

South-east Peru to north-east Argentina and south-west Brazil. Deciduous woodland. Dusky featureless jay, showing purplish-brown colour in good light, especially on tail upperside. Possibly meets rare Azure Jay which is brighter and bluer. Violaceous Jay overlaps in south-east Peru, greyer and bluer, with blacker hood and breast and pale nape patch; here Purplish favours Andean foothill forest, Violaceous in riverine forest. Juvenile even duller. Adult shown.

3 Azure Jay *Cyanocorax caeruleus* **Text page 85**

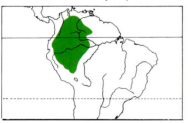

South-east Brazil and north-east Argentina. Rare and declining. Forest, especially *Araucaria*. Dark purplish-blue jay, with contrasting blackish hood and chest; looks all dark in dull light. Compare Purplish Jay with which it might overlap. Juvenile duller and greyer.

3a. adult: typical bluish-mauve bird.
3b. adult: greenish-blue morph, recorded throughout species range.

4 Violaceous Jay *Cyanocorax violaceus* **Text page 85**

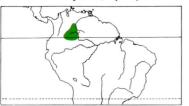

Western Amazon and upper Orinoco basins. Riverine forests, including open forest. Dull bluish-grey jay with wings and tail bluer, contrasting black head and breast and whitish nape patch. Appears drab greyish in poor light. Overlaps with rare Azure-naped which has pale iris, more extensive pale blue nape and white vent and tip to tail. See also Purplish Jay in Peru.
Juvenile greyer. Two races, adult nominate shown.

5 Azure-naped Jay *Cyanocorax heilprini* **Text page 86**

Colombia/Brazil/Venezuela border region. Forest edge and savannah woodland. Rare and little known. Pale iris and white vent and tail tip distinguish this greyish-blue jay from more numerous Violaceous, the nape is also brighter pale blue. Adult shown.

Hilary Burn

PLATE 7: South American Cyanocorax Jays

1 Plush-crested Jay *Cyanocorax chrysops*   **Text page 89**

Woodland and scrub, up to 1500 m. Black crown and breast contrasts with violet-blue upperparts and creamy-white underparts and broad white tail tip. Compare Curl-crested (plate 6) and White-naped Jays. Three races, two shown.

1a. adult nominate race (most of species range).
1b. juvenile nominate race: slightly duller, especially facial pattern.
1c. adult race *diesingii* (northern Brazil): crown tufts longer and facial spots smaller than nominate.

2 White-naped Jay *Cyanocorax cyanopogon*   **Text page 89**

Woodland and scrub, up to 1100 m. No known overlap with Plush-crested from which it differs in having brown upperparts and whiter nape, it is also relatively smaller and longer-tailed. Overlaps with Curl-crested (plate 6) but prefers denser woodland. Adult shown.

3 Cayenne Jay *Cyanocorax cayanus*   **Text page 87**

The Guianas and adjacent parts of Venezuela and Brazil. Open woodland, up to 1100 m. No similar jays within range, resembles White-tailed Jay but tail merely tipped white. Compare Black-chested Jay (plate 8).

3a. adult.
3b. juvenile: duller facial pattern, white of tail and face washed buffish-mauve.

4 White-tailed Jay *Cyanocorax mystacalis*   **Text page 90**

Peru/Ecuador border region. Dry woodland and scrub, up to 1200 m on Pacific slope. The only jay in its range. Juvenile has duller, mauve-tinged, face spots and iris probably dark. Adult shown.

1a

1b

1c

2

3a

3b

3a

4

Hilary Burn

1 Black-chested Jay *Cyanocorax affinis* **Text page 87**

Costa Rica to west Venezuela. Forest and woodland, up to 2200 m. No similar jay within range. Juvenile duller, with face spots vestigial, upperparts browner and belly buffer, iris brown. Two races, adult nominate shown.

2 Green Jay *Cyanocorax yncas* **Text page 91**

Relatively small greenish or yellowish-green forest jay, showing distinctive yellowish outer tail feathers in flight. Forages in lower canopy and shrubbery. Twelve described races fall into two widely-separated groups (see text). Northern races are lowland forest birds, found up to 1800 m; South American races inhabit Andean forest between 800 and 3000 m. An example of each group is depicted.

2a. adult race *glaucescens* (northernmost race).
2b. adult race *galeatus* (western Colombia): frontal crest well-developed.

3 Unicoloured Jay *Aphelocoma unicolor* **Text page 73**

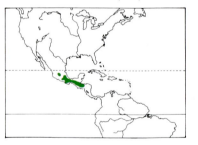

Cloud forest, 1500-3400 m. Completely uniform rich blue plumage prevents confusion with any other jay if seen well, but looks wholly dark in dull light. Juvenile duller and greyer, with pale yellowish bill base. Five races described, varying in degree of purplish in plumage tones and slightly in size (see text). Two extremes shown.

3a. adult nominate race (Chiapas and Guatemala).
3b. adult race *guerrensis* (central Guerrero): relatively longer-tailed and shorter-winged than nominate, with plumage very purplish blue.

4 Brown Jay *Psilorhinus morio* **Text page 94**

Woodland and scrub, up to 1700 m. Large, sluggish dusky brown jay, unlike any other jay within range. Five similar races, varying in overall size and presence of white tipping to tail, southernmost birds smallest with white-tipped tails, northern races largest and plain-tailed.

4a. adult plain-tailed morph.
4b. juvenile: bill yellow, black in adults.
4c. adult white-tipped morph.

Hilary Burn

1 Black-throated Magpie-Jay *Calocitta colliei* **Text page 92**

Restricted to north-west Mexico (south Sonora to Colima). Open woodland, especially by rivers. Pacific lowlands to 1650 m. Overlaps marginally with White-throated Magpie-Jay in Colima. Differs in having relatively longer tail and black face and throat when adult. Immature birds have crown feathers tipped white, face and throat mottled whitish and shorter tails. Thus more easily confused with the next form. Adult male shown.

2 White-throated Magpie-Jay *Calocitta formosa* **Text page 93**

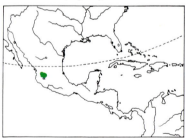

Open woodland, dry scrub, up to 1250 m. Long curving crest and white face and underparts provide easy distinctions from other jays; compare Black-throated Magpie-Jay with which it marginally overlaps and perhaps interbreeds. Three races, two shown, other race *azurea* of Chiapas and Guatemala is brighter blue above, has throat washed violet and more white in tail.

2a. adult male nominate race (Colima to Oaxaca).
2b. adult female nominate race: duller and shorter-tailed than male.
2c. juvenile nominate race: duller and shorter-tailed than female.
2d. adult male race *pompata* (Guatemala to Costa Rica): shorter-tailed than nominate, paler blue above, crown feathers less black.

3 Tufted Jay *Cyanocorax dickeyi* **Text page 88**

Very restricted range, the Sierra Madre Occidental on borders of Sinaloa, Durango and Nayarit. Montane forest, 1350-2150 m. No other similar jay in region. Stiff bristle-fan crest, white nape and terminal half of tail distinctive. Juvenile has duller facial pattern, dark iris and short crest. Adult shown.

Hilary Burn

PLATE 10: Perisoreus and Lanceolated Jays

1 Grey Jay *Perisoreus canadensis*   **Text page 101**

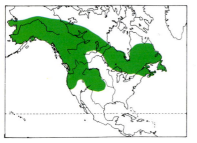

Coniferous forests. Small-billed, fluffy, uncrested greyish or grey and whitish jay, often tame. Marked variation in pattern, see text for details. Nine races, three shown, others somewhat intermediate.

1a. adult nominate race (Canada and northern USA).
1b. juvenile nominate race: all races similarly drab.
1c. adult race *capitalis* (Rocky Mountains): very pale-headed.
1d. adult, race *obscurus* (Pacific coastal slope of USA): contrastingly pale below and dark above.

2 Siberian Jay *Perisoreus infaustus*   **Text page 100**

Coniferous forests. Small-billed, fluffy, uncrested brownish jay, with rusty tail and rump. Often tame. Clinal variation in intensity of rufous or grey plumage tones, but no marked races, despite ten recognised subspecies (see text), two extremes shown.

2a. adult race *ruthenus* (Scandinavia and west Siberia): a very rufous form.
2b. juvenile race *ruthenus*: softer plumage than adult, duller browner.
2c. adult race *yakutensis* (Eastern Siberia): a very grey form.

3 Sichuan Jay *Perisoreus internigrans*   **Text page 99**

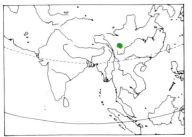

Restricted to montane coniferous forest between 3350-4300 m in Central China (west Sichuan to south Kansu). Rare and little known. A drab sooty grey jay with darker head, unmistakable within range, recalling juvenile Grey Jay. Adult shown.

4 Lanceolated Jay *Garrulus lanceolatus*   **Text page 97**

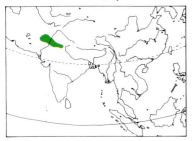

Himalayas (east Afghanistan to Nepal). Thinly-wooded slopes, 1500-3000 m. Overlaps with Eurasian Jay (plate 11), but is slimmer, with black hood and barred blue (not all black) tail.

4a. adult.
4b. juvenile: duller, with tail tipped greyish, rather than white as adult.

1 Eurasian Jay *Garrulus glandarius*   **Text page 95**

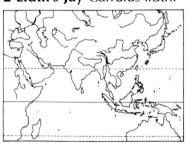

Widespread, but relatively shy, jay of woodland and broad-leaved forests. Black tail and white rump obvious in flight, providing an easy distinction from Lanceolated in the Himalayas. Very complex racial variation, with some 35 races falling into eight groups (examples depicted are adults).

1a. Nominate group (European forms): crown streaked.
1b. *cervicalis* group (North Africa): rufous nape and grey mantle, very pale head sides, crown black (*cervicalis*) or broadly streaked.
1c. *atricapillus* group (Middle East, Crimea and Turkey): mantle and nape uniform in colour, crown black, face very pale.
1d. race *hyrcanus* (Caspian forests of Iran): an isolated small form, with black forecrown and broadly streaked hindcrown.
1e. *brandtii* group (Siberia and northern Japan): streaked crown, dark iris, reddish hood and greyish mantle.
1f. *leucotis* group (south-east Asia): no white in wing, forecrown white, hindcrown black, much white on sides of head.
1g. *bispecularis* group (Himalayan region): unstreaked rufous crown and no white wing patch.
1h. *japonicus* group (southern Japanese islands): large white wing patch, blackish face and scaled crown.

2 Lidth's Jay *Garrulus lidthi*   **Text page 98**

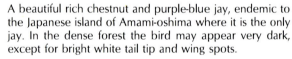

A beautiful rich chestnut and purple-blue jay, endemic to the Japanese island of Amami-oshima where it is the only jay. In the dense forest the bird may appear very dark, except for bright white tail tip and wing spots.

2a. adult.
2b. juvenile.

1a

1b

1c

1d

1e

1f

1g

1h

2a

2b

Hilary Burn

1 Clark's Nutcracker *Nucifraga columbiana*　　　　Text page 129

Often tame about picnic and camp sites in Rocky Mountain forests. Combination of dove-grey body plumage, white secondary patch and outertail feathers in otherwise black wings and tail makes confusion unlikely.

2 Spotted Nutcracker *Nucifraga caryocatactes*　　　Text page 128

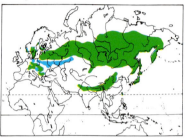

Coniferous forests, especially in mountainous regions. Spotted plumage, white vent and tail corners. All plumages similar but races form two distinct groups:-

2a. Northern group (Europe and northern Asia to Japan). Spotting heavy, extending over flanks. White in outertail only at tips. Nominate race of Europe shown, eastern Siberian birds similarly stout-billed; most of Siberia inhabited by thinner-billed race *macrorhynchos*, prone to occasional eruptive movements over most of northern Europe.

2b. Southern group (China and Himalayas)
Spotting weak, typically none below breast or on scapulars. At distance looks brown with blackish crown and wings. White in outertail extends almost to base. Well-marked *hemispila* of western Himalayas shown, other forms have less extensive, smaller spots (see text)..

3 Larger-spotted Nutcracker *N. (c.) multipunctata*　　Text page 129

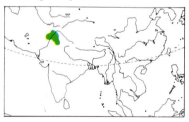

West Himalayan forests, chiefly north-west of *hemispila*. Heavy spotting extends to uppertail coverts. Has an overall whitish appearance, except for blackish crown and wings and pied tail. Less white in outertail than in *hemispila* and tail relativley longer. A few intermediates known.

4 Azure-winged Magpie *Cyanopica cyana*　　　　Text page 111

Open woodland and parks. Relatively small magpie with black hood and dull blue wings and tail. All plumages and races similar, of which very isolated *cooki* of Spain and Portugal is the most distinct.

4a. adult nominate race (north-west of Asian part of range): typical of Asian races, with whitish tips to central tail feathers.

4b. adult race *cooki* (Spain and Portugal): differs from Asian races in lacking whitish tips to central tail feathers and in being a little browner, slightly smaller and relatively shorter-tailed.

1

2a

2b

3

4a

4a

4b

Hilary Burn

1 Black-billed Magpie *Pica pica*   **Text page 120**

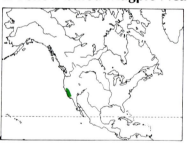

One of the most distinctive and widespread of all corvids, only possible confusion is with Yellow-billed Magpie of California but ranges do not meet. Some twelve races varying in extent of white in wings and rump patch, and to a certain degree in social behaviour and voice indicates that other isolated forms (i.e. North Africa and Arabia) possibly equally as worthy of distinction (see text).

1a. adult nominate race (Europe, except north and south-west).
1b. adult race *camtschatica* (Kamchatka and north-east Siberia): white in wings very extensive.
1c. adult race *mauretanica* (North Africa): bare blue eye-patch, no white on rump, a distinctly short-winged form.
1d. adult race *asirensis* (south-west Arabia): very dull black, large bill, little white in wings.

2 Yellow-billed Magpie *Pica nuttallii*   **Text page 122**

Restricted to valleys in California, west of the Sierra Nevada, where Black-billed Magpie absent. At all ages easily distinguished by bright yellow bill and bare skin about eye, also a little smaller and slimmer than North American race of Black-billed Magpie.

PLATE 14: Blue Magpies

Blue magpies are arboreal birds, feeding within the forest canopy; they are typically encountered in small flocks, flying in follow-my-leader fashion from tree to tree, with long tails billowing out behind.

1 Taiwan Magpie *Urocissa caerulea*   Text page 103

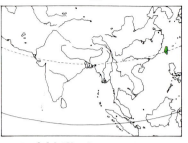

Endemic to Taiwan, where it is the only blue magpie and unlikely to be confused. Hill forest, between 300 and 1200 m. Adult shown.

2 Gold-billed Magpie *Urocissa flavirostris*   Text page 104

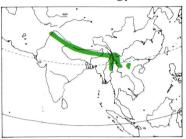

Himalayan forests from Pakistan east to Vietnam, chiefly at higher elevations (1600-3350 m) than Blue Magpie with which it overlaps in range. Difficult to separate from Blue Magpie unless good views obtained but bill and legs yellow or orange-yellow (not red or orange-red), whitish nape patch smaller (extends to rear crown and upper mantle on Blue Magpie), upperparts duller and greyer and underparts with pale yellow wash (but not in western race *cucullata*). Four races, two extremes shown.

2a. adult race *cucullata* (Pakistan to central Nepal): bluer upperparts, whiter underparts and larger nape patch than eastern races, thus closer to Blue Magpie.
2b. juvenile race *cucullata*: duller overall, especially bare part colours, nape and crown more extensively whitish (recalling Blue Magpie).
2c. adult race *robini* (north-west Tonkin): the race with olive and yellowish plumage tones most developed.

3 Blue Magpie *Urocissa erythrorhyncha*   Text page 105

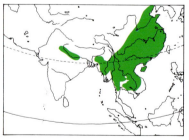

Hill and foothill forest with clearings, locally in wooded plains in China, chiefly below 1500 m but up to 2200 m in summer (*cf* Gold-billed Magpie). Only confusion is with Gold-billed Magpie with which it widely overlaps in southern part of range (see above). Strangely absent from north-east India. Five races, two shown.

3a. adult nominate race (southern China).
3b. adult race *occipitalis* (Himalayas): very white under parts and nape, larger white tertial markings.
3c. juvenile race *occipitalis*: duller overall, with more extenive pale on crown, bill greyish and legs yellowish at first, colours gradually developing.

1 White-winged Magpie *Urocissa whiteheadi* Text page 106

Bulky forest magpie of tropical China and Vietnam, forages in small parties in waterside trees in hill forest. In flight shows Three broad yellowish-white wing bands and extensive yellowish-white sides and tip of tail. Unlikely to be confused. Two distinct races. Immature drab grey-brown instead of blackish, with dingy bill and iris.

1a. adult nominate race (Hainan).
1b. adult race *xanthomelana* (mainland Asia): slightly larger and blacker, with blackish, rather than grey, tail.

2 Crested Jay *Platylophus galericulatus* Text page 65

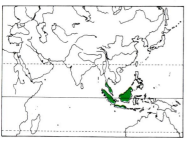

Distinctive dusky forest jay with remarkable upstanding long crest and white ear-patch. Small noisy parties work through foliage uttering rattling cries. Three races, all shown. Juvenile unbarred, with whitish belly and short crest, moulting into immature plumage stage (2c).

2a. adult nominate race (Java): the darkest race.
2b. adult race *ardesiacus* (Malaysia and Thailand).
2c. immature race *ardesiacus*: underparts barred, plumage more rufous above, with buff spotting on wing coverts.
2d. adult race *coronatus* (Sumatra and Borneo): rich reddish-brown.

3 Black Magpie *Platysmurus leucopterus* Text page 65

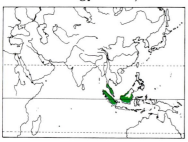

Bulky long-tailed jay-like bird of lowland forests and scrub, forages in tree canopy in small, parties, uttering bubbling calls. Wholly black (Borneo) or with conspicuous white wing patch. Unlikely to be confused, but Bornean birds could suggest a small long-tailed crow. Juvenile greyish-black. Two races, both shown.

3a. adult nominate race (Malaysia and Sumatra).
3b. adult race *aterrimus* (Borneo): lacks white in wing, longer frontal tuft forming short crest when raised.

4 Ratchet-tailed Treepie *Temnurus temnurus* Text page 119

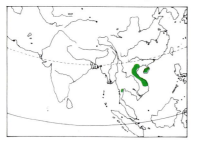

Small black forest treepie, rather dumpy and sluggish by nature, easily confused with Racket-tailed Treepie (plate 18) but tail does not flare at tip and shows distinctive jagged outline if seen well. Recently discovered breeding in Thailand, well away from previously known range. Adult shown.

PLATE 16: Ceylon and Green Magpies

1 Ceylon Magpie *Urocissa ornata*　　　　Text page 103

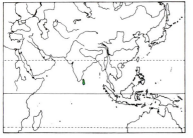

Endemic to Sri Lanka, where there are no similar birds. Forages in small parties in hill forest. Declining. Juvenile duller. Adult shown.

2 Green Magpie *Cissa chinensis*　　　　Text page 107

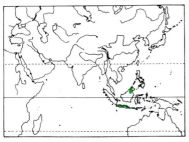

Small parties in low canopy of foothill forests, the emerald green plumage and chestnut wings being conspicuous as they move between trees. Overlaps with Yellow-breasted Magpie and Short-tailed Magpie (on Borneo), which see. When worn, plumage fades to bluish. Juvenile duller, with yellowish bill and legs. Five races, two extremes shown.

2a. adult nominate race (India to Thailand and China): both fresh and bleached (bluish) examples shown.

2b. adult race *margaritae* (isolated on Mt. Lang Bian, Vietnam): tail slightly longer than nominate and crown bright yellow.

3 Short-tailed Magpie *Cissa thalassina*　　　　Text page 110

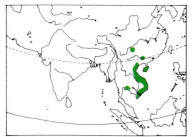

Two isolated populations, which are often lumped with Yellow-breasted Magpie (see text). On Borneo at higher altitudes than Green Magpie (above 1000 m, whereas Green Magpie only up to 400 m), also has much shorter tail, pale (not red) irides, darker red legs and plain-tipped tertials.

3a. adult nominate race (Java): the only 'green' magpie of the island.

3b. adult race *jefferyi* (Borneo): more extensive chestnut on tertials and whitish tips to tail feathers than Javan birds.

4 Yellow-breasted Magpie *Cissa (thalassina) hypoleuca*　　　　Text page 109

Overlaps with Green Magpie over northern Indochina, but replaces it further south. Differs in having yellower underparts, relatively shorter tail and plain, unbarred, tertials. When worn, plumage fades to bluish. Five races, two shown. Often considered conspecific with Short-tailed Magpie (see text).

4a. adult nominate race (southern Indochina).

4b. adult race *jini* (isolated on Yaoshan Massif, Kwangsi): relatively longer-tailed and greener below than other races.

1

2a

2a

2b

3a

3b

4a

4b

Hilary Burn

PLATE 17: 'Grey' Treepies

Treepies on this plate are all rather closely related, and no doubt evolved after long isolation from similar ancestors.

---

1 Andaman Treepie *Dendrocitta baylei* **Text page 116**

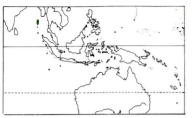

A small treepie of dense forest, endemic to the Andaman Islands, where there are no other treepies. Adult shown.

2 Grey Treepie *Dendrocitta formosae* **Text page 113**

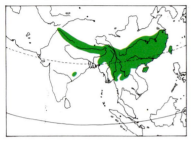

Widespread treepie, the only one over most of China; in India almost confined to Himalayan foothills, except for isolated population in Eastern Ghats. Much duller, less rufous than Rufous Treepie (plate 18), with white patch at base of primaries (wing-coverts and tertials pale, but primaries all dark in Rufous) and grey (not rufous) rump. See also Collared Treepie (plate 18). Seven races, two extremes shown (see text).

2a. adult nominate race (Taiwan): rump whitish, tail blackish.
2b. adult race *occidentalis* (north-west India): rump grey, tail relatively longer with most of central feathers grey.

3 White-bellied Treepie *Dendrocitta leucogastra* **Text page 116**

Endemic to southern India, differs from Rufous Treepie (plate 18) in having white underparts, nape and rump and white flash at base of primaries.

4 Sumatran Treepie *Dendrocitta occipitalis* **Text page 114**

Endemic to Sumatra, where it is the only treepie. Adult shown.

5 Bornean Treepie *Dendrocitta (occipitalis) cinerascens* **Text page 115**

Endemic to Borneo, where it is the only treepie. Adult shown.

The treepies of Sumatra and Borneo are usually regarded as isolated races of one species (Sunda Treepie). In view of striking differences in head pattern, they are here given specifc status (see Goodwin 1986).

1

2a

3

2b

4

5

Hilary Burn

1 Rufous Treepie *Dendrocitta vagabunda*   **Text page 112**

Widespread throughout India, extending eastwards over lowland south-east Asia. Foxy-rufous body, blackish head and silvery 'shoulders' prevent confusion with Grey and White-bellied (plate 17) with which it overlaps, see also Collared (below). Eight races, two shown.

1a. adult nominate race (India).
1b. adult race *sakeratensis* (eastern Thailand): a richly-coloured race.

2 Collared Treepie *Dendrocitta frontalis*   **Text page 117**

A rare treepie of dense forest, recorded in the Himalayan foothills up to 2100 m, from north-east India to Tonkin. Black face and throat contrasts with clear grey nape and breast, unlike Rufous; rufous-chestnut upperparts, grey 'shoulders' and lack of white at base of primaries prevent confusion with Grey (plate 17). Adult shown.

3 Racquet-tailed Treepie *Crypsirina temia*   **Text page 118**

Small black forest treepie, with very long tail, expanding at tip; feeds inside canopy of lowland forest. Easily confused with rarer Ratchet-tailed Treepie (plate 15), but tail longer and of different shape.

3a. adult.
3b. juvenile: tail narrower at tip, plumage duller, irides brown.

4 Hooded Treepie *Crypsirina cucullata*   **Text page 118**

Rare little treepie, known only from lowland forest in central Burma. Possibly now endangered. Adults are pale grey with contrasting black hood, wings and long, spoon-ended tail. Unlikely to be confused.

4a. adult.
4b. juvenile: browner, with darker brown hood, orange patch at gape (see text for discussion on later plumages).

PLATE 19: Ground-Jays

The four Podoces species form two pairs: Henderson's and Biddulph's are northern, with long uppertail-coverts; Pander's and Pleske's are southern and have short uppertail-coverts.

---

1 Henderson's Ground-Jay *Podoces hendersoni*   **Text page 124**

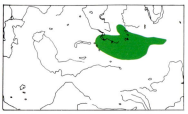

Mongolia. Stony desert with some bushes. Black of head only on crown, tail wholly black with long sandy coverts. In flight inner wing black, outer wing white.

2 Biddulph's Ground-Jay *Podoces biddulphi*   **Text page 125**

Sinkiang. Sandy desert with shrubs. Black face and crown (looks black-throated in profile); otherwise head and body very pale. Tail almost white. In flight has outerwing and band along secondary tips white.

3 Pander's Ground-Jay *Podoces panderi*   **Text page 125**

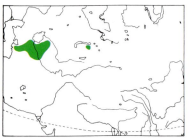

Turkmenia, Uzbekistan and Lake Balkash. Sandy desert with shrubs. No black on crown but black breast patch when adult. Tail all black; wings chiefly white, with some black on coverts in flight.

3a. adult.
3b. juvenile: no chest patch, bill and legs fleshy-grey, black parts of plumage duller (typical of genus).

4 Pleske's Ground-Jay *Podoces pleskei*   **Text page 126**

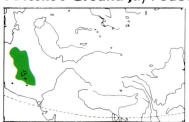

Iran. Sandy desert with shrubs. Differs from Pander's in range and in having more black in wing - secondaries black with white trailing edge.

5 Hume's Ground-Jay *Pseudopodoces humilis*   **Text page 127**

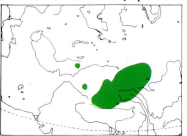

Tibetan plains and slopes. Very small, recalls a drab wheatear in size and behaviour, mouse-brown with dull whitish outertail feathers.

5a. adult.
5b. juvenile: faintly barred below, bill and legs fleshy-grey

Hilary Burn

PLATE 20: Choughs and Jackdaws

1 Red-billed Chough *Pyrrhocorax pyrrhocorax* Text page 133

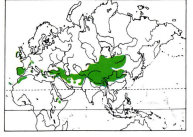

Mountains and high altitude pastures; also rugged coasts in western Europe. Note isolated populations in Canaries and Ethiopia. Often in flocks. Small black crow with diagnostic red legs and slender red bill. In flight note rectangular wings, long fingered primaries and square-ended tail, in length tail equals width of wing base. Nominate race shown.

1a. adult.
1b. juvenile: shorter and yellower bill than adult, legs reddish

2 Alpine Chough *Pyrrhocorax graculus* Text page 132

Mountains. Usually in flocks. Small black crow with small yellow bill and short red legs. In flight note wings less rectangular than Red-billed, with primaries shorter and less fingered; tail longer than width of wing base and less square at tip. Nominate race shown.

2a. adult.
2b. juvenile: dingy bill and dusky legs, brownish until first-summer.

3 Western Jackdaw *Corvus monedula* Text page 136

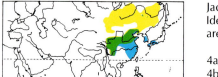

Farmland, towns and coasts. Usually in flocks. Small black crow with   diagnostic pale iris, grey nape and small black bill. In flight note small head and bill, blunt-tipped wings and relatively long tail.

3a. adult race *spermologus* (western Europe).
3b. juvenile race *spermologus*: nape darker than adult, iris also dark.
3c. adult race *soemmerringii* (eastern Europe and Asia): very pale grey nape, often with obvious whitish collar.

4 Daurian Jackdaw *Corvus dauuricus* Text page 138

Jackdaw ranges almost meet in northern Baikal region. Identical in size,   shape, behaviour and most calls. Adults are piebald but immatures are dusky, has dark iris at all ages.

4a. adult.
4b. immature: differs from adult Western in having darker grey nape, dark iris, and shows 'ghost' of breast pattern of adult; from juvenile Western only by silver streaks on ear-coverts. Birds attaining pale collar are at first very pale on upper nape, remaining dark on lower nape (reverse of Western, which is palest on lower nape).

1a

1b

2a

2b

2a

3a

3b

3c

4a

4b

4a

Hilary Burn.

1 Rook *Corvus frugilegus*   **Text page 149**

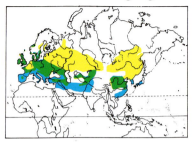

Widespread sociable crow of open farmland. Also intro-duced into New Zealand. Bare whitish bill base and face diagnostic of adults. In flight primaries longer and more fingered than in Carrion Crow and tail more wedge-shaped at tip (cf Northern Raven, plate 30).

1a. adult nominate race (Europe and west Asia).
1b. juvenile nominate race: face fully-feathered, very similar to Carrion Crow, but bill straighter and more pointed and 'thighs' more shaggy.
1c. adult race *pastinator* (eastern Asia): face feathered but has bare whitish bill base as nominate race.

2 Carrion Crow *Corvus corone*   **Text page 159**

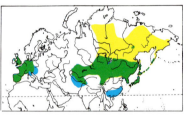

Widespread over western Europe and eastern Asia as two disjunct races of wholly black crow, separated by conspecific Hooded Crow. Solitary when breeding, Rook colonial. See Rook for distinctions, juvenile Rook very similar. Compare also Northern Raven (plate 30) and, in Asia, Large-billed Crow (plate 22) with which it widely overlaps. Nominate race shown.

3 Hooded Crow *Corvus (corone) cornix*   **Text page 160**

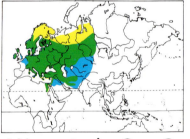

Distinctive crow of eastern Europe, the Middle East and western Asia, freely hybridising with both western and eastern races of black Carrion Crow at zones of contact, therefore treated as conspecific (see text).

3a. adult race *cornix* (northern Europe).
3b. hybrid Carrion x Hooded Crow: rather variable, a typical example.

4 Mesopotamian Crow *Corvus (corone) capellanus*   **Text page 161**

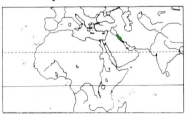

Replaces Hooded Crow in riverside cultivation along Euphrates of lowland Iraq and adjacent south-west Iran, with little evidence of interbreeding. Much whiter body plumage than Hooded, slightly larger and with relatively larger bill. Calls seemingly also differ (see text discussion).

5 Collared Crow *Corvus torquatus*   **Text page 174**

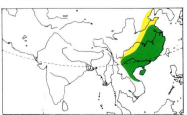

Replaces Carrion Crow in lowlands of eastern China, favouring waterside cultivation. Contrasting white nape and breast band prevents confusion with other crows within range, but compare smaller Daurian Jackdaw (plate 20).

1a

1c

1a

1b

2

3b

4

3a

3a

5

1 House Crow *Corvus splendens*   Text page 139

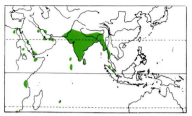

Abundant in towns and cities, widely introduced at ports in Middle East and Africa. Small, slender-billed, crow with greyish nape and breast and glossy black crown and face. Confusion unlikely with any other crow, but compare smaller, short-billed Western Jackdaw (plate 20) in Kashmir.

1a. adult race *zugmayeri* (Pakistan): the palest race.
1b. adult race *insolens* (Burma): the darkest race.

2 Large-billed Crow *Corvus macrorhynchus*   Text page 162

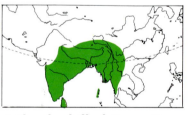

Widespread large crow of eastern Asia, the Indian Himalayas, Philippines and a number of East Indian islands. Loud, almost mocking caws, longer and more arched bill, stepped forehead and broader wings distinguish this crow from widely-overlapping Carrion Crow (plate 21). Northern Raven (plate 30) has longer, more wedge-shaped tail, longer primaries and deep, croaking, calls. Situation complex in Malaysia, Philippines and East Indian islands where Slender-billed and Violaceous Crows occur (see text for discussion). Races vary greatly in size over wide range (see text). Status on Borneo needs clarifying (few records).

2a. adult race *colonorum* (south-east Asia): small and dull race.
2b. adult race *tibetosinensis* (Tibetan region): large and very glossy.

3 Jungle Crow *Corvus (macrorhynchus) levaillantii*   Text page 164

India and Burma. Distinctly smaller and with more square-ended tail and higher-pitched voice than overlapping Large-billed, which it meets in Himalayan foothills. However in view of complex size variation in races of Large-billed, probably conspecific. Race *culminatus* (India) shown.

4 Slender-billed Crow *Corvus enca*   Text page 141

Forest crow of Malaysia, Sumatra, Java, Borneo and some other nearby islands, widely overlaps with Large-billed which replaces Slender-billed in cultivated and cleared areas. Slender-billed has a slimmer, less arched, bill with bare culmen base and its calls are faster and higher in pitch. Large race *compilator* (Borneo, Sumatra, Java) shown. See text.

5 Violaceous Crow *Corvus (enca) violaceus*   Text page 142

Several forms of short-billed forest crows from the Philippines and the island of Ceram in the Moluccas. Probably conspecific with Slender-billed but bill much shorter and plumage more glossy. On the Philippines replaced by larger Large-billed in more open habitats. See text for discussion on this complex problem, race *violaceus* of Ceram shown.

1a

1b

1

2a

2

2b

3

4

5

Hilary Burn

1 Hawaiian Crow *Corvus hawaiiensis*   **Text page 174**

Endemic to the main island of Hawaii, where it is the only crow. Now only in higher altitude forest, declining and severely endangered.

2 Mariana Crow *Corvus kubaryi*   **Text page 144**

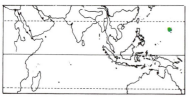

Endemic to islands of Guam and Rota in the Marianas Islands, West Pacific, where it is the only crow. Population reasonably stable on Rota but now rare and declining on Guam. Chiefly in forest.

3 Piping Crow *Corvus typicus*   **Text page 143**

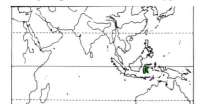

Endemic to Sulawesi, where quite numerous in forest in central and southern part of the island. Slender-billed Crow (plate 22) also present on the island, but Piping easily distinguished by pattern and smaller size.

3a. adult.
3b. juvenile: whitish areas suffused brownish.

4 Banggai Crow *Corvus unicolor*   **Text page 143**

Endemic to tiny island of Banggai, off east coast of Sulawesi. Virtually unknown, perhaps extinct. Presumably a forest crow. Resembles an all dark Piping Crow and might be vocally similar. Recent crow sightings on the Banggai islands are thought to be colonising Slender-billed (plate 22), which is larger, longer-billed and probably differs vocally (see text).

5 Flores Crow *Corvus florensis*   **Text page 144**

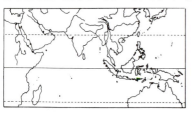

Endemic to island of Flores in the Sundas, where it occurs in lowland forest. Overlaps with Large-billed (plate 22) but is markedly smaller and small-billed and unlikely to be confused given reasonable views.

6 Long-billed Crow *Corvus validus*   **Text page 145**

Endemic to forest areas on the Moluccan islands of Morotai, Obi and Halmahera. Massive, long bill and forest habitat prevent confusion with overlapping Torresian Crow (plate 29) which has smaller, insignificant bill and prefers areas cleared for cultivation.

PLATE 24: Island Crows: New Guinea and south-west Pacific

Torresian Crow (plate 29) also occurs throughout New Guinea.

---

1 White-billed Crow *Corvus woodfordi*　　　　Text page 146

Endemic to islands of Choiseul, Isabel and Guadalcanal in the northern Solomon Islands where it is the only crow.

2 Bougainville Crow *Corvus meeki*　　　　Text page 146

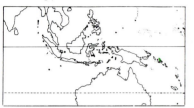

Endemic to islands of Bougainville and Shortland in the Solomon islands where it is the only crow. Often considered conspecific with the previous form as Solomon Islands Crow, but striking differences in bill colour and form of nasal bristles suggests specific status.

3 Brown-headed Crow *Corvus fuscicapillus*　　　　Text page 146

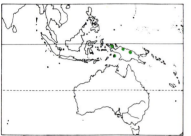

Known only from a few sites and islands in north-west New Guinea and the Aru Islands; mangroves and lowland forest. A scruffy-looking crow with large, arched, bill (black or yellowish according to sex and age), brownish head and relatively short, square tail. Grey Crow is longer-tailed, has pinkish, bare, facial skin and bill; latter stout, but is not arched. two races, one shown, other is race *megarhynchus* of islands of Waigeu and Gemien, which is slightly larger-billed than nominate.

3a. adult nominate race: male has black bill, female has yellowish bill.
3b. juvenile: yellow bill, plumage very scruffy and browner than adult.

4 New Caledonian Crow *Corvus moneduloides*　　　　Text page 147

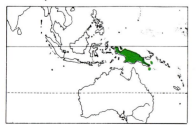

Endemic to New Caledonia and Mare (Loyalty Islands) where it is the only crow. Relatively common in both forest and cleared habitats.

5 Grey Crow *Corvus tristis*　　　　Text page 140

Widespread forest crow over most of New Guinea up to 1400 m. Plumage very variable but relatively long tail, stout bill and bare facial skin obvious at any age. Adults blackish on head and upperparts, browner underparts. Immature plumages often very pale brownish-grey, with very pale bill. See text for plumage variation discussion.

5a. adult, dark type.
5b. sub-adult.
5c. juvenile.

Hilary Burn

1 Stresemann's Bush Crow *Zavattariornis stresemanni*   Text page 123

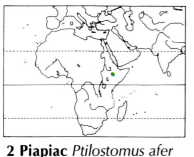

Endemic to acacia savanna in central-south Ethiopia. A small grey, starling-like crow, with black wings and tail; unlikely to be confused, but Wattled Starling is superficially similar (see text). Adult shown.

2 Piapiac *Ptilostomus afer*   Text page 135

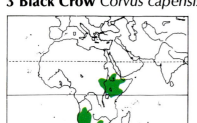

Savannas and palms over Central Africa (except east). Small black crow with remarkable long, graduated tail which gives superficial resemblance to one of the long-tailed glossy starlings (see text) but stout bill distinctive.

2a. adult.
2b. juvenile: pinkish bill.

3 Black Crow *Corvus capensis*   Text page 148

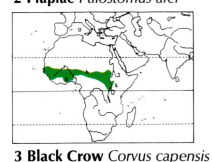

Medium-sized glossy black crow of farmland in southern and eastern Africa, the only wholly black crow over most of its range, but in parts of east Africa meets Dwarf (plate 30) and Fan-tailed (plate 26) Ravens, but only former likely to be confused (see text, but note slim bill of Black Crow).

4 Pied Crow *Corvus albus*   Text page 176

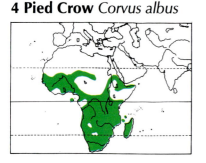

The most widespread crow in Africa, with distinctive white lower breast (and nape) and relatively weak bill which help distinguish it from larger, shorter-tailed, massive-billed White-necked Raven (plate 26). In Ethiopia compare Thick-billed Raven (plate 26). In Somalia and Ethiopia seems not infrequently to hybridise with Dwarf Raven (see text).

4a. adult.
4b. hybrid Pied Crow x Dwarf Raven: pattern varies, typical example shown.

PLATE 26: African Ravens

1 Fan-tailed Raven *Corvus rhipidurus*

Text page 181

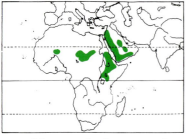

Distinctive wholly black crow with stumpy tail of arid canyons in the Middle East and central and north-east Africa. Shape suggests White-necked Raven but Fan-tailed much smaller, with small bill and lacks white on nape.

2 White-necked Raven *Corvus albicollis*

Text page 182

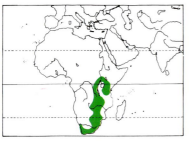

Very large raven, with broad wings, short tail and massive bill of hills in eastern and southern Africa. Range does not overlap that of Thick-billed of Ethiopia (which see) but marginally meets Fan-tailed in Kenya. Massive white nape patch, sometimes extending thinnly onto breast recalls Pied Crow but size and shape quite different.

3 Thick-billed Raven *Corvus crassirostris*

Text page 183

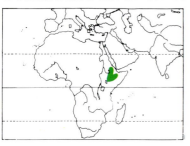

Huge raven, endemic to Ethiopia where it is widespread in hilly country. Recalls White-necked (which does not overlap in range) but tail longer and white on nape less extensive.

Hilary Burn

PLATE 27: North American Crows

Northern Raven (plate 30) is also widespread in North America.

---

1 Northwestern Crow *Corvus caurinus*　　　　**Text page 151**

Coasts from south Alaska south to Washington. Virtually inseparable from American Crow but much more sociable and only overlaps from British Columbia to Washington. Calls are lower in pitch and upperparts less glossy than western race *hesperis* of American Crow and on average is slightly smaller and has weaker legs and toes. However note that *hesperis* is smaller and vocally rather different to nominate. See text.

2 American Crow *Corvus brachyrhynchos*　　　**Text page 152**

Widespread over most of North America in a variety of habitats. Weaker-billed and with more rounded tail tip than Chihuahuan or Northern (plate 30) Ravens, and with different voice. Compare Fish and Northwestern Crows with which it also overlaps, although only marginally with the last. Four races, two shown, others are *pascuus* of Florida (smaller but relativley stouter-billed than nominate) and *paulus* of south-east USA which resembles Florida race but is smaller-billed. See also Tamaulipas Crow (plate 28).

2a. adult nominate race.
2b. adult race *hesperis* (western North America): smaller and vocally different to nominate race (see text).

3 Fish Crow *Corvus ossifragus*　　　　　　　**Text page 154**

Eastern USA, coastal marshes and lowland rivers. Very similar to American Crow with which it may form mixed feeding parties. Plumage more glossy, and is smaller, smaller-billed, longer-legged and has more rounded tail tip. Most easily identified by short, nasal, call. See text and compare Tamaulipas Crow (plate 28).

4 Chihuahuan Raven *Corvus cryptoleucus*　　　**Text page 175**

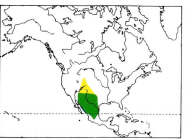

Crow-sized raven of Mexico and the arid interior of southern USA, overlaps with American Crow from which it is separated by longer, deeper, bill with more extensive nasal bristles, relatively longer wings and more wedge-shaped tail. Smaller, slighter overall and with less wedge-shaped tail than Northern Raven (plate 30) replacing it in arid, flatter country; call different to either (see text)

1

2a

2b

3

4

Hilary Burn

1 Tamaulipas Crow *Corvus imparatus*

Text page 153

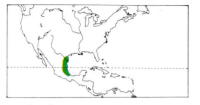

Endemic to Gulf coast of Mexico from Texas border to north Veracruz. Lowland scrubby farmland and open woodland. Small, small-billed, very glossy crow, with short frog-like croaked calls. Very sociable. Recalls a small Fish Crow but ranges do not overlap and voice quite different.

2 Sinaloa Crow *Corvus sinaloae*

Text page 154

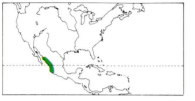

Endemic to Pacific coast of Mexico from south Sonora to Colima. Open woodland and bushy farmland. Virtually identical to Tamaulipas Crow (with which it was formerly lumped as Mexican Crow) but voice totally different and tail slightly longer. See text.

3 Palm Crow *Corvus palmarum*

Text page 155

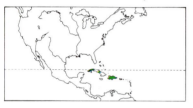

Cuba and Hispaniola, forest clearings, very local on Cuba. Smaller and smaller-billed than either Cuban or White-necked Crows, with which it freely associates when feeding. Readily flicks tail when calling, a habit not shared by the other two. Voice also differs (see text).

3a. adult nominate race (Haiti and Dominican Republic).
3b. adult race *minutus* (Cuba): smaller than nominate.

4 Jamaican Crow *Corvus jamaicensis*

Text page 157

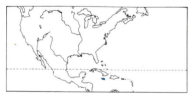

Endemic to forests on Jamaica, where it is the only crow. See text.

5 Cuban Crow *Corvus nasicus*

Text page 157

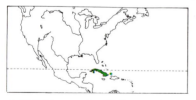

Widespread on Cuba; also on Caicos Islands of the nearby Bahamas. On Cuba mixes with very local Palm Crow (which see). See text.

6 White-necked Crow *Corvus leucognaphalus*

Text page 158

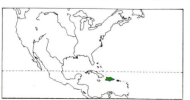

Endemic to Hispaniola, almost certainly now extinct on Puerto Rico. Mixes with smaller Palm Crow when feeding (which see). See text.

All species have white eyes when adult, brown when immature. Identification extremely difficult (see text), range of limited help.

---

1 Australian Raven *Corvus coronoides*   Text page 169

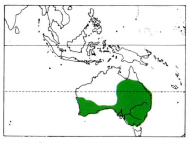

Throat bulge on upper breast, especially when calling. Crown slopes from bill to peak on rear crown. Calls harsh and guttural with prolonged terminal moan, latter often given in flight but without missing a beat. Full call in horizontal posture with throat bag extended. Wings and tail relatively longer and more slender than in crows. Pairs or mall flocks. Does not fly high.

2 Little Raven *Corvus mellori*   Text page 171

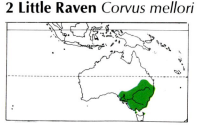

Throat lacks obvious bulge. Calls harsh, lacks terminal moan of Australian Raven. Flips wings with each call note, but with no special posture adopted. Sociable. Often flies high.

3 Forest Raven *Corvus tasmanicus*   Text page 172

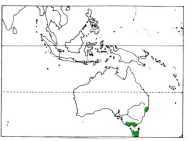

Tasmania and adjacent wooded coastal mainland. Very stocky with heavy bill. Calls harsh and deep, with terminal note rolling. Wings and tail shorter that other ravens, contributing to blunt-winged look in flight. Two races, both shown.

3a. adult nominate race (Tasmania and adjacent south coast mainland).

3b. adult race *boreus* **New England Raven** (New South Wales): relatively longer tail and slimmer bill than Forest Raven, possibly this form is specifically distinct (see text).

4 Little Crow *Corvus bennetti*   Text page 168

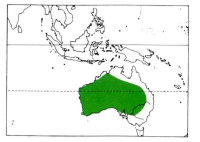

Throat smooth, bill shorter than head, crown slightly more domed than in Torresian. Calls quick, abrupt and nasal. Does not prolong final note or wing shuffle after alighting. In territorial flight, gives two calls and 'misses a beat'. Sociable, in arid country often in flocks. Often flies high and performs aerial acrobatics. Underwing slightly two-toned.

5 Torresian Crow *Corvus orru*   Text page 165

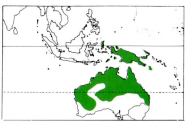

Lower throat slightly ruffled when calling, calls with barking, almost 'musical' quality, often prolongs final note. Repeatedly shuffles wings after alighting. In territorial flight, gives one note and 'misses a beat'. Does not fly very high. Where food abundant, forms flocks. In arid country in pairs by tree-lined watercourses. Compare Long-billed Crow in Moluccas and see also plate 24.

1 Brown-necked Raven *Corvus ruficollis*

Text page 178

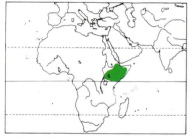

Widespread in desert plains of North Africa, the Middle East and central Asia, overlapping in some places with Northern Raven. A little smaller than most races of Northern, with slightly narrower wing-tip and slimmer body, more developed brown tones in plumage and different voice (see text). When perched wing tips fall well short of tail tip, almost equal in Northern. Northern Ravens in arid country become distinctly brown with wear, but where ranges overlap Northern tends to be in mountains rather than plains.

1a. adult, in reasonably fresh plumage.
1b. adult, in worn plumage.

2 Dwarf Raven *Corvus (ruficollis) edithae*

Text page 177

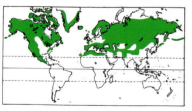

Arid country in north-east Africa, but replaced on Socotra island by Brown-necked. Very similar to Brown-necked in colouration but markedly smaller, crow-sized. Range not known to meet Brown-necked but where overlap occurs with Pied Crow hybridisation takes place (see plate 25). Compare also Black Crow (plate 25). Usually treated as conspecifc with Brown-necked Raven.

3 Northern Raven *Corvus corax*

Text page 179

Chiefly in wild upland regions, but also in forest, on coasts and locally in plains. Large size, heavy bill, shaggy throat hackles, relatively long, fingered wing-tip and wedge-shaped tail helps separate from other large black crows, including Large-billed (plate 22) but deep, croaking calls often easiest feature. Compare Brown-necked and Chihuahuan (plate 27) Ravens with which it overlaps. Several races which vary in size over wide range, see text for discussion on variation.

3a. adult nominate race (Europe and western Siberia, south to Caucasus).
3b. adult race *subcorax* (Greece, Middle East to Pakistan): slightly larger and with shorter throat hackles, bleaches very brown on neck and underparts in worn plumage (as shown).
3c. adult race *tingitanus* (Canaries and North Africa): smallest race, bill very stout and plumage rather oily, bleaching brown with wear.

1a

1a

2

1b

3a

3b

3c

Hilary Burn

SYSTEMATIC
SECTION

CRESTED JAY *Platylophus*
BLACK MAGPIE *Platysmurus*

These two monotypic genera share a pattern of distribution in the Malay peninsula and the Greater Sundas (except that the Black Magpie is absent from Java), where they inhabit dense lowland forest. It is possible that both are very primitive corvids, *Platylophus* being an early jay and *Platysmurus* an early treepie. The Crested Jay not only looks strange with its extraordinary crest, but has other peculiar features; the nasal bristles so typical of other corvids are vestigial, leaving the nostrils exposed, the juvenile has buff spotting at the tips of the wing and body feathers. Such juvenile features are more typical of other passerine groups; amongst other corvids juvenile wing spotting is only shown by nutcrackers. It has been suggested that *Platylophus* might be more closely allied to the Helmet-shrikes of Africa, but Sibley and Monroe (1990) have retained it with the corvids.

CRESTED JAY   Plate 15

Platylophus galericulatus

A striking and peculiar bird; its inclusion in the crow family has been doubted by some authorities.

IDENTIFICATION: A dark forest bird, with an extraordinary long erect crest and gleaming white neck patches. Populations of the Malay peninsula and Java are very dusky overall, those of Sumatra and Borneo almost reddish-chestnut. All forms however are so distinctive, that they are highly unlikely to be confused with any other bird. Typically encountered in small parties low down in dense forest, proclaiming their presence with chattering rattles.
DESCRIPTION: Length 31-33 cm. Head dominated by very long crest arising from rear crown. Bill medium, slightly hook-tipped. Nasal tuft very short, not concealing nostrils, but rictal bristles long and prominent. Tail medium, slightly rounded at tip. Adult race *ardesiacus*: crest and most of head down to upper breast blackish, shading to very dark grey on rest of underparts. Upperparts very dark olive-brown. Very dark plumage relieved by a broad white patch at the sides of the upper neck, almost meeting behind the base of the crest and two white spots to rear of the eye forming a broken crescent. Juvenile and immatures different (see below). Bill and legs blackish. Irides reddish or brownish.
SEX/AGE: Sexes similar. Juvenile has short crest and reddish-brown body plumage, shading buffer on underparts, weakly mottled with paler feather tipping; wings paler olive-brown than in adult, with warm buff tips to wing-coverts and tertials. First-year birds closer to adult, but retain juvenile spotted wing feathers and have underparts variably mottled or weakly barred whitish.
MEASUREMENTS: Race *ardesiacus*: wing 138-143, tail 114-122, tarsus 34-36, bill 28-30, weight unrecorded.
GEOGRAPHICAL VARIATION: three races, differing in colour of body plumage.
   P. g. ardesiacus: Malay peninsula north to Thailand. Described above.
   P. g. galericulatus: Java. Much darker, almost black, on body plumage.
   P. g. coronatus: Sumatra and Borneo, a strikingly differ-ent bird, being rich tawny-rufous overall, including the head, with black only at borders of white neck patches. Crest averages a little shorter than in the other races. Birds from the northern part of Borneo tend to be a little paler and have been named *lemprieri*, but they seem to be the end of a

cline rather than forming a separate population.
VOICE: Call an excited, often rather explosive, staccato chattering rattle, varying somewhat in intensity and speed of delivery; some are better described as a high-pitched chittering, rather than chattering, with clearer and sharper individual notes. However there may be geographical significance in this variation, which needs further clarification. Also gives a single 'chik' note as it hops in the foliage.
HABITS: Surprisingly poorly-documented for such a widespread, distinctive and unique large bird. Generally located in pairs or small (family ?) parties working through forest foliage, keeping to the lower and middle levels of the canopy. Rather inquisitive, will jauntily approach observers, uttering chattering calls and raising and lowering crest in an excited manner. Feeds mainly on invertebrates, those recorded include beetles, grasshoppers, cicadas, wasps, cockroaches and millipedes.
BREEDING: Essentially unknown. Said to construct a 'jay-like nest'.
HABITAT: Lowland forest, both primary and secondary forest, recorded up to 750 m in Thailand, 1000 m on Sumatra and 1800 m on Borneo.
DISTRIBUTION: Throughout the Malay peninsula and peninsular Thailand, lowland Sumatra, Java and Borneo.
STATUS: Locally common in lowland forest throughout its range, but population sparse in Thailand which is at the edge of its range. Its dependence on the presence of lowland forest must have created local decreases as these are extensively logged-out.
REFERENCES: Goodwin 1986, Robson, C. (sound-recordings), Smythies 1981.

BLACK MAGPIE   Plate 15

Platysmurus leucopterus

Alternative names: Black Jay, White-winged Black Jay.

A heavily built long-tailed forest 'jay' of uncertain affinities, not quite a treepie, magpie or a jay. Shares a remarkably similar distribution to the Crested Jay.

IDENTIFICATION: A bulky black forest magpie, with a moderately long, broad tail; the race of Thailand, Malaysia and Sumatra has massive white wing patches and is quite unmistakable. Bornean race is wholly black and might recall a crow in a brief view but is smaller, with a short bill and has a much longer tail; heavy, broad tail also recalls that of a coucal in flight and plumage and basic shape suggests male Koel, but latter has pale green bill, is sleeker and is merely a migrant to coastal areas of Borneo.

DESCRIPTION: Length 39-41 cm. Nominate race: feathers of forecrown stiff, short and blunt, merging into nasal tuft of stiff, upcurving, bristles which form a short crest on forehead. Bill short, with curved culmen. Tail moderately long, broad and very graduated. Almost entire plumage deep black, with slight sheen on the wings, crown feathers more glossy, with slight blue-green sheen. A large white area on the wing is formed by extensively white greater coverts and tertials. Bill and legs blackish. Irides deep red.

SEX/AGE: Sexes similar. Juvenile duller, more greyish-black, than adult, with juvenile wing and tail feathers retained until first-summer moult.

MEASUREMENTS: Nominate race: wing 187-200, tail 190-220, tarsus 35-38, bill 35 (one), weight 178 and 182 (two).

GEOGRAPHICAL VARIATION: The two subspecies are strikingly different and it is tempting to suggest that they might well be worthy of specific treatment. Further research is needed.

P. l. leucopterus: Sumatra, Malay peninsula, southern Thailand. Described above, has a huge white wing patch.

P. l. aterrimus: Borneo. Entirely black, with no white in wings; feather of forecrown longer, forming a more obvious bristled crest.

VOICE: A noisy bird with a varied vocabulary. Recordings from Borneo contain a harsh, chattering phrase of three to eight rapidly-repeated notes (recalling Black-billed Magpie), a short 'kip', plaintive, high-pitched and irregularly repeated and a plaintive, high-pitched mewing cry, varying in length and pitch, given singly or repeated three or four times. Smythies (1981) also refers to a "short, staccato, high 'pip' followed by two lower prolonged notes of a peculiar hoarse tone" and refers to its "enormous range of voice" which includes mimicry of other birds, especially barbets. Recordings of the nominate race from Thailand include a similar magpie-like chattering to the Bornean birds, but the phrases are of eight to twelve rapidly repeated notes

which are slightly less grating in tone, also a low, hoarse 'grrraah' and a metallic, ringing note, both of which are repeated. There might be geographical significance in the vocal variety but a thorough analysis of a long series of recordings is necessary.

HABITS: Usually encountered in pairs or small parties of up to six birds, moving restlessly between trees, in follow-my-leader fashion. Feeds entirely amongst tree cover, from lower to upper level of canopy, perhaps mostly at mid-level, on fruits and invertebrates (beetles and caterpillars specifically recorded), but also said to take small mammals. When perched repeatedly bows and bobs its head in a nervous manner and seems to be constantly on the move. The birds do not call in flight but a soft 'boobooboo' sound is produced by their wings which no doubt helps keep the group in contact as they move through the forest. In flight the tail is partially opened and appears distinctly broad and heavy; the wing-beats are short, even and deliberate. Normally flies between trees at mid-level height, not rising above the canopy, but readily crosses clearings and open roads.

BREEDING: Seemingly a solitary nester. The nest is a rather large, but somewhat crudely-constructed, platform of twigs, with a shallow cup lined with fibres and strips of bark. Placed in trees and bushes between 1 and 8 m above ground level. Clutch two to three eggs, which are whitish, finely speckled with brown or grey, these markings may be concentrated at either end of the egg. Eggs recorded June on Borneo, nests recorded February to April of nominate form. No information on incubation, fledging, etc.

HABITAT: Prefers dense lowland forest, but also found in swampy woodland, secondary forest and forest edges, reaching 900 m in foothills.

DISTRIBUTION: Throughout the lowlands of the Malay peninsula and peninsular Thailand, lowland Sumatra and Borneo.

STATUS: Locally common in lowland forest over most of the range, but less common at northern range limits in southern Thailand. Vulnerable to forest clearance but also found in secondary forest and bushy clearings.

REFERENCES: Goodwin 1986, Robson, C. (sound-recordings), Smythies 1981.

PINYON JAY *Gymnorhinus*

Monotypic genus. Despite its rather dull colouration this is a most interesting corvid, its highly social behaviour is comparable only to that of the Rook, whereas its bill shape and feeding habits recall the nutcrackers. However the nostrils are bare and exposed, a feature shared amongst corvids only by adult Rook and Crested Jay. On the ground unlike other jays, it walks and hops in the manner of a nutcracker or crow.

PINYON JAY　　　　　Plate 1

Gymnorhinus cyanocephalus

This peculiar corvid recalls a small crow in its actions, yet in colour it suggests a plain bluish jay. Its close association with pines is shared only by the nutcracker and its colonial habits only by Rook.

IDENTIFICATION: Western USA only. A distinctive

dull bluish corvid of dry pine slopes. Usually occurring in flocks, even in breeding season. Fine bill and relatively long wings and short tail, uniform colouration and flocking habit renders it unmistakable. Compare Clark's Nutcracker.

DESCRIPTION: Length 25-28 cm. Bill relatively fine and sharply pointed; nostrils bare and exposed. Tail short. Wings relatively long. Entire plumage dull blue, darkest on head, brightest on breast, crown and forehead and palest on rump; throat whitish, slightly mottled. When worn becomes dark greyish overall, but the forecrown remains bright blue. Bill and legs blackish. Irides brown.

SEX/AGE: Sexes similar, but male relatively longer-billed than female and female said to be paler blue. Juvenile dull smoky grey overall, with bluish tinge to forehead, wings and tail; bill and legs greyer than adult when very young. First-summer bird resembles juvenile until summer moult, after which not separable from adult.

MEASUREMENTS: Male averages slightly larger than female. Wing 142-159 (male 148-159), tail 101-116 (male 104-116), tarsus 34-39, bill 32-38, mean weight 103.

GEOGRAPHICAL VARIATION: Monotypic.

VOICE: Vocabulary quite varied. Most frequently heard calls are a high-pitched, quickly uttered, 'kwa-kwa-kwa-kwa', a mewing 'kraa-aha' and a slower, lower, 'kura, kura, kura'. Several other calls have also been noted from this well-studied species.

HABITS: Highly gregarious. Flocks exist as separate units and there is little interchange between them. They forage over hill slopes, both on the ground and in trees, breaking up into smaller family groups whilst feeding. Each foraging flock has a number of individuals delegated as look-outs whilst the rest are feeding responding immediately to their warning calls at the approach of a potential predator. If a flock is threatened by a bird-of-prey, the birds silently gather into a compact group and make a sudden dash for dense cover. They will also mob owls and raptors until the offending bird departs from the area. Flock size varies but 250 birds is typical, a study group of this size roamed over an area of 21 sq. kms. They have several roost sites in their home range, and fly up to 5 kms to roost, but hardly ever roost near the day's chosen feeding spot. Birds roost in small units within the roost, probably composed of pairs or family parties. Pair-bonds are long-standing, pairs remaining together throughout the year within the flock; they rarely breed until in their third calendar year. Pinyon Jays rely heavily on the seeds of conifers, especially those of the Pinyon Pine, but they also take a wide variety of other items, especially invertebrates and flocks will even visit gardens to feed on seeding sunflowers. They store surplus seeds near nesting area, either in crevices in tree bark or dug into the soil. Unlike nutcrackers, these caches are often raided at times of need by the storer's mate or offspring. On the ground, walks like a crow. Where unmolested becomes very confiding of man. Flight action direct and crow-like but much swifter than American Crow, flocks fly in tight units when underway and follow changes of direction suddenly in manner of waders. During colder, winter months flocks descend to lower elevations and move back up again in early spring. Dependence on one main food source causes chaos to their complex lifestyle at times of crop failure and, like the nutcrackers, they are given to periodic dispersal well-away from normal range and habitat in search of fresh feeding areas. Much more information can be found in the monograph, Marzluff and Balda (1992).

BREEDING: Colonial breeder, but nests widely spread over quite a large area and generally only one, but sometimes two or three, in one tree. Nest is a bulky construction of sticks and weeds, with a deep cup lined with soft plant materials and wool. Usually situated between 1 and 6 m, rarely as high as 25 m, in juniper, pine or oak trees. Clutch three to six, usually three or four, pale bluish or pale greenish eggs, speckled brown or black. Incubation by female for 16 days, being fed by male at the nest. Both sexes feed young, and often other adults will help as chicks become larger or when they have fledged. Young leave nest when three weeks old, and join families from nearby nests, together with parents. Breeding season varies from year to year according to pine seed crop, in good years as early as February, in poorer years not until May; will re-nest up to three times if first nest fails, therefore eggs have been recorded at various times between February and October.

HABITAT: Dry mountain slopes and foothills, dominated by Pinyon Pine or Yellow Pine and Junipers, descending onto adjacent plains outside breeding season and at times of pine-seed failure; during irruptions may occur in almost any situation from gardens to desert scrub. Generally between 1000 and 3000 m.

DISTRIBUTION: The Great Basin of west-central USA. Eastern slope of Rocky Mountains and associated lower ranges, extending from central Oregon east to western South Dakota, south to northern Baja California, central New Mexico and western Oklahoma. Dispersal takes birds further into the interior; subject to irregular irruptions when birds occasionally recorded east to central Texas, north to southern Washington and southern British Columbia and south to north-west Mexico.

STATUS: Locally abundant.

REFERENCES: Hardy 1990, Marzluff and Balda 1992.

BLUE and STELLER'S JAYS *Cyanocitta*

Both of the these two northern jays incorporate mud in their nest construction and have prominent wing and tail barring, features not shown by other American jays. Although strikingly different in plumage colour, these two medium-sized crested jays geographically replace each other and are very closely-related. Where marginal overlap in distribution occurs, occasional mixed pairing has been recorded.

BLUE JAY   Plate 1

Cyanocitta cristata

Widespread over eastern North America, where it is one of the most colourful and familiar birds of the region.

IDENTIFICATION: Readily identified by combination of short, not always prominent, crest, white underparts and barred blue wings and tail, the latter with a clear white tip which is particularly obvious in flight. Steller's Jay has head and body sooty with longer crest and lacks white tail border and tips to secondaries. Scrub Jay is uncrested and also lacks white in tail or wings. Blue Jay is gradually spreading westwards and is becoming more frequent in western USA, where occasionally hybridises with Steller's Jay.

DESCRIPTION: Length 24-30 cm. Bill relatively weak. Tail medium-long, graduated at tip. Head with moderate crest arising from mid to rear crown. Nominate race: nasal tuft bluish-white. Crown and crest light violet-blue. Narrow black band encircles crown under base of crest, narrowest from eye to nape and across forehead, widest at sides of neck and under crest; an extension continues as a narrow collar across lower breast. Ear-coverts, short supercilium above eye, throat and remainder of underparts off-white, washed pale dull mauve or violet-grey. Upperparts of body rather dull bluish-grey, washed with violet-blue, becoming brighter blue on rump and uppertail-coverts. Wings bright sky-blue, heavily barred with black on secondaries and secondary greater coverts, both also broadly tipped white. Tail bright sky-blue with prominent narrow black barring (weakest on outermost feathers) and broad white tips to all but central pair of feathers. Underside of wings and tail dull grey, except for white feather tips. Legs blackish. Bill black. Irides blackish-brown.

SEX/AGE: Sexes similar. Juvenile duller overall, with greyer upperparts, almost unbarred wing-coverts, barring on secondaries and tail more disjointed, and white at tips more restricted.

MEASUREMENTS: Male averages somewhat larger than female. Nominate race: Wing 125-148, tail 117-147, tarsus 31-39, bill 22-28, weight 65-109.

GEOGRAPHICAL VARIATION: Four similar subspecies differing in size and subtle plumage tones, but variation clinal and ill-defined (therefore not compared below):-

C. c. cristata: Eastern seaboard of USA from North Carolina south to central Florida and north Texas.

C. c. semplei: southern Florida, the smallest race.

C. c. cyanotephra: interior and western part of range, extending west to foothills of the Rockies and south to west Texas. A little paler and cleaner than other forms.

C. c. bromia: north and west of nominate, north to Manitoba and Newfoundland, west to Illinois. The largest race.

VOICE: Vocabulary very varied. Most typical call is a shrill, penetrating but short scream 'peeeah, peeeah', repeated two or three times. This and similar sounds vary in pitch, some recall the mewing cry of a Red-tailed Hawk. Another popular phrase is a liquid, but high and almost metallic 'too-doodle-up-to'. Many of its calls are quite musical, including various sharp clicking, rattling, squeaking and almost bell-like notes which are uttered in various combinations.

HABITS: A familiar jay of woodlands, parks and large gardens. Usually alone or in pairs, but forms small flocks after breeding season and on passage. Feeds within tree canopy and on the ground, very agile and lively in trees where family parties flit one-by-one across clearings at mid-canopy level. Readily visits garden bird-tables and becomes remarkably confiding where unmolested, conversely can be remarkably shy and wary where persecuted. Its diet is chiefly vegetarian, where various nuts (especially acorns, beech-mast and chest-

nuts) and seeds (chiefly Palmetto) make up the bulk of its food intake. It is an opportunist feeder and will freely take a variety of human food waste and invertebrates (especially grasshoppers, beetles and caterpillars). Occasionally takes eggs and nestling birds, small rodents and even, day-flying small bats. Habitually hides surplus food items, either by burying them in the soil or pushing them into crevices of tree bark; it is believed that only resident populations indulge in food-hiding, the more northerly migratory forms apparently do not. Generally noisy and very active, especially in winter and spring but quiet and even furtive when breeding. Mobs predators such as cats and owls, dive-bombing and even pecking ground predators near nest, including humans. Anting behaviour frequently recorded, rubbing ants over feathers to extract formic acid and deter feather parasites. Flight action direct, with rapid, regular wingbeats, usually low keeping below tree-top level, but rises high above trees to mob passing raptors. Migrating flocks also fly high, but avoid crossing large open stretches of water; these may number as many as 100, and sometimes even more.

BREEDING: Solitary nester. Nest of twigs, roots, feathers, paper etc. usually mixed with mud, lined with fine plant fibres and other soft materials. Constructed in fork of tree or large branches in shrubs, rarely old buildings, by both sexes. A 'false' nest is often constructed nearby before 'real' nest is commenced. Clutch two to six, usually four to five, eggs varying from pale green to pale buff, even marked with brown, olive and grey spotting and speckling. Incubation by female, very rarely male recorded as taking turns, for 16-18 days. Male feeds incubating female and shares in feeding nestlings and fledged young, the latter fledge at 17-21 days. Young capable of independence some three weeks after fledging, but remain with adults for about two months. First eggs recorded late March and April in south of the range, but later in the north where egg-laying may not commence until late May or early June. Usually single-brooded, certainly so in north of range, but two successful broods not infrequent and an exceptional third brood is sometimes recorded.

HABITAT: Mixed and deciduous woodlands, especially those with clearings; also frequent in parks and large gardens, even in cities.

DISTRIBUTION: Widespread over eastern North America, reaching northern limits in Newfoundland, southern Quebec, central Manitoba and central Alberta and southern limits in Louisiana and eastern Texas. Western limit of range runs through eastern Wyoming, Nebraska and eastern Colorado to west Texas. The breeding range is gradually spreading to the north-west and since the 1970s has become a regular rare autumn and winter migrant in very small numbers to south-east British Colombia and eastern Washington, much rarer further south on west coast and merely a vagrant to California. Has recently nested in Oregon and future breeding and colonisation likely elsewhere in the west. Northernmost populations partially, some wholly, migratory.

STATUS: Very common over most of main part of range, and population increasing, with gradual range extension in west (see distribution).

REFERENCES: Goodwin 1986, Terres 1980.

STELLER'S JAY

Plate 1

Cyanocitta stelleri

Western counterpart of Blue Jay, with the most extensive range of all American Jays, extending from Alaska to Nicaragua.

IDENTIFICATION: Combination of dusky head and body, very prominent crest and blue wings and tail makes this an easy bird to identify in North America, but the situation becomes not quite so straightforward in southern parts of Central America where some races have appreciably shorter crests and are much more bluish in colour. However even here the crest is normally visible, the body is very dark blue and the wings and tail are finely barred. These features are not shown by other Central American jays. Can appear wholly dusky in dull light.

DESCRIPTION: Length 28-32 cm. Bill relatively weak. Tail medium-long, graduated at tip. Head with prominent upstanding crest from mid to rear crown. Legs relatively longer and bill slimmer than in Blue Jay. Nominate race: Crest, head and upper breast brownish to greyish-black, shading a little paler on mantle, back and sides of neck. Forehead feathers with light blue tipping. Chin and throat with whitish fine streaks. Underparts below breast dark greenish-blue with brighter blue on ventral region, rump and uppertail-coverts. Wings bright purplish blue, becoming lighter and more sky-blue on primaries; greater coverts and tertials barred narrowly with black. Tail bright blue, with varying purplish tones and variable amounts of fine barring. Underwing and tail underside dark grey. Bill and legs blackish. Irides blackish-brown.

SEX/AGE: Sexes similar. Juvenile duller overall, with blue of rump and uppertail-coverts dull grey, wings and tail duller blue; bill pale but darkens in first autumn. Juveniles of blue-crested races are dull, greyish-blue on body. Races which have crest streaks or eye-spots when adult either lack these, or have them much reduced in juvenile plumage.

MEASUREMENTS: Male averages somewhat larger than female. Nominate race: Wing 142-161, tail 128-150, tarsus 40-50, bill 28-32, weight 111-142.

GEOGRAPHICAL VARIATION: Very complex. Some 16 races as treated here, with southern forms based on review by Browning (1993). Basically races of North America south to central Mexico (Jalisco) are dusky, black-crested forms and those further south are blue overall, with shorter blue crests. The exception is *azteca*, a black-crested form in the centre of a ring of blue-crested races.

Black-crested races

C. s. *stelleri*: coastal south Alaska to north-west Oregon, described above.
C. s. *carlottae*: Queen Charlotte Islands, British Colombia. The largest and blackest race.
C. s. *annectens*: interior, from British Colombia south to north-east Oregon, east to Alberta and Wyoming. Slightly paler than nominate, more contrast between greyer mantle and blackish head, with a white spot above eye and markings on forehead.
C. s. *carbonacea*: central coastal California (Marin

south to Monterey), smaller than last, with longer crest and no eye-spot.
C. s. *frontalis*: central Oregon south through remainder of California, smaller and paler than last, with blue streaking in crest.
C. s. *macrolopha*: Rocky Mountains, south into north Mexico (Sierra Madre Occidental), east to west Texas. Crest and face glossy black, clear whitish streaks in crest and patch above eye.
C. s. *diademata*: Sierra Madre Oriental, north Mexixo. Similar to last but a little more contrasting, throat also streaked white.
C. s. *azteca*: Central Mexico in north Puebla, Mexico state, Morelos, Distrito Federal and adjacent parts of Veracruz and east Michoacan. Isolated amongst blue-crested races. Slightly bluer than *macrolopha*, with more prominent white marks about eye, crest long with the feathers tipped blue. Wing 149, crest 69. Intergrades with blue-crested race *purpurea*.

Blue-crested races
Mean wing and crest lengths of males given, from Browning (1993).

C. s. *coronata*: north Veracruz and probably adjacent south-east San Luis Potosi. Dark blue, becoming purplish blue above, including head and crest. Wing 144, crest 6l.
C. s. *phillipsi*: south-west San Luis Potosi, northern Guanajuato, west Hidalgo and probably north Queretaro. Lighter and duller blue than *coronata*, lacking purplish tones. Wing 142, crest 60.
C. s. *restricta*: Oaxaca. Paler and purer blue than *coronata*, paler below, throat whiter and crest shorter than *teotepecensis*. Wing 142, crest 67.
C. s. *purpurea*: West and central Michoacan. Darker and more purplish-blue than other blue-crested races. Wing 149, crest 70.
C. s. *teotepecensis*: Central and southern Guerrero. Paler blue and less purplish than *purpurea*. Wing 143, crest 67.
C. s. *ridgwayi*: Chiapas and west Guatemala. Darker blue than *restricta*, with bluer (less whitish) streaks in crest. Wing 146, crest 56.
C. s. *lazula*: El Salvador. Darker and purer blue than either *suavis* or *ridgwayi*. A little known form. Wing 150, crest 58.
C. s. *suavis*: Honduras and Nicaragua. Paler blue than *ridgwayi*, with less white on throat and more contrast between upperparts and crest. Wing 143, crest 58.

VOICE: Vocabulary very varied. Most typical call is a harsh, repeated 'shaaak, shaaak, shaaak'. Also a mellow liquid 'klook, klook' and a variety of shrill squeaks, squawks, clicks and rattles in manner of Blue Jay but most sounds less thin. Like Blue Jay produces mewing cry recalling that of a buzzard. There is some geographic variation with the pitch of the sounds produced, but this has yet to be properly documented. See Brown (1964) for full discussion on the voice of this jay.

HABITS: Familiar about camp sites and picnic spots, especially in the Rocky Mountains, where it can become very confiding. Otherwise generally shy and wary of man. Forages singly or in pairs during late winter and spring but family parties stay together through the autumn, parties often assemble in larger numbers at favoured feeding spots. Feeds both in trees and on the ground, flicking aside leaves and other debris in search for invertebrates, especially caterpillars, beetles, wasps and bees. Also takes a variety of human food scraps. Like most other jays, feeds primarily on nuts and seeds, especially acorns and pine seeds, berries and fruits. Hides acorns and also raids nut stores of woodpeckers. Its omnivorous diet is sometimes supplemented by eggs and nestlings of small birds, frogs and even small snakes. Seen to eat snow even when water available. In winter, parties descend to lower altitudes, even to edges of desert plains, where they visit farmsteads and gardens of small towns. Where ranges overlap, Scrub Jay is dominant over Steller's but latter drives Scrub Jays away from vicinity of its nest site. Occasionally irrupts, as do other conifer-haunting species, into areas where normally absent.

BREEDING: Solitary nester. Nest a bulky structure of twigs, etc., cemented by mud, similar to that of Blue Jay. Constructed between 3 and 5 m up in trees or large shrubs in open forest or by clearing, sometimes as high as 30 m in huge trees and occasionally in tree hollow or buildings. Built by both sexes. Clutch two to six, usually four, eggs similar to those of Blue Jay. Incubation by female, very rarely recorded as shared by male, for about 16 days. Male feeds incubating female and shares in feeding nestlings and fledged young, the latter fledge at about 18 days. Young fed by parents for at least a month after fledging, but remain with adults well into the winter months. Eggs recorded mid to late April in Mexico, April to June in California and May to July in Alaska, but latest dates could be re-nesting attempts after earlier failures.

HABITAT: Coniferous forests and mixed pine-oak woodlands, preferring open forest and forest clearings. Also in open mixed park woodland and large gardens bordering forests. Breeds between 1350-3900 m.

DISTRIBUTION: Widespread over western North and Central America, from southern Alaska and south-west Alberta southwards. Eastern limits in western Montana, Wyoming, south-west South Dakota, western Nebraska, east-central Colorado, New Mexico and south-west Texas. Range extends south through central mountains of Mexico, to Guatemala, Honduras, El Salvador and north-central Nicaragua.

STATUS: Common over most of main part of range, but very local and patchy in parts of southern Mexico and Central America, where some populations little known.

REFERENCES: Brown 1963, 1964, Browning 1993, Goodwin 1986.

APHELOCOMA JAYS *Aphelocoma*

The precise number of genera of the American jays is debatable; there is so much variation within them that they could all (except the very distinct Pinyon Jay) be united into one large polymorphic genus, *Cyanocorax* (Hardy 1969). The genus *Cyanolyca* is a good example of the problem, members of that genus are close to *Aphelocoma* in structure and differences, other than basic colouration, are difficult to define. The more traditional approach is followed here, with merely three species of relatively plain-coloured, crestless jays included in *Aphelocoma*.

SCRUB JAY Plate 2

Aphelocoma coerulescens

Alternative names: see Geographical Variation.

Some populations of this distinctive jay have been very well studied. The social behaviour and voice of the Florida population seem to differ from the others races and it is probably a different species. In view of the similar situation with Grey-breasted Jay, however, a more cautious treatment is followed here.

IDENTIFICATION: A relatively long-tailed jay of dry, shrubby habitats. In flight easily separated from Blue Jay by the lack of white tips to the wing feathers and tail border; the two are most likely to be found together in Florida. Often overlaps with Steller's Jay but much duskier head and body and long crest of latter prevents confusion. Only Grey-breasted Jay is really similar, but latter is uniform dull bluish above, relatively stockier, has unpatterned underparts which lack dark breast band and favours more heavily wooded, rugged habitats. Southern races of Scrub Jay are duller below and can be confusing (see Grey-breasted Jay for discussion). Almost uniform blue Pinyon Jay is shorter-tailed, thinner-billed and is generally found in larger flocks. See also Unicoloured Jay in Mexico.

DESCRIPTION: Length 27-31 cm. Nominate race (Florida): Bill moderately weak. Tail relatively long, graduated at tip. Forehead and short diffuse supercilium whitish, becoming powder blue on crown, nape and sides of neck. Lores dark bluish-grey, becoming dull bluish on ear-coverts and sides of head. Throat and upper breast whitish, diffusely streaked greyer, bordered below by dark, dull blue sides of breast which extend narrowly towards breast centre. Underparts below band dingy pale greyish-buff, darker on flanks and undertail coverts. Mantle and back light greyish-brown or greyish-fawn, contrasting with hood and light powder blue of lower rump, uppertail-coverts. Wings and tail rather dull powder blue. Bill and legs dull blackish. Irides dark brown.

SEX/AGE: Sexes similar. Juvenile duller, with head greyish-brown, flight and tail feathers duller, toned greyish-fawn.

MEASUREMENTS: See Geographical Variation.

GEOGRAPHICAL VARIATION: Complex. There are some 17 described races, varying in degree of colour saturation, strength of breast band, size and to a certain extent in behaviour and voice. The most isolated forms, from Florida and Santa Cruz island, have been proposed as separate species. Accordingly Sibley and Monroe (1990) have accepted three 'allospecies' as indicated below:-

A. coerulescens (Florida Jay): confined to Florida, described above. A very isolated form differing from the others in its smaller size, relatively longer tail, extensively whitish forehead and greyer ear-coverts. Wing 106-113, tail 129-145, tarsus 36-40, bill 24-27, weight mean 80.

A. insularis (Santa Cruz Jay): Santa Cruz island, California. Also isolated, differing from other races in its markedly large size and very bright and rich colouration, being deep blue on head, wings and tail, dark purplish-blue on sides of head and on breast band, almost creamy-white on underparts and with pale blue undertail coverts. The forehead is bright blue and the supercilium thin but clear white. In this form the male is distinctly stouter-billed than the female. Wing 128-140, tail 139-163, tarsus 43-47, bill 32-33, weight mean 116.

A. californica (Scrub Jay): remainder of the range, 15 subspecies which can be assembled into at least three further groupings:-
A. c. californica group: eight races, western USA north to south Washington, east to central Oregon and west Nevada, south into Mexico through Baja California. Colour pattern as *insularis* but smaller and less bright, more fawnish, brown and lacking blue on undertail coverts. Race *californica*: Wing 116-132, tail 125-147, tarsus 38-46, bill 21-27, weight mean 80.
A. c. sumichrasti group: south-central Mexico, two races, *sumichrasti* (Tlaxcala to central Oaxaca) and *remota* (east-central Guerrero). Compared to *californica*, paler above and below with breast band obscure and confined to sides.
A. c. woodhouseii group: five races, south-central USA west to south-east Oregon and Arizona, east to central Texas and south into north-central Mexico to north Tlaxcala (adjoining *sumichrasti*). Compared to *californica*, paler blue, with mantle suffused bluish and less defined, throat heavily smudged with greyish streaks and underparts washed dull bluish-grey making breast band less contrasting.

VOICE: Marked geographical variation, but the full extent of this is not yet fully understood. Florida birds have different calls to studied populations of western races. Vocalisations also vary within defined races; certainly in Florida strong vocal differences are detectable over quite short distances. Typical calls from the Florida populations include a short, rasping squawked 'creep' or 'rheep' rather flat in tone and regularly repeated; also a sweet, loose 'ch,leep'. The Western race *obscurus* utters a louder, excitedly repeated rasping call but it is markedly shriller and has a rising inflection; also given is a loud, ringing chattering 'kay-kay-kay-kay-kay....' and a lower pitched chattering recalling that of Black-billed Magpie (although the notes are more clipped). A magpie-like chatter is also reported from the Santa Cruz form.

HABITS: Normally encountered in pairs or family parties. Pairs are quite strongly territorial, those in Florida average some 12 ha in extent and may also be defended by one or two of their offspring of previous years who may also act as nest helpers. Apparently social breeding is confined to the Florida population. Rich food sources, however, are shared by several territory holders. Feeds primarily on the ground, usually not far from bushy cover, hopping and digging for invertebrates and acorns. Some western races feed chiefly on pine seeds rather than acorns, particularly those of the Pinyon Pine and have been seen to rob Clark's Nutcrackers of both seeds and opened pine cones. Scrub Jays also store both acorns and pine seeds and are important as tree-planting agents. The diet of all races is very varied; a great variety of invertebrates is taken as well as small rodents, eggs and nestlings of small birds, small frogs and lizards. Vegetable matter includes seeds, acorns, berries and fruits. They sometimes search cattle for ectoparasites. They generally keep within bushy cover and are rather furtive in behaviour but at other times they can be quite noisy and conspicuous; they often become tame at feeding stations in gardens and at picnic sites. Intruding predators near the nest may be attacked from behind, cats and other ground predators often have their tails pecked and the birds are away before the animal can turn. Flight action is strong and slightly undulating, a mixture of flapping and gliding; remarkably agile when flying through dense cover. See also monograph, Woolfenden and Fitzpatrick (1984).

BREEDING: Solitary breeder, but social breeding typical of Florida race. Nest of twigs, lined with plant fibres, situated up to 3 m in thickets of shrubs and bushes. Built by both sexes. Clutch two to six, eggs varying from pale green to pale grey, speckled and shaded with brown, reddish and grey. Incubation 16-19 days by female, being fed at the nest by the male. Young fledge at about 18 days, being attended by both sexes. The Florida race is unique amongst the Scrub Jays in that most breeding pairs are assisted in territorial and nest defence and in the feeding of the nestlings by one to three helpers, usually young birds from that pair of the previous year. Helpers however do not assist with incubation, brooding or nest building. Eggs laid late March and April in Florida, a little later, in April to early May, in interior western populations.

HABITAT: Florida Scrub Jays are found in scrubby thickets of mixed shrubs and trees, favouring areas adjacent to clearings; they freely visit nearby gardens. Western races inhabit a variety of open, bushy country including semi-desert scrub, mangroves, orchards and hillsides of mixed pines and oaks, often in almost arid canyons with sparse tree cover. Ascends as high as 3000 m in Colorado.

DISTRIBUTION: Florida race isolated in peninsular Florida but absent from south-central region north to Osceola. Santa Cruz race endemic to Santa Cruz Island off southern California. Other forms widespread over south-central and west USA., from south-east Washington, southwards through Oregon, California and the Baja California peninsula into Mexico. Eastwards across southern Idaho to southern Wyoming, through Nevada and Utah to central Colorado and from Arizona and New Mexico to west and central Texas. In Mexico along the Baja California peninsula, and rather patchily through the central mountains of the north in isolated forms from central Chihuahua and east-central Coahuila south to eastern Guerrero and central Oaxaca.

STATUS: Locally common throughout its range.

References: Peterson 1991, Pitelka 1951, 1961, Woolfenden and Fitzpatrick 1984.

GREY-BREASTED JAY   Plate 2

Aphelocoma ultramarina

Alternative names:
  Mexican Jay

An arboreal stocky relation of the Scrub Jay, with which it overlaps in range but only marginally in habitat.

IDENTIFICATION: Resembles Scrub Jay, especially the drabber southern races with which it overlaps, however is distinctly bulkier, larger-billed, relatively longer-winged and shorter-tailed, and is more arboreal by nature, favouring forested rather than scrubby habitats. Upperparts are more uniformly bluish-grey, washed grey on mantle in some races but typically lacks clearly contrasting brownish 'saddle' of Scrub Jay, some abraded Grey-breasted Jays however have quite brownish-grey backs but other features, including underpart colour, provide easy distinctions. Grey-breasted Jay is dull pale below with strong wash of fawny-grey, except for whiter throat and belly. Scrub Jays even of southern races have at least the start of a band at the side of the breast, diffuse streaking on the wide pale throat and duller grey-toned lower underparts.

DESCRIPTION: Length 28-32 cm. Bill heavier than in Scrub Jay, tail relatively shorter but wing relatively longer. Nominate race: Head, sides of neck and nape and upperparts blue, tinged brownish-grey on mantle and back (grey-brown feather bases show through). Lower back, rump, uppertail-coverts and tail blue. Wings blue, with grey-brown wash to wing-coverts and bases of secondaries when worn. Throat whitish, with faint shaft streaks. becoming pale ashy-grey on remainder of underparts and whitening on undertail-coverts. Bill and legs black. Iris dark brown.

SEX/AGE: Sexes similar. Juvenile duller, with head and upperparts greyer-brown in tone, especially brownish on mantle and wing-coverts; flight feathers and tail almost as blue as in adult. Bill pale fleshy-yellow, tip darker, legs brownish. After first moult, much as adult, but immatures of western races may be pale-billed for several years, whereas eastern races become dark-billed during post-juvenile moult.

MEASUREMENTS: Male averages slightly larger than female. Race *arizonae*: Wing 157-173, tail 136-154, tarsus 41-44, bill 27-32, weight 105-144.

GEOGRAPHICAL VARIATION: Complex. seven races have been described, differing slightly in size and degree of blue and grey tones in upperparts, but more obviously in bill colour of immatures. Eastern races attain blackish bills during their first moult; these are perhaps all territorial forms. Western races may be pale-billed for several years and have social lifestyles (see Habits). Other differences between the races are relatively minor, thus they are merely listed, but in view of similar differences within the Scrub Jay complex, these two racial groupings might also be considered as 'allospecies'. Clearly more intensive field research within Mexico is required, especially in southern parts of the species range where ranges of the groups might meet.

Eastern races (dark-billed post-juvenile stages).
  A. u. couchii: south Texas to south Nuevo Leon and

west Tamaulipas.
  A. u. potosina: eastern central Mexico.
  A. u. colimae: west and central Jalisco and north-east Colima.
  A. u. ultramarina: central Mexico, from south-east Jalsico and north-west Michoacan to central west Veracruz.

Western races (pale-billed immature stages). These forms also rather whiter on throat and lower underparts and more silvery-bluish on upperparts than eastern forms.
  A. u. arizonae: Arizona, New Mexico and north-west Mexico.
  A. u. wollwebberi: western Mexico.
  A. u. gracilis: east Nayarit and north Jalisco.

VOICE: Some geographical variation. Based on most studied races *couchii* and *arizonae*. Typical call remarkably finch-like, a repeated ringing chirped 'wink-wink' - querulous, high-pitched and almost metallic in quality, similar in both forms but squeakier in *arizonae*. Uttered at varying pitches, some quite guttural in quality. The territorial race *couchii* also has a mechanical rattle, lacking from repertoire of *arizonae* but considered to be an aggressive call probably used in territorial defence.

HABITS: Social habits differ between eastern and western groups of races, at least in northernmost populations. Western races sociable, living in flocks of six to 20 birds throughout the year; these flocks contain one or two breeding pairs plus a number of non-breeding immatures, offspring of previous years, which act as nest helpers. Race *couchii* of Texas is territorial when breeding and it seems that bill colouration of immatures is an important symbol in territorial defence. Other aspects of their behaviour are similar (but note egg colour differences). Flocks noisily forage amongst leaf litter under trees, where their diet is similar to that of the Scrub Jay. However their lightly wooded and rugged habitat is distinctly different; the birds forage and perch at mid canopy level in trees as well as on the ground and follow walkers and picnickers for scraps. They are often remarkably tame and will take food from the hand in areas where protected. Their flight is strong, flocks flying up to perch on rocky outcrops above forest to catch the last of the sun before going to roost and vice versa in the cool of the early morning.

BREEDING: Solitary and social breeder (see Habits and below). Nest of twigs, lined with plant fibres, situated in trees (usually oaks) between 2 and 15 m from ground (usually between 5 and 8 m). Built by both sexes, but actual construction mostly by female; in social units sometimes a helper will also bring materials. Clutch three to seven, usually four beautiful unmarked green eggs in *arizonae*, pale yellowish or bluish-green, speckled dark brown in eastern forms. Incubation 17-18 days by female, being fed at the nest by the male and often also by a procession of helpers, incubation possibly occasionally shared by another female. Young fledge at 24 to 26 days, being fed and tended by the flock. Eggs recorded late March to mid April.

HABITAT: Mountainsides, canyons and hillsides with mixed pine-oak woodland or mainly oak forests, generally from 1200 - 1800 m.

DISTRIBUTION: Mexico and extreme southern USA. Northern limit of eastern group of races is the Chisos

72

Mountains in south-west Texas, from here they range into Mexico through the eastern central mountain chain south to Puebla, Guerrero and central Veracruz and west to Jalisco and Colima. Western races occur from central Arizona and south-west New Mexico south through western central mountains to north Jalisco.

STATUS: Locally common throughout its range, even locally common at sites in extreme southern USA.

REFERENCES: Brown 1963, 1970, Brown and Horvath 1989, Ligon and Sandra 1974.

UNICOLOURED JAY   Plate 8

Aphelocoma unicolor

A beautiful and very local uniformly blue 'Scrub Jay' of cloud forests, foraging both low in undergrowth and quite high on large tree branches.

IDENTIFICATION: Uniform deep slate-blue colouration, size and shape (which recall that of Grey-breasted Jay) and flocking behaviour render this lovely jay quite unmistakable if seen well, but it can appear quite blackish in dull light. Black-throated Jay may appear similarly dark, is also sociable and has 'Scrub Jay-like' calls but is smaller and slimmer, with black face and throat and has narrow whitish line above eye if seen well. Both are likely in similar habitats.

DESCRIPTION: Length 27-32 cm. Structure recalls Grey-breasted Jay but bill stouter and finer at tip. Nominate race: Almost entire plumage deep dark blue, changing in overall tones with angle of light. Wings and tail a little duller blue. Loral region blackish. Underwing dark brownish-grey. With wear, grey feather bases become exposed making the bird appear more greyish-blue. Irides dark brown. Bill and legs black.

SEX/AGE: Sexes similar. Juvenile markedly duller, brownish-grey with bluer wings and yellowish bill; as in western races of Grey-breasted Jay the pale bill colouration is retained and does not darken until the completion of the first summer moult.

MEASUREMENTS: Male averages slightly larger than female. Nominate race: Wing 155-169, tail 144-160, tarsus 41-43, bill 28-30, weight 121-130.

GEOGRAPHICAL VARIATION: Complex. Five races have been described, differing slightly in degree of purplish in plumage and minor size features, the most different being *guerrensis*.

A. u. unicolor: Chiapas and Guatemala, described above.

A. u. concolor: west central Veracruz, Puebla, presumably this form recently discovered eastern Hidalgo, duller and slightly more purplish.

A. u. griscomi: El Salvador and west Honduras, more

purplish and bill larger.

A. u. oaxacae: central Oaxaca, slighter longer-tailed and smaller-billed than the last.

A. u. guerrensis: south-central Guerrero, bright purplish-blue with relatively longer tail and shorter wings than nominate. The most distinct form.

VOICE: The only recorded calls sound not unlike the finch-call of Grey-breasted Jay but are rather fuller; a loud ringing chirped 'chink-chink...', more frequently uttered, almost becoming a chattering outburst, interspersed with quiet chittering notes.

HABITS: Social habits seem to be remarkably similar to those of the western races of Grey-breasted Jay. Highly sociable, usually met with in small flocks foraging either near or on ground under shrubby cover or investigating branches of large forest trees, searching clumps of bromeliads, lichens and other epiphytes for invertebrates. These small parties typically consist of from four to nine birds, composed of a breeding pair plus 'secondary' members of both sexes. 'Secondary' males will occasionally attempt copulation with the main female but this is usually foiled by the dominant male. The group forages over an area of some 30 ha, the boundaries of which all members help defend. The group noisily scold, mob and will even attack potential predators. Foraging parties are often joined by other birds including woodcreepers and orioles.

BREEDING: Social breeder. Nest a bowl of twigs, lined with finer plant materials. Placed chiefly in oaks at between 6 and 24m from the ground. Constructed by the primary pair of the group, helped to a small degree by other group members. Eggs not described. Incubation by main female being fed by all group members. Three or four nestlings noted in study nests, were fed by all of group members, fledging at 21-26 days. Feeding continues for at least 50 days after leaving nest. Egg laying period March.

HABITAT: Montane cloud forest, both mixed oak-pine and pure oak, generally between 1500-3400 m. Descending lower into secondary growth in winter.

DISTRIBUTION: Somewhat patchily distributed in the mountains of south-central Mexico; from west-central Veracruz, eastern Hidalgo, Puebla and east Mexico, central Guerrero, central Oaxaca and Chiapas into Guatemala and adjacent areas of northern El Salvador and western Honduras.

STATUS: Little known species, now diminishing through habitat destruction, perhaps no longer in Veracruz, Mexico state or Puebla (a 1985 record was the first recent record for that state). Apparently still reasonably common in parts of Guerrero. Distribution seems always to have been rather patchy, but it is becoming more and more fragmented by forest clearance and the species must rank as threatened.

REFERENCES: Peterson 1991, Pitelka 1951, Webber and Brown (in press).

CYANOLYCA JAYS *Cyanolyca*

A complex of nine species of Central American and Andean jays, all of which are smaller and sleeker birds than *Cyanocorax* jays and lack crests or frontal tufts. Structurally the genus is poorly differentiated from *Aphelocoma*, its members being uniformly deeper and darker blue, with a black mask and more arboreal in their habits.

THE COLLARED JAYS

Black-collared, Turquoise and White-collared Jays are very similar and have at times been treated as races of one polymorphic species, the Collared Jay *C. viridicyana*. They do replace each other ecologically in the upper levels of Andean forests from Venezuela to Bolivia, but Turquoise and Black-collared overlap and it is now known that vocalisations of all three differ. In view of the complex relationships of several groups of Neotropical jays it seems reasonable to assume that speciation has occurred.

BLACK-COLLARED JAY   Plate 3

Cyanolyca armillata

Alternative name: Collared Jay.

Northern counterpart of White-collared Jay with which it was formerly treated as conspecific, but it differs vocally as well as in plumage and range.

IDENTIFICATION: Andes from west Venezuela, through central and eastern Colombia to north Ecuador. Slim deep-blue jay with a black mask and thin black line across lower throat, crown lighter blue. Range overlaps with very similar Turquoise Jay in southern Colombia and north Ecuador, but Black-collared generally much scarcer and intolerant of degraded forest; Turquoise Jay shows more contrast between blue of head and greenish-blue of rest of plumage, especially on underparts, has relatively shorter tail and much paler, almost bluish-white crown and throat. Replaced by (but does not meet) even rarer Beautiful Jay on Pacific slope of Andes, which is smaller, more violet-blue, lacks thin black collar and has much paler, almost whitish throat, crown and nape; this species also favours forest understorey and gulleys at lower elevations than Black-collared.
DESCRIPTION: Length 30-34 cm. Nominate race: Bill relatively weak. Tail relatively long, graduated at tip. Forehead, lores and sides of head black. Throat almost ultramarine-blue, bordered by a narrow black line which connects to rear of black ear-coverts. Crown and nape light violaceous-blue, hardly contrasting with remainder of body, wings and tail which are bright dark-blue. Wings and tail upperside slightly duller blue. Underwing and underside of tail blackish. Bill and legs black. Irides brown (needs confirmation).
SEX/AGE: Sexes similar. Juvenile duller, with greyer throat, body feathers greyish with blue only at tips.
MEASUREMENTS: Nominate race (other forms are larger): Wing 124, tail 165, tarsus 38, bill 29 (one specimen measured), weight 190 and 210 (two).
GEOGRAPHICAL VARIATION: three races differing in size and colour tone of blue in body plumage.

   C. a. armillata: By Rio Chiquito in south-west Tachira, Venezuela and along eastern Colombian Andes, south to Cundinamarca. Described above.
   C. a. meridana: Andes of west Venezuela in Trujillo,

Merida and northern Tachira. Similar but darker and more purplish-blue overall. Irides said to be bluish.
   C. a. quindiuna: Andes of central Colombia south into extreme north Ecuador. Larger than the other two forms, with relatively heavier bill and plumage tinged greenish on body, wings and tail, offering some contrast with mauve blue of crown and throat.
VOICE: Has quite a complex vocabulary composed of a variety of short and often musical notes. Most freely uttered are a rising, almost twanging 'shrwee', various shrill rising and falling notes, a sharp, stuttered 'jet-jtjtjtjt', a low guttural 'wowr' and a soft, liquid 'craa'. These various sounds seem to be uttered in various combinations in quite rapid sequences.
HABITS: Poorly documented. Typically encountered in small, loose, parties working middle and upper canopy levels of the forest, keeping in vocal contact with each other. Forages along branches festooned with epiphytes, hopping along and pausing to peer through foliage. Occasionally descends to gulleys with tree ferns and bamboo thickets.
BREEDING: Nest and eggs undescribed. Birds in breeding condition have been collected between June and October in Colombia.
HABITAT: Humid, mossy, cloud forest between 1600 and 3250 m.
DISTRIBUTION: Two disjunct ranges in the northern Andes. The bluest races along the eastern Andes of Colombia from Cundinamarca northwards into extreme north-west Venezuela through Tachira and Merida to Trujillo. The larger and greener-blue form is found at the north end of the west slope of the central Colombian Andes in Antioqua and along the entire length of the eastern slope, south into northern Ecuador (extreme eastern Carchi and north-west Napo).
STATUS: Distinctly scarce and poorly known over most of its range. Quite numerous in western Venezuela. Uncommon, even rare, throughout most of the Colombian Andes, even in areas of good habitat, and only reasonably common in southern Colombia in eastern Narino. Exceptionally rare in Ecuador, where only known from two records.
Reference: Hardy 1990, Hilty and Brown 1986, Ridgely and Tudor 1989.

TURQUOISE JAY   Plate 3

Cyanolyca turcosa

Replaces Black-collared Jay in the Andes of Ecuador, but quite widely overlaps with it over northern part of range, proving its validity as a good species.

IDENTIFICATION: Very similar to race *quindiuna* of Black-collared Jay with which it overlaps in northern Ecuador and southern Colombia but latter is not quite so greenish-blue, and has darker blue crown and throat (both much paler, almost whitish-blue in Turquoise) and is slightly longer-tailed, additionally the narrow black collar is even narrower in Turquoise. Also locally meets rarer Beautiful Jay on Pacific slope of Andes, which is smaller, more violet blue, lacks thin black collar and has more extensively whitish crown and nape.

DESCRIPTION: Length 32 cm. Bill relatively stronger than nominate Black-collared, but close to race *quindiuna*. Tail relatively long, but shorter than all races of Black-collared. Forehead, lores and sides of head black. Throat very pale almost turquoise blue darkening to purplish-blue towards lower throat and narrow black collar. Crown and nape pale turquoise-blue, becoming paler on forecrown. Remainder of plumage greenish-blue except for blackish underwing and underside to tail. Bill and legs black. Irides probably brown.

SEX/AGE: Sexes similar. Juvenile apparently duller, probably similar to that of Black-collared Jay.

MEASUREMENTS: Wing 137, tail 142, tarsus 39, bill 34, (one specimen measured) weight unrecorded.

GEOGRAPHICAL VARIATION: Monotypic.

Voice: Most typical calls are a loud, piercing, descending 'tsrrrp' and a liquid explosive 'kworrr', both may be repeated three or four times. Also has several other short calls, including a repeated clicked snapping sound.

HABITS: Poorly documented. Forages in small parties in mid and upper canopy of forest trees, more tolerant of open and secondary forest than is Black-collared Jay.

BREEDING: No information.

HABITAT: Humid forests, both primary and secondary, extending to lower growth of elfin forest, in degraded woodland has a tendency to favour stands of Alders. Chiefly between 1500 and 3000 m.

DISTRIBUTION: Centred on the Ecuadorian Andes. Northern limit of range is in Narino (but probably extends north to Cauca) in southern Colombia, ranging south over both Pacific and eastern slopes of Andes through central Ecuador to southern limit in northern Peru (north Piura and north-western Cajamarca).

STATUS: Quite common in Ecuador, but rare and little known in Colombia and Peru.

REFERENCES: Hardy 1990, Hilty and Brown 1986, Ridgely and Tudor 1989.

WHITE-COLLARED JAY   Plate 3

Cyanolyca viridicyana

Alternative name: Collared Jay

Southernmost of the three species within this complex, with a range that does not quite meet the Turquoise Jay.

IDENTIFICATION: Very similar to Black-collared and Turquoise Jays but range does not overlap with either. Almost meets latter in northern Peru but White-collared only on eastern slope of the Andes and is unknown in range of Turquoise. Northern race of White-collared is clear dark purplish-blue (lacking green tones of Turquoise), with throat and crown chiefly dark blue (both very light blue in Turquoise) and if seen well, the narrow white collar is diagnostic.

DESCRIPTION: Length 34 cm. Nominate race: Bill relatively weak. Tail relatively long, graduated at tip. Forehead, lores and sides of head black. Throat dark greenish-blue, bordered by a narrow white line which curves to meet rear of black ear-coverts, in some birds white of supercilium curves behind ear-coverts to join white collar. Forecrown and sides of crown white, forming a narrow border to ear-coverts, central and rear crown and nape bright pale greenish-blue. Remainder of plumage relatively dull greenish-blue. Underwing and underside of tail blackish. Bill and legs black. Irides dark brown.

SEX/AGE: Sexes similar. Juvenile presumed to be duller and similar to that of Black-collared.

MEASUREMENTS: Nominate race: Wing 134, tail 162, tarsus 38, bill 33 (one specimen measured), weight 82-127.

GEOGRAPHICAL VARIATION: three races differing in tone of blue in body plumage and extent of white on crown.

   C. v. viridicyana: North-west Bolivia. The greenest race, described above.
   C. v. cyanolaema: South-east Peru. Bluer than nominate, less greenish, with throat dark blue.
   C. v. joylaea: Central and Northern Peru, south to Junin. The bluest race, almost purplish-blue, with white of crown restricted to forecrown; chin very pale blue becoming purplish-blue on throat; white collar narrower than in nominate race.

VOICE: Has quite a complex vocabulary, but tends to be more repetitive when calling than Black-collared, thus more like Turquoise in this respect. Sound recordings of race *joylaea* include a rapid, dull chatter not unlike a tinny burst of fire from a machine-gun 'chdchdchdchdchd...', a repeated piped, mellow 'wau' at regular intervals, a series of hollow clicks and explosive piercing whistles.

HABITS: Poorly documented. Encountered in small, relatively quiet, parties working along branches, peering into clumps of epiphytes and crevices. Said to be oblivious to the presence of human observers.

BREEDING: Undocumented.

HABITAT: Humid luxuriant cloud forest and higher up in more stunted elfin forest, favours bushy clearings. Chiefly between 2000 and 3000 m, but in Peru up to 4000 m.

DISTRIBUTION: Eastern slope of the Andes of eastern Peru, north to Amazonas, extending into north-western Bolivia in provinces of La Paz and Cochabamba.

STATUS: Generally uncommon over most of its range, but locally fairly commn in parts of Peru.

REFERENCES: Hardy 1990, Ridgely and Tudor 1989.

AZURE-HOODED JAY — Plate 4

Cyanolyca cucullata

One of the most widespread of the genus, occurring throughout most of Central America. Forms a species-pair with Beautiful Jay of Colombia.

IDENTIFICATION: An extremely dark jay, the overall blue-black colouration being relieved by striking bright sky-blue crown and nape, bordered by a narrow white line, which in northern race curves widely down behind rear ear-coverts. This combination shared by no other jays within its range; but the rare and restricted Black-throated Jay recorded sharing same trees, is markedly smaller, with rich blue crown and nape concolourous with remainder of upperparts and body and, if seen well, shows only very fine whitish line bordering sides of crown. Compare Silvery-throated Jay in Costa Rica (which does not actually overlap in range or habitat).
DESCRIPTION: Length 26-31 cm. Bill relatively heavy. Tail medium-long, graduated at tip. Feathers of forehead and lores short, dense and tufted. Nominate race: Forehead, sides of head, throat, breast and mantle black. Forecrown and sides of crown narrowly silvery-white, shading bright sky-blue over remainder of crown and nape. Rest of body, wings and tail dark blue, becoming purplish-blue on back and breast. Bill and legs black. Irides dark red.
SEX/AGE: Sexes similar. Juvenile duller, more sooty on head and breast, blue of body darker and duller, crown ad nape dull blue without whitish, irides presumably dull brown.
MEASUREMENTS: Nominate race: Wing 115-131, tail 115-146, tarsus 40-43, bill 25-33, mean weight 88.
GEOGRAPHICAL VARIATION: three subspecies differing in size and crown pattern.
C. c. cucullata: Costa Rica and Panama. Described above.
C. c. hondurensis: Caribbean slope of western Honduras. Extent of white at crown sides intermediate between the other two races, underparts duller, less purplish-blue.
C. c. mitrata: Mexico to Guatemala. Larger than nominate (wing 126-139, mean weight 100), with black forehead extending further back onto crown and white border to ear-coverts wider at sides of neck, forming more obvious white area behind and below rear ear-coverts.
VOICE: Most frequent call is a loud, explosive 'djeek-djeek-djeek' with varying emphasis. This call freely uttered by moving parties, interspersed with soft whistles and rasping notes. Also has a soft, clear, upslurred 'woyt' and a dry, scolding, raucous 'raaaaah'.
HABITS: Roams through lower and middle levels of forest canopy in pairs or small parties of up to ten birds, favouring dense, tall shrubbery of forest understorey and edges but also ascends to upper level of canopy. Forages quietly, probing clumps of moss and epiphytes, peering into and gleaning invertebrates from amongst foliage and crevices of tree trunks. Only really vocal when on the move, but then can be quite noisy. Food items recorded include various invertebrates, berries and small fruits.
BREEDING: Solitary nester. Nest a crudely-constructed platform of twigs, with a cup of smaller twigs, lined roughly with plant fibres. Situation at 5-7 m in small trees at edge of forest. Eggs not described, the two nests so far discovered each contained two young. Breeding noted April-June in Costa Rica.
HABITAT: Humid mossy cloud forest, forest borders and oak woodland, between 900 and 2100 m.
DISTRIBUTION: Widespread through Central American highland forest, from south-eastern Mexico (Gulf slope in south San Luis Potasi, Veracruz and adjacent Oaxaca, also in interior Chiapas) through Guatemala to western Honduras. Another population occurs along Caribbean slope of Costa Rica from Volcan Arenal to western Panama (Veraguas), with range locally extending over onto Pacific slope of mountains.
STATUS: Despite wide range it is comparatively uncommon overall, but this could be a reflection of its less conspicuous behaviour compared to a number of other Central American jays.
REFERENCES: Hardy 1990, Stiles and Skutch 1989.

BEAUTIFUL JAY — Plate 3

Cyanolyca pulchra

A little-known, rare and decreasing, jay of the Pacific slope of Colombia. The shortly tufted frontal feathering is shared by Azure-hooded of Middle America, with which it probably forms a species-pair.

IDENTIFICATION: A dull violet-blue jay with contrasting wide black mask, bright blue upper mantle and very pale throat, crown and nape. Less sociable than Turquoise Jay with which it overlaps, usually only in pairs in lower canopy of forest, and at lower elevations (900-2300 m, whereas Turquoise above 1500 m). Further differs in lacking black collar on lower throat, lacking green in plumage tones (but often washed brown on upperparts) and in being a little smaller and relatively shorter-tailed.
DESCRIPTION: Length 27 cm. Bill relatively heavy. Tail medium-long, graduated at tip. Feathers of forehead and lores short, dense and tufted. Forehead, lores and sides of head black. Chin black, throat light violet-blue, darkening on upper breast. Crown and nape bright whitish-blue, narrowly whiter along upper border of black ear-coverts. Upper mantle and band across upper breast bright violet-blue. Remainder of plumage dark violet-blue, brightest on the wings and uppertail-coverts. Underside of wings and tail blackish. Mantle, lower breast, scapulars and wing-coverts often strongly washed brown. Bill and legs black. Irides brown.
SEX/AGE: Sexes similar, but females usually with brownish tones on upperparts as in first-year birds. Juvenile drabber and browner than adults, but poorly documented. First-year birds retain brown feathering on mantle and wing-coverts and it is possible that only older males loose brown more or less completely.
MEASUREMENTS: Wing 135, tail 120, tarsus 34, bill 33, weight unrecorded (one specimen measured).
GEOGRAPHICAL VARIATION: Monotypic.
VOICE: Calls recorded include a quickly repeated, mellow 'chew,chew,chew', which can be more piercing and explosive in delivery; also a repeated short dry

'graasp' of varying intensity, and a variety of short, single notes based on variants of these. A common call is a double 'click' followed by a rising whistle, repeated by a single 'click' and whistle.

HABITS: Poorly documented. Found singly or in pairs in low growth in gulleys and forest understorey; a lively bird, bouncing and bobbing when calling and peering into foliage and flitting across forest trails whilst foraging. Choice of lower-level foraging and solitary habits renders it more likely to be overlooked than congeners, but very vocal and most easily located by voice. One bird was watched 'mobbing' in a very forceful fashion, trying to chase away a Plate-billed Mountain-Toucan by repeatedly flying into it.

BREEDING: Undocumented.

HABITAT: Humid mossy cloud forest, forest borders and secondary forest, between 900 and 2300 m.

DISTRIBUTION: Pacific slope of western Andes from central Colombia (extreme southern Choco and Valle), south Pichincha in north-western Ecuador.

STATUS: Always rare and little known, but it seems to have suffered marked decline in recent years, especially in Ecuador. Reasons for this are as yet unknown, but probably not forest destruction as habitat still intact over large areas of its range.

REFERENCES: Hardy 1990, Hilty and Brown 1986, Ridgely and Tudor 1989, Pearman 1993.

BLACK-THROATED JAY   Plate 4

Cyanolyca pumilo

Alternative name: Black-throated Dwarf Jay

A little known jay, confined to a small area of mountains in central Middle America.

IDENTIFICATION: A small, slim dark blue jay, with black throat and face, the general dark appearance being relieved by an inconspicuous fine whitish border to upperside of black mask, but latter only visible under exceptional viewing conditions. Small size and black throat prevents confusion with other similar jays, although only known to overlap with Azure-hooded. Latter is markedly larger with striking sky-blue nape and whitish sides to neck and is darker blue overall.

DESCRIPTION: Length 26-28 cm. Bill relatively weak. Tail long, graduated at tip. Feathers of forehead and lores short, dense and tufted. Forehead, sides of head and throat black. Forecrown and sides of crown with fine whitish border to black of forehead and mask. Crown, nape, mantle and breast deep purplish-blue, becoming a duller, slightly greener-blue over remainder of plumage. Wings and tail brighter blue. Underwing dark grey. Bill and legs black. Irides probably brown.

SEX/AGE: Sexes similar, but female duller. Juvenile duller, with black of head more greyish-black shading to blue-grey on throat; lacks narrow whitish border to crown.

MEASUREMENTS: Wing 110-119, tail 109-120, tarsus 30-33, bill 21-24, weight 47 (one measured).

GEOGRAPHICAL VARIATION: Monotypic.

VOICE: Calls bear a striking resemblance to some populations of Scrub Jays from western USA. Record-

ings indicate that calls are short and rapidly repeated. A soft, almost contented, low, chuckled 'cheecheecheecheeche...' and a repeated squeaked 'kirwik-kirwik-kirwik-kirwik. Literature references also include a soft, querulous 'shrreee' and a short whining note interspersed with sharper calls.

HABITS: Typically encountered in parties of up to 12 birds, working various levels of forest from the understorey to the upper canopy, foraging in hanging vines and in canopy of tall shrubbery and trees. Favours dense shrubbery of forested ravines. Probes and pokes for invertebrates amongst clumps of leaves and lichens along branches and trunks. Although descends to quite low levels, not recorded as feeding on ground. Generally quite approachable and more confiding than most other species of jays. Has been observed feeding in same trees as Azure-hooded Jays but parties did not mix.

BREEDING: Undocumented.

HABITAT: Humid cloud forest, especially forest ravines; occasionally in more open forests of mixed oaks, alders and pines. Between 1200 and 3050m.

DISTRIBUTION: Very restricted range in mountains of south-eastern Mexico (south-western Chiapas) and adjacent regions of El Salvador, western Honduras and western and southern Guatemala.

STATUS: Not uncommon over restricted range, but detailed information lacking.

REFERENCES: Hardy 1990, Goodwin 1986.

DWARF JAY   Plate 4

Cyanolyca nana

The smallest of the American jays, confined to a small area of forest in southern Mexico. It feeds in the tree canopy with great agility, showing none of the cumbersome actions of other jays.

IDENTIFICATION: A small, slim dull-blue jay, with a wide black mask and very pale, almost whitish throat and supercilium; the throat is highlighted by a diffuse dusky breast band. No other similar jays occur within its range or habitat, but compare more strikingly patterned, slightly bulkier, and equally rare, White-throated Jay elsewhere in southern Mexico. Feeding habits recall smaller passerines, rather than the jays.

DESCRIPTION: Length 20-23 cm. Bill small and weak. Legs thin and slender. Tail long, graduated at tip. Lores, malar region and ear-coverts black. Forehead very pale, almost whitish-blue with very light blue supercilium bordering black mask and curving down behind rear of ear-coverts. Throat silvery whitish-blue, bordered below by a dusky blue, but somewhat diffuse, band across upper breast. Remainder of underparts dull, greyish-blue. Crown and nape violet-blue, becoming slightly duller violet-blue over remainder of upperparts, brightest on wing and tail feathers. Underwing and underside of tail dull greyish. Bill and legs black, irides red-brown.

SEX/AGE: Sexes similar, but female slightly duller. Juvenile duller, with dull greyish-blue throat; forehead and supercilium dull greenish-blue and not noticeably paler than rest of crown.

MEASUREMENTS: Wing 107-117, tail 111-117, tarsus

29-33, bill 17-20, weight 40 and 42 (two specimens measured).

GEOGRAPHICAL VARIATION: Monotypic.

VOICE: Vocabulary limited, most typical call is a two-syllable, rather harsh and nasal, but high-pitched 'yeeyip, yeeyip' usually soon repeated. A more raucous and longer, harsh squawk is also given, but more rarely.

HABITS: Much less sociable than most other Neotropical jays, generally being found in well-scattered pairs, but after breeding season forms small, loose, gatherings of up to a dozen birds which associate with other forest passerines in mixed foraging flocks, typified by the presence of the Grey-barred Wren *Camylorhyncus megalopterus*. Feeds relatively high in forest trees, where it works the foliage and branches of the sub-canopy with great agility. It hovers briefly and hangs upside-down in the manner of tits as it investigates clumps of bromeliads, lichens and ferns for invertebrates. Also pokes and probes cracks and crevices and under loose bark in more typical jay-like manner. Unlike most other jays it seems to have no association with acorns; its diet seems to be entirely insectivorous.

BREEDING: Solitary nester. Nest relatively large for such a small jay, constructed with mosses, lichens, pine-needles and some twigs, cup lined with rootlets or needles and some strands of grass. Placed near end of branch or in the crown of an oak between 3 and 15 m from the ground. Nest-building shared apparently by both sexes. Clutch two or three, pale greenish-blue eggs, mottled olive. Incubation by female only for about 20 days, being fed at or near the nest by male. Both sexes feed the young. Eggs laid from late March to late April.

HABITAT: Humid montane mixed pine and oak forests between 1500 and 3000 m. Forest types vary from those which are predominately oak with a few large scattered pines and a dense shrubby understorey to more evenly mixed oak, pines and firs with abundant epiphytic growth.

DISTRIBUTION: Endemic to south-central Mexico, where known from Veracruz, Puebla and Oaxaca.

STATUS: Not uncommon within restricted range, but in the breeding season population densities are low. Hardy (1971) has shown that this rare bird is particularly prone to deserting if humans disturb it at the nest that its canopy feeding habits make it vulnerable to Sharp-shinned Hawks. The forests in its range are being gradually destroyed by logging and it may already be extinct in Veracruz and Puebla, as all recent observations come from its remaining habitat in Oaxaca. Former reports of its occurrence in the adjoining state of Mexico are probably erroneous.

REFERENCES: Hardy 1971, 1990, Goodwin 1986.

WHITE-THROATED JAY   Plate 4

Cyanolyca mirabilis

Alternative name: Omilteme Jay

A strikingly-patterned small jay, confined to a small area of southern Mexico, where it is threatened by habitat destruction. Closely-related to Silvery-throated Jay of

Costa Rica, with which it forms a species-pair.

IDENTIFICATION: A small, slate-blue jay, with a striking head pattern created by conspicuous white throat and supercilium, which join at the sides of the neck to isolate the black mask. This bridled head pattern renders this rare jay quite unmistakable. Compare Dwarf Jay, but ranges do not overlap.

DESCRIPTION: Length 23-25 cm. Bill moderately stout. Tail long, graduated at tip. Forehead and lores with an inconspicuous tuft of very short stiff feathers. Forehead, lores, malar region and forepart of ear-coverts black. A conspicuous white band over forecrown, extends above the mask as a supercilium to join white rear ear-coverts and throat at sides of neck. Remainder of crown, nape, sides of neck and upper breast black. Remainder of plumage dull slate-blue with a weak greenish tone. Underwing dark grey. Bill and leg black. Irides probably brown.

SEX/AGE: Sexes similar. Juvenile said to be duller, but head pattern remains obvious.

MEASUREMENTS: Wing 103, tail 108, tarsus 30, bill 22 (one specimen measured), weight 50-54.

GEOGRAPHICAL VARIATION: Monotypic.

VOICE: Like Dwarf Jay, calls are typically uttered in twos and quickly repeated, but are less high-pitched, less nasal and somehow sweeter. Recordings indicate a rather squeaked, chirping 'chi-eery, cherrup' but this call varies in pitch and emphasis, one example being much more nasal and closer to that of Dwarf Jay. A nasal 'reek' of alarm has also been noted from a distressed bird.

HABITS: Virtually undocumented. Reported to be found in pairs and very small (family ?) parties. Presumably much as Silvery-throated Jay.

BREEDING: Undocumented.

HABITAT: Montane humid forests, favouring oak forest, but also recorded in mixed and coniferous forests. Recorded as occurring up to 3500 m.

DISTRIBUTION: Endemic to south-west Mexico, where it is known from the Sierra Madre del Sur in Guerrero and in adjacent Oaxaca in the Sierra de Miahuatlan and Sierra de Yucuyacua.

STATUS: Presumably not uncommon in restricted range, but detailed information lacking. This area of Mexico is under pressure from forest clearance and overgrazing, which could well confine its range to the higher forests and reduce its population to dangerously low levels.

REFERENCES: Hardy 1971, 1990, Goodwin 1986.

SILVERY-THROATED JAY   Plate 4

Cyanolyca argentigula

Closely-related to White-throated Jay of Mexico, but confined to high altitude forests in Costa Rica and adjacent west Panama.

IDENTIFICATION: A small, dark blue jay, with a gleaming white throat and eye-brow; quite unmistakable within its range, which almost meets that of the Azure-hooded Jay.

DESCRIPTION: Length 25-27 cm. Bill moderately stout. Tail long, graduated at tip. Forehead and lores with an inconspicuous tuft of very short stiff feathers. Race *albior*: forehead, lores, malar region and ear-coverts black. Throat and upper breast shining silvery-white, tinged with violet in fresh plumage. A narrow but conspicuous white band over forecrown extends above the mask as a supercilium (tinged violet in fresh plumage). Black of head extends onto mantle, lower breast and sides of neck but becomes rich, dark purple-blue over remainder of plumage. Wings and tail clearer, brighter blue with a hint of greenish in some lights. Underwing and tail underside blackish. Bill and leg black. Irides dark red.

SEX/AGE: Sexes similar. Juvenile duller, with dull greyish-black areas on head, crown dusky blue and lacks whitish on forecrown and in supercilium, irides presumably duller.

MEASUREMENTS: Race *albior*: Wing 118-129, tail 119-123, tarsus 32-37, bill 27-30, weight mean 65.

GEOGRAPHICAL VARIATION: Despite limited range, two subspecies recognised.

C. a. *argentigula*: eastern Costa Rica and western Panama. White of throat, forecrown and supercilium strongly washed violet.

C. a. *albior*: central Costa Rica. Described above, has whiter throat, forecrown and supercilium.

VOICE: Most typical call a harsh, nasal, rather scratchy 'jew-jeah-jeah' or a single 'nyaaaah'; also has a harsh scolding 'zhraaank'. When taking flight utters two to four sharper 'nyat nyat nyat'. Young birds give a quicker,

higher-pitched 'nyaah nyaah'.

HABITS: Usually encountered in small parties of four to ten birds which forage over quite extensive areas of high montane forest, after end of breeding season larger gatherings of up to 30 birds may form. Such parties also roost communally, being quite noisy when going to roost. Feeding parties move through foliage in rather loose association, feeding high in canopy or subcanopy but descending lower at forest edges and clearings. They feed on invertebrates, small frogs, small lizards, salamanders, berries and small fruits. Foraging parties search quietly and methodically through each tree before moving on, probing and pecking into clumps of epiphytes such as lichens, mosses and bromeliads.

BREEDING: Nest undescribed, breeding season considered to be March to June.

HABITAT: Montane humid cloud forests, favouring oak forest, chiefly between 2000 and 3200 m, but seasonally descends as low as 1300 m.

DISTRIBUTION: Virtually endemic to Costa Rica. In Costa Rica it occurs from the Irazu-Turrialba massif, southwards along the Cordillera de Talamanca to just extend into extreme western Panama in the Chiriqui highlands.

STATUS: Overall rather uncommon, with a low-density population in Costa Rica and seemingly very uncommon in Panama.

REFERENCES: Hardy 1990, Stiles and Skutch 1989.

CISSILOPHA JAYS subgenus *Cissilopha*

A group of four superficially similar Central American jays, characterised by their black heads and body plumage and unmarked bright blue upperparts and tails. Unlike most other corvids they have prolonged immature stages involving complex changes to the colours of their bare parts. Despite their obvious plumage similarities, the species differ in habitat choice, social behaviour, age process and voice. Only two species actually overlap (San Blas and Purplish-backed) but even here, the degree of sympatry is slight. The other two (Bushy-crested and Yucatan) are quite well separated by altitude and habitat (see distribution and maps).

All have complex social relationships, in which breeding pairs are helped in the rearing of their young by several non-breeding flock members. Flocks are of mixed ages, the colour and pattern of whose bare parts varies in each species. The colour changes to the bare parts are complex and have been summarised in a table. Its value as a field aid is however rather limited as there is a degree of individual variation.

BUSHY-CRESTED JAY   Plate 5

Cyanocorax melanocyaneus

Alternative name: Hartlaub's Jay

One of the most distinct of the black-and-blue jays; the only one with black legs and bluish lower underparts at all ages.

IDENTIFICATION: The only *Cissilopha* in its range and the only one with blue lower underparts and black legs. Some eastern birds however have wholly blackish underparts suggesting Yucatan Jay but latter has yellow (not black) legs at all ages. Range does not actually meet Yucatan Jay which is a lowland bird, although both occur in Guatemala, where Yucatan is uncommon in foothills of the north (Peten) and Bushy-crested in the central and southern highlands. Also differs from Yucatan

by having a yellowish (not dark) iris when adult, dark-eyed immatures lack the yellow orbital ring and whitish tail tips of immature Yucatan.

DESCRIPTION: Length 28-30 cm. Bill relatively weak. Tail relatively long, graduated at tip. Head bulky when crown feathers erected, the feathers of the forecrown somewhat stubble-like, but hardly crested. Nominate race (adult): Head, neck, upper mantle and breast black. Underparts from lower breast downwards relatively dull greenish-blue. Upperparts, including wings and tail blue with greenish and violet tones, somewhat brighter and more violet-blue on tail. Underwing grey, underside of tail blackish. Legs blackish. Bill black. Irides pure yellow.

SEX/AGE: Sexes similar. Juvenile dull blackish-grey, paler grey on lower underparts, wings and tail blue, bill yellowish-horn with darker tip, iris dark brown, legs dark grey. Acquires blackish head and body feathering and bill darkens from tip in first few weeks after leaving nest;

by January much as adult; but irides still quite dark (olive-brown), some pale visible at bill base and overall plumage lacks sheen of adult. By second-year irides yellow and only separable from adult by some pale areas on inside of bill (all black in adult).

MEASUREMENTS: Nominate race: Wing 130-139, tail 133-153, tarsus 39-42, bill 25-28, weight 103-115.

GEOGRAPHICAL VARIATION: two subspecies differing in overall plumage tones, the two forms seem to intergrade.

C. m. melanocyaneus: Guatemala, described above.
C. m. chavezi: Honduras and Nicaragua, darker, less greenish, blue above with underparts richer mauve-blue; some individuals of this race are wholly blackish on underparts.

VOICE: The alarm call is most frequently heard, given as a social warning of possible danger: a rather thin, high-pitched, rapidly-repeated, rasping 'kreep, kreep, kreep' or 'kwarrr-kreep, kreep, kreep'. Other calls are less often heard.

HABITS: Poorly documented (even though social behaviour well-studied in captivity). Like most others of the subgenus this a social species, living in small groups which behave as a unit, the whole group taking part in nest care and feeding the young (see breeding). They forage at low to mid canopy levels in trees and bushes, descending to the ground noisily to search through the leaf-litter for invertebrates, fruits and nuts.

BREEDING: Social breeder. Nest of twigs, lined with plant fibres and other soft materials, constructed in dense shrubbery, vine tangles, etc. Clutch three to four, pinkish-buff to pale reddish eggs, with darker markings. Only one female lays the clutch, but two females share incubation duties and the brooding of the young, and many more individuals help feed the young. A study nest with four young was attended to by at least eleven individuals. Juveniles from earlier nests also help. Eggs recorded late April to mid May.

HABITAT: Humid woodlands, especially edges of mixed pine and oak, with clearings and scrubby shrubbery, including coffee plantations. Usually between 1000 and 2450 m, sometimes lower into the foothills.

DISTRIBUTION: Range extends from central and southern Guatemala and northern El Salvador, eastwards through Honduras to north-central Nicaragua.

STATUS: Little information, but not uncommon and seems to be thriving, despite widespread forest degradation over much of its range. It favours forest clearings which has enabled it to become particularly well established in areas cleared for agriculture, especially coffee plantations.

REFERENCES: Hardy 1973, 1974, 1976, 1990.

SAN BLAS JAY   Plate 5

Cyanocorax sanblasianus

This jay is widespread along the Pacific coast of northern Mexico, where it just about meets with the larger Purplish-backed.

IDENTIFICATION: The only *Cissilopha* over most of the Pacific coastal plain of north-west Mexico, meeting with Purplish-backed in a small area of central coastal Nayarit. It is markedly smaller, has duller yellow legs and is purer, less shining purplish, blue above, lacking contrast between mantle and wings of Purplish-backed.

DESCRIPTION: Length 27-31 cm. Bill relatively weak. Tail relatively long, graduated at tip. Race *nelsoni* (adult): Head bulky, with shortly tufted feathers on loral region and over eye, which are inconspicuous, some feathers here are of irregular length and thinly elongated. Nostrils partially exposed. Head, neck, upper mantle and underparts black. Undertail-coverts and tibia, dark purplish-blue. Upperparts, including wings and tail, blue with varying green tones, purer blue on uppertail-coverts, slightly more violet-blue on tail. Underwing grey, underside of tail blackish. Legs greenish-yellow. Bill black. Irides yellow or greenish-yellow.

SEX/AGE: Sexes similar, but in race *nelsoni* adult male has dull greenish-yellow irides, whereas in adult female have pure yellow irides. Both sexes of the nominate form have them pure yellow. Age changes of race *nelsoni*: Juvenile has elongated, erectile frontal crest, is dull blackish-grey, paler grey on lower underparts; wings and tail blue, bill yellowish, iris dark brown, legs brownish. Acquires blackish head and body feathering during first few weeks of leaving nest, by end of October much as adult in body plumage but black duller and bill still largely pale, but darkening at tip. Bill remains chiefly pale throughout first year as legs become greenish-yellow as adult. During the moult towards the end of their first year (August-September) the bill becomes mainly black, with vestiges of pale towards the base, the crest is still largely evident. Towards the end of the second year, there is a complete moult after which the body plumage is glossy black and resembles the adult; long wispy crest feathers remain, the bill is partially pale only on the interior, and the irides become paler, olive-brown in some birds. By the end of the third year the crest has all but gone, and the only sign of immaturity is the darkish iris, which in many birds does not become yellowish until the end of the fourth year. Nominate race: Differs from *nelsoni* in having a crest only up to end of first (not second or third) year, after which they are virtually as adults; the bill becomes black early in the first year (not second) and the irides are yellowish in many by their third (not fourth) year.

MEASUREMENTS: Male markedly heavier than female, but measurements widely overlap. Race *nelsoni*: Wing 127-142, tail 135-151, tarsus 38-42, bill 28-31, weight male 117-123, female 92-112.

GEOGRAPHICAL VARIATION: Two subspecies differing chiefly in age progression of bare part colours and crest prominence.

C. s. nelsoni: central Nayarit to extreme west Guerrero, described above.

C. s. sanblasianus: central coastal Guerrero, completely lacks crest after juvenile stage and very similar to adult after first-year (see sex/age section above for details). Adults are brighter, more purplish or violet in tone in the blue of the upperparts.

VOICE: The alarm, a quickly repeated, hoarse, squawked, rhythmic chatter 'geeup, geeup, geeup..' or 'gee, gee, gee...' is the most frequently heard vocalisation. There is a small difference between these calls in the two races, each individual note being more uniform in *nelsoni*, with a downward inflection in the nominate; thus nelsoni call sequences lack the somewhat undulating rhythm of the nominate, see Hardy and Raitt (1977). The contact call is a two-syllable, hoarse, ringing 'geyip-geyip'.

HABITS: A social jay, like others of this subgenus, living in groups of up to 30 birds. These social groups have quite extensive territories, although there is little direct contact or conflict with neighbouring groups; their territories being merely mutually avoided. Each group has some six to ten breeding pairs, which have prolonged, perhaps even life-long, pair-bonds; the remaining few birds of the social group are non-breeders. Most birds do not breed until three years old, but a surprising number of immature, even first-year, birds also breed. Within the extensive foraging territory of a large flock will be a smaller breeding area, which may be half-heartedly defended against other flock members. There is minimal interchange between groups, the outsiders being chiefly immature females. In the breeding season, birds tend to forage alone, but after breeding they roam their territories in flocks. They feed at varying heights, from ground level to the canopy of palm trees, and are omnivorous, taking various invertebrates, small lizards and fruits, especially the pericarp of palm nuts.

BREEDING: Social breeder. Nest of twigs, lined with plant fibres and other soft materials, constructed in shrubbery, trees and vines. Those of the nominate race are found almost exclusively in crowns of palm trees. Clutch three to four eggs, pinkish-buff mottled with darker rufous spots and blotches. One female lays in each nest but a 'helper' female will take brief turns at incubation which lasts for 17-18 days. As many as 13 individuals of both sexes help feed the young, although most of these only feed them after fledging. Eggs and young recorded June and July.

HABITAT: Lowland open wooded areas, including mangroves and cultivation mixed with wooded scrub, has a special liking for coconut palm groves.

DISTRIBUTION: Pacific west Mexico from central Nayarit (San Blas area) south along coastal lowlands of Jalisco, Colima and Michoacan to vicinity of La Lagunella in exteme west Guerrero (race *nelsoni*). There is then an inexplicable break for some 200 km southwards along coastal Guerrero, until near Tecpan de Galeana where the nominate race is found and inhabits the coastal strip for the subsequent 175 km along central Guerrero. Four individuals collected in the USA near Tucson, Arizona in 1937, 1938 and 1939 cannot easily be explained as the species is sedentary; presumably they were the survivors of a small flock that had arrived following storms from the south (Phillips 1950).

STATUS: Not uncommon but rather patchy in distribution throughout its range, like Bushy-crested it has adapted well to living in mixed cultivation and its native shrubby wooded habitats.

References: Hardy 1973, 1974, 1976, 1990, Hardy and Raitt 1977, Hardy, Webber and Raitt 1981, Phillips 1950.

YUCATAN JAY   Plate 5

Cyanocorax yucatanicus

The Caribbean replacement of the San Blas Jay, with which it presumably forms a species-pair. Because of its isolation a uniquely white juvenile plumage has evolved, which is soon moulted out after fledging.

IDENTIFICATION: The only *Cissilopha* along the Caribbean coastal lowlands. Yucatan Jay is the only *Cissilopha* to have dark irides and yellow legs at all ages, a yellow eye-ring and whitish tips to tail underside when immature and a white juvenile plumage stage. See Bushy-crested for field comparisons.

DESCRIPTION: Length 31-33 cm. Bill relatively strong. Tail relatively longer than San Blas, and more strongly graduated at tip. Head bulky, with shortly tufted feathers on forecrown. Nostrils partially exposed. Head, neck, upper mantle and underparts black. Undertail-coverts and tibia, with scattered blue tipping. Upperparts, including wings and tail pure bright blue, with weak greenish tones in certain lights; tail brighter with slight violet sheen. Underwing grey, underside of tail blackish. Legs bright orange-yellow. Bill black. Irides blackish-brown.

SEX/AGE: Sexes similar. Age changes: Juvenile has head and body white, with dull bluish upperparts, underside of tail has obvious white feather tipping, bill and legs fleshy-yellow, irides dark. Acquires blackish head and body plumage and brighter leg and bill colour during first moult, only a few weeks after fledging. Through the first year it resembles a dull adult in plumage but has a bright yellow bill and orbital ring and retains whitish tips to tail feathers. By its second year it has a bright plumage like adults, the bill becomes variably mottled during the year, though some are black-billed and the orbital ring becomes broken by black. By third year, some pale areas might persist on bill but most are black billed. Even some fourth year birds show some whitish markings inside the mandibles but are otherwise as adults.

MEASUREMENTS: Wing 137-148, tail 134-150, tarsus 40-43, bill 21-23, weight 105-128.

GEOGRAPHICAL VARIATION: two subspecies differing marginally in colour and size.

C. y. yucatanicus: Most of species range.

C. y. rivularis: westernmost birds, from Tabasco and south-west Campeche. Slightly larger; lighter, more silvery-blue above.

VOICE: Vocally very varied. The alarm is a rapid, raucous, chattering, lower in pitch and more abrupt than the thin, high rasping chatter of Bushy-crested. Contact call a two or three note, hollow, incisive 'chuduk-chuduk. Amongst other calls is a far-carrying repeated, mellow purred 'prrrauwk'.

HABITS: Has similar complex social flock-living lifestyle to that of San Blas. See Raitt and Hardy (1976) for detailed study. In winter, flocks of 45-55 birds may be found in prime areas, with about half of these being first-year birds. Breeding flocks are smaller, having broken up into groups of some ten birds which occupy an area some 400 m in diameter. Breeding groups generally consist of a pair of breeding adults, plus several non-breeding adults and immatures. They forage chiefly within cover at the edge of the forest, often quite low or on the ground but working all levels right up into the canopy. They feed well within cover of the dense foliage, hopping and flying between perches in scattered groups. The species follow swarms of army ants to take advantage of the invertebrates that the ants disturb during their merciless progression through the forest. Their diet is varied and omnivorous. They take a variety of invertebrates, especially beetles and caterpillars, but they also eat seeds and fruits. The birds make use of the seasonal abundance of various insect larvae and fruits.

BREEDING: Social breeder. Nest a rather flimsy platform of twigs, sparingly lined with plant fibres and other soft materials, built at height of between 4 and 9 m in subcanopy of forest trees, but close to forest edge. Nest may be constructed by either sex; in a study pair, it was built chiefly by the female, but the following year by the male. Clutch four to six, average five, eggs, pinkish-buff speckled with reddish-buff. One female lays in each nest and does all the incubation (unlike San Blas and Bushy-crested where duties shared by two females). Incubation 17 days, the female being fed at the nest by her mate and several 'helpers'. Young fledge at about 26 days. Eggs laid in May and June. Some breeding flocks have at least two simultaneous nests to attend to, which limits the number of helpers in attendance at each nest.

HABITAT: Lowland humid forest, with clearings, sometimes in more open scrubby habitats; in Belize and Guatemala in pine woodland with scrubby undergrowth, along ridges up to 500 m.

DISTRIBUTION: The Caribbean and Gulf coastal lowlands of Mexico, over most of the Yucatan peninsula, extending south-west to north-eastern Tabasco; eastwards the range extends to northern Belize and the Peten district of northern Guatemala.

STATUS: Not uncommon over much of the Mexican part of its range in the right habitat. It has benefited from the opening up of forest roads and clearings for agriculture. However may be locally endangered by excessive forest clearance. In Guatemala and Belize, it is distinctly local and uncommon.

REFERENCES: Hardy 1973, 1974, 1990, Raitt and Hardy 1976.

PURPLISH-BACKED JAY   Plate 5

Cyanocorax beecheii

Alternative name: Beechey or Beechey's Jay

The largest and northernmost of the *Cissilopha* jays. Its range extends north from that of San Blas, along the coast of north-west Mexico where it is declining.

IDENTIFICATION: The only *Cissilopha* over most of the coastal lowlands of Sinaloa and northern Nayarit in north-west Mexico, but range occasionally meets that of San Blas Jay in the region of Sauta, central Nayarit. It differs from San Blas Jay of the northern race in being distinctly larger and bulkier, with bright purplish-blue upperparts (clearer blue in northern San Blas but southern San Blas Jays are more violet-blue), brighter yellow legs and in having a more obvious short ruffled crest (latter only when crown raised). Calls also differ to the practised ear (see Voice below).

SUMMARY OF COLOUR CHANGES TO BARE PARTS. Purplish-Backed Jay.				
	Juvenile	1st year	2nd year	3rd year	Adult

	Juvenile	1st year	2nd year	3rd year	Adult
Legs :	Yellowish	Yellow	Yellow	Yellow	Yellow
Bill :	Yellowish	Yellow	Bicoloured	Black	Black
Iris :	Dark brown	Dark brown	Olive-yellow	Yellow	Yellow

DESCRIPTION: Length 35-41 cm. Bill relatively strong. Tail relatively long, graduated at tip. Head bulky, with shortly tufted feathers on loral region, forecrown and over eye, which are inconspicuous, unless feathers erected. Nostrils more or less concealed. Head, neck, upper mantle and underparts black. Undertail-coverts and tibia, dark purplish-blue. Upperparts, including wings and tail bright purplish-blue, brightest on mantle and rump, a little duller on wings and tail. Underwing and underside of tail blackish. Legs yellow. Bill black in full adults. Irides yellow.

SEX/AGE: Sexes similar. Age changes: juvenile has dark grey head and body, with distinctly darker hood and almost blackish breast, wings and tail bluish, bill and legs yellowish horn, irides dark brown. By August, the head and body have moulted and the plumage resembles a fully adult bird, juvenile bare part colours are retained; the bill begins to become marked with black from the base during August of the second calendar year and this gradually increases during the second year and the irides become greenish-yellow, by the third year the irides are yellow and the bill is wholly black on the outside (but pale patches remain on the interior) and the bird is essentially fully adult in appearance.

MEASUREMENTS: Male averages a little larger than female. Wing 156-175, tail 165-199, tarsus 47-52, bill 25-30, weight mean 195.

GEOGRAPHICAL VARIATION: Monotypic.

VOICE: The alarm is a harsh, grating 'craaaa, craaaa, craaaa' not unlike the call of the Eurasian Jay in tone, but more quickly repeated and without the fading finish; lower in pitch and longer than the almost chattered notes of San Blas.

HABITS: Like others of this group has a social lifestyle, but flocks do not attain the size of its smaller congeners, generally in parties of two to five birds throughout the year. These groups seem to roam over larger territories than other *Cissilopha* (up to 30 ha) and are more aggressive in defending them from intruding groups from outside the unit. The groups consist of a breeding pair plus one or two first-year birds; non-breeding adults are apparently not tolerated. They are rather more elusive than other *Cissilopha* jays, partly because of the low-density population and the fact that they spend most of their time within the forest interior. Birds forage on the ground as well as within the tree canopy and adopt a varied series of foraging techniques from gleaning foliage and probing bark and searching leaf-litter on the forest floor to brief bouts of hawking for flying insects. Regular food sources near the forest such as orchards, small garbage dumps and roadsides are regularly visited. They feed on a variety of invertebrates, small lizards, small rodents as well as vegetable matter. They take grain, both from growing corn as well as fallen grain by roadside and railway lines, fruits (especially mangos), berries and human food scraps.

BREEDING: Social breeder, but occasional solitary nesting recorded (perhaps due to low density of population). Nest a rather untidy platform of twigs, sparingly lined with finer twigs, situated in tree canopy at about 6 m. All members of the group assist in nest construction but the bulk of the work is undertaken by the female. Clutch three to six, average five, eggs pinkish-buff to reddish-buff speckled chestnut and shaded with grey. Incubation is solely by the mated female for about 15 days, being fed only by her mate. Young fledge at about 12-14 days (data from captive pair which might have fledged prematurely); all members of the group help feed the young. Eggs laid in first half of May.

HABITAT: Lowland and foothill dry deciduous forests, especially secondary growth, also coastal scrub and mangroves. Up to 500 m.

DISTRIBUTION: The Pacific coastal lowlands of northwest Mexico, over southern Sonora (north to Alamos), Sinaloa, and northern Nayarit (south to Sauta). Like all members of this group it is sedentary, therefore the appearance of a bird in southern USA near El Paso, Texas in 1985 is odd, but compares with the assumed vagrancy of a party of San Blas Jays in Arizona 50 years earlier.

STATUS: Uncommon and thinly-distributed, declining because of intensive clearance of lowland forests. Extensive areas of its native deciduous forest habitat in Sonora and northern Sinaloa have been destroyed in recent years. Although it feeds in secondary growth this jay disappears from areas where primary woodland has been cleared. This jay is clearly endangered.

REFERENCES: Hardy 1973, 1974, 1990, Raitt and Hardy 1979.

CYANOCORAX JAYS Cyanocorax

The bulk of Neotropical jays, especially the South American species are in this genus; indeed, because of the gradual variation between genera of the New World jays, some former genera are now relegated to subgenus level. There is also a good case for expanding Cyanocorax to include Aphelocoma, Cyanolyca and Cyanocitta. These may be linked by Cyanolyca, members of which show affinities with Aphelocoma yet have vestigial frontal tufts akin to Cyanocorax. Members of Cyanocorax as treated here are heavily-built jays, the majority of which show some white in the tail and underparts; they have fairly prominent to very obvious frontal tufts, are chiefly lowland in distribution and, as far as is known, have a social breeding lifestyle like Aphelocoma jays.

CURL-CRESTED JAY   Plate 6

Cyanocorax cristatellus

Boldly-patterned black and white jay of savanna woodland in central Brazil, with a unique erect curved frontal crest.

IDENTIFICATION: A very distinctive large jay with violet-blue upperparts and black hood and breast contrasting with white lower underparts and terminal half of tail. Underpart and tail pattern is shared by both Plush-crested and White-naped Jays, both of which have pale (not dark) eyes, a flat, ruffled crown shape, pale on the nape and a preference for denser woodland. Remarkable stiff erect frontal crest is diagnostic (but short in juveniles).
DESCRIPTION: Length 35 cm. Bill strong. Wings long and broad. Tail moderate, broad and only slightly graduated at tip. Nasal tuft short, just covering nostrils. Frontal crest elongated, front feathers longest, erect and slighlty recurving. Head, neck, breast and crest black becoming brownish-black on nape and sides of neck. Rest of underparts including tibia pure white. Whole of upperparts and wings violet-blue, becoming washed brown on mantle and back (brownest in worn plumage), brightest on wings and tail base. Basal half of tail violet-blue, terminal half of tail pure white on both surfaces. Underwing-coverts pure white contrasting with blackish underside to flight feathers in flight. Basal portion of underside of tail blackish. Bill and legs black. Irides dark brown or blue.
SEX/AGE: Sexes similar. Juvenile duller, with short frontal crest, terminal half of tail washed mauve and brownish fringes to wing-coverts.
MEASUREMENTS: Wing 188, tail c 150, tarsus 36, bill 35 (one specimen measured), weight unrecorded.
GEOGRAPHICAL VARIATION: Monotypic.
VOICE: Most freely uttered is an excited, sharp 'kyaar', frequently repeated. Also has an abrupt, piercing 'kyap' and penetrating shrill 'kiyeeee'. Song a soft conglomeration of muted croaks, chittering and piping sounds.
HABITS: Little documented. Fairly conspicuous outside breeding season, when encountered in straggling groups in 'cerrado' grassland, flying strongly over the open landscape. Bold and inquisitive but conversely, if startled, the flock will fly off for a considerable distance before alighting. In the heat of the day will resort to shade of denser forest canopy. Perhaps in view of its specialised habitat, this jay does not mix with other species. Hardy (1961) thought it probably nomadic by nature and in view of the 'unity of the flocks' a highly social breeding species.
BREEDING: Nest undescribed. Three eggs taken in November, described as light blue, thickly covered in dark sepia dots and fine streaks, most concentrated towards larger end of egg.
HABITAT: 'Cerrado' woodland: savanna-like grassland, with thin cover of short gnarled trees, also forest edges. Between 150 and 1100 m.
DISTRIBUTION: Tablelands of central Brazil, from south-west Para, south Maranhao and south Piauf south over the Mato Grosso and Goias to Minas Gerais and Sao Paulo. Also in adjacent north-east Paraguay.
STATUS: Locally common but sparsely distributed in its specialised habitat, easily seen near Brasilia; in Paraguay only recorded from San Luis de la Sierra, Concepcion.
REFERENCES: Hardy 1969, 1990, Ridgely and Tudor 1989.

PURPLISH JAY   Plate 6

Cyanocorax cyanomelas

The drabbest of all Neotropical jays, but a bold and noisy character.

IDENTIFICATION: A featureless bulky jay, lacking plumage pattern and often appearing dusky unless in good light. Violet may then become apparent on the upperside of the tail (i.e. when tail spread on alighting) and the head and breast appear blacker and slightly contrasting. The superficially similar, but very rare Azure Jay probably does not overlap in range (but see Azure Jay for discussion). Violaceous Jay which overlaps in south-east Peru, is bluer and greyer with blacker hood and breast and has pale nape patch; favours lower and especially lowland riverine forest whereas Purplish prefers Andean foothill forest (and is much scarcer in Peru). Often associates with flocks of Plush-crested Jays.
DESCRIPTION: Length 37 cm. Bill strong. Tail moderately long, only slightly graduated at tip. Nasal tuft short, just covering nostrils. Frontal crest shortly tufted and inconspicuous, of stiff feathers on lores and about eye. Loral region black; forecrown, sides and front of head, throat and upper breast sooty. Remainder of crown purplish-brown, becoming dull purple with brown wash on nape. Remainder of body plumage and wings dull bluish-purple washed brownish, a little browner above than below; brightest on primaries, secondaries and uppertail-coverts. Underwing dark grey-brown. Tail brighter, dark, violet-blue. Underside of tail blackish. With wear, body plumage becomes duller and browner and contrasts more strongly with brighter tail. Bill and

legs black. Irides dark brown.

SEX/AGE: Sexes similar. Juvenile slightly paler and overall duller.

MEASUREMENTS: Wing 185, tail 158, tarsus 43, bill 37 (one specimen measured), weight mean 222.

GEOGRAPHICAL VARIATION: Monotypic.

VOICE: A raucous repeated 'craa-craa-craa-craa-craa', recalling repeated short call of a small crow in quality, is the most frequent call.

HABITS: Sociable birds of forest and secondary scrub, they nosily forage in parties of six to eight birds and often join roving flocks of Plush-crested Jays or other large passerines. They seem to be quite bold and inquisitive, readily investigating 'squeaks' or 'pishing' from observers. Although spending most of their time in the canopy, they sometimes descend to the ground. They feed chiefly on invertebrates, fruits and berries but will also take carrion from predator kills. Flight action distinctly laboured when covering longer distances, alternating a series of slow with quicker wingbeats, terminating in quite a long upward glide to perch.

BREEDING: Nest described as built of twigs and creeper stems, lined with leaves, in low trees covered in vines at about 3m from ground. Clutch two to six, chiefly three to four. Eggs whitish to light green or pale blue, heavily marked with dark brown spots and blotches and lilac shading. Eggs recorded early October to early December in Paraguay, November in Argentina.

HABITAT: Deciduous woodland and adjacent secondary scrub, in lowlands but recorded up to 2000m in Bolivia.

DISTRIBUTION: From extreme south-east Peru (scarce in Madre de Dios and Cuzco regions), through northern and eastern Bolivia, Paraguay, south-west Brazil (western Mato Grosso), northern Argentina (eastern Formosa, eastern Chaco, northern Santa Fe and Corrientes), rarely recorded east to Misiones.

STATUS: Locally common in parts of Paraguay and northern Argentina, but rare and little known in Peru. See also comment under Azure Jay. In Brazil deforestation is reported to have aided a range expansion, culminating in the exceptional record of a single bird as far east as Sao Paulo in 1987.

REFERENCES: Hardy 1990, Ridgely and Tudor 1989, Willis and Oniki 1993.

AZURE JAY   Plate 6

Cyanocorax caeruleus

Perhaps the most endangered of all South American jays, this species has declined considerably in recent years, for reasons that are not obvious.

IDENTIFICATION: Very similar to much more numerous Purplish Jay with which it may have been confused in the past, as very few recent records from Argentina and Paraguay (see Status). Rather larger than Purplish Jay and brighter dark-blue, without brown tones, and with more contrasting black head and breast; some birds are more greenish-blue. In dull light appears wholly dark like Purplish Jay, but stouter bill and more prominent frontal tuft might help in silhouette views. More or less confined to remaining forests dominated

by Araucaria 'pines'. Like Purplish Jay also often associates with flocks of Plush-crested Jays.

DESCRIPTION: Length 38 cm. Bill strong and stout. Tail moderately long, only slightly graduated at tip. Nasal tuft short, just covering nostrils. Frontal crest bristled and tufted, forming short bushy crest on forehead. Head, neck and upper breast black or sooty. Remainder of body plumage varies from cobalt-blue, through violet-blue to greenish-blue, which merely seems to be individual variation, the most frequent colour being purplish-blue. Underwing blackish. Bill and legs black. Irides dark brown, possibly blue.

SEX/AGE: Sexes similar. Juvenile slightly greyer and overall duller.

MEASUREMENTS: Wing 205, tail 168, tarsus 47, bill 44, weight 272 (one specimen measured).

GEOGRAPHICAL VARIATION: Monotypic.

VOICE: The typical call phrase is very similar to that of Purplish Jay but slightly thinner and higher in pitch.

HABITS: Little documentation. Recorded as forming small parties, often associating with flocks of Plush-crested Jays. Feeds in canopy of dense tropical forest, primarily on fruits of the Acromia palm. Flight action has been described as rather undulating and quite weak. Anting recorded from captive birds.

BREEDING: Nest undescribed. Eggs light greenish-blue, profusely speckled and blotched dark brown and olive, with underlying grey and lilac markings. Clutch (possibly incomplete) of two eggs recorded early October in Brazil.

HABITAT: Subtropical and tropical humid forests, dominated by Araucaria 'pines' and Acromia palms, in lowlands and foothills up to 1000 m.

DISTRIBUTION: Recorded from south-eastern Brazil (Rio Grande do Sul north to south Sau Paulo), adjacent eastern Paraguay and north-eastern Argentina, but perhaps now mainly in Rio Grande do Sol.

STATUS: Threatened. Formerly recorded widely from eastern Paraguay, with records west to the Paraguay River around Asuncion, but only recent Paraguay record is of a pair to the west of Puerto Stroessner in 1977. A similar situation exists in north-east Argentina, where there are only old records for east Formosa and east Chaco (although there are Purplish Jays in those regions, no Azure Jays have been found for many years). In Misiones there have been very few recent observations at Iguazu National Park. It is still locally common in remaining habitat in Rio Grande do Sul in Brazil. Reasons for the decline are worrying, as suitable habitat remains both in east Paraguay and north-east Argentina. Competition with the more successful Purplish Jay has been suggested and this is plausible. Obviously some of the older records could have been identification errors but it seems that a real and inexplicable decline is taking place. Destruction and subsequent fragmentation of remaining lowland forests will also be an important factor.

REFERENCES: Hardy 1969, 1990, Ridgely and Tudor 1989.

VIOLACEOUS JAY   Plate 6

Cyanocorax violaceus

A widespread dark bluish jay from the forests of the

upper Amazon, over most of which it is the only jay.

IDENTIFICATION: Chiefly in riverine forests in the Upper Amazon. A dark bluish-grey jay with no obvious pattern unless seen well, when close views will reveal the whitish nape and contrasting black face and breast. Range meets Purplish Jay in extreme south-east Peru (which see) and in the north-east of its range with rare Azure-naped, but latter has a more extensive pale nape, a distinctive white tip to the tail, whitish undertail-coverts and pale eye.

DESCRIPTION: Length 37 cm. Bill strong. Tail moderately long, only slightly graduated at tip. Nasal tuft and forehead feathering stiffly erect but short, forming inconspicuous stubbled frontal crest. Nominate race: Head, throat and upper breast black. Hindcrown almost whitish, tinged violet-blue becoming pale violet-blue on nape. Remainder of plumage dull mauvish-blue, lighter on underparts and darkest on wings and tail, often tinged greyish on upperparts. Underwing and of underside tail blackish. Bill and legs black. Irides dark brown.

SEX/AGE: Sexes similar. Juvenile slightly greyer and duller.

MEASUREMENTS: Nominate race: Wing 186, tail 155, tarsus 44, bill 40 (one specimen measured), weight 262.

GEOGRAPHICAL VARIATION: Two subspecies.

C. v. violaceus: most of range, described above.

C. v. pallidus: coastal Anzoategui, Venezuela, paler overall.

VOICE: Usual call a repeated short, piercing scream, with a rising inflection, 'jeeer..jeeer..' Other sounds recorded include a sharp 'clop-clop-clop-clop...', various quiet chortling gurgles, a descending ripple, and a guttural clicking.

HABITS: A lively and noisy jay invariably found in flocks of six to twelve birds, working through the mid to upper canopy level of stands of trees in more open areas, such as forest clearings or along riverbanks. Violaceous Jays are very excitable and inquisitive and quite readily come towards a 'squeaking' or 'pishing' observer, whom they will mob as they would potential predator, bouncing and bowing and uttering their shrieking calls. Parties also accompany mixed bird flocks, especially *icterids*. The flock seems to stay together throughout the year and although little is known about their breeding behaviour, they are almost certainly social breeders. Flock members move one-by-one across forest clearings and rivers, where they seem to favour stands of waterside Cerropia trees. They hop and pick amongst the foliage for insects and fruits; small lizards are also taken.

BREEDING: Poorly documented. Probably a social breeder. Nest a bulky structure of sticks and large twigs, lined with plant fibres, placed in a fork at some 9m. Clutch five, eggs bluish-white thickly speckled reddish-brown to dark-brown. Eggs recorded early April in Orinoco basin; flock feeding two large young recorded July in llanos of Venezuela.

HABITAT: Subtropical and tropical deciduous forests of lowlands and foothills, avoiding areas of dense forest, favours clearings with stands of trees, especially along rivers. Also mangroves. Recorded up to 1350m.

DISTRIBUTION: Range extends through southern and central Venezuela, reaching the north coast in Anzoategui, but absent north of the Orinoco in the east of the country; local southern Guyana. It is widespread

in north and western Brazil, west of the Rio Purus and upper Rio Negro region. On the west side of the Amazon basin, along the eastern foothills and lowlands of Colombia, Ecuador and Peru reaching southern limit in extreme northern Bolivia (Pando).

STATUS: Widespread and common over most of the main part of its range.

REFERENCES: Hardy 1969, Ridgely and Tudor 1989.

AZURE-NAPED JAY Plate 6

Cyanocorax heilprini

A little known jay with a very restricted range on sandy soils of the Venezuela-Colombia-Brazil border region.

IDENTIFICATION: Confined to the region of the upper Rio Negro. Only likely to be confused with Violaceous Jay which lacks the pale eye, white tail tip and vent of Azure-naped, and has most of crown, not merely forecrown, black. Note that the white tail tip of Azure-naped is most obvious on the tail underside, when the white vent should also be apparent. Range does not extend far enough east to meet that of Cayenne Jay which has similar tail pattern, latter however has distinctive white underparts and nape.

DESCRIPTION: Length 34 cm. Bill strong. Tail moderately long, only slightly graduated at tip. Nasal tuft and forehead feathering stiffly erect but short, forming inconspicuous stubbled frontal crest. Forehead, sides of head and neck, throat and upper breast black; throat sides with pale blue malar stripe. Crown bluish-white (except for black forecrown), becoming sky-blue on nape and hind-neck. Upperparts grey-blue washed with violet-brown. Underparts dull violet, paler on lower belly and becoming yellowish-white on undertail-coverts. Tail darker violet-brown with comparatively narrow white tips to all feathers, more conspicuous on underside. Bill and legs black. Irides pale yellowish-white.

SEX/AGE: Sexes similar. No information on juvenile.

Measurements: Wing 162, tail 150, tarsus 50, bill 36 (one specimen measured), weight unrecorded.

GEOGRAPHICAL VARIATION: Monotypic.

VOICE: Call remarkably similar to repeated 'jeeer..jeeer..' of Violaceous Jay, probably indistinguishable in the field but recordings sound slightly thinner, higher in pitch and more descending.

HABITS: Virtually undocumented. Has been found in small trees and bushes between forest edge and more lightly wooded savanna grassland.

BREEDING: Virtually undocumented. Nest described as a 'basin-shaped' construction of twigs, 'appearing carelessly made' and placed between 2 and 3m from ground. Juveniles noted March and April in Venezuela.

HABITAT: Forest-edge, secondary growth and savanna woodland, on sandy soils. Possibly also in dense rain forest. Recorded between 100 and 250m.

DISTRIBUTION: Range centred on borders of Colombia, Brazil and Venezuela. In Brazil recorded in extreme north-west of the upper Rio Negro drainage. In Venezuela in tropical west Amazonas. In Colombia reported from extreme eastern Guainia (opposite mouth of Rio Casiquiare) and from near Mitu in eastern Vaupes, but range probably extends north to south-east

Vichada.

STATUS: Local and uncommon, but no precise information.

REFERENCES: Hardy 1990, Ridgely and Tudor 1989, de Schauensee 1978.

CAYENNE JAY   Plate 7

Cyanocorax cayanus

A distinctive jay of lowland north-eastern South America; despite the huge range gap, perhaps most closely-related to White-tailed Jay of Ecuador.

IDENTIFICATION: Combination of white nape and underparts and broad white tail tip prevents confusion with all other jays of the region, although the only likely species marginally to overlap is Violaceous Jay.

DESCRIPTION: Length 33cm. Bill strong. Tail moderately long, slightly graduated at tip. Nasal tuft and forehead feathering form shortly tufted frontal crest. Forehead, sides of head and neck, throat and upper breast black; throat sides with whitish malar stripe; small whitish spots above and below eye. Crown (except for black forecrown), nape and hindneck white diffusing to violet-brown on back, mantle and rump, uppertail-coverts cleaner bluish-purple. Lower underparts creamy-white. Wings dark bluish-purple. Underwing with whitish coverts and blackish flight feathers. Tail dark bluish-purple with broad white tips to all feathers. Bill and legs black. Irides pale bluish-white or white.

SEX/AGE: Sexes similar. Juvenile duller, with eye spots smaller or absent and like the malar stripe are bluish, the latter becomes white before eye spots; white of tail band suffused violet-fawn, especially in centre.

MEASUREMENTS: Wing 156-164, tail 140, tarsus 46, bill 36, weight 170-196.

GEOGRAPHICAL VARIATION: Monotypic.

VOICE: Quite varied, includes a number of yapping and crowing sounds, some of which suggest a trogon or toucan. Typical calls include a repeated mellow, enquiring 'keyow' (recalling that of Black-chested Jay) and a short, nasal buzzing note. A variety of other short notes have been described, some quite harsh and others quite mellow and plaintive.

HABITS: Poorly documented. Forages in small parties in tree canopy, moving from tree to tree in short glides, seemingly flapping wings only reluctantly. Food items recorded include insects, berries and fruits. Generally shy and wary of man, but perhaps only where persecuted, as also reported coming into gardens of settlements and even towns to feed on fruit trees.

BREEDING: Seemingly unrecorded. Recently fledged young have been collected in late December, January and late March.

HABITAT: Woodland of various types, from wooded savannas to edges of humid forests and riverine trees; avoids dense continuous forests, recorded up to 1100 m in Venezuela.

DISTRIBUTION: From the Guianas, west into south-east Venezuela (Bolivar) and south into northern Brazil, where recorded south to Manaus and north Amapa.

STATUS: Relatively common, although distinctly local in the Guianas and Venezuela; very scarce and little known in Brazil.

REFERENCES: Hardy 1990, Ridgely and Tudor 1989, de Schauensee 1978.

BLACK-CHESTED JAY   Plate 8

Cyanocorax affinis

Strikingly patterned jay of dense forest edge in southern central and north-west South America, where no similar species occur.

IDENTIFICATION: The only jay in its range with white underparts and tail band; range does not meet that of Cayenne Jay which has white nape as well as underparts. Black-chested has a distinctive combination of black head and breast and whitish underparts, contrasting with violet or violet-brown upperparts and white terminal band to tail. Keeps well hidden in foliage, but proclaims presence by call.

DESCRIPTION: Length 36cm. Bill strong. Tail moderately long, slightly graduated at tip. Nasal tuft and forehead feathering form shortly tufted frontal crest. Nominate race: Crown, sides of head and neck, throat and upper breast black; throat sides with violet-blue malar stripe; small violet-blue spots above and below eye. Remainder of underparts creamy-white. Nape and hindneck dull violet, suffused brown, browner on mantle and back, becoming purplish on uppertail-coverts. Wings violet-blue. Tail darker violet-blue with white tips to all feathers. Underwing coverts whitish, underside of flight feathers dusky. Underside of tail blackish with broad white tip. With wear upperparts fade to pale dull fawn. Bill and legs blackish. Irides yellow or yellowish-white.

SEX/AGE: Sexes similar, although female tends to be browner, less violet in tone above than male. Juvenile duller, with little or no violet on body upperparts, wing-coverts washed brownish; eye spots vestigial or absent; malar stripe narrower and duller; irides brownish-yellow. First-year birds as adult except that eye spots are small and drab.

MEASUREMENTS: Male averages a little larger than female. Wing 159-175, tail 154-161, tarsus 45-52, bill 30-36, weight 194-232.

GEOGRAPHICAL VARIATION: Two subspecies, which intergrade.

C. a. *affinis*: Colombia and Venezuela, described above.

C. a. *zeledoni*: Costa Rica and Panama, brighter overall, bluer, less brown-toned above; brighter blue malar and eye marks; underparts and tail tip pale creamy-yellow rather than white.

VOICE: Quite varied, includes a number of harsh, squeaky and metallic short notes, including clicks and rattles. Most typical call a repeated, ringing, incisive 'kyop-kyop-kyop...'. In alarm utters a nasal rattled 'chep-chep-chep..'.

HABITS: An inconspicuous jay of dense foliage, where it usually keeps well concealed, it is not given to flying over open spaces. Forages in small parties of six to eight birds in middle canopy of dense foliage, often working higher towards crowns but sometimes descending to ground level where they hop about under cover. Diet omnivorous, includes various fruits, berries and invertebrates also the occasional small lizard or frog. Often attends an army ant trail to feed on disturbed insects. Moves through trees with long hops, keeping in vocal contact; when potential predator is spotted, such as a snake or owl, it is mobbed and scolded with vocal gusto. Normally keeps well hidden in foliage, proclaiming presence with repeated 'chopping' call. However, typically also quite confiding and inquisitive of presence of human observer. Flocks keep together throughout the year and it assumed that they have a social lifestyle.

BREEDING: Probably a social breeder. Nest bulky, of sticks and twigs, lined with finer twigs and plant fibres, built towards the end of a branch or in an upright fork in densely-foliaged small and somewhat isolated trees. Clutch three to five, pale buff or brownish-white, heavily spotted and blotched olive-brown and marbled grey. Eggs recorded early April to early May in Colombia.

HABITAT: Broken, rather than dense, woodland and forest of various types, both humid and dry. From borders of forest clearings to dense secondary growth at fringes of cultivation i.e. small cocoa and banana plantations, and riverine trees; avoids dense continuous forests. Chiefly in foothills but locally down to coast; in hills up to 2200 m (in Colombia).

DISTRIBUTION: From Caribbean slope of eastern Costa Rica (limit is Rio Estrella), south through Panama into northern Colombia (Pacific lowlands to Valle and to Huila in Magdalena valley), eastwards to north western Venezuela (Maracaibo basin east to extreme east Falcon).

STATUS: Relatively common in Colombia and Venezuela, uncommon and rather local in Panama and scarce in limited range in Costa Rica.

REFERENCES: Hardy 1969, Ridgely and Tudor 1989, Stiles and Skutch 1989.

TUFTED JAY   Plate 9

Cyanocorax dickeyi

Alternative name: Dickey's Jay

This strikingly beautiful jay was discovered as recently as 1934; and is remarkable in having a very restricted range in a tiny area of west Mexico. These limitations have attracted a deal of attention; indeed its habits and breeding biology are better known than many quite widespread Neotropical jays. Its nearest relative seems to be the White-tailed Jay of Ecuador.

IDENTIFICATION: Quite unmistakable; the white nape and underparts, almost entirely white tail (or so it appears in flight), dark-blue upperparts and black and white head topped by a stiff fan of a crest are features shared by no other jay. Within its range could only be confused with poorly seen Black-throated Magpie-Jay, which however lacks extensive white in longer tail and has a bluish nape, uniform with the upperparts.

DESCRIPTION: Length 37 cm. Bill medium. Tail moderately long, rather broad and graduated at tip. Wings relatively bluntly rounded at tip. Prominent stiff, bristly, fan-shaped crest over crown starting at base of bill. Crest black, becoming dark-blue towards feather bases. Large white patch above eye and very extensive white patch below eye, extending over malar region. Forehead, loral region, narrow eye-line, sides of neck, throat and upper breast black. Nape, hind-neck, upper mantle, lower sides of neck and rest of underparts white. Mantle, scapulars, wings, rump and uppertail-coverts very rich, dark, purplish-blue. Basal portion of tail similarly rich dark-blue, remainder of tail white (terminal half of central feathers widening to terminal two-thirds on outermost). Bill and legs black. Irides bright yellow.

SEX/AGE: Sexes similar. Juvenile has short crest, blue (not white) patch on side of head, lacks patch above eye, has dark irides and fleshy base to bill; first-year birds similar but still wholly blackish after first few months of life. Second-year birds as adults, the yellow irides being attained early in the year.

MEASUREMENTS: Wing 173, tail 158, tarsus 40, bill 39 (one specimen measured), weight 176 (mean of three).

GEOGRAPHICAL VARIATION: Monotypic.

VOICE: Well studied. Vocabulary varied, indeed it is a habitual mimic. Typical call a staccato double 'chuk-chuk' or 'ca-ca-ca-ca', uttered with varying emphasis. Mobbing call an agitated, faster and higher version of this call. A number of chattering phrases resemble agitated chatter of thrushes or 'robins', some also recall chatter of *Pica* magpies. A low, nasal 'aaagh' of plaintive quality is uttered by single birds joining a resting group. Feeding groups utter a bell-like 'pid-ee' prior to moving on to fresh foraging site. Other sounds are more closely linked to nesting behaviour or song, the latter is subdued but includes mimicry of other bird sounds.

HABITS: Well studied. A highly social jay, living in flocks of from four to 16 birds, the larger flocks tend to break up into smaller units towards the end of March at the onset of the breeding season. Breeding flocks consist of one breeding pair of adults plus several non-breeding immature birds. They feed on invertebrates, fruits, berries and acorns. They rarely descend to the ground, spending most of the day in the tree canopy. Here they search the foliage for insects, especially katydids (crickets), acorns, berries and fruits. They have been watched peering and probing into clumps of bromeliads, tearing them apart to retrieve berries and acorns; it is not certain whether such fruits were previously hidden there or were merely windfalls. They will even hang briefly upside down and hover whilst feeding. During the hottest part of the day several hours are spent resting and preening in the shade of foliage. Breeding and roosting sites are quite close to each other. The male of the nesting pair spends a good part of the day 'on guard' near the nest during the incubation period. When the young are being fed, the whole social unit is busy flying to and from the nest with food.

BREEDING: Social breeder. Nest bulky, of sticks and twigs, lined with finer twigs and plant fibres, decorated with fresh green leaves about the rim; it is typically constructed between 5 and 15 m from the ground in the dense canopy of a tree, situated in a shady spot such as near the head of a ravine. Most flock members bring material for the nest, which is probably built chiefly by the female. Clutch three to five; eggs dull greenish-white, fading to olive-buff, speckled and blotched brown, with underlying lavender markings. Incubation 18-19 days by female, which is fed at the nest by the male and several helpers. Young are similarly fed by most of the flock and fledge at about 24 days. Eggs are laid during

April and early May.

HABITAT: Wooded hillsides, with oak and mixed oak-pine on the ridges and dense deciduous and evergreen forest by watercourses in the lower valley bottoms. 1350-2150 m.

DISTRIBUTION: Endemic to small area of west Mexico, the Pacific slope of the Sierra Madre Occidental, which straddles the borders of south-eastern Sinaloa, south-western Durango and north-eastern Nayarit.

STATUS: Very localised range and social lifestyle makes this species particularly vulnerable to forest destruction. It certainly is distinctly uncommon and should be regarded as a threatened species. No precise details on population numbers are available.

REFERENCES: Crossin 1967, Hardy 1990, Moore 1938.

PLUSH-CRESTED JAY   Plate 7

Cyanocorax chrysops

Alternative names: Plush-capped Jay, Urucca Jay

The most widespread South American jay, inhabiting most of lowland Brazil, except the east where replaced by similar White-naped Jay.

IDENTIFICATION: The only jay over most of lowland central Brazil. The short ruffled crest gives a peculiar flat-topped look to the head, with a bulge at the rear crown; unless birds are close the impression is of medium-sized jay with blackish face and breast, contrasting whitish underparts and blue or dark upperparts. In flight the tail shows a broad white terminal band. Although distribution widely overlaps that of Curl-crested their habitats differ. Curl-crested favours cerrado woodland (stunted trees in savanna country), Plush-crested prefers 'islands' of tall gallery forest. Curl-crested is bulkier and rather shorter-tailed, with whole head and neck black (Plush-crested has pale patch above blue of upper nape), has dark (not pale) eyes and distinctive upright crest; calls also differ. Very similar White-naped not known to overlap with Plush-crested, although ranges virtually meet (see White-naped for discussion).

DESCRIPTION: Length 36 cm. Bill medium. Tail moderately long, slightly graduated at tip. Feathers of forehead shortly tufted and stiff becoming softer and velvety in texture over whole crown forming a soft, velvet cap which bulges on rear crown. Nominate race: crown, sides of head and neck, throat and upper breast black; throat sides with violet malar stripe; small violet-blue or greenish-blue spots above and below eye, latter merging with malar stripe. Remainder of underparts creamy-yellow. Nape and rear crown almost whitish-blue becoming dark violet on hind-neck. Upperparts and wings dull, dark, violet-blue. Tail similar but with wide pale yellow or whitish band at tips of all feathers, narrowest but still broad on central pair, widest on outermost pair. Underparts and tail band fade to whitish, with wear. Bill and legs blackish. Irides lemon-yellow or pale yellow.

SEX/AGE: Sexes similar. Juvenile lacks eye spots and has vestigial malar stripe; irides browner. First-year birds as adult except that eye spots are small and drab, becoming as adult after second moult.

MEASUREMENTS: Male averages a little larger than female. Nominate race: Wing 146-165, tail 155-179, tarsus 42, bill 30-32, weight mean 157.

GEOGRAPHICAL VARIATION: Three subspecies are recognised.

C. c. chrysops: Most of species range, described above.

C. c. tucumanus: north-east Argentina, similar but averages larger.

C. c. diesingii: a distinct form, probably isolated on lower Rio Madeira and lower Rio Tapajos in northern Brazil; longer and more upright crest gives rather more domed crown shape, eye spots and malar stripe smaller and lacks whitish patch on upper nape.

VOICE: Quite varied, includes a number of short harsh, squeaks, rattles and chortles and includes mimicry of other birds. Typically includes various chattering phrases which vary in pitch, some of these recall the 'yaffle' of a woodpecker, others are more thrush-like. Most distinct phrase an emphatic incisive chopping, double or treble 'chyup-chyup'.

HABITS: A fairly conspicuous forest jay; it usually keeps within the canopy and is not given to flying over open spaces. Forages in groups of up to twelve birds at varying levels of the trees, and is often accompanied by Purplish Jays and even the very rare Azure Jay. The flock is active and very noisy as they peer and peck amongst the foliage, occassionally descending to ground level. They are inquisitive and will cautiously approach a quiet observer, flicking their tails nervously. They are omnivorous, taking a variety of invertebrates, fruits and berries, they occasionally take eggs and nestling small birds; even visiting settlements for human food scraps and in Paraguay reported as following people planting maize, sometimes digging up the grains.

BREEDING: Little studied. Nests reported 4 to 6 m from ground in forest trees. Clutch varies, two to four in Paraguay, six to seven in Brazil reported. Variable in colour, from buff or cream to pale greenish, spotted and blotched with various shades of brown. Eggs reported from early October to early December in Paraguay.

HABITAT: Various types of lowland and temperate forest, including 'islands' of forest in the open pampas, quite extensive rain forest and secondary scrub. Visits adjacent orchards and agricultural land for foraging. Generally below 1500 m, but locally as high as 2800 m (in Bolivia).

DISTRIBUTION: Wide ranging over central and southern Brazil, south of the Amazon (but not beyond) in Para, south through Mato Grosso to Sao Paulo, Parana and Rio Grande do Sul; through northern and eastern Bolivia (west to Beni and Cochabamba), Paraguay and Uruguay into northern Argentina, where occurs from Salta and Tucuman east to Entre Rios.

STATUS: Relatively common over most of its wide range, but race *diesingii* little known and in need of investigation.

REFERENCES: Hardy 1969, Ridgely and Tudor 1989, Stiles and Skutch 1989.

WHITE-NAPED JAY   Plate 7

Cyanocorax cyanopogon

Alternative name: Blue-bearded Jay

Forms a species-pair with Plush-crested Jay, which it replaces in eastern Brazil; the ranges of the two are mutually exclusive.

IDENTIFICATION: The only jay over most of eastern Brazil; it virtually meets the similar Plush-crested Jay in eastern Mato Grosso but they have not been found at the same localities and no hybrids have been proven. Compared to Plush-crested it lacks the bulge towards the rear crown, the entire nape is white and the upperparts are brown, not dark blue. It overlaps in range, but not habitat, with bulkier, shorter-tailed Curl-crested, but stunning white nape is an easy distinction even at long range.

DESCRIPTION: Length 35 cm. Slightly smaller and relatively longer-tailed than Plush-crested. Feathers of forehead stiff becoming softer and velvety in texture over crown forming a soft, velvet cap, but not bulging as in Plush-crested. Crown, sides of head and neck, throat and upper breast black; throat sides with violet malar stripe; small bright-blue spots above and below eye. Remainder of underparts creamy or creamy-white. Nape and rear crown white, washed very pale mauve in fresh plumage. Upperparts and wings dull dark-brown, darker on flight feathers. Tail similar but with wide white at tips of all feathers, narrowest, but still broad on central pair, widest on outermost pair. Bill and legs blackish. Irides bright yellow.

SEX/AGE: Sexes similar. Juvenile has very small, dull eye spots and narrower and duller malar stripe than adult, but subsequent plumages much as adult.

MEASUREMENTS: Wing 142, tail 147, tarsus 37, bill 33 (one specimen measured), weight unrecorded.

GEOGRAPHICAL VARIATION: Monotypic.

VOICE: Quite varied and very similar in range and content to that of Plush-crested, including much mimicry and the incisive double chopping 'chyup-chyup' call.

HABITS: Seem to be virtually the same as those of Plush-crested, including visiting settlements to raid fruit trees.

BREEDING: Undocumented in the wild.

HABITAT: Forest, including 'islands' of gallery forest in wooded savanna, riverine forest and secondary woodland. Up to 1100 m.

DISTRIBUTION: Eastern Brazil, from south-east Para, Maranhao, and Ceara south through Goias and much of Bahia to Minas Gerais and eastern Mato Grosso. Specimens collected in Sao Paulo and Parana as reported in older literature, have proven to be Plush-crested Jays.

STATUS: Relatively common over parts of its range, although seems to have declined in recent decades; at least in Bahia trapping for the cagebird trade is considered to be the likely cause of the decline.

REFERENCES: Hardy 1969, Ridgely and Tudor 1989.

WHITE-TAILED JAY   Plate 7

Cyanocorax mystacalis

An extremely local and beautiful jay, confined to the Pacific lowlands of the Peru-Ecuador border. Probably most closely-related to Tufted Jay of Mexico, which has an even more restricted range.

IDENTIFICATION: The only jay in its small range along the dry, semi-arid Pacific slope of south-west Ecuador and north-west Peru. A beautiful blue-and-white jay with so much white in the tail that it appears to be almost wholly white with a narrow dark centre in flight.

DESCRIPTION: Length 33 cm. Bill relatively long. Tail moderately long, slightly graduated at tip. Feathers of forehead shortly tufted and stiffly erect. Crown, loral region, eye-line, sides of neck, throat and upper breast black. Small white patch above eye and very extensive white patch below eye, extending over malar region. Nape, hind-neck, upper mantle, lower sides of neck and rest of underparts white. Mantle, scapulars, wings, rump and uppertail-coverts dark blue, brightest on wings. Tail white, except for central pair of feathers which are dark blue with a wide white tip and some dark markings towards base of the next pair. Bill and legs black. Irides bright lemon-yellow.

SEX/AGE: Sexes similar. Juvenile has white of malar patch washed blue and lacks spot above eye; this spot attained at the first moult after which much as adult.

MEASUREMENTS: Wing 146, tail 147, tarsus 40, bill 40 (one specimen measured), weight unrecorded.

GEOGRAPHICAL VARIATION: Monotypic.

VOICE: Less varied than most other jays of the genus. Typical is a scolding chatter, varying somewhat in pitch, 'cha-cha-cha-cha-cha....' Also gives a double, high-pitched, clipped 'clewp-clewp'.

HABITS: A conspicuous jay, closely associated with mesquite woodland and shrubby cactus steppe where it forages in scattered parties of up to ten birds, but often singly or in pairs. This jay works both the tree canopy and lower down in scrubby habitats, including foraging openly on the ground. It is far less skulking than many of its congeners, because of its habitat limitations; mesquite consists of quite tall trees with little canopy lower down. They are quite bold and inquisitive and live freely in the vicinity of human habitation, nesting in trees adjacent to houses and foraging in gardens. They feed on a variety of invertebrates and seeds and have been accused of stealing eggs of chickens and domestic ducks. Hardy, 1969, reported watching a pair raiding the nest of a Pale-legged Hornero *Furnarius leucopus*, having apparently excavated a hole in the side of the baked-mud nest to get the eggs.

BREEDING: Little information. Probably a solitary breeder. Nest constructed in trees, often in large trees adjacent to villages. Eggs pale buff, profusely speckled with drab brown, with underlying greyish markings and sparse blackish speckles.

HABITAT: Dry woodland, chiefly park-like mesquite forest, shrubby cactus steppe; also orchards and streamside shrubby thickets. From coast up to 1200 m.

DISTRIBUTION: Limited range in south-western Ecuador (Guayas, El Oro and west Loja) and north-western Peru (south to western La Libertad).

STATUS: Very local but quite common over small range, the fragile wooded habitats are vulnerable to cutting and overgrazing, which presumably has created local descreases but there is no precise information on numbers.

REFERENCES: Hardy 1969, Ridgely and Tudor 1989.

GREEN JAY   Plate 8

Cyanocorax yncas

Alternative name: Inca Jay.

The only green jay. Sometimes divided into at least two species, treated here, as in most recent reviews, as a single polymorphic species.

IDENTIFICATION: An unmistakable small jay of humid forests, primarily green or green above and yellow below, but always with yellow outer tail feathers and black face and throat.
DESCRIPTION: Length 25-27 cm. Bill small. Tail relatively long and narrow, graduated at tip. Wings relatively short and bluntly rounded. Feathers of forehead tufted and stiffly erect, varying according to race (see Geographical Variation). Nominate race: nasal tuft forms prominent bushy crest on forecrown. Crown and nape yellowish-white, lower nape washed bluish. Loral region, sides of head, ear-coverts and throat black. Small spots above and below eye and malar stripe blue. Remainder of underparts yellow. Upperparts and wings green. Underwing yellowish. Tail slightly darker green, outermost tail feathers yellow. In worn plumage crown and nape almost white, underparts fade to creamy-yellow and upperparts and tail have distinctly bluish tone. Bill black. Legs reddish-brown. Irides variable, brown (Colombia to central east Peru) or yellow (central Peru to Bolivia).
SEX/AGE: Sexes similar. Juvenile has shorter frontal tuft, white of malar patch washed blue and lacks spot above eye; this spot attained at the first moult, after which much as adult.
MEASUREMENTS: Sexes very similar in size. Race glaucescens: Wing 104-117, tail 118-131, tarsus 34-39, bill 23-25, weight 66-92.
GEOGRAPHICAL VARIATION: Complex, eleven races. Strangely absent from Nicaragua to Panama. This natural break divides the races into two groupings, at times given specific status. Many of these races intergrade.

Andean (nominate) group (Inca Jay): five races, Venezuela and Colombia, south to Bolivia. Montane forest, 1400 to 3000 m (lower in Venezuela). Slightly larger than Central American races, with larger frontal crest and yellow underparts. Upperparts darker green, bluish in some; nape whitish or blue. Irides yellow, but dark south Colombia to central Peru.

C. y. yncas: subtropical south-west Colombia, eastern Ecuador to north Bolivia, described above.
C. y. longirostris: high altitudes Rio Maranon valley, northern Peru, very similar but larger.
C. y. galeatus: subtropical Pacific slope, west Colombia, yellow irides (brown in Colombian population of nominate race) and larger frontal crest.
C. y. cyanodorsalis: subtropical, central and eastern Colombia and north-west Venezuela, smaller than last, with large deep-blue frontal crest, narrow white band on forecrown, rest of crown and hindneck deep-blue; upperparts darker green, washed blue (bluest in worn plumage). Irides yellow. Legs darker.
C. y. guatemalensis: northern Venezuela, sometimes down to coast; like the last but crest shorter, less blue

wash above and narrower white band on forecrown.

Central American (luxuosus) group (Green Jay): six races, Texas to Honduras. Lowlands to 1800 m. Smaller than Andean races, with short and inconspicuous frontal tuft. Crown and nape blue. Underparts variable, green in northern races, yellow in southern. Irides yellow, but dark in northernmost race.
C. y. luxuosus: east and south-central Mexico; short blue frontal tuft, crown and nape blue, underparts greenish-yellow, yellower towards vent. Irides yellow. Legs brown.
C. y. glaucescens: south Texas, Tamaulipas and Nuevo Leon (Mexico); slightly paler and duller, with dark brown irides and blackish legs.
C. y. centralis: south-east Mexico, Guatemala, Belize, Honduras; underparts yellow or yellowish.
C. y. vividus: Pacific slope south Mexico and west Guatemala; slightly larger with brighter yellow lower underparts.
C. y. maya: Yucatan; underparts bright light-yellow, forecrown white.
C. y. cozumelae: Cozumel island, Mexico; small with pale-blue crown and bright yellow underparts.
VOICE: Very varied. Generally quiet whilst feeding but noisy at other times. Repertoire includes various mewing, chattering, clicking, rattling, buzzing, squeaking and rasping notes, the definition of which is complicated by much vocal mimicry. Typical calls include a double or treble incisive 'cleeop', a nasal treble 'nyaa-nyaa-nyaa' and a metallic clicking.
HABITS: A forest jay of the lower canopy, where it generally forages in small parties in shrubby undergrowth. Solitary birds are often very shy but flocks are typically inquisitive and bold, coming forward to peer at observer. They freely come to bird feeders and gardens adjacent to forests, and have even been reported to enter tents and houses. Like the Grey-breasted and Scrub Jays, populations differ in their social behaviour, although a number of races remain to be studied in detail. Northern populations seem to be solitary breeders but assemble into larger parties after breeding, whereas southern forms are social birds. In Colombia territorial flocks consist of three to nine birds, with one breeding pair of adults and several non-breeding immature 'helpers'. The flock is very bold in mobbing predators, especially in nest defence. When protecting nestlings, the mobbing flock will surround the predator, calling incessantly in an attempt to force it, through confusion and frustration, to leave the area. Meanwhile, the young are being fed by other birds, some of whom might leave the mobbing flock to do so. If one of their group is taken the others will mob or even attack the predator. Green Jays do not like flying over clearings or other exposed places, but when doing so their flight is quite laboured and flapping. Their diet is omnivorous; a variety of invertebrates such as beetles, earthworms and crickets, the eggs of lizards and probably of small birds and seeds, berries and fruits. They have a special liking for acorns and the fruits of the Palmetto Palm, often venturing well out in the open to obtain these. They have been seen bathing in smoke near smouldering logs, a habit similar to 'anting' as an aid to rid their plumage of parasites.
BREEDING: Solitary (Central American forms) and

social (Andean forms) nester. The nest is a platform of thorny twigs and roots, lined with mosses, lichens, dried grasses and leaves, constructed by the breeding pair. It is well hidden in a fork or outer branches of a small tree in dense shrubbery, some 2 or 3 m from the ground, rarely as high as 15 m. Clutch three to five, usually four, eggs very pale greyish, buffish or greenish, speckled and spotted various shades of brown with underlying lilac shading. Incubation period unrecorded. Young are fed in the nest for 19 to 22 days and for at least three weeks after fledging, by both parents. A team of 'helpers' in Andean forms, feed both the incubating female and the young. Eggs recorded April to June in northern races, March to August in various parts of Colombia, the later dates being from further south. Northern races are occasionally nest-parasitised by the Bronzed Cowbird *Molothrus aeneus*.

HABITAT: Humid forest edge, shrubby woodland and brushy thickets. In lowlands and foothill forest in northern forms, reaching 1800 m in Mexico. Andean forms generally between 1400 and 3000 m, but locally as low as 900 m on Pacific slope of Colombia and down to sea level in Venezuela.

DISTRIBUTION: Widespread through Central America and northern South America, but with wide break in range in southern Central America where absent El Salvador, Nicaragua, Costa Rica and Panama. Central American forms reach northern limit in lower Rio Grande valley of southern Texas, extending throughout Gulf coast slope of Mexico to Belize and north-central Honduras; on the Pacific slope range extends from Nayarit to western Guatemala. South American races extend throughout most of Colombia, into north-western Venezuela (east to Sucre) and south through eastern Ecuador, central and eastern Peru to west-central Bolivia (La Paz and Cochabamba).

STATUS: Generally common over most of range, but rather local; in very limited range in USA; most easily seen at the Santa Ana Refuge near McAllan where birds very tame and readily come to feeders by park trails.

REFERENCES: Alvarez 1975, Gayou 1986, Goodwin 1986, Hardy 1990.

MAGPIE-JAYS *Calocitta*

Hardy (1969) considered *Calocitta* merely a subgenus of *Cyanocorax*. The two magpie-jays form a distinct group; they both have long tails and tall, curving frontal crests and are unlikely to be confused with any other birds. The two are closely related and have often been considered conspecific, indeed possible hybrids have been reported from Jalisco and elsewhere. Both forms vary; immature and variant Black-throated showing whitish patches on the throat and breast which can be quite extensive (see Black-throated). Variant White-throated conversely can show more black than usual on the sides of the head and breast. Where they overlap in Colima, the two species show no evidence of hybridisation. Thus birds with mixed features are reported from areas where only one of the species occurs. In view of this it seems preferable to follow most recent authorities in treating them as species.

BLACK-THROATED MAGPIE-JAY   Plate 9

Calocitta colliei

Alternative name: Collie's Magpie-Jay

The longest-tailed of all jays, confined to a small area of west Mexico, a range it shares with the even more localised Tufted Jay.

IDENTIFICATION: A large jay with an incredibly long tail, black face and throat and erect, tall crest. In flight the tail is so long that it undulates with the wing action. Marginally overlaps with the similar but slightly smaller White-throated Magpie-Jay from which it differs in having a straighter crest, black face and throat and longer tail; in northernmost areas of its range (Sonora) some birds show areas of white on throat and face suggesting hybrid influence, but as White-throated only overlaps in southern part of range (Colima) these are more likely to be variants. Immature Black-throated has whitish feather tipping on throat and chest but not on lower breast, thus at any distance can appear pale-throated with a black pectoral band suggesting White-throated.

DESCRIPTION: Length 58-75 cm (male has longer tail than female). Bill medium-long, with curved culmen. Crest long, erect, slightly recurved. Nasal tuft short and insignificant. Male: Tail very long, strongly graduated with exceedingly elongated central two pairs of feathers and short outermost, rest intermediate in length. Crest black, feathers tipped blue. Crown, lores, face, sides of head, ear-coverts, throat and chest black. Malar stripe and patches above and below eye blue or whitish, white patches on throat and chest of some birds, especially in Sonora. Remainder of underparts white. Rear crown (below crest), nape, sides and rear of neck and entire upperparts deep-blue, brightest on nape, dullest on mantle and back, which can have weak green tinge. Wings deep-blue, underwing-coverts white, contrasting somewhat with grey underside of flight feathers. Tail dark blue with wide white outer border and tip to all but central two pairs of feathers which are wholly blue. Bill and legs black. Irides dark brown.

SEX/AGE: Sexes similar, although female relatively shorter-tailed than male. Juvenile inadequately described, probably very much as next stage but lacking bluish face and eye-patches, tail shorter and bill and legs probably paler. First-year birds differ from adults in having clear white tips to crest and crown feathers and black feathers of throat and chest tipped whitish and bluish, but lower breast blacker. Thus have pale-throated appearance, with black breast band; upperparts lighter and duller than in adult and with greenish tones. Probable second-year birds seem to be much as adult but have some white tips as well as blue tips to crown feathers.

MEASUREMENTS: Sexes similar in size, apart from

average tail length. Wing 198-221, tail male 435-508, female 407-508, tarsus 48-52, bill 32-36, weight 225-251.

GEOGRAPHICAL VARIATION: Monotypic.

VOICE: Vocabulary remarkably rich, indeed an incredible variety of sounds are produced. The majority are rhythmically repeated several times. They include various notes and chattering sounds, some high in pitch and musical in tone, others low and more guttural; barking, yelping, bubbling, stuttering, whistling, clicking and rattling sounds may be heard.

HABITS: A sociable and quite conspicuous jay, perching on tops of shrubs and bushes as well as inside crowns of larger trees. Invariably encountered in small noisy parties moving from tree to tree with tails waving. Often feeds in company of other large passerines, especially Yellow-winged Cacique *Cacicus melanicterus*. Feeds on invertebrates, berries and fruits. General behaviour much as in the White-throated Magpie-Jay.

BREEDING: Social nester. Nest a very bulky structure of twigs, lined with mosses, lichens and roots, placed in thorny trees. Eggs greyish-white, spotted, blotched and clouded with various shades of brown and grey. Eggs recorded April.

HABITAT: Arid bushy country, thorn forest and deciduous open woodland. From lowlands up to 1650 m.

DISTRIBUTION: Endemic to north-west Mexico. Range extends from southern Sonora and south-western Chihuahua, through Sinaloa and Jalisco to Colima, and possibly Guanajito. Occasional dispersal north to central Sonora, with an exceptional record of a presumed vagrant individual in extreme south USA at Douglas, Arizona.

STATUS: No precise information on numbers, presumed to be reasonably common in its restricted range, although no doubt has locally suffered from deforestation and intensive overgrazing.

REFERENCES: Goodwin 1986, Hardy 1990.

WHITE-THROATED MAGPIE-JAY Plate 9

Calocitta formosa

The more widespread of the two magpie-jays, extending over much of the central part of Central America.

IDENTIFICATION: A large and conspicuous jay with a long tail, white throat and face, narrow black collar and erect tall crest. Unmistakable over most of its range with the exception of the extreme north, where it overlaps with similar Black-throated Magpie-Jay (which see for discussion).

DESCRIPTION: Length 46-56 cm (male has longer tail than female). Bill medium-long, with curved culmen. Crest long, erect, slightly recurved. Nasal tuft short and insignificant. Male nominate race: Tail very long, strongly graduated with exceedingly elongated central two pairs of feathers and short outermost, rest intermediate in length. Crest black, feathers barred bluish-white at bases. Central forehead blackish, crown behind crest, nape and hindneck deep blue. Lores, supercilium, ear-coverts, sides of head, throat and breast white. Some dark feathering about eye. Malar stripe blue-black, often mottled, does not reach bill. Blackish area borders rear ear-coverts and extends as narrow 'U' shaped band across lower breast and over base of hindneck. Remainder of underparts white. Mantle, back and scapulars greyish-blue. Rump and uppertail-coverts darker greyish-blue often tinged greenish. Wings brighter, a more violet-blue; underwing-coverts white contrasting somewhat with grey underside of flight feathers. Tail darker, rich violet-blue, with wide white outer border and tip to all but central two pairs of feathers which are wholly blue. Bill and legs black. Irides dark brown.

SEX/AGE: Sexes similar, although female relatively shorter-tailed than male, with more extensive blackish on ear-coverts, blackish rear crown, narrower breast band and slightly duller on upperparts. Juvenile similar to female but central tail even less elongated, bill and legs greyer, duller greyish-blue above, narrower breast band, whiter crown and has shorter crest, the feathers of which are tipped blue and/or white. Much as adult after first moult except tail shorter.

MEASUREMENTS: Sexes similar in size, apart from average tail length. Nominate race: Wing 178-193, tail male 284-334, female 267-314, tarsus 39-46, bill 29-34, weight 205-213.

GEOGRAPHICAL VARIATION: Three intergrading races are recognised.

C. f. formosa: Colima, Michoacan and Puebla south to Oaxaca, intergrading with *azurea* towards Chiapias, described above.

C. f. azurea: Pacific slope of Chiapas and Guatemala, slightly larger with a little more white in tail, brighter, less grey, blue on upperparts; dark of rear ear-coverts much more bluish, blue wash above breast band on chest.

C. f. pompata: interior east Oaxaca, interior Chiapas, north slope of Guatemala, El Salvador and Honduras south to Costa Rica. Smaller, paler and duller blue than *azurea*, with more dusky rear ear-coverts, often with crest feathers extensively bluish-white with black tips.

VOICE: Vocabulary very similar to, and as rich and varied as Black-throated Magpie-Jay, but many of the phrases more nasal and shriller in quality.

HABITS: A sociable and quite conspicuous jay, roaming over open bushy country in small, noisy parties of five to ten birds. Also frequents larger clumps of trees and broken forest, especially along watercourses. More conspicuous than most jays, readily perching on tops of shrubs and bushes as well as feeding inside canopy of larger trees. Although generally shy and wary of man, they can also be very bold jumping about in trees uttering loud scolding chattering, if observer near nest. Similarly mobs predators, including roosting owls. Parties fly across open areas quite low in loose, straggling lines, flying with several flaps and a glide, their long tails undulating. Feeds inside foliage of shrubs and trees at various levels, also descending onto the ground where they move about with bouncing hops. Diet very varied, includes large invertebrates, small lizards and frogs, eggs and nestlings of small birds, seeds, fruits and berries, including grain; also sips nectar from large Balsa blossoms.

BREEDING: Social nester. Nest a very bulky mass of large twigs, lined with fine rootlets, placed in a tree 6-30 m and constructed by both sexes. Clutch three to four, eggs grey, finely freckled with brown. Incubation by female, which is fed at the nest by male and several helpers. No information on incubation or fledging periods. Young fed in nest and after leaving by several members of the social flock. Eggs recorded late December and early January in west Guatemala, mid April in El Salvador, June and July on Caribbean slope of Guatemala, February to July in Costa Rica. Protracted breeding season probably reflects on re-nesting attempts after failures rather than second-broods.

HABITAT: Bushy open country, thorn forest, deciduous woodland, gallery forest, fringes of cultivation and coffee plantations. Lowlands from sea-level to 800 m, locally up to 1250 m.

DISTRIBUTION: Widespread over central America, from central Mexico to northern Costa Rica. In Mexico it reaches its northern limit in the Pacific lowlands and slope of Colima, Michoacan and western Puebla, but is widespread through the southern part of the country along the Pacific slope, through Guatemala, El Salvador, Honduras and Nicaragua, locally extending over onto the Gulf-Caribbean side in valleys in Chiapas, Guatemala and Honduras. In Costa Rica on northern Pacific slope south to San Mateo and Orotina, irregularly to Carara, avoids Central Valley, but extends onto northwest Caribbean slope as far as Brasilia.

STATUS: Common and widespread throughout most of its range.

REFERENCES: Goodwin 1986, Hardy 1990, Stiles and Skutch 1989.

BROWN JAY *Psilorhinus morio*

BROWN JAY
Plate 8

Psilorhinus morio

Alternative names: Plain-tailed Brown Jay, White-tipped Brown Jay.

The only really drab Neotropical jay, further differing from all the others in having two colour phases and a bare inflatable sac on the chest. This extra air sac presumed to help in regulating its body temperature, but it also produces strange clicking sounds when the bird is calling.

IDENTIFICATION: A large, bulky dark-brown featureless jay, with whitish lower underparts and white tips to the tail feathers in southern populations. Juveniles with yellow bills and immatures, with blotched bills, add a little to its otherwise total lack of contrast. With its broad wings, relatively long graduated tail and raucous cries however it is obviously a jay and quite unmistakable.

DESCRIPTION: Length 39-44 cm. Bill medium-long and stout, with curved culmen. Frontal tuft stiff and wiry, but short and inconspicuous. Loral feathering short and velvet-like. Small bare inflatable area on chest (the furcular sac), not visible unless calling. Tail relatively long and very strongly graduated. Nominate race: Head almost blackish-brown, velvety feathers of loral region contrast with malar region, making latter appear browner. Underparts become increasingly paler towards belly, with belly and ventral region dingy off-white. Entire upperparts, wings and tail dull, dark earthy-brown, but paler than head. Wings and tail have indistinct grey sheen in fresh plumage. Small patch of bare skin behind eye black. Irides dark brown. Orbital ring black. Bill and legs black.

SEX/AGE: Sexes similar. Juvenile a little lighter brown overall, with bright yellow bill; legs, narrow orbital ring and tiny bare eye-patch also yellowish, becoming greenish in many soon after fledging. First-year birds have patchy yellow and black bills and legs. Ageing process seems to be individually variable. In many birds yellowish patches remain on the bill for several years.

MEASUREMENTS: Male distinctly larger than female when seen together. Nominate race: Wing male 202-216, female 198-206; tail male 210-226, female 201-214; tarsus male 48-52, female 49-51; bill male 26-32, female 26-28; weight (both sexes) 173-224.

GEOGRAPHICAL VARIATION: Some six races have been described, chiefly on minor mensural differences, southern birds being smallest and northern birds largest. It occurs in two colour phases (morphs), differing in underpart colouration and tail pattern:-

Plain-tailed morph: Underparts dark brown shading paler from lower breast downwards to brownish-white on belly, tail wholly dark. South Texas, south-eastern Nuevo Leon and Tamaulipas to eastern Oaxaca, northern Tabasco and north-eastern Chiapas.

White-tipped morph: Underparts from lower breast down quite cleanly white, all but central pair of tail feathers broadly tipped white. From central Veracruz, Chiapas and Yucatan south-east to west Panama.

Thus there is quite an extensive area of Mexico (Tabasco to central Veracruz) where the two occur side-by-side. Formerly these were thought to represent two species, southern birds being known as White-tipped Brown Jay (*P. mexicanus*). It is now known that these are merely colour morphs, not even races (see Selander 1959).

VOICE: Vocabulary less complex than most other Neotropical jays. The main call is a rather high pitched, nasal 'peeeeah' or 'eeeeurr' which is usually quickly repeated with varying intonations, pitch and speed. Interspersed between the individual calls is a rapid clicking sound, or hiccuping which is often given alone, this sound is produced through the furcular sac.

HABITS: A highly social arboreal jay, roaming open woodland in noisy but somewhat scattered parties of six to ten birds. Flocks generally consist of one, sometimes two, breeding pairs plus a number of immature non-breeding birds; the variable age process of the bare parts of individual birds is believed to aid their recognition of each other. They forage at all levels, readily descending to the ground, where they forage amongst the leaf litter, moving with bounding hops. In the canopy, the birds glean the foliage for insects and probe rotten wood or under loose bark. Occasionally they will fly out to catch insects on the wing. Their diet is very varied, consisting of all manner of invertebrates, including dragonflies caught on the wing, small lizards and frogs, the eggs and nestlings of small birds and a great variety of fruits, berries and seeds. Nectar is sipped from banana and balsa flowers. Their flight action is heavy and slightly undulating, several deep flaps followed by a long glide, generally at about tree top height. Noisily and persistently mobs potential predators and will noisily follow and scold humans.

BREEDING: Social nester. Nest a very bulky mass of large twigs and vines, lined with fibrous roots. Occasionally built against main trunk of a tree, amongst a vine tangle, or in crown of a banana plant but more typically far out on slender tree branch, at some 8 to 22 m from the ground. Built by both sexes, sometimes aided by a 'helper'. Clutch two to seven, usually three to four, larger clutches due to more than one female sometimes sharing same nest; eggs grey, finely freckled with brown. Incubation 18-20 days by female, being rarely briefly relieved by both a male and a helper. Incubating female and the young fed by a whole team of helpers, fledging at 23-24 days. Eggs recorded March to June, chiefly April.

HABITAT: Open woodland, riverine forest, edges of plantations and other farmland, preferring secondary forest to primary forest. Occurs from coastal areas up to 1700 m, reaching 2500 m in Costa Rica.

DISTRIBUTION: Widespread over central America, from extreme south-east Texas (lower Rio Grande valley), throughout the Gulf-Caribbean slope of Mexico, Belize, Guatemala, Honduras, Nicaragua and Costa Rica, reaching the southern limit of its range in extreme north-western Panama (west Colon).

STATUS: Common and widespread, increasing in many parts of its range, aided by forest degradation which has created the more open habitats that it favours. In Costa Rica it has spread into the Pacific lowlands in recent decades. In Panama it is very local, but increasing and occasional birds have been recorded south to central Panama. At the other end of its range it is very local and sparsely distributed along the banks of the lower Rio Grande of Texas, inland from Brownsville.

REFERENCES: Goodwin 1986, Hardy 1990, Selander 1959.

PALEARCTIC JAYS *Garrulus and Perisoreus*

These two genera are considered together, as although the six species fall fairly well into their respective genera, they are somewhat bridged by the extremely localised and poorly known Sichuan Jay. The latter is included, probably correctly, in *Perisoreus*, but shows certain features, i.e. bill shape, closer to the Lanceolated Jay of *Garrulus*.

Garrulus is represented by the widespread and incredibly variable Eurasian Jay, and two localised species, Lanceolated and Lidth's Jays which are similar in both having longer and more graduated tails than Eurasian Jay. *Perisoreus* has three allopatric members, two are widespread (Siberian and Grey Jays) and the third, the Sichuan Jay is isolated in western China. Although not strictly a Palearctic bird, the Grey Jay is the American cousin of the Siberian Jay and is unrelated to the other American jays.

EURASIAN JAY   Plate 11

Garrulus glandarius

Alternative names: Jay, Common Jay, Red-crowned Jay (India)

One of the most important natural planters of acorns; the distribution of several oak species is quite dependant on its presence. This lovely bird exhibits the most extreme racial variation of any corvid, and is also one of the most widespread, occupying wooded habitats as diverse as the Siberian taiga and the rainforests of Thailand.

IDENTIFICATION: Despite the variety of plumage colours and patterns, this jay is highly unlikely to be confused with any other bird. It is a relatively large pinkish-brown (at least in Europe, other races vary in body and head colour) woodland bird. The wings show fairly obvious white patches and blue shoulders (latter not obvious in flight) but the most constant feature over its wide range is the all black tail, contrasting well with white rear of both upper and undersides of the body. On the ground the pinkish-brown body, with black moustache, bold stance and ruffled crown is unlike any other bird, but both head and wing pattern, as well as body colour, vary with the subspecies concerned (see Geographical Variation). Usually seen in flight, which is slow and direct with a peculiar jerky flapping action, on relatively broad wings. Overlaps with Lanceolated Jay in the western Himalayas, with which it is unlikely to be confused, although alarm call very similar.

DESCRIPTION: Length 32-36 cm. Bill relatively short. Tail medium, narrow, almost square at the tip. Wings relatively broad and blunt. Crown feathers slightly elongated forming ruffled appearance when erect. Nasal tuft short, soft, just covering nostrils. Nominate race: Nasal tuft whitish or pale warm buffish. Forehead and crown whitish streaked with black. Loral and eye areas whitish. Chin and throat whitish bordered by prominent black malar stripe. Rear crown, sides of head and most of body plumage light rufous-brown to pinkish-brown, weakly washed grey on scapulars and mantle (actually very finely and indistinctly barred grey). Belly, and both under and uppertail-coverts white. Tail black, becoming slightly greyish towards base, which is also finely barred bluish. Wing pattern complex, simplified description given. Lesser and median coverts rufous, primary coverts and outer greater coverts bright blue, finely barred black; inner greater coverts black. Primaries brownish-black, with whitish edges to outer webs. Secondaries black with white bases to outermost five; innermost tertial deep chestnut with black tip. Underwing pinkish-rufous, with greyish flight feathers. Bill dark brownish-horn. Legs light fleshy-brown. Irides bluish-white with very narrow brown outer-ring and ring around pupil.

SEX/AGE: Sexes similar. Juvenile very similar, but body colour darker, more rufous, legs fleshy-yellow, irides bluish, bill greyer. By first autumn much as adult and not easily distinguished except in hand, but black barring on blue wingcovert feathers irregular.

MEASUREMENTS: Sexes very similar in size. Nominate race: Wing 170-188, tail 134-147, tarsus 40-44, bill 29-35, weight 140-187.

GEOGRAPHICAL VARIATION: Very complex, with some 33 subspecies recognised. For convenience these may be amalgamated into eight groups following Stresemann (1940) and Vaurie (1959). Goodwin (1986), reduced these to five groups by combining the first four of those listed below. The majority of mainland races intergrade, indeed some are distinctly clinal.

Nominate group: Europe, Crete and Cyprus. Nine very similar races, with streaked crowns and pinkish-grey or pinkish-rufous body plumage, described above.

"cervicalis" group: North Africa. Three races with contrast between rufous nape and grey mantle. Race *cervicalis* (north Algeria and Tunisia) has whitish sides of head and neck, wholly black crown and extensive grey over basal portion of tail; races *whitakeri* (north Morocco to west Algeria) and *minor* (Moroccan Atlas) have crown partially, but broadly streaked and rear sides of head pinkish-rufous.

"atricapillus" group: Turkey, Rhodes, Crimea, Caucasus, the Middle East to southern Iran. Four races. Mantle and nape uniform in colour, crown black, face whitish but more rufous in race *krynicki* (Turkey and the Caucasus).

G. g. hyrcanus: Caspian forests of northern Iran. A small rufous form, with greyish-black forehead and crown, blackest on forecrown, becoming mottled rufous, greyish and black on hind-crown. Intergrades with race *krynicki* of previous group in west Caspian region.

"brandtii" group: northern Russia and Siberia, south into western and north-eastern China, including northern Japan (Hokkaido). Four races. Foxy red on head, breast and nape, contrasting with grey mantle and scapulars, face dusky, irides dark blue. Western race *sewerzowii* (east to Urals) is an intergrading form with nominate race, south-eastern race *pekingensis* (Hopeh, China) has variable mixed characters with race *sinensis* (east and central China) of the *"bispecularis"* group.

"japonicus" group: Japan, from Honshu to Yakushima (off kyushu). Replaced by *brandtii* on Hokkaido. Four races. Crown and nape very white, streaked black, contrasting with buffy-rufous of sides of head (in *japonicus* of Honshu south to northern Kyushu), more heavily streaked and less white in other races, loral region and face blackish, very extensive white secondary patch (except in race *orii* of Yakushima). Irides white.

"bispecularis" group: Himalayas and central and eastern China, to west and north Burma and Taiwan. Six races. Head and body plumage uniform rufous (eastern races) to uniform light buffy-rufous (western races), uniform with unstreaked crown. Secondary patch blue with black, not white barring. Tertials

virtually lack chestnut. Irides black (western races) or grey (eastern races). Most races rather small, especially the bill. Race *haringtoni* (Chin Hills, Burma) has whiter throat and sides of head and larger bill, approaching *leucotis* group. Race *taivanus* (Taiwan) has blackish mottling on forehead and dusky nasal tuft.

"leucotis" group: South-east Asia, west to Burma. Two races. Crown and nape black, forehead streaked, throat and sides of head contrastingly whitish, body plumage becomes light brownish or more pinkish-brown when worn, but of varying hues when fresh; irides dark and wing (lacks white secondary patch) as in *bispecularis* group, bill large. Race *oatesi* (central Burma) intermediate between race *haringtoni* of *"bispecularis"* group, but has crown streaked.

VOICE: See Goodwin (1986) for detail. The most obvious call is the alarm, a dry, rasping screech 'skaaaak-skaaaak'. A weak mewing note is also often heard. A variable, subdued warbling song is easily overlooked in the wild, but more frequently noticed in spring is an almost crow-like 'kraah'.

HABITS: A shy and wary bird of woods and forests, typically first noticed flying away through the trees uttering harsh screech of alarm. Normally solitary by nature, mated pairs have very long bonds and defend their territories, but do not keep in very close contact over much of the year. Small gatherings of five to 30 birds form in late winter and early spring; these are unmated birds seeking partners, smaller groups almost certainly consist of an unmated female being courted by several unmated males. Eurasian Jays feed primarily on the ground, where they hop as they search the leaf litter for fallen acorns and invertebrates. In the autumn and winter, very large numbers of acorns are brought back to the birds' territories and hidden or stored for future retrieval. Acorns are typically pushed individually under dead leaves, brambles and hollows formed by low cover. It has been estimated that a single bird could 'plant' as many as 3000 acorns in one month. Eurasian Jays have learnt to recognise that a germinating oak seedling has a hidden acorn attached and select these seedlings when foraging in summer. As well as acorns, Eurasian Jays also take chestnuts, beech mast and hazel nuts, invertebrates, young birds and eggs and to a lesser extent, berries, fruits and some grain. Siberian races also feed on pine-seeds. Where unmolested they are fairly bold, visiting garden bird-tables for human food scraps, but these tend to be city park jays rather than the shy and wary country jay. There are records of more unusual feeding behaviour e.g. a jay pausing in its flight over a river to dip down and pick a small dead fish from the surface, one carrying a live toad, and in Britain, of feeding on peanuts in suspended bags and baskets intended for tits. Races occurring in the Himalayas and south-east Asia form small parties in winter and join up with roaming bands of mixed forest birds, such as laughing thrushes, minivets and tits. Eurasian Jays love to bathe in woodland puddles, and also freely indulge in 'anting', the latter activity often followed by a vigorous bath. They are reluctant to leave the shelter of the woodlands; when they do venture across clearings or roads they do so one at a time, the following bird not breaking cover until the previous one has made it safely across. Their flight action is usually laboured and flapping but when flying high and well underway, is steadier and more direct. When they irrupt flocks fly high in straggling parties, often invading open areas where not normally encountered. Irruption occurs sporadically in northern populations and is associated with acorn crop failure after some good years of acorn production. The Siberian race *brandtii* seems particularly prone to such movements. At such times many hundreds or even thousands may be seen flying in search of more productive feeding grounds. The most recent massive movement (of the nominate group) was in northern and central Europe west to Britain in the autumn of 1983, and consisted of birds which moved west in vast numbers. Jays avoid crossing water if at all possible.

BREEDING: Solitary nester. The nest is a platform of small twigs and roots, lined with rootlets and other fine plant fibres, (Siberian race *brandtii* also uses feathers and lichens in the cup); typically well-hidden near the main trunk or secondary fork of densely-foliaged trees or shrubs, between 3 and 6 m from the ground, sometimes higher; rarely in tree cavities. Both sexes share construction. Clutch three to seven, average five. Eggs variable, typically bluish-green, so densely freckled with brown that the green often obscured. Incubation 16-19 days by female, fed at nest by male. Young fed at the nest by both sexes for 18-23 days. Eggs recorded April and May over most of its wide range; but earlier in Israel, where generally mid February and March.

HABITAT: Woodland, orchards and forests, both mixed and deciduous, northern races in conifer forests. Often in city parks and large gardens. From lowlands up to 3965 m

DISTRIBUTION: Widespread throughout Europe (absent Iceland, north Scotland, northernmost Scandinavia and smaller offshore islands), south to north-west Africa (Morocco, northern Algeria and Tunisia), eastwards through northern Mediterranean including Sardinia, Corsica, Sicily, most Aegean islands, Crete, Rhodes and Cyprus. Through Turkey, to the Caucasus region, and east along the forests of the Caspian lowlands of northern Iran. South through the forested hills of Syria and Lebanon to central Israel and adjacent Jordan, across western and northern Iraq and throughout the Zagros mountains of western Iran. Absent Afghanistan and Central Asia. Range extends across Russia through Siberia to the Pacific, northern limit being approximately 60° North and the mouth of the Amur river; also Sakhalin, the southern Kuriles and Japan south to Kyushu and Yakushima. Southern limit in Russia is the boundary of the taiga/steppe zones, with an isolated population in the Crimea. Further east the southern boundary runs through northern Mongolia, to Ussuriland and Korea. South again throughout eastern and central China, including Taiwan (but absent Hainan) and into south-east Asia through most of Vietnam, northern Laos, northern Cambodia, northern Thailand and most of Burma. The range then extends westwards through the Himalayan forests across northern India, Bhutan and Nepal to northern Pakistan. Vagrant to Malta.

STATUS: Generally common, even locally abundant, over most of its range.

REFERENCES: Goodwin 1986, John and Roskell 1985, Stresemann 1940, Vaurie 1959.

LANCEOLATED JAY   Plate 10

Garrulus lanceolatus

Alternative name: Black-throated Jay

An elegant black-hooded jay of western Himalayan slopes, with a wing and tail pattern strangely reminiscent of the North American Blue Jay.

IDENTIFICATION: Distinctive jay of west Himalayan forests, the ruffled black hood contrasts with light pinkish-grey body and barred blue wings and tail, both of which are tipped white. It is a longer-tailed and slimmer bird than Eurasian Jay with which it overlaps in all but the western part of its range but is unlikely to be mistaken for it although the alarm screech is similar. It also favours more open forest, often perching on low scrub and might suggest a species of laughing-thrush rather than a jay, with its long, round-tipped and white-tipped tail. The black hood suggests Black-headed Sibia, *Heterophasia melanoleuca*, which inhabits the same forests, but latter is a smaller, predominantly bright rufous bird of dense canopy.

DESCRIPTION: Length 33 cm. Bill stout. Tail relatively long, distinctly graduated or rounded at tip. Nasal tuft short but dense. Crown feathers shaggy, forming ruffled crest when raised and a slight tuft at rear crown when relaxed. Head and nasal tuft black, chin and throat heavily streaked white on black background, bordered below by grey patch. Hindneck, sides of neck and most of body plumage pinkish-grey, rather greyer on upperparts, clearer dull pinkish on lower underparts. Wing pattern complex, simplified description given. Lesser and median coverts black. Primary coverts white. Outer secondaries bright blue, with narrow black barring, with broad black subterminal band, narrowly tipped white. Tertials soft grey, with wide black subterminal band and small white tips. Primaries dark grey, outer webs marbled bluish and narrowly edged with whitish outer fringe. Tail bright blue, heavily but narrowly barred black, with black subterminal band and white tips to all feathers. Bill light olive-grey or olive-horn. Legs bluish grey. Irides dark brown or reddish-brown.

SEX/AGE: Sexes similar, female possibly slightly shorter-tailed than male. Juvenile has duller black hood, less streaked throat, browner body plumage, lacks white tips to secondaries and tertials (but has white subterminal marks on secondaries), has greyer tips to tail feathers and shorter crest. After autumn moult, head and body much as adult, but juvenile wing and tail feathers retained well into first year.

MEASUREMENTS: Sexes similar in size but male seemingly has relatively slightly longer tail than female (in the small sample cited). Wing 144-158, tail 141-169, tarsus 32-34, bill 20-23, weight 84-104.

GEOGRAPHICAL VARIATION: Monotypic.

VOICE: Surprisingly similar to Eurasian Jay (see Goodwin (1986) for detail). The alarm is a dry 'skaaaak', slightly thinner than that of Eurasian Jay and invariably given singly. Goodwin describes it well, stating that it is flatter, lacking the crispness or incisiveness of Eurasian; even when given in intense alarm there is a pause between screeches, whereas they tend to run together

97

in Eurasian. The mewing call is higher in pitch and the 'kraah' call is a little flatter, less resonant, although more freely uttered than in Eurasian. A subdued song of soft mewing, bubbling and whistling notes interspersed with considerable mimicry has been recorded from captive males.

HABITS: Favours more open wooded slopes than Eurasian Jay, although in autumn and winter the two species often associate loosely, together with Gold-billed Magpies. Usually encountered in pairs or family parties, which often gather together into larger flocks of up to 20 or 30 in winter. Like Eurasian Jay these birds are closely linked with oaks, and feed primarily on acorns in the autumn, many of which are taken away and hidden. They also feed on pine seeds, but take a variety of other items into their diet, from human food scraps to a wide variety of invertebrates, small lizards, and the eggs and nestlings of small birds; in season they also devour berries and fruits and can be something of a nuisance in small orchards. They are noisy birds and vigorously mob potential predators such as roosting owls, screeching and bobbing with crests raised until the predator departs, often followed by the scolding birds. Not particularly shy of man, these jays come to isolated houses, mountain huts and small villages to feed on food waste and in nearby terraced fields. Although primarily arboreal by nature they tend to feed more on the outside of the canopy, rather than inside like Eurasian Jay, and readily alight on exposed perches such as bush tops, bare trees and rocky outcrops as well as being quite at ease feeding on the ground. Their flight action is more undulating than that of Eurasian Jay, perhaps an effect created by their slimmer shape and longer tails. In winter many descend to lower elevations and at least in Afghanistan, where their habitats are less lush, come into trees and cultivation at the edges of large towns, as at Jalalabad; but further east they remain in the hills through the winter.

BREEDING: Solitary nester. Nest a deep, untidy, loose base of twigs, with cup lined with roots, black fungal rhizoids (resembling horse-hair) and grass stems. Placed in a fork towards the top of a small tree (especially oak), or large shrub on open hillsides or near forest edge, at some 5 to 7 m from the ground. Built by both sexes. Clutch three to five, usually three to four, eggs olive-brown to olive-green, minutely freckled and blotched brown, the markings coalescing towards wider end, where there are some black lines. Incubation by female, for at least 16 days (captive birds), being fed on or off nest by male. Fledging period unrecorded, but male assists in feeding young. Eggs recorded April and May.

HABITAT: Montane forests, from open hillsides and ridges with scattered trees and shrubbery to forest edges; mixed pine-oak and cedar-oak forests preferred. Also near shrubby cultivated terraces by villages in winter. Breeds between 1500 m and 3000 m, descending a little lower in winter.

DISTRIBUTION: Western Himalayas. Western limit is eastern Afghanistan (west to Kabul and Paktia provinces), through northern Pakistan (south to Safed Koh), Kashmir (but not the vale of Kashmir), Himachal Pradesh, Garwhal and Kumaon in India and through western Nepal, reaching eastern limit in region of Kathmandu.

STATUS: Relatively common on exposed slopes throughout its range, but perhaps less numerous in Nepal than further west.

REFERENCES: Ali 1949, Goodwin 1986, Paludan 1959.

LIDTH'S JAY   Plate 11

Garrulus lidthi

A beautiful jay, endemic to the northern Nansei islands of Japan. In shape, comparable to the Lanceolated Jay of the western Himalayas, to which it must be related. Some aspects of its behaviour are strange for a jay; it is a habitual cavity-nesting bird, lays plain coloured eggs, and has been observed to use its stout bill as a climbing aid in the manner of a parrot.

IDENTIFICATION: A large, stout-billed, beautiful rich chestnut and purple-blue jay, with striking white tertial and tail tips. It is the only jay within its range, therefore quite unmistakable.

DESCRIPTION: Length 38 cm. Bill very stout. Tail relatively long, graduated or rounded at tip. Nasal tuft short but dense. Crown feathers only very slightly elongated. Forehead and loral feathering slightly stiffened. Nasal tuft, forehead, loral region, chin and throat black, the throat marked with small white streaks. Remainder of head, neck, upper mantle and breast rich dark purplish-blue. The lower breast gradually changes from dark reddish-purple to rufous-chestnut, with mauve tones on belly, flanks and ventral region. Upperparts darker rufous-chestnut, with purplish tones, this most apparent in fresh plumage when feathers have purplish tips, with wear appears more chestnut. Wings almost wholly dark purplish-blue, finely barred black on wing-coverts and outer secondaries. Secondaries have diffuse dark subterminal markings and white tips, most obvious on the innermost (i.e. tertials). Tail dark purplish-blue, with blackish subterminal band and clear white terminal band. Bill clear pale yellowish, tinged green over basal portion. Legs dark grey. Irides dark violet-blue.

SEX/AGE: Sexes similar. Juvenile much duller, lacking white tips to wing and tail feathers, has chestnut of body plumage a dull brown and blue of head and neck greyish-brown to brownish-black.

MEASUREMENTS: Wing 179-183, tail 175-187, tarsus 41-43, bill 39-42, weight unrecorded.

GEOGRAPHICAL VARIATION: Monotypic.

VOICE: The most frequently heard call is a harsh, grating 'kraah' which is the usual alarm given when flushed or when mobbing; the 'kraah' call is given in a variety of pitches and stresses. Another call, a high-pitched mewing seems to be contact note used by foraging pairs. Has a 'flattened' screech comparable to Lanceolated, but seemingly only uttered in display.

HABITS: A sociable jay of woodland and woodland edges, in pairs or small parties, but in autumn family parties gather together into flocks of up to 100 birds and roam through the forest and adjacent habitats. These jays, despite their limited range, are quite abundant and seem to live in high densities for forest corvids. Breeding pairs maintain a nesting territory of some 150 to 300 sq. m, which is not aggressively defended, but males stake their territories with much vocal activity. Birds call from exposed tree-top perches, call period lasting up to three minutes, speeding-up the frequency rate towards the end and stopping abruptly. They noisily attack and chase-off intruding potential predators such as Large-billed Crow, *Corvus macrorhyncus*. Lidth's Jays forage at all levels of the forest, in adjacent cultivation, and even along nearby seashores. They feed with rather heavy, ponderous movements in the canopy and undergrowth, inspecting almost every nook and cranny. During a brief study, Bruce (1979) reported observing a bird using its large bill as a climbing aid, 'in the mannner of parrots'. Bruce also reported seeing birds run for a few steps, as well as hopping, whilst foraging on the forest floor, which is also exceptional. These jays feed principally on acorns, but also take a variety of invertebrates, small reptiles, seeds, fruits, berries and small sweet potatoes. Like the others in the genus it is recorded to hide acorns. Flight action, said to resemble that of Eurasian Jay. Formerly considered shy and very wary of man, but following a long period of protection in some areas, it is now quite bold and confiding.

BREEDING: Solitary nester. Nest resembles that of the Eurasian Jay but is constructed in tree holes, cliff crevices and on ledges in and around buildings, between 1 and 5 m from ground level. Clutch three to five, eggs pale greenish-blue, usually plain but sometimes with a few brownish speckles. Eggs laid February and March.

HABITAT: Various forest types, both in the hills and lowlands, from coniferous, to mixed and deciduous woodland. Also in relatively small shady woods in cultivated areas near villages.

DISTRIBUTION: Endemic to Nansei (formerly Ryukyu) islands of Japan, where only presently known on the island of Amami-oshima and adjacent small island of Kakeroma-jima. A single bird on the island of Iriomote-jima in the Yaeyama Islands in 1984 was considered to have been an escaped individual which had been illegally transported there.

STATUS: Formerly quite abundant on the islands of Amami-oshima and Tokunoshima but population devastated by uncontrolled shooting and trapping for the feather trade in the early part of this century. It formerly occurred in the central mountains of Tokunoshima but has not been seen there since the 1920s. Protection on Amami-oshima, where it has been declared one of Japan's Natural Monuments, has resulted in a dramatic increase in population and it is now widespread and quite common there; with a population estimated at some 5,800 birds in 1973. It is also common on the nearby small island of Kakeroma-jima.

REFERENCES: Brazil 1991, Bruce 1979, Goodwin 1986

SICHUAN JAY Plate 10

Perisoreus internigrans

Alternative names: Szechuan Grey Jay, Sooty Jay

Despite being the drabbest of all jays, even duller in appearance than the Brown Jay, its rarity and the remoteness of its environment makes it as enigmatic as the Giant Panda which shares the same habitats.

IDENTIFICATION: Rarely seen and easily overlooked due to rather skulking behaviour (see Habits). A drab uncrested greyish jay with distinctly dusky hood and contrastingly pale, stubby bill. Despite the lack of plumage features it unlikely to be confused with any other bird. Similar Siberian Jay does not occur in this region, has rusty rump and tail and weaker blackish bill.

DESCRIPTION: Length 30 cm. Bill stouter than that of Siberian Jay, with lower mandible distinctly angled, similar in shape to bill of Lanceolated Jay. Wings short. Tail relatively long and slightly rounded at tip. Nasal tuft short and dense. Head and throat sooty blackish-brown merging into overall drab medium-dark grey of remainder of plumage, bases of throat feathers greyer, possibly losing dark tips when worn. Thighs sooty. Wings and tail slightly darker and more brown-tinged than body plumage. Bill dull yellowish-olive to horn. Legs blackish. Irides brown.

SEX/AGE: Sexes similar, juvenile undescribed.

MEASUREMENTS: Wing 167, tail 157, tarsus 41, bill 29 (one specimen measured), weight unrecorded.

GEOGRAPHICAL VARIATION: Monotypic.

VOICE: Vocally has much closer affinities with the Siberian Jay than it has with the *Garrulus* jays. Tape recordings show two types of call. Both of these calls were given by a foraging pair of birds; neither were very far carrying and seemed to be forms of contact call. It is possible that the 'kyip' call might be a kind of alarm or warning note prompted by the sight of a human observer. One of the calls is a plaintive high pitched 'kyip, kyip' with rising inflection, occasionally speeded up into an increasingly rapid longer phrase 'kyip, kyip, kyip,kyip,kyip,ip,ip,ip,ip', this has something of a woodpecker-like quality in tone, but the speed is not unlike the 'chipper' phrase given by a displaying Common Snipe *Gallinago gallinago*, although much thinner and more plaintive. The other call is a plaintive mewing note, very much like the call of a buzzard, 'meeeoo-meeeoo' with a rising inflection.

HABITS: Little documented. Most observations have been of single birds or pairs. They are very unobtrusive birds which are easily overlooked, but draw attention to themselves by their mewing calls. Pairs forage inside the dense foliage of conifers, peering and pecking into crevices of the main trunk in their search for invertebrates. They forage at about mid-height of the trees, methodically working their way along, progressing by hopping from twig to twig close to the main trunk. The birds then move at a low level to the next tree or drop down a slope to work another patch of forest. They are not particularly wary, and readily come closer to inspect humans. One report mentions a bird perching briefly on the top of a tall conifer before flying off. The slight chisel shape to the lower mandible might be an aid to prising pieces of bark off the trunk or to allow it access to pine seeds by opening cones. It possibly produces sticky saliva like the other two *Perisoreus* jays.

BREEDING: Undocumented.

HABITAT: High altitude spruce and pine forest, with marked preference for extensive forest on steep mountainsides, or smaller patches of conifers on ridges and upper slopes; avoids the gentler slopes of the valley bottoms. Occurs between 3350 and 4300 m.

DISTRIBUTION: Endemic to central China, where its range extends along the mountains of the Min Shan range, on the borders of northern Sichuan, extreme south-east Qinghai and south-west Kansu.

STATUS: Rare. This jay is frustratingly difficult to observe, even in areas where it is known to occur. Forest destruction in the region has possibly fragmented its range in recent decades, but much remains on the steeper slopes. Most ornithological work in this region takes place in May and June when weather conditions are favourable, however, it is possible that the jays nest in this season and consequently remain very unobtrusive. Visits to the region in autumn would probably be more productive in locating this difficult species .

REFERENCES: Goodwin 1986; Robson, C (tape recordings).

SIBERIAN JAY   Plate 10

Perisoreus infaustus

A small dull brownish jay of the taiga forests, spanning the entire length of the Palearctic region. Replaced by the Grey Jay in equivalent habitats in North America.

IDENTIFICATION: Rather small, long-tailed jay of northern forests; the dull and rather loose greyish-brown plumage being relieved by darker head and rusty wing patch, rump and tail, the latter being concealed by brown central feathers when at rest. Generally an inconspicuous inhabitant of dense forest, typically seen gliding and swooping through the trees, usually singly or in pairs but sometimes in small parties.

DESCRIPTION: Length 25-31 cm. Bill very short, lower mandible upturned, culmen almost straight. Wings short. Tail relatively long and slightly rounded at tip. Nasal tuft short and fluffy. Nominate race: Nasal tuft pale buff. Head darkish brown, very dark about eye. Throat and breast buffy grey-brown, becoming more buffish on lower breast, lower underparts dull buffy rufous. Hindneck, sides of neck and most of upperparts lighter greyish brown. Lower rump and uppertail-coverts bright rufous. Wings grey brown, with rusty-rufous primary coverts and outer greater coverts. Underwing rusty-buff shading dull greyish on flight feathers. Most of tail orange-rufous, with greyish shade at very tip, central pair of feathers dull grey-brown, concealing rufous when perched. Bill blackish. Legs blackish. Irides very dark brown.

SEX/AGE: Sexes similar, juvenile has softer and fluffier plumage than adult, but colour virtually the same; they tend to be rather paler below, have head less contrastingly dark and the upperparts a shade darker. Adults have a complete moult late May to early August, juveniles moult only body July to September; therefore adults have moulting flight feathers and tail in summer and are in very fresh plumage in first autumn and winter; juveniles have abraded flight and tail feathers which might be apparent by late autumn or winter.

MEASUREMENTS: Male averages larger than female. Nominate race: Wing 134-154, tail 135-149, tarsus 35-38, bill 22-23, weight 73-97.

GEOGRAPHICAL VARIATION: Overall basic colour tones vary over wide range but differences are distinctly clinal and difficult to define. Vaurie (1959) recognises ten subspecies, but many others have been described. These clinal variations are summarised briefly below, but as Vaurie cautions, such a complicated variation,

intergrading where clines meet, is open to different interpretations.

Northern, west to east cline: birds become gradually greyer towards the east, from the nominate race (Lapland to Kola peninsula), through *ostjakorum* (north-west Siberia to the Yenisei), to the very grey and least rufous race *yakutensis* (Yenisei east to north-east Siberia).

Southern, west to central cline: warmer, more rufous than northern forms, more greyish at tail tip and larger rufous wing patch. Race *ruthenus* (central Scandinavia south-east to west of the Altai) and much darker rufous, darker headed race *opicus* (west Altai to western Sayan) which also has extensive rufous in wing.

Central cline: very grey forms with large rufous wing patches, *rogosowi* (central Siberia east to Baikal region) and *sibericus* (Baikal and north Mongolia to Yakutia) which is paler and greyer than *rogosowi*.

Eastern, north to south cline: darker than Central and northern forms, becoming more saturated towards the south, from *varnak* (upper Amur basin) which is greyer and darker-headed than *sibericus*, through *sakhalensis* (Sakhalin and adjcent coastal Siberia) to the darker *maritimus* (Ussuriland to north-east China) which resembles western forms but has a blacker crown and much more rufous in wing.

VOICE: Not very vocal, but sometimes draws attention to itself by calling. Calls include a buzzard-like mewing cry, a harsh, high 'hearrr-hearrr' and a jay-like hoarse 'skaaaak' but latter is rather less dry and more nasal than that of jay, and fuller at the beginning. It has an inconspicuous song of various whistling, creaking and trilling notes, interspersed with some mimicry; but this is only audible at close range.

HABITS: Usually a fairly inconspicuous inhabitant of dense forest, but along popular forest trails and at picnic sites they are often very tame and seem to appear from nowhere to wait for scraps. Elsewhere they can be very elusive, birds seem to 'melt' into the forest, their dingy colouration blending well with darkness of the conifers. Usually encountered in pairs or family parties, mated birds apparently pair for life and hold permanent territories of between 50 and 150 ha depending on population density. When breeding, birds with larger territories tend to restrict their foraging to the vicinity of the nest and do not exploit the whole area until later in the year when food is less abundant. Breeding pairs will tolerate young from the previous year within the territory until well into the following breeding season. Non-breeding birds form small parties but odd individuals of either sex will be tolerated within an established territory, sometimes for years, and often take the place of a partner if one of the pair dies. Occasional promiscuous couplings occur and two females have been recorded sharing incubation and rearing the young at the same nest. They feed both in trees and on the ground, occasionally swinging in tit-like fashion beneath the branches. As with other jays they are omnivorous, feeding on a variety of berries, fruits, insects and their larvae, slugs, snails, voles, and the eggs of small birds as well as carrion and human food scraps. They build up winter stores of berries, chiefly bilberries, which are hidden behind loose bark or amongst hanging tufts of lichens. Shares with Grey Jay the ability to stick balls of food together for winter stores with its special salivary glands (see Grey Jay for more information). Occasionally perches on the tops of conifers at a prominent view point, but usually keeps low, perching at mid canopy level. Flight action delicate, silent and buoyant, sweeping low across forest trails.

BREEDING: Solitary nester. Nest materials my be collected and stored for some time before construction commences. Nest variable in size, but a strongly built, thick construction of twigs and lichens, feathers and mosses, with a thickly-lined deep cup of feathers, fur and soft plant materials. Situated against the main trunk of a conifer between 2 and 6 m from the ground. It is built by both sexes, though sometimes just by the female. Clutch three to five, average four. Eggs bluish-green or greenish-grey, spotted and blotched brown and grey, with a concentration at the wider end. Incubation 19 days, by female, being fed at the nest by the male. Fledging period 21-24 days, young being tended by both sexes and sometimes remaining in their territory for up to a year before moving on. Eggs laid late March and April in Scandinavia, late April and May in central Siberia. As with many resident taiga species breeding commences early and young have been recorded in the nest whilst snow is on the ground; presumably this gives the fledged young a better chance of survival during the short summer period when food is abundant.

HABITAT: Dense coniferous forest, but sometimes in birch in the very far north. Occurs in both lowlands and uplands, ascending as high as 2200 m in the Altai mountains.

DISTRIBUTION: Widespread across the boreal Palearctic, from Norway in the west to the Pacific,;absent from the tundra regions of the far north and the extreme north-east of Siberia; range includes Sakhalin but not Japan. Southern limit is the southern edge of the Taiga: central Norway and central Sweden, Estonia, north of Moscow, southern Urals, extreme northern Mongolia, Ussuriland and extreme north-eastern Heilungkiang (China). Central Siberian birds wander to a certain extent and occasional minor irruptive movements are reported. Vagrants have occurred south to Latvia, Denmark, Czechoslovakia, Hungary and the Ukraine.

STATUS: Despite very extensive range, is by no means common throughout; it seems to be patchily distributed across the main land mass. There is also some evidence that it has descreased or disappeared from many areas at the southern edge of its range. In Finland numbers have steadily declined throughout the 1970s and 1980s, perhaps because of competition or predation from Eurasian Jay which is gradually increasing and spreading northwards. In one study area in Scandinavia 80% of nests failed, because of predation by corvids, including other Siberian Jays.

REFERENCES: Blomgren 1964, 1971, Dement'ev and Gladkov 1970.

GREY JAY   Plate 10

Perisoreus canadensis

Alternative name: Canada Jay

Replaces Siberian Jay in North America and like that species, produces a sticky saliva with which it glues together berries and other food items into balls for easier winter storage.

IDENTIFICATION: Distinctive fluffy-plumaged dark-grey and white jay of coniferous forests in western and northern North America. Adults with their dark grey upperparts, dark hood and white forecrown and underparts are quite unmistakable (see however Geographical Variation). Juveniles are dingy grey overall and may be quite puzzling, although readily identified by size, shape and attendant adults. Often remarkably tame, entering tents and lodges which they ransack for food. Compare Clark's Nutcracker.

DESCRIPTION: Length 25-28 cm. Bill very short, lower mandible upturned, culmen almost straight. Wings short. Tail relatively long and slightly rounded at tip. Nasal tuft short and fluffy. Nominate race: Nasal tuft, forehead, lores and forecrown white. Rear crown, sides of head behind eye, nape and hindneck dusky greyish-black, diffusing into white of forecrown. Lower hindneck greyish-white becoming whiter at sides of neck and joining white throat and breast. Remainder of underparts light grey, with ashy tinge, darkening to medium grey on flanks and sides of breast. Upperparts including wings and tail slate-grey with ashy tones, wings and tail rather purer grey with bluish tones in fresh plumage. Underwing dusky grey. Diffuse whitish edges to all wing feathers, widest and most obvious on tertials and primaries. Tail diffusely tipped greyish-white. Bill and legs black. Irides dark brown.

SEX/AGE: Sexes similar, juvenile quite different, being slate-grey or blackish-grey all over (depending on race), except for ill-defined whitish malar stripe. Bill has pale fleshy base. By first winter much as adult.

MEASUREMENTS: Male averages slightly larger than female. Nominate race: Wing 140-148, tail 135-151, tarsus 34-37, bill 19-23, weight 62-73.

GEOGRAPHICAL VARIATION: Quite marked, with some eight races currently recognised, as usual with such a variable species, several other forms have been named which are generally regarded as intergrading populations.

P. c. canadensis: most of Canada and northern USA, described above.
P. c. nigricapillus: Nova Scotia, Newfoundland, Quebec and Labrador, darker overall, with more extensive black on crown (almost reaching upper forehead), underparts darker grey and white of throat and breast sullied very pale grey. Juvenile almost sooty-black on head and breast.
P. c. pacificus: Alaska and north-west Canada, white areas of plumage sullied grey, with buff tones, especially on forehead.
P. c. arcus: central coastal British Columbia, like last but darker and with forehead greyish-white.
P. c. capitalis: Rocky Mountains from Idaho to New

Mexico, very pale with greyer and more restricted black on head (virtually only on nape), paler grey above. Juvenile quite a light grey.

P. c. albescens: from north-east British Columbia, east of the Rockies to South Dakota and Nebraska, like last but even paler with even less dark on head. Juvenile light grey.

P. c. obscurus: coastal Washington south to north California, smaller than nominate, dark of head browner and extending further foreward, collar wider and whiter, underparts white down to belly; upperparts more ashy-grey, with weak whitish shaft streaks on mantle. Juvenile like nominate but more sooty-brown.

P. c. griseus: south-west British Columbia and Vancouver south to central Oregon and north-east California, slightly larger and greyer than the last. Juvenile like nominate but more sooty-brown.

VOICE: Has a number of different calls, most noticeable perhaps is a harsh, grating, churring scold of alarm, uttered especially when a potential predator such as a snake, owl or small mammal is spotted. Other calls include a soft whistle 'wheeeoo' with several variations, including some which are almost of human quality. Also has a low 'chuck' and like other northern jays has a subdued song, consisting of soft modulated trills.

HABITS: Its behaviour is similar to that of the Siberian Jay. Usually encountered in pairs or family parties in coniferous forests. At the appearance of people it often appears as if from nowhere, sweeping in suddenly and silently, gliding with hardly a flap. Despite its association with humans, this jay is very much a bird of remote forests; it does not frquent towns and villages. Its bold and cunning behaviour is both endearing and annoying; it will enter forest camps, log cabins and tents with amazing boldness and fly-off with anything it can carry, whether edible or not. It is reported to steal food from frying-pans and plates, even perching on heads or hands just prior to the theft. One of several folk-names is 'Camp-robber'. It is apparently attracted by the sight of camp-fires and the sound of gunshots. As well as human food scraps and carrion from hunters' camps, it feeds on a variety of natural items, including various invertebrates, small rodents, young birds, eggs, fungi, lichens (latter two eaten as a last resort), berries and fruits. Both this species and the Siberian Jay have a special pair of

mucous-secreting glands inside the bill; the sticky saliva coats the tongue and enables the bird to form berries into sticky balls which can then be stuck onto branches or lichen clumps and retrieved when required; the sticky tongue also helps the bird to get at food items stored in crevices. These glands are similar to those of woodpeckers and are not known to be present in any other corvids.

BREEDING: Solitary nester. Nest similar to that of Siberian Jay, a thick construction of twigs and strips of bark, padded with mosses and lichens; inner cup thickly-lined with feathers, fur and soft plant material, decorated with spider webs, nests and cocoons around the outside of the rim. Built by both sexes, but chiefly by the female; situated in the crown of a conifer, or near the end of a large branch from 2 to 9 m from the ground. Clutch two to five, usually four. Eggs pale greenish or whitish, spotted and blotched brown and grey, with underlying grey markings. Incubation 16 to 18 days, by female, being fed at the nest by the male. Young fledge from 15 days, after being fed by both sexes. Eggs laid late March and April over most of its range, sometimes as early as late February.

HABITAT: Coniferous forests, but sometimes in mixed forests, with a preference for wilderness-like country.

DISTRIBUTION: Widespread across the boreal Neartic. Range extends from north-central Alaska and central Yukon eastwards across Canada to northern Labrador and Newfoundland, on the eastern seaboard south to north New York, north New England, New Brunswick and Nova Scotia. Westwards the southern limit goes through extreme north USA to the foothills of the Rockies in South Dakota and turns south into the eastern boundary of its range, south to Colorado and northern New Mexico. The south-western boundary then runs through central Arizona, central Utah, central Idaho and central Oregon and south again to northern California. Mainly resident but occasional irruptive movements occur when birds move into various parts of the US interior.

STATUS: Seemingly not uncommon, even locally common over its wide range, with no precise information available on population changes.

REFERENCES: Dow 1965, Goodwin 1986

BLUE MAGPIES *Urocissa*

A small genus of colourful tropical and subtropical corvids from the forests of southern and eastern Asia, they are closely-related to the green magpies *Cissa*. In reality there is little difference between the genera, although obviously the green magpies form a species-group amongst themselves. The isolated Ceylon Magpie and perhaps the White-winged Magpie bridge the gap between the two.

CEYLON MAGPIE   Plate 16

Urocissa ornata

Alternative names: Sri Lanka Magpie, Ceylon Blue Magpie

One of the most colourful of all corvids, restricted to hill forest in Sri Lanka, where its numbers are declining through habitat destruction.

IDENTIFICATION: Confined to humid forests on Sri Lanka, this beautiful bird is quite unmistakable; its chestnut head, breast and wings contrast with its brilliant blue body and long white-tipped tail are shared by no other bird on the island, or elsewhere.
DESCRIPTION: Length 42-47 cm (including tail). Bill relatively stout, with curved culmen. Nasal tuft soft, moderate. Area of bare skin about eye. Crown slightly crested towards rear. Wings relatively short and broad. Tail long and graduated. Head, neck and upper breast deep chestnut-red, remainder of body plumage bright deep purplish blue becoming lighter blue over rump and uppertail-coverts and belly and undertail-coverts. Wing-coverts darker purple-blue, the lesser coverts being lighter; primaries and secondaries chestnut-red, lighter and less brown than chestnut of head and neck; secondaries with purplish-blue inner webs forming a bluish panel on closed wing and showing as blue wedges on inside of tertials. Tail purplish-blue, with central feathers lighter blue, each feather with wide white tip and black subterminal band, the white being narrowest on central pair, and widest on shorter outermost feathers. Bill and legs coral-red. Irides brown with red orbital ring and deeper-red bare skin about eye.
SEX/AGE: Sexes similar. Juvenile duller, with grey wash to blue of body plumage; eye-ring brownish and colour of other bare parts duller than adult.
MEASUREMENTS: Female averages a little smaller than male, and tail also probably shorter. Wing 155-170, tail 235-255, tarsus 40, bill 36-37 (from feathers, not skull), weight 196 (one).
GEOGRAPHICAL VARIATION: Monotypic.
VOICE: Has quite a wide vocabulary, which includes mimicry. Feeding groups are rather quiet apart from low conversational squeaks and chirps, mixed with occasional loud raucous and rasping notes. A very distinctive call is a far-carrying loud jingle uttered with bill wide-open 'chink-chink' or 'cheek-cheek', repeated with variations. It has a rasping 'crakrakrakrak' and a loud 'whee-whee' or 'tweewi-kraa'. A subdued song of various squeaks, chattering and sucking noises, mixed with some mimicry of other bird calls is also recorded. Said to be most vocal during wet weather.
HABITS: A lively bird of wet hill forests, roaming through the forest in parties of up to seven birds, sometimes singly or in pairs. Parties seem to forage through quite an extensive territory. They often feed in low shrubbery, even descending to ground level but are chiefly birds of the tree canopy. They noisily work through the foliage, hopping from branch to branch, peering into bunches of leaves, poking under loose bark, sometimes hanging upside-down like overgrown tits, or clinging on to the side of a large leaf. Food items recorded include a number of arboreal invertebrates such as crickets, caterpillars, beetles, also tree-frogs and small lizards. It does take some fruits but is chiefly carnivorous; hairy caterpillars are vigorously and carefully rubbed against mossy branches to remove their hairs. They prefer to fly only relatively short distances between trees and when leaving trees they tend to drop out of them to within a few feet of the ground, flying low and rising to sweep up onto next perch.
BREEDING: Probably a solitary nester. Nest recalls that of a crow, but smaller, a stick construction, with the cup lined with fine roots and fine beard-like lichens. It is placed in the canopy of tall saplings, or the outer branches of small trees, between 5 and 13 m from the ground. Clutch three to five, average three. Eggs whitish, profusely speckled and spotted with brown, obscuring ground colour. Eggs recorded between mid January and late March.
HABITAT: Dense evergreen forests, including fringes of tea plantations, in both the lowland wet zone and the hills, between 150 m and 2100 m
DISTRIBUTION: Endemic to Sri Lanka where confined to the wet south-west of the island.
STATUS: Rare and declining, forest destruction, particularly in the lowlands, has severely reduced the population in recent decades. No precise information on population available.
REFERENCES: Henry 1971, Collar and Andrew 1988.

TAIWAN MAGPIE   Plate 14

Urocissa caerulea

Alternative name: Formosan Blue Magpie

A beautiful and distinctive pie confined to hill forest on Taiwan, where there are no other blue magpies.

IDENTIFICATION: This beautiful bird is quite unmistakable; its black head and breast, rich blue underparts, stunning yellow eye and scarlet bill are quite unlike the other blue magpies, neither of which occur on Taiwan.
DESCRIPTION: Length 63-68 cm (including tail). Slightly bulkier and with less elongated tail than Blue Magpie. Bill relatively stout, with curved culmen. Nasal tuft

moderate. Wings relatively broad. Tail long and graduated, central pair of feathers greatly elongated (not as extreme as in Blue Magpie). Head, neck and upper breast black, feathers tipped dark blue. Entire body plumage, including underparts rich azure-blue, being only relieved by whitish fringing to undertail-coverts and broad black scale-tipping to uppertail-coverts. Wings bright azure-blue, with very small white tips to tertials. Underwing-coverts dark grey, darker than light grey of flight feathers. Tail bright azure-blue, each feather with wide white tip and blackish subterminal band. Bill and legs scarlet-red. Irides clear lemon-yellow, with narrow scarlet orbital ring.

SEX/AGE: Sexes similar. Juvenile duller, head and breast blackish-grey, body plumage a duller, more greyish-blue; bill and legs fleshy-pink, irides brown (as nestlings); wings and tail as adult.

MEASUREMENTS: Wing 200-207, tail 340-418, tarsus 52-57, bill 45-46, weight not recorded.

GEOGRAPHICAL VARIATION: Monotypic.

VOICE: Basic alarm or warning call a high-pitched, cackling chatter, slower and higher-pitched than chatter of Black-billed Magpie; has been rendered as 'kyak-kyak-kyak-kyak'. A soft 'kwee-eep' or 'swee-eee' is given by relaxed perched birds.

HABITS: As the other blue magpies. Encountered in parties of six or more birds, which are shy and wary. Feeding parties work the canopy of hill forest, flying between with several short flaps and a glide in typical blue magpie fashion. Food items recorded include wild figs, berries and insects. See Severinghaus (1987) for details of social behaviour.

BREEDING: A social breeder see Severinghaus (1987). Nest a large, bulky construction of twigs, placed on large, almost horizontal, bough of a tree at junction of several small branches. Eggs five or six, creamy-white with greenish tinge, blotched and spotted dark brown. Eggs recorded mid to late May.

HABITAT: Deciduous hill forests, also down into lowlands in winter. Between 300 and 1200 m.

DISTRIBUTION: Endemic to Taiwan.

STATUS: No population details available but reported 'elusive' by Brazil (1992) who mentions the wooded areas around the huge reservoir at Shihmen Dam near Taipei as a precise site.

REFERENCES: Goodwin 1986, Severinghaus 1987, Brazil 1992.

GOLD-BILLED MAGPIE   Plate 14

Urocissa flavirostris

Alternative name: Yellow-billed Blue Magpie

A Himalayan forest bird, replacing Blue Magpie at higher elevations; differences between the two species are complicated by racial variation.

IDENTIFICATION: Very similar to Blue Magpie with which it overlaps in distribution, but rarely in elevation. Blue Magpie generally below 1500 m, Gold-billed above 1800 m, but in summer Blue Magpie occasionally recorded as high as 2200 m and has been exceptionally reported at 3050 m; conversely in winter Gold-billed

sometimes descends to 1000 m. Gold-billed most easily distinguished by lemon-yellow (not red) bill, smaller white patch in centre of nape (extends vertically from mantle to rear, or even mid crown on Blue Magpie), narrower white tertial tips (western birds) and in eastern part of range by pale yellow underparts in fresh plumage. Problems arise with western race which is purer blue-grey and white than eastern races and, chiefly juveniles, sometimes have larger white patch on nape, thus more like Blue Magpie; however white does not extend as far as mantle. Blue Magpie does not occur in Pakistan, Kashmir or between Nepal and Burma along the Himalayan foothills (although it is present in hills south of the Brahmaputra in north-east India); the main problem areas of overlap are from the Kulu region of India through Nepal. It is possible that Gold-billed with large nape patches might be the result of occasional hybridisation, but this has not been reported or suspected.

DESCRIPTION: Length 61-66 cm (including tail). Slightly smaller than Blue Magpie. Bill medium, with curved culmen. Nasal tuft moderate, soft. Wings relatively broad. Tail long and very graduated, central pair of feathers greatly elongated and drooping towards tip. Nominate race: Head, neck, upper mantle and upper breast black, with small white transverse patch in centre of hindneck. Underparts below breast off-white, with pale yellow wash in fresh plumage. Upperparts greyish-blue, washed faintly with olive in fresh plumage; uppertail-coverts scaled black. Wings similar but with white tips to secondaries, most obvious on tertials. Primaries narrowly edged whitish on outer webs. Underwing grey. Tail greyish-blue, each feather broadly tipped white, with blackish subterminal band, latter narrow and less defined on elongated central pair; white of tail tips and wing feathers washed pale yellow in fresh plumage, except on central pair of tail. Bill clear yellow, varying from lemon-yellow to deep yellow, rarely orange-yellow. Legs orange-yellow or orange, sometimes yellow. Irides yellow, narrow orbital ring variable, from yellow to dark brown - significance of variation unknown, seemingly not sexual, possibly age-related.

SEX/AGE: Sexes similar. Juvenile duller, with ashy-olive wash to upperparts, white of nape patch slightly mottled grey; bill brownish-horn, soon becoming yellow; legs dusky-yellowish.

MEASUREMENTS: Nominate race: Wing 175-195, tail 345-423, tarsus 48-51, bill 37-42, weight 132-180.

GEOGRAPHICAL VARIATION: Four races recognised, differing in size and degree of olive or yellow tones in plumage. These tones are most apparent in fresh plumage, fading considerably when worn (and in skins).

U. f. cucullata: western race, from Pakistan (Hazara) east to central Nepal, where it intergrades with the nominate. Smaller than nominate race (wing 123-165), purer white below and bluer above, lacking olive or yellow tones even in fresh plumage. Juveniles sometimes have extensive white on nape, extending to mid crown or have whitish tipping to crown feathers.

U. f. flavirostris: central Nepal east to northern Burma, described above.

U. f. schaferi: Chin Hills, Burma. Slightly smaller, wing 162-177.

U. f. robini: north-west Tonkin, Vietnam. Brighter green wash to upperparts and yellow wash to under parts than nominate.

VOICE: Similar to that of Blue Magpie and equally varied. A variety of loud and harsh creaking and grating calls. Vocabulary includes squealing whistles mixed with mimicry of other birds' calls. No detailed comparative studies have been made but Fleming *et al.* have attempted this by transcribing typical calls as a wheezy 'bu-zeep-peck-peck-peck', 'pop-unclear', 'pu-pu-weer' and a high 'clear-clear' (compare Blue Magpie).

HABITS: As of Blue Magpie. Found singly, in pairs or in small groups of up to ten birds, foraging at forest edge or on nearby terraced slopes, hopping about boldly when on the ground with tails carried high in an arch as if to prevent long feathers from becoming soiled. Parties often accompany mixed bird flocks roaming through montane forest, jumping with squirrel-like agility from bough to bough as they search epiphytic bunches of orchids and ferns, or clumps of foliage. They stream across gaps between the trees in single file, with long tails waving and fanned. When moving over longer distances parties skim low over tree tops, with several flaps followed by a short glide. Rarely the occasional Gold-billed might be found amongst a flock of Blue Magpies in winter. Diet includes a great variety of invertebrates, fruits and berries, also small frogs, snakes, lizards, nestling birds, eggs, rodents and carrion. Apparently one of the few birds seen to take terrestrial leeches. Much more of a true forest bird than Blue Magpie and typically wary and unapproachable; when unmolested they do however, become more confiding and about isolated hill stations and small villages they take a variety of human food scraps.

BREEDING: Solitary breeder(?) ,though perhaps a social breeder as has now been established for related Taiwan Magpie. Nest a bulky construction of twigs, lined with rootlets and plant fibres, not unlike a small crow's nest, placed 5 or 6 m above ground in fork or canopy of a small, leafy tree just outside edge of forest. Built by both sexes. Clutch three or four, eggs creamy-white, blotched and freckled various shades of brown, markings concentrated towards broader end. Incubation probably only by female. Males feed females at nest and assist in tending the young. Eggs recorded mid May and June.

HABITAT: Deciduous and mixed mountain forests, with oaks, chestnut, pines and rhododendron, also in adjacent secondary scrub, tea plantations and cultivated slopes. Breeds between 1600 and 2700 m, descending lower in winter, exceptionally recorded as low as 1000 m and as high as 3700 m.

DISTRIBUTION: The wet temperate zone along the southern faces of the Himalayas, from Hazara in Pakistan eastwards through Kashmir, northern Himachal Pradesh and Nepal, Bhutan, south-east Tibet, north-east frontier states of India, northern Burma, Yunnan and extreme north-west Tonkin in Vietnam.

STATUS: Fairly common or locally common over most of range although preference for higher altitude forests renders it less frequently observed than Blue Magpie. Tonkin race *robini* little known.

REFERENCES: Fleming *et al.* 1976, Goodwin 1986, Ali 1962, Ali and Ripley 1972

BLUE MAGPIE   Plate 14

Urocissa erythrorhyncha

Alternative names: Red-billed Blue Magpie, Red-billed Magpie

The most widespread blue magpie; a lowland hill species with a range extending over most of the far east of mainland Asia.

IDENTIFICATION: Differs from Gold-billed in having bright red (not yellow) bill and extensive white on nape which extends from mantle to mid-crown (small central nape patch on Gold-billed) and in being bluer and whiter. There are some reservations about the extent of white on the nape but there are also marked differeces in elevation and range which are discussed under Gold-billed. Over most of mainland China (except west Yunnan) it is the only blue magpie. On Taiwan replaced by the Taiwan Magpie. Compare also Azure-winged Magpie.

DESCRIPTION: Length 65-68 cm (including tail). Slightly larger than Gold-billed Magpie. Bill medium, with curved culmen. Nasal tuft moderate, soft. Wings relatively broad. Tail long and strongly graduated, central pair of feathers greatly elongated, drooping towards tip. Nominate race: Head, neck, upper mantle and upper breast black; large pale bluish-white area from rear or mid crown down nape and hindneck onto upper mantle; mid crown also mottled white. Underparts below breast off-white, with pale greyish wash, whitest on ventral region; underparts with weak salmon-pink wash in very fresh plumage. Upperparts dull medium blue, washed mauve; uppertail-coverts scaled black. Wings similar but coverts darker and brighter mauve-blue, white tips to secondaries and primaries, most obvious on tertials. Primaries narrowly edged whitish on outer webs. Underwing grey. Tail mauve-blue, each feather broadly tipped white, with blackish subterminal band, latter narrow and less defined on elongated central pair. Bill bright coral-red or reddish-pink. Legs coral-red or pinkish-red. Irides dark brown.

SEX/AGE: Sexes similar. Juvenile duller, with face and throat greyish-white (but not in race *occipitalis*), more extensive and whiter nape patch, often extending to forecrown, giving effect of a pale head with a blackish mask; upperparts duller and greyer; bill and irides bluish-grey; legs dusky yellow-flesh.

MEASUREMENTS: Nominate race: Wing 180-210, tail 375-425, tarsus 48-55, bill 32-39, weight 196-232.

GEOGRAPHICAL VARIATION: Five races recognised, differing in degree of grey or blue of upperparts, extent of white on nape and, in juvenile plumage, blackness of throat and face.

U. e. brevivexilla: northern China, duller and greyer on upperparts than nominate.

U. e. erythrorhynca: central and eastern China, described above.

U. e. alticola: northern Yunnan and adjacent part of Burma, bluer upperparts than nominate.

U. e. magnirostris: north-east India and south-east Asia, very blue upperparts, smaller white nape area, bill larger.

U. e. occipitalis: Nepal to Himachal Pradesh, India,

very blue upperparts, larger white spots on tertials, very white nape patch. Juvenile with blackish throat and face.

VOICE: Calls varied. In flight gives an explosive, almost metallic 'penk' which is repeated two or three times and seems to be a contact note; this call may also be rapidly repeated turning into a rather high-pitched ringing chatter when alarmed. Also has a short grating rattle, which is preceded by several liquid whistling notes. Fleming et al. have attempted to compare the calls of these two species, by transcribing those of the Blue Magpie as: a piercing 'quiv-pig-pig', a softer and repeated 'beeee—trik', a subdued 'kluk' and a sharp 'chwenk-chwenk' (compare Gold-billed Magpie).

HABITS: An arboreal magpie. Typically encountered in small parties of up to twelve birds in foothill and lowland valley forests, especially by clearings and in ravines. Forages in similar fashion to that of Gold-billed Magpie. Unlike Gold-billed, is rarely seen in ones and twos, which suggests a social lifestyle, as flocks seem to be together throughout the year and to work a large feeding territory. Often found close to villages, where they will sometimes forage on the ground at the edges of cultivation. Also spends a lot of time within the canopy of fruiting fig trees. Despite being such gaudy birds they can easily be overlooked whilst feeding inside the canopy, though they proclaim their presence with their ringing contact calls. General attitudes, behaviour and diet are close to those of Gold-billed Magpie except that they are birds of subtropical lowland hill forests.

BREEDING: Solitary breeder (?), though perhaps a social breeder as has now been established for related Taiwan Magpie. Nest a crow-like construction of twigs, lined with rootlets and plant fibres, placed 3 to 6 m above ground near the outside of a large branch or in the canopy of a sapling. Built by both sexes. Clutch three to five, eggs creamy-white, buff or pale green, blotched and freckled with various shades of brown markings, concentrated towards broader end. Incubation by female. Male feeds female at nest and assists in tending the young. Eggs recorded April in southern China, June in northern China, March to June in Burma and April to June in India.

HABITAT: Subtropical and temperate foothill evergreen forests, favouring broken valley forest, with small clearings and patches of cultivation, chiefly between 300 and 1500 m, but in summer ascends into Himalayan valleys up to 2200 m, exceptionally recorded at 3050 m in Nepal.

DISTRIBUTION: Eastern and south-eastern mainland Asia, range seemingly broken by its absence from the east Himalayan foothills. In the Indian region western limit is the Kangra area of Himachal Pradesh, from where it extends east along the Himalayan foothills to eastern Nepal. Another population occurs to the south of the Brahmaputra river in the Cachar area of Assam, Meghalaya, Nagaland, Manipur and probably adjacent parts of Bangladesh, extending east over the hills of Burma, western Thailand, Laos, northern Cambodia and northern Vietnam. It is widespread over almost the whole of eastern China, including Hainan (but not Taiwan), west to east Kansu and east Sichuan, reaching its northern limits in southern Jilin. A feral population which became established from escaped cagebirds on

Oahu in the Hawaiian islands has now probably been exterminated.

STATUS: Fairly common or locally common, over most of range although scarce in extreme northern part of range in China (Liaoning and Jilin). However it has recently been reported to be increasing in northern China, at least in the Beidaihe area (Hebei) of the northeast.

REFERENCES: Fleming et al 1976, Goodwin 1986, Ali 1949, Ali and Ripley 1972

WHITE-WINGED MAGPIE   Plate 15

Urocissa whiteheadi

Alternative name: Whitehead's Magpie

A little studied large, bulky magpie, perhaps the most aberrant of the group, sometimes allocated its own monotypic genus Cissopica.

IDENTIFICATION: Distinctive heavily-built large magpie with relatively long tail of southern China and northern Indochina. Its yellowish-white wing and tail bands and lower underparts provide a striking contrast to the blackish, greyish or brownish (depending on age and race) head, breast and upperparts and yellow eye. In flight wings are broadly banded blackish and pale yellow and the long, graduated tail has a wide pale yellow tip and surrounding border. Roams through forests in quite large parties of mixed age groups. Very distinctive.

DESCRIPTION: Length 46 cm (including tail). Relatively larger than blue magpies. Bill heavy and quite long. Nasal tuft moderate, soft. Small patch of bare skin behind eye. Wings relatively broad. Tail quite long and stongly graduated, central pair of feathers elongated but not greatly so. Race xanthomelana: Head, neck and breast black, crown feathers narrowly fringed brownish. Black of throat and breast with slight yellowish bloom, becoming progressively greyer and with stronger yellow wash on lower breast and flanks, shading into pale yellow on belly and ventral region. Upperside of body black, with yellowish rump (formed by yellowish feather tips) and uppertail-coverts, the latter greyish with yellow tips and white bases to feathers. Wings strikingly patterned on blackish background, lesser and median coverts pale yellow (forming band along leading edge of wing); greater coverts pale yellow with black bases (forming central wing band); outer secondaries with narrow yellowish-white fringe, becoming increasingly wide towards inner wing, tertials extensively yellowish-white with black basal portion of inner web (large whitish area at rear base of wing forming progressively narrower trailing edge towards primaries); primary coverts and primaries black with small white tips to latter. Underwing coverts and axillaries pale yellow. Tail black with yellowish-grey base and wide pale yellow tips to all feathers, tips narrowest on central pair of feathers, widest on short outermost, rest intermediate in length and extent of pale yellow. It is likely that the yellow markings fade whiter with wear, as they do in skins. Bill orange becoming greenish at base. Legs black. Irides pale greenish-yellow. Small bare eye-patch brownish-green.

SEX/AGE: Sexes similar. Juvenile inadequately documented (birds which have been described as juvenile are probably first-year birds - see Goodwin (1986). 'First-year' birds have black areas of adults' head and body plumage replaced by dark yellowish-grey. Tail and wing as adult but secondaries and primaries have grey outer webs forming lighter panel on closed wing. Bill brownish-grey. Irides brownish. Presumed older birds attain orange bill tip and greenish bill base at same time as iris becomes yellowish-brown, followed by mantle becoming blacker.

MEASUREMENTS: Race *xanthomelana*: Wing 224-238, tail 230-243, tarsus 52-54, bill 42-52, weight unrecorded.

GEOGRAPHICAL VARIATION: Two rather different subspecies.

U. w. xanthomelana: southern China, Laos and Vietnam, described above.

U. w. whiteheadi: Hainan, slightly smaller in all proportions, tail pattern differs, each feather grey with black restricted to a subterminal band and black areas of plumage replaced by sooty-brown. Irides clear yellow and bill red with brownish-yellow base. The pale wing bands and tail surround appear to be white rather than yellow in this race, but it is possible that a yellow wash might be present in fresh plumage.

VOICE: Recordings from Vietnam give four call types. They seem not to be loud or piercing as was described by Delacour (1927), but vocabulary is probably more varied than recordings indicate. The most conspicuous call is a repeated, short, hoarse but rising 'shurreek'. Also recorded was a low, hoarse, almost purring 'churrree', a repeated soft, liquid rippled 'brrriii...brrriii...' and a similar but rather harsher, also repeated 'errreep...errreep...', the latter with a rising inflection.

HABITS: Poorly documented. A very social magpie, roaming through the forest in parties of 20 to 25 consisting of both adults and immature birds. They are quite active, flighting about the forest trees and bamboos in the narrow valleys. Their diet is said to consist of both invertebrates and fruits. Their social habits and the relatively large number of eggs in the only described nest, indicate social breeding.

BREEDING: The nest described was of the nominate form from Hainan; it was a concave platform of closely interwoven dry stems of creepers and roots. It contained a clutch of six eggs, pale greenish-blue, flecked and spotted with brown. A nest under construction reported from Vietnam in early July.

HABITAT: Subtropical and tropical evergreen lowland and montane forests, favouring forest borders and clearings along ravines and watercourses. In Vietnam recently reported to tolerate logged forest and secondary forest and even plantations of Manglietia. In Vietnam occurs from 50 to 1400 m.

DISTRIBUTION: South eastern China, extending into north and central Laos, and in Vietnam in Tonkin and north and central Annam. In China the isolated nominate form is confined to Hainan; the mainland race has been found in extreme south Sichuan and in Guangxi and presumably occurs in intervening Guizhou.

STATUS: Nominate race of Hainan now very rare and endangered due to massive destruction of natural forests on the island during the Chinese Cultural Revolution. Patches of forest remain at the south side of the island, where there have been a few sightings of small parties in recent years. The mainland race is rare and little known in China but in Vietnam is not uncommon in remaining forest south to central Annam, especially in the Cat Bin area where it is described as still quite common. No recent information from Cambodia or Laos.

REFERENCES: Delacour 1927, Goodwin 1986, Robson et al. 1989, 1993

GREEN MAGPIES *Cissa*

Beautiful pea-green magpies with velvet black masks, chestnut-red wings and red bills and legs. The feathers of the crown are slightly elongated, giving a tufted look to the rear of the head. Despite their gaudy plumage they blend well with their lush rain forest habitats where they keep well hidden in the foliage and can be surprisingly difficult to see.

The plumage of the green magpies can lose its green, yellow and red pigments, and 'fade' to blue, white and brown respectively, this is frequent with captive birds, and with skins, and is also not infrequent in the wild. Prolonged exposure to direct sunlight is one of the factors involved; wild birds living in more open or dry forest are most prone to this loss of pigmentation, which can be total or partial and patchy.

Green magpies are closely related to the blue magpies *Urocissa*, indeed there are good reasons to cassify them together. The two genera are somewhat linked by the Ceylon Magpie and White-winged Magpie, both of which are difficult to place, possible both should be placed in separate monotypic genera.

The relationships between the various forms of green magpies are controversial. Isolation has produced some interesting forms, the precise relationships of which are in need of further review. Delacour (1929) in his review of the genus recognised six species. Vaurie in Peters (1962) however, recognised only two. Goodwin (1976) and (1986) considered that three was the most sensible option and this is followed in the present work. These opinions are listed overleaf for comparison.

Delacour, 1929 Six species	Vaurie, 1962 Two species	Goodwin, 1976, 1986 Three species
C. chinensis	**C. chinensis**	**C. chinensis**
C. c. chinensis	C. c. chinensis	C. c. chinensis
C. c. minor	C. c. minor	C. c. minor
C. c. robinsoni	C. c. robinsoni	C. c. robinsoni
C. c. klossi	C. c. klossi	C. c. klossi
C. c. margaritae	C. c. margaritae	C. c. margaritae
C. hypoleuca	**C. thalassina**	**C. hypoleuca**
C. h. hypoleuca	C. t. thalassina	C. h. hypoleuca
C. h. chauleti	C. t. hypoleuca	C. h. chauleti
	C. t. chauleti	C. h. concolor
C. jefferyi	C. t. jefferyi	C. h. jini
	C. t. katsumatae	C. h. katsumatae
C. katsumatae	C. t. jini	
	C. t. concolor	**C. thalassina**
C. concolor		C. t. thalassina
C. c. concolor		C. t. jefferyi
C. c. jini*		
C. thalassina		

* Summary amended to include this form, described by Delacour in 1930 as a new subspecies of his previously monotypic C. concolor.

GREEN MAGPIE   Plate 16
Cissa chinensis

Alternative names: Green Hunting Crow, Hunting Cissa

The most widespread of the genus and the only one with obvious black and white spots at the tips of the tertials.

IDENTIFICATION: Large headed, bulky bodied bright green jay-like bird with long, graduated tail, striking wide black mask, chestnut wings and bright red bill and legs. Widespread over much of mainland tropical southeast Asia; it overlaps with the very similar Yellow-breasted Magpie in northern and central Laos and Vietnam. The two species are most easily separated by tertial pattern; in Green boldly tipped with black and white spots to form a spotted longitudinal stripe along the upper border of the chestnut wing, whereas in Yellow-breasted the tertials are virtually unmarked. See Yellow-breasted for further discussion. On Borneo it occurs together with the Short-tailed Magpie, which see for discussion.

DESCRIPTION: Length 37-39 cm (including tail). Bill relatively long and stout. Nasal tuft short, dense and soft. Eye relatively large with prominent fleshy orbital ring. Rear crown and nape feathers elongated, forming short horizontal tuft at rear of head. Tail long, strongly graduated, central pair of feathers somewhat elongated but blunt-tipped. Wings short and broad. Nominate race: Nasal tuft, forehead and crown yellowish-green. Lores black extending to form wide black band across sides of head, meeting on upper nape under base of tufted crest. Remainder of body plumage bright pea-green or leaf-green. Wings bright rusty-chestnut, with dusky blackish primaries and underwing. Tertials with prominent black

subterminal bar and wide white tip. Tail bright green, central pair of feathers with broad greenish-white tip, remainder with broad black subterminal band and wide white tip. Tail underside (when closed) looks whitish with blackish band towards base. In flight the chestnut wings contrast with the brilliant green plumage. Plumage can fade to light bluish (see introduction to genus). Bill coral-red, often whitish at very tip, or duller orange-red. Legs orange-red to bright coral-red. Irides dark brown to red. Orbital ring bright coral red or brownish-red.

SEX/AGE: Sexes similar. Juvenile with horny yellow bill and legs, dull brown iris, plumage duller, with whitish undertail-coverts, tail feather tips more pointed. Much as adult after first moult but pointed tail tips and duller bare parts might help age first year birds.

MEASUREMENTS: Male averages only a little larger than female on measurements but average weight distinctly heavier. Nominate race: Wing 137-157, tail 171-210, tarsus 43-47, bill 34-42, weight male 130-133, female 120-124.

GEOGRAPHICAL VARIATION: Five subspecies are recognised, of which only the isolated *margaritae* is strikingly different, its bright yellow crown and longer tail making it one of the most beautiful of all corvids; it is however linked to the nominate form through *klossi*.

C. c. chinensis: India, Burma, Thailand, east to northern Annam (Vietnam), described above.

C. c. minor: Sumatra and Borneo, similar but a little smaller.

C. c. robinsoni: Malay peninsula, smaller, with larger white tertial spots.

C. c. klossi: central Annam (Vietnam) and central Laos, forehead yellow, crown yellowish green.

C. c. margaritae: Mt. Lang Bian, southern/central Annam (Vietnam), slightly longer tailed than nominate, with crown bright golden yellow.

VOICE: Calls are typical sounds of rainforest, shrieking whistles and hoarse chattered phrases. Recordings from Thailand and Vietnam differ somewhat but perhaps only individually variable rather than of geographical significance. Race *margaritae*: A shrill, loud and penetrating piped whistle 'peeep', repeated in a series of three spaced notes, followed by a quick gruff, soft 'chak' of reply from presumed mate: 'peeep—peeep—peeep-chak'. Nominate race (Thailand): a quickly repeated series of three rapid soft harsh 'chaks' followed by a single short 'peep'; a soft chattered 'churrk chak-chak-chak' or a shorter 'chuurk-chak', latter repeated at shortly spaced intervals. The mobbing call is a hoarse scolding chatter not unlike that of Black-billed Magpie but slower in delivery and rather higher in pitch. Other transcriptions refer to vocal mimicry.

HABITS: An inconspicuous magpie of forest understorey or shrubbery by forest streams, reveals presence by piping whistling call, generally calling from low, partially exposed branch. Also moves higher into foliage of forest trees, especially when flanked by shrubby overgrown ravines. Outside breeding season gathers into small parties of up to six birds and roams through forest, often joining forces with mixed bird parties, especially laughing thrushes. Feeds low down and also quite freely on the ground, but under cover of shrubbery. Diet mainly insects such as beetles, crickets and mantises, also small frogs, small reptiles and birds, probably fruits and berries and has been observed feeding on carrion. Flies quite low, but avoids flying over large open areas.

BREEDING: Solitary breeder. Nest a large, rather flat platform of twigs, interwoven with leaves, bamboo and roots, cup lined with finer plant materials. Built in low dense shrubbery, bamboo thickets, vine tangles or the canopy of a small tree. Clutch three to seven, usually five. Eggs whitish, pale buff or pale greenish, profusely speckled brown, often obscuring background colour. No information on incubation or fledging periods. Egg laying dates vary April and May in India, April in Burma, but January and February in Borneo.

HABITAT: Subtropical and tropical evergreen hill and lowland forests, favouring forest borders, bamboo thickets and shrubbery along watercourses. Recorded from lowlands up to 1800 m, but reaches 2100 m on Sumatra.

DISTRIBUTION: Mainly south eastern Asia. Western limit is in Garwhal, north-west India, from where it is found throughout the Himalayan foothills to Burma. In India also occurs south of the Himalayas, in the north east from the hills of southern Assam and eastern Bangladesh eastwards into Burma. Widespread over Burma and the hill forests of western and north-central Thailand, across north and central Laos, northern Cambodia and in Vietnam in Tonkin and locally on borders of central and south Annam (Lang Bian area). Range extends just into southern China in south Yunnan and Guangxi. More isolated populations are found in the hills of the Malay peninsula, throughout Sumatra and in mountain foothills of north-eastern Borneo.

STATUS: Relatively uncommon to locally common throughout its main range.

REFERENCES: Ali and Ripley 1972, Robson, C. (tape recordings), Smythies 1981.

YELLOW-BREASTED MAGPIE   Plate 16

Cissa (thalassina) hypoleuca

Alternative names: Eastern Green Magpie, Yellow-breasted Green Magpie

Although sometimes considered conspecific with the Short-tailed Magpie, its striking vocal differences justify its treatment here.

IDENTIFICATION: Very similar to Green Magpie, but conveniently their ranges only overlap over quite a limited area, replacing Green Magpie over much of Vietnam and adjacent parts of Laos. Relatively easily distinguished from Green Magpie by the plain tertials (boldly tipped black and white, forming a line of spots in Green), much yellower underparts (not so obvious in the two isolated Chinese races) and relatively bigger head and shorter tail.

DESCRIPTION: Length 34-35 cm (including tail). Build and structure as Green Magpie, except tail relatively shorter and central feathers hardly project beyond the next pair. Head appears relatively larger, perhaps due to rather shorter tail. Nominate race: Plumage as nominate race Green Magpie except entire underparts from throat to undertail-coverts strongly washed lemon-yellow, tinged greenish on sides of throat and neck. Upperparts a little darker green, giving quite marked contrast between upper and underparts. Tertials broadly tipped and fringed green, with no spotting. Tail feathers, broadly tipped light grey (not white), except plain central pair. Bare parts as in Green Magpie.

SEX/AGE: As in Green Magpie.

MEASUREMENTS: Nominate race: Wing 143-155, tail 114-157, tarsus c. 44, bill c.36, weight not recorded.

GEOGRAPHICAL VARIATION: Five subspecies are recognised, differing in intensity of yellow on body plumage and colour of tips of outer tail feathers.

C. h. hypoleuca: south Annam and Cochinchina, north and west to southern Laos and south-east Thailand, described above.

C. h. chauleti: central Annam, underparts deeper yellow, yellower wash to green overall, especially on head. Tail washed brownish-buff, especially tips of outer feathers.

C. h. concolor: north Annam, less yellow, darker green above, below light green but obviously washed yellow. Tail feathers tipped light buff.

C. h. jini: south Sichuan and southern Guangxi, China. Slightly longer tail than *concolor* and less yellowish overall, tail tipped buff.

C. h. katsumatae: Hainan, similar to last, but central tail yellower green and tipped blue-grey, not buff; tertials tipped bluer green.

VOICE: Rather different in pitch from that of the Green Magpie, although has a similar selection of calls. The piercing rising, whistle 'peeee' notes of that species are more plaintive, less shrill and either drop in pitch or are flatter in tone. Recordings from Vietnam are described below, although the differences may reflect individual rather than geographical variations. A plaintive prolonged note uttered in pairs and repeated, 'peeeoo-peeeoo, peeeoo-peeeoo'; a plaintive, more clipped and shrill 'peu-peu-peu' (Central Annam); a plaintive and enquiring whistle 'po-puueeee' answered by a gruff 'chuk'; an abrupt, plaintive 'weep' which is repeated; a long enquiring, rising 'eeeoooeeep' followed by a full rich 'graak'; a more piercing long, dropping 'peeeeooo' (North Annam); a high-pitched scolding chatter, recalling that of Black-billed Magpie but higher in pitch and a little looser in delivery (Cochinchina).

HABITS: Much as Green Magpie.

BREEDING: Solitary breeder. Nest a platform of sticks, lined with dry grass and feathers, similar to that of Green Magpie. Built by both sexes. Female incubates. Eggs presumably May; nest with young found North Annam in late June.

HABITAT: Subtropical and tropical evergreen hill and lowland forests, often in lower elevation forest where range meets Green Magpie. Recorded from lowlands up to 900 m (China) and 1500 m (Thailand).

DISTRIBUTION: Northernmost populations are in southern China, isolated on Hainan and the Yao Shan hills of east-central Guangxi and recently discovered near Maupin in south Sichuan. Widespread throughout Vietnam from south Tonkin to Cochinchina; presumably in Cambodia but no published records; range extends west into northern-central Laos and into extreme south-eastern Thailand.

STATUS: Locally not uncommon in Vietnam; rare and little known in China, where Hainan population probably endangered by forest destruction. Distinctly uncommon and very local in Thailand.

REFERENCES: Goodwin 1986, Robson, C. (tape recordings).

SHORT-TAILED MAGPIE   Plate 16

Cissa thalassina

Alternative name: Short-tailed Green Magpie

Two very isolated green magpie forms are included together under this species, one on Java, the other on Borneo.

IDENTIFICATION: Easily distinguished from Green Magpie, which overlaps in range on Borneo, by very short tail, greener crown (lacking yellow wash), lack of obvious tertial spotting, obscure subterminal black tail marks and very different voice. They are also separated by elevation: on Borneo Green Magpie is widespread in the foothills of the northern uplands, only rarely as high as 1000 m, whereas Short-tailed replaces it above 1000 m on the same mountain and hill ranges. On Java there are no other green magpies.

DESCRIPTION: Length 31-33 cm (including tail). Build and structure as Green Magpie, except tail much shorter, bluntly graduated, and crest feathers relatively shorter.

Race *jefferyi*: Plumage as nominate race Green Magpie except darker green overall and lacking yellow wash on crown. Tertials lack obvious pattern, the exposed larger tertials and tips being almost plain light greenish-white; tail pattern also differs, the black subterminal bar on each feather of Green Magpie is very narrow and ill-defined and does little to highlight the broad whitish tips. Irides white (not brown or red as in Green Magpie). Bill and legs darker red.

SEX/AGE: As in Green Magpie.

MEASUREMENTS: Nominate race: Wing 141-145, tail 97-110, tarsus 42-48, bill 39-40, weight not recorded.

GEOGRAPHICAL VARIATION: Two subspecies are recognised.

> *C. t. jefferyi*: Borneo, described above.
> *C. t. thalassina*: Java, differs in having more extensive light green areas on tertials, outer tail feathers almost plain, lacking dark subterminal bars and with tips merely diffusely pale, irides dark (not white).

VOICE: Quite different to that of either Green or Yellow-breasted Magpies, at least on Borneo. No recordings heard of Javan form. The voice is remarkably sweet and musical; the notes put together into a rhythm recalling a small passerine. One of the recorded phrases is of five notes, repeated after a short break; it is uttered with a rising and falling rhythm; the notes are clear short whistles, uttered with incisive clarity and in rapid succession: 'swe-swi-swee-swi-swe sweet' or 'swe-si-si-swe-sweep', with variations from different individuals. Other notes and phrases recorded include a thin, penetrating 'sweeeii' and a repeated three note 'swe-swe-gurg' or simply two note 'swe-gurg....swe-gurg.....swe-gurg.

HABITS: Much as Green Magpie. Little information on Javan race but Bornean race described as a true forest bird of the wooded mountain slopes; higher up near the limits of the tree-line it is sometimes encountered feeding on the ground amongst gnarled mossy trunks. Food items mentioned by Smythies include insects, caterpillars, snails and probably small frogs.

BREEDING: Poorly documented. On Borneo, family parties recorded in April, typically of two young per family. The only description of the eggs is of the Javan race; they are described as like those of the Green Magpie.

HABITAT: Higher elevation mountain forests; Bornean race occurs between 950 and 2500 m.

DISTRIBUTION: Java and Borneo; on Borneo it is found from Mt. Kinabalu to Mt. Murud, the Usan Apau Plateau and Mt. Dulit.

STATUS: Locally not uncommon over limited range on Borneo, fairly easily found on slopes of Mt. Kinabalu which is a National Park. No information on status of Javan subspecies.

REFERENCES: Goodwin 1986, Robson, C. (tape recordings), Smythies 1981.

AZURE-WINGED MAGPIE *Cyanopica*

This magpie is unique. It is the only corvid in which the juvenile replaces its flight feathers at the first moult. It shares with Crested Jay and nutcrackers, a juvenile plumage which shows buff tips to wing-coverts and tertials, more typical of other passerine bird families. In other respects it seems closer to the American jays than to the Old World corvids. Like the Blue and Steller's Jays of North America it uses mud during nest construction. Co-operative breeding has recently been proven in Japan, also a character of some American jays and in the Old World only proven in the Taiwan Magpie, although it possibly occurs in the less studied blue magpies. This bird is probably a very ancient form of magpie and possibly even close to the ancestral 'American jay'.

This magpie has a remarkable distribution occurring in eastern Palearctic Asia and Spain and Portugal. It has been said that it was brought back to Spain by early traders with China and subsequently became established in south-west Europe. The fairly marked racial difference of the Iberian forms suggests however, that it has been isolated in Europe for an exceedingly long time. The centres of the two elements of its range are on latitude 40°N, in comparatively seasonally hot, maritime climates. It therefore seems more likely, especially in view of its presumed ancient origins, that it had a more continuous range in the distant past. This is somewhat supported by the rather fragmentary range in the Baikal region where the most western site at Uliastay in north-west Mongolia is nearly 1000 km west of the nearest sites. A number of closely related species-pairs share a similar distribution i.e. White Stork *Ciconia ciconia* and Oriental White Stork *C. (c.) boyciana*, Dunnock *Prunella modularis* and Japanese Accentor *P. rubida*, Greenfinch *Carduelis chloris* and Oriental Greenfinch *C. (c.) sinica*, Marsh Tit *Parus palustris* and Asian Marsh Tit *P. p. brevirostris* possibly even Red-necked *Caprimulgus ruficollis* and Grey Nightjars *C. indicus*.

AZURE-WINGED MAGPIE   Plate 12

Cyanopica cyana

A strange magpie, with an even more peculiar distribution.

IDENTIFICATION: Distinctive small magpie of south-west Europe and eastern Asia. Striking bird with its combination of black hood, pale blue wings and long, graduated pale blue tail. Gregarious, being usually found in small parties following each other from tree to tree, sweeping up into canopy after low flight.

DESCRIPTION: Length 34 cm (including tail). Head relatively large, very slightly crested at nape. Bill medium stout. Nasal tuft short and dense. Legs short and slight. Tail long and graduated, pointed. Race *cooki*: Hood black, lightly glossed, reaching base of lower mandible and central ear-coverts. Throat white, fairly cleanly becoming dull pinkish-buff on remainder of underparts. Upperparts slightly darker pinkish buff-brown. Wings sky-blue, washed violet, especially on coverts; primaries blackish on outermost two; inner primaries with white outer webs. Tail sky-blue, with violet tones, sometimes with narrow whitish tips to outer tail feathers. Bill and legs black. Irides brownish black.

SEX/AGE: Sexes similar. Juvenile duller, browner on body plumage, feathers fringed lighter (including black of hood), wing-coverts and tertials dull greyish-brown with whitish-buff tips, outer tail feathers narrowly tipped white, central tail feathers short and weak. At first moult juvenile moults vestigial central tail feathers and all flight feathers as well as those of head and body. After which is virtually as adult, although most retain some juvenile greater coverts, which are dull and have whitish tips, into first year.

MEASUREMENTS: Race *interposita*: Wing 135-142, tail 199-240, tarsus 32-36, bill 24-28, weight 62-82.

GEOGRAPHICAL VARIATION: Slight, with isolated *cooki* of Europe most distinct, variation chiefly clinal in the Far East. There are nine subspecies, the European race differing from all of the others in lacking white tips to central tail feathers; it is also the smallest race. The Asiatic races are best compared by discussion. Westernmost of these is the nominate form of Transbaicalia and northern Mongolia, which is very grey both above and below; this intergrades further east into *pallescens* of the Amur valley and Ussuriland, a rather paler and browner form. To the south, in Heilongjiang is the darker and greyer *stegmanni* and to the south-east in Korea, *koreensis*, which is whiter below and browner above. The populations of Shanxi and Shaanxi in central China, *interposita*, are darker than *stegmanni*, whereas those to the east and south, *swinhoei*, are darker and browner. Western Chinese birds, *kansuensis*, are very grey above and very pale below and have small bills. In Japan, *japonica*, is small and quite dark grey compared to mainland forms. Other forms have been described but are considered to be intergrading populations

VOICE: Usual call a dry shivering, almost trilled 'screeep', often given when birds move between trees. Other calls include a harsh chatter, a sharp whistled 'wee-wee-wee-u' and a harsh 'krarrah' of alarm, latter often followed by a series of metallic 'kwink' notes.

HABITS: A very sociable magpie, always in small parties, feeding in tree canopy and generally keeping well inside cover. Flocks vary in size, generally in family parties in breeding season but later in the year will gather into larger congregations, sometimes exceeding well over 100 birds in China. Flocks also congregate to form large communal roosts in winter. Parties scatter once inside tree cover and work through the foliage and branches as they search for insects, fruits and berries. Food hiding has been reported in the wild. In parts of Asia they scavenge around villages, towns and city parks, where human food scraps are taken. As well as feeding in trees they readily descend to the ground, but keep close to cover. In Spain they seem to inhabit more open countryside, and are more likely to be seen in full flight moving between copses of trees across open fields. Asian populations keep very much to tree cover, merely moving between trees across quite small gaps. In some city parks in Japan and China they are quite bold and allow humans to approach closely; elsewhere they seem to be more wary and, especially in the breeding season, can be remarkably inconspicuous. Parties keep together throughout the year and breed in small colonies, their social lifestyle has locally evolved into co-operative breeding, at least in Japan, where this magpie has been intensively studied.

BREEDING: Sociable nester. Nests in loose colonies, normally not more than one nest per tree but colonies can be quite large, with as many as 70 nests. Nest of sticks and twigs, with cup lined with softer plant materials and animal hair, mud incorporated into basal construction. Built by both sexes in fork of side branch or open decayed hollow in trees or shrubs, up to 12m from ground, though sometimes virtually at ground level. Clutch five to eleven, usually five to seven. Eggs buff or light greenish, speckled brownish. Incubation 15 days by female, being fed at nest by male. Sometimes immature birds from a previous brood help male feed the nestlings; female helps as young become larger. Occasionally produces two broods in Asia, with juveniles of first brood still being fed by male, whilst females incubates next clutch. Eggs recorded late March to May in Spain, later in the Far East where late May and June is more typical in Ussuriland and Japan. In Europe their nests are sometimes parasitised by the Great Spotted Cuckoo *Clamator glandarius*, in Asia by both Indian

Cuculus micropterus and Common Cuckoos *C. canorus*.
HABITAT: Woodland and forest edge, both mixed and deciduous. Locally in city parks and large gardens. In Europe favours sheltered valleys with groves of trees and orchards. Chiefly in lowlands but ascends to 1600 m in Japan.
DISTRIBUTION: Remarkably disjunct. Western population in southern and central Spain and Portugal. Otherwise widely distributed in eastern Asia, from extreme north-west Mongolia (Uliasutay) eastwards to the south of Lake Baikal across northern Mongolia and Transbaicalia to the Khabarovsk region, with northern boundary following the valley of the Amur river. In the Far East its range extends south over Ussuriland and Korea and much of eastern China, west to extreme east Qinghai and south Sichuan, with southern boundary following the valley of the Yangtze to Shanghai. In Japan now only on Honshu.
STATUS: Locally common and increasing in Spain and Portugal and over main part of range in Asia, but very local in western part of Asian range in the Baikal region. Increasing on Honshu in Japan, but now extinct on Kyushu where it was still common in the north up to the 1950s, probably through competition with the introduced Black-billed Magpie.
REFERENCES: Dementiev and Gladkov 1954, Dos Santos 1968, Goodwin 1986, Honsono 1966 to 1983.

TREEPIES *Dendrocitta*

Treepies are a group of Oriental arboreal corvids, most of which are easily located through their loud musical clanging calls or seen as they flap with jerky undulating flight between trees, across open spaces or rivers. They feed in the tree canopy and are particularly fond of fruiting and flowering trees. Within the genus the ranges of most species are allopatric, but, where there is overlap, two species do not occur together but specialise in their own favoured habitats. Between them they occupy most of south-east Asia. The genus presents little in the way of identification problems.

RUFOUS TREEPIE   Plate 18

Dendrocitta vagabunda

Alternative name: Indian Treepie

The commonest and most conspicuous treepie in India, and the only one likely to be found in gardens and parks away from forested areas.

IDENTIFICATION: A relatively large treepie with bright rusty body and blackish head and breast. In flight and when perched look for conspicuous wide silver-grey wing-coverts and lack of white at base of primaries, which distinguish it from Grey Treepie when body colour not visible. In overhead flight the whitish subterminal band to the tail is quite striking (absent in Grey). Grey marginally overlaps throughout northern part of range, although where the two occur together Grey replaces it in hill country. In southern India compare White-bellied, and in forests of the north-east the more similar but now rare Collared Treepie.
DESCRIPTION: Length 46-50 cm (including tail). Bill short, stout, with down-curved culmen. Nasal tuft short,

stiff. Wings short and broad. Tail long and graduated, with central pair of feathers elongated, slightly expanding to a blunt tip. Nominate race: Head, neck, breast and upper mantle sooty, shading to almost black on forehead, face and throat. Entire body plumage, rusty-orange, upper and undertail-coverts shading paler and buffer; mantle, back and scapulars slightly darker and browner rusty-orange. Wing-coverts and tertials very pale grey, contrasting with brownish-black of rest of the wing. Central tail feathers pale grey, shading paler and almost white towards tip, ending in a wide black terminal band; remaining tail feathers similar but gradually shorter, with outermost shortest and with over half the feather black. Bill dark grey or blackish. Legs blackish-brown. Irides red or brown.
SEX/AGE: Sexes similar. Juvenile duller, with narrow central tail feathers, paler more yellowish-rusty body colour, browner hood, all wing and tail feathers with buffish tips; inside of mandibles probably pink rather than black of adult. First-year birds may be aged by retained flight and tail feathers.
MEASUREMENTS: Male on average has longer tail than female. Nominate race: Wing 144-173, tail male 218-297, female 219-279, tarsus 32-37, bill 30-37, weight 90-130

GEOGRAPHICAL VARIATION: Nine subspecies are recognised, although variation is basically clinal and all forms intergrade; the general colour is much affected by feather wear and bleaching.

D. v. bristoli: Pakistan and north-west India, the largest and longest tailed race (tail 265-363), with rich colour as in the nominate.

D. v. pallida: western India from Rajasthan south to Maharashtra, less richly coloured and bigger than nominate, with pale buff belly and vent and dingy mantle and scapulars.

D. v. vagabunda: eastern half of India, described above.

D. v. vernayi: south-east India, size as nominate, but brighter although paler, lower underparts almost creamy-buff.

D. v. parvula: south-west India, smallest form (tail 189-239), with richest colours, upperparts dark rufous-brown.

D. v. sclateri: western Burma, darker above than nominate with nape and mantle colour diffused.

D. v. kinneari: Burma and west Thailand, similar to last but darker.

D. v. saturatior: Tennaserim and south-west Thailand, the darkest and smallest race, with upperparts dark rufous-brown.

D. v. sakeratensis: eastern Thailand to Vietnam, like nominate but hindneck darker.

VOICE: The advertising call is one of the most familiar sounds of the Indian countryside, but difficult to describe: a loud metallic flute-like 'ko-ki-la' or similar, often mixed with a loud harsh rattling cry. Alarm is a chatter not unlike that of Black-billed Magpie. Has a variety of other harsh, metallic and mewing notes.

HABITS: One of the most familiar of Indian birds, feeding and nesting in large trees in villages, city parks and large gardens. Often in pairs or family parties, but at good food sources larger congregations of 20 or so birds form. Outside breeding season often follows mixed groups of woodland birds, feeding on moths and crickets flushed by them. Also joins barbets, green pigeons, Koels and other larger birds to feed in fruiting trees. Rarely descends to the ground for other than the briefest moment to drink, but will do so to feed on carrion. Diet very varied with a variety of invertebrates, seeds, fruits and berries recorded, also nestlings and eggs of small birds, lizards, rodents, carrion and human food scraps. Although always wary, often becomes very bold and inquisitive where unmolested and will enter houses to search for geckos. Will also tear open nests of weaver birds to get at the contents. Locally regarded as a pest of orchards. Perches quite high, generally just inside canopy. Flight very strongly undulating and rather heavy on broad wings, with alternate periods of flapping and short glides over longer distances, generally not above tree-top height. Birds move up into hills for the breeding season, descending lower in winter; this is particularly true of Himalayan foothill populations.

BREEDING: Solitary nester. Nest rather small for its size, a rather flimsy platform of sticks and thorny twigs, the deep cup lined with finer plant materials, such as rootlets. Built by both sexes at 6 to 8 m in a large, prominent and rather isolated tree, often in villages. Clutch two to six, average four or five. Eggs variable both in size and colour, reddish to pale greenish, pale buffish, variably spotted and blotched with various shades of brown or grey, sometimes unmarked whitish. Incubation said to be both sexes, period unrecorded. Both sexes feed young. Eggs recorded from February and March in south of range, later in April and May in the north.

HABITAT: Both dry and moist broken deciduous woodlands, open cultivation with scattered trees, towns and villages, city parks. Avoids dense forest. Lowlands and low hills, locally to 2100 m on sparsely wooded, cultivated slopes and valleys.

DISTRIBUTION: Throughout the Indian subcontinent, except Sri Lanka, with western limit in Hazara, Pakistan, eastwards through lowland Burma (including Tennaserim), Thailand (except central and most of east), Laos (except north) and Cambodia to extreme southern Vietnam (Cochinchina).

STATUS: Generally common to very common over most of Pakistan and India, thinning out in the east of its range and decidedly rare and little known in Vietnam.

REFERENCE: Ali and Ripley 1972.

GREY TREEPIE   Plate 17

Dendrocitta formosae

Alternative name: Himalayan Treepie

Its adaptation to a cooler environment allows this treepie to survive much further north than the others.

IDENTIFICATION: Rather dull-coloured treepie of hill forest and cultivation. Small but clear white patch at base of primaries on otherwise wholly black wing and grey or white rump are crucial features; additionally the black face, throat and forecrown contrast with the pale grey nape and there is a chestnut patch on the vent. Chinese populations have black tails which strikingly contrast with white rump in flight; Himalayan races have basal two-thirds of tail grey with wide black tip and pale grey rump. This is the only treepie likely to be seen in the hills in China. Southernmost populations overlap with Rufous (fox-coloured body, wholly black primaries, pale grey wing coverts and tertials); rare Collared Treepie of Burma region has bright russet upper and underparts, contrasting with grey nape and breast and lacks white primary patch. Note isolated population in hills of Eastern Ghats in India, surrounded by Rufous Treepie.

DESCRIPTION: Length 36-40 cm (including tail). Shape as Rufous Treepie, but a little smaller, with slightly longer bill and shorter tail. Race *himalayensis*: Forecrown, sides of crown, sides of neck and throat blackish-brown, shading lighter on rear ear-coverts and upper-breast; very black on forecrown and above eye. Rest of crown and nape light, pure grey, shading into brownish-grey on mantle. Breast drab brownish grey shading paler on lower underparts, undertail-coverts chestnut. Mantle, scapulars, back and upper rump dark tawny-brown. Lower rump and uppertail-coverts pale grey or whitish-grey. Tail with two central feathers elongated and broad-tipped, the basal two-thirds of the central pair being silver-grey with wide black terminal area; remainder of tail feathers show decreasing amounts of grey

towards outermost which are short and all black. Bill black. Legs blackish-brown. Irides red or reddish-brown.
SEX/AGE: Sexes similar. Juvenile duller, with less black on forecrown, nape browner grey, narrow central tail feathers, small rufous tips to all feathers, including those of wings and tail. This reduces contrast between throat and breast. Inside of mandibles probably pink rather than black of adult. First-year birds may be aged by retained flight and tail feathers.
Measurements: Little difference between the sexes. Race *himalayensis*: Wing 133-151, tail 191-230, tarsus 28-35, bill 30-40, weight 89-121.
GEOGRAPHICAL VARIATION: Seven subspecies are recognised, which fall into two quite well defined groups of races; all forms do however intergrade.

Western group: birds with grey or greyish-white rump, at least basal half of central tail feathers grey and longer tails than eastern group.
    D. f. occidentalis: Pakistan to west Nepal, differs from next race only in larger size (tail 241-261).
    D. f. himalayensis: west Nepal east to northern Burma, with an isolated population in the Eastern Ghats of India, described above.
    D. f. assimilis: southern Burma and Thailand, slightly smaller, with a stouter bill, relatively shorter tail and drabber underparts.

Eastern group: darker, less patterned birds with very white rump and shorter wholly black tails (except nominate).
    D. f. sapiens: south Sichuan (Omei Shan), similar to the next form.
    D. f. sinica: mainland China, darker, with contrasting white rump, slightly shorter and all black tail.
    D. f. insulae: Hainan, slightly smaller and duller than the last, with very small white patch on wing.
    D. f. formosae: Taiwan, quite brown above and light below, with basal third of central tail feathers grey.
VOICE: As with all of the genus the vocalisations are difficult to describe. The most frequent call is a loud, stumbling series of rapid notes, uttered with an explosive undulating rhythm: a metallic, clucking, squawked 'klok-kli-klok-kli-kli'. Also has several shorter calls, both harsh and musical. Alarm is a chatter very much like that of Black-billed Magpie.
HABITS: A sociable treepie, often in small groups of five or six about hill forest clearings with mountain and foothill villages and tea plantations. Overall behaviour much as Rufous Treepie but less closely-associated with human activity. Descends to forage on the ground more frequently than Rufous Treepie, foraging by hopping with tail cocked; also frequents terraced hillsides. The diet is almost as varied as the Rufous Treepie, being a mixture of invertebrates and small vertebrates, seeds, fruits, flower nectar and berries. It does some damage to orchards and semi-wild silkworms in Assam. Also follows parties of laughing thrushes along the forest edge and joins mixed groups of forest birds feeding in fruiting trees. Flight action is similar to that of the Rufous Treepie, in fact even more jerky, with steep lifts on the downbeat and short nose-dives on the pauses.
BREEDING: Solitary nester. Nest rather small for the size of the bird, a rather flimsy platform of sticks with a shallow cup lined with finer plant materials, such as rootlets. Built by both sexes. Placed between 2 and 6 m in trees, shrubs or bamboos; sometimes in quite an exposed situation or even almost on ground. Clutch two to five, average three or four. Eggs vary from whitish to buffish or pale green, variably spotted and blotched with various shades of brown or grey. Incubation said to be by both sexes, period unrecorded. Both sexes feed young. Eggs recorded May to July in the Indian Himalayas; May and June in Burma.
HABITAT: Deciduous mountain forests, preferring open forest with adjacent cultivation and scrub, chiefly between 800 m and 2300 m, but as low as 550m in China.
DISTRIBUTION: Throughout the Himalayan foothills reaching western limit in the Murree hills of Pakistan. In eastern India there is an isolated population in the Eastern Ghats of Orissa and north Andhra. Further east is widespread throughout the hills of the north-east Indian states and extreme east Bangladesh, eastwards across western and northern Burma, west and north Thailand, north Laos and northern Vietnam (Tonkin). In China it is widespread north to the Yangtze in southern Jiangsu, and west to Yunnan, with isolated populations on Omei Shan (south Sichuan), Hainan and Taiwan.
STATUS: Fairly common to common over main part of range, although less so along the western Himalayas. Hainan race probably endangered by forest destruction, although perhaps less affected than some other forest corvids.
REFERENCE: Ali and Ripley 1972.

SUMATRAN TREEPIE   Plate 17

Dendrocitta occipitalis

Alternative names: Malaysian Treepie (part), Sunda Treepie (part).

A close relative of the White-bellied Treepie of southern India, endemic to Sumatra, where it is the only treepie.

IDENTIFICATION: Differs from similar and possibly conspecific Bornean Treepie in its blackish head and upper breast, contrasting with pale grey nape and weaker bill.
DESCRIPTION: Length 40 cm (including tail). Bill stout, although less so than Bornean Treepie. Legs short and weak. Wings very short and broad. Tail graduated, with central tail feathers much elongated, narrower than in Grey Treepie. Head and centre of upper breast blackish-brown, blackest on crown. Underparts below breast tawny rufous becoming richer and more orange-tawny on undertail-coverts. Nape and hindneck pale silvery grey, becoming almost white on upper nape. Mantle, back and scapulars tawny brown. Rump and uppertail-coverts very pale grey, almost whitish (feathers fringed rufous in fresh plumage). Wings black with small white patch at base of primaries. Outer-tail feathers black, elongated central tail feathers silver-grey with wide black tip. Bill black or greyish-black. Legs greyish-black. Irides red or reddish-brown.
SEX/AGE: Sexes similar. Juvenile with narrower, more pointed central tail feathers, probably has pinkish inside mandibles rather than black of adults; overall colouration duller, with light buff fringes to body feathers and

borders to tertials; dull sooty face and throat, rather than blackish-brown. First year birds may be aged by retained flight and narrower central tail feathers.

MEASUREMENTS: Wing 144-148, tail 276-284, tarsus 30-32, bill 31-32, weight not recorded.

GEOGRAPHICAL VARIATION: Monotypic as treated here.

VOICE: Similar to that of Bornean Treepie as far as is known; no recordings available.

HABITS: Similar to those of Bornean and White-bellied Treepie as far as is known.

BREEDING: Undocumented.

HABITAT: Mountain and foothill forests, preferring open forest with plantations and bamboo thickets, between 400 m and 2300 m.

DISTRIBUTION: Endemic to Sumatra.

STATUS: Fairly common throughout the mountains of the island.

REFERENCES: Goodwin 1986, van Marle and Voous 1988.

BORNEAN TREEPIE   Plate 17

Dendrocitta (occipitalis) cinerascens

Alternative names: Malaysian Treepie (part), Sunda Treepie (part).

Endemic to Borneo, where it is the only treepie. The treepies of Sumatra and Borneo are usually regarded as isolated races of one species and termed together as Malaysian or Sunda Treepie. In view of striking differences in head pattern, they are here given specific status.

IDENTIFICATION: Differing from similar and possibly conspecific Sumatran Treepie in having the face, throat and breast pinkish rufous concolorous with the rest of the underparts, crown almost white and bordered by a narrow blackish eyestripe and frontal band and a stouter bill (Sumatran has head and throat blackish-brown contrasting with pale nape).

DESCRIPTION: Length 40 cm (including tail). Bill markedly thick, with strongly curved culmen. Legs short and weak. Wings very short and broad. Tail graduated, with central tail feathers much elongated, narrower than in Grey Treepie. Crown very pale grey, almost whitish, shading greyer on nape, the grey becoming mixed with pinkish-rufous on hindneck. Narrow chocolate-brown band across forehead, joining eyes, extending back behind eye and tapering above rear ear-coverts. Nasal tuft, loral region, ear-coverts, throat and entire underparts dull pinkish-rufous, with indistinct greyer shade across breast. Mantle, back and scapulars pinkish-rufous with strong grey wash. Rump and uppertail-coverts very pale grey, almost whitish. Wings black with small white patch at base of primaries. Outer-tail feathers black, elongated central tail feathers silver-grey with wide black tip. Bill black or greyish-black. Legs greyish-black. Irides red or reddish-brown.

SEX/AGE: Sexes similar. Juvenile (based on photograph of first-year bird) with narrower, more pointed central tail feathers, probably has pinkish inside mandibles rather than black of adults; overall colouration probably

duller, with light buff fringes to body feathers and tertials. First-year birds may be aged by retained flight (showing vestiges of pale fringes to tertials) and narrower central tail feathers.

MEASUREMENTS: Wing 136-153, tail 210-283, tarsus 32-33, bill 30-32, weight not recorded.

GEOGRAPHICAL VARIATION: Monotypic as treated here. The population inhabiting the higher altitude forests of Mt. Dulit has been separated as race *tuckeri* but differences are minor and it is not generally recognised.

VOICE: Typical selection of treepie squawks and clangs, with musical bell-like, metallic and harsh tones. Difficult to transcribe, but shorter call phrases than those produced by Grey Treepie. Recordings include the following short phrases, all loud and rather explosive: a metallic clang not unlike the sound of an old motor horn - 'kli-awk', a raucous squawk followed by a metallic clunk - 'sqwaaaaak-tonk', a metallic note followed by ringing fading resonance - 'b,clunk-eee' and a liquid sound followed by a pair of short harsh notes - 'plonk, grah-grah'. The literature describes a rapid harsh magpie-like cackling and refers to its ability to mimic the sounds of other forest birds.

HABITS: A sociable treepie, found in small noisy parties feeding in tree canopy; their loud and varied calls being the predominant bird sound of the forests. They can become quite bold and fearless where unmolested, as on Kinabalu, where they come to the forest trails in search of human food scraps. Their short legs and long tails makes them clumsy in their movements both in the canopy and particularly if they come down to ground level. In the valleys they visit cultivated fields and villages. Their diet includes cockroaches, beetles and other insects, seeds and berries, which are their main food source.

BREEDING: Little documented. Nest a shallow construction of fine twigs placed in a low tree in scrub jungle. The two nests described each contained two eggs, which seems small for a complete clutch. Eggs greenish-white, freckled with brown markings, concentrated into a ring at the wider end. Eggs recorded early January and mid March.

HABITAT: Montane forests, favouring foothill and valley forests with clearings and cultivation, secondary scrub jungle and bamboo thickets. Between 300 and 2800 m.

DISTRIBUTION: Endemic to Borneo.

STATUS: Common throughout the northern and central hills and mountains of the island, most numerous in lower altitude valleys, least numerous at higher elevations.

REFERENCES: Goodwin 1986, Robson, C. (tape recordings), Smythies 1981.

WHITE-BELLIED TREEPIE   Plate 17

Dendrocitta leucogastra

Alternative name: Southern Treepie

This beautifully patterned treepie is one of several endemics of the Western Ghats of southern India. Only its wing pattern suggests a relationship with the Grey Treepie; it is perhaps closest to Sumatran.

IDENTIFICATION: An unmistakable treepie of the lush forests of south-west India where it only overlaps with Rufous, but the white underparts, rump, nape and primary flash are easy distinctions. It is also a bird of lush, humid evergreen forests whereas Rufous inhabits sparsely wooded cultivated areas; however the two species occur together where their habitats meet.
DESCRIPTION: Length 48 cm (including tail). Bill stout, with strongly curved culmen. Legs short and weak. Wings short and broad. Tail graduated, with central tail feathers very elongated and broadening towards slightly concave tip. Crown, sides of head, throat and breast black. Nape, hindneck and underparts below breast almost completely white, except for black thighs and chestnut undertail-coverts. Mantle, back and scapulars chestnut-brown. Wings black with white patch at base of primaries. Rump and uppertail-coverts white. Central pair of tail feathers silver-grey with black terminal third, remainder of tail feathers shorter and black. Bill black or greyish-black. Legs greyish-black. Irides red or reddish-brown.
SEX/AGE: Sexes similar. Juvenile with narrower, shorter and more pointed central tail feathers, probably has pinkish inside mandibles rather than black of adults; overall colouration duller, with light buff fringes to white body feathers.
MEASUREMENTS: Wing 141-157, tail 278-324, tarsus 32-33, bill 32-34, weight 99 (one).
GEOGRAPHICAL VARIATION: Monotypic.
VOICE: Several of its calls are strangely similar to those of the Greater Racket-tailed Drongo, a forest bird with which this treepie has a close association; these are presumably produced as part of typical treepie mimicry. Calls are typical of the genus but are louder, harsher and more metallic than those of Rufous Treepie. Whilst feeding it utters a short, dry rattle which ends in a short frog-like croak. Also gives a throaty 'chuff-chuff-chuff' and a rhythmical creaking. Another call has been described as like that of a duck. Other sounds produced by this treepie include clicking notes followed by a short dove-like but rather liquid 'ko-koo' in display and a harsh 'kraa' (possibly of alarm). Voice in general poorly studied and seemingly unrecorded.
HABITS: An arboreal treepie of dense forest, foraging in pairs or small family parties. Habitually follows mixed foraging parties of other forest birds, especially Greater Racket-tailed Drongo, but the reasons for this association are unclear. Flight action is jerkily bounding as with Grey Treepie of the Himalayas (which is also often seen in the company of the forest drongos). Occasionally feeds in low shrubbery and even on the ground close to cover. Food items recorded include fruits, seeds, nectar, various invertebrates and small reptiles, nestling birds, eggs and rodents.

BREEDING: Solitary nester. Nest a deepish construction of prickly twigs, lined with smaller twigs and rootlets. Placed in dense rainforest tree or shrub, well away from human habitations. Clutch three or four. Eggs variable, creamy through greenish to reddish-white, marked with all shades and shapes of brown markings. Much more like eggs of Grey Treepie, rather than Rufous. Eggs recorded February to April, most frequently in March and April.
HABITAT: Humid evergreen hill forests, and associated secondary growth, and ravines, often around abandoned overgrown rubber plantations. Inhabits forest between 60 and 1500 m.
DISTRIBUTION: Endemic to southern India, where it is found from Goa and western Mysore, south to Kerala and western Tamil Nadu. Has also been recorded from further east, in southern Andhra Pradesh from Bangalore east to Palmaner but is not known to be resident in that region. A remarkable mid 19th century record of a bird collected far to the north-west in Gujarat is regarded as dubious by Ali and Ripley (1972), but it is possible that it was formerly more widespread in western India, cf. presence of Grey Treepie isolated in the Eastern Ghats way south of rest of Indian range. However the habitat in Gujarat is dry, deciduous scrub forest and quite unsuitable for this species.
STATUS: Locally quite common, but status in southern Andhra Pradesh needs clarification.
REFERENCE: Ali and Ripley 1972.

ANDAMAN TREEPIE   Plate 17

Dendrocitta bayleyi

A small treepie of dense forest, endemic to the Andaman Islands, where there are no other treepies.

IDENTIFICATION: An unmistakable treepie of the lush forests of the Andamans, it is the smallest and slightest of the genus, rich rufous in colour with a dark hood and has a very large white band across the flight feathers of its otherwise black wings.
DESCRIPTION: Length 32 cm (including tail). Bill small and stout, with strongly curved culmen. Legs short and weak. Wings short and broad. Tail long and graduated, central pair of feathers shortly elongated. Head and neck dark grey shading to blackish on face and forecrown. Underparts deep tawny-rufous shading greyer on upper breast and almost chestnut on ventral region. Upperparts similar but duller, dark tawny-brown on mantle and back, brighter rufous on rump, becoming grey on uppertail-coverts. Wings black with large white bases to primaries and outer secondaries. Tail blackish, shading dark grey over basal half of the central pair of feathers. Bill black or greyish-black. Legs greyish-black. Irides yellow.
SEX/AGE: Sexes similar. Juvenile has sooty reddish-brown hood, upperparts darker and redder, with rusty feather fringes; wing coverts more greyish, with brownish fringes to lesser and median coverts; shorter and greyer tail feathers; probably has pinkish inside mandibles rather than black of adults; irides olive-green, becoming brighter green and then yellow.
MEASUREMENTS: Wing 117-124, tail 180-206, tarsus

27-28, bill 26-28, weight 92-113.

GEOGRAPHICAL VARIATION: Monotypic.

VOICE: Little documented. Said to have a harsh, repeated alarm note, and to produce a metallic sound recalling 'a coarse file being drawn across the teeth of a saw'.

HABITS: An arboreal treepie of dense forest, foraging in pairs or small family parties; often gathers together in large congregations of 20 or more birds. Like the Grey and Southern Treepies, follows mixed foraging parties of other forest birds, especially parties of Andaman Drongos, which are also a very sociable species.

BREEDING: Solitary nester. Nest a flimsy construction of fine twigs and grasses, lined with rootlets. 5 m from ground in small, thickly-foliaged forest sapling. Clutch three. Eggs pale creamy yellow, well marked with small blotches of light brown and dark grey, concentrated at the larger end. Eggs recorded from March to May inclusive.

HABITAT: Dense evergreen forests.

DISTRIBUTION: Endemic to the Andaman Islands, absent from the Cocos and Nicobar islands to the south.

STATUS: Although it is quite numerous in its preferred habitat, the forested areas of the islands have been depleted in recent years, especially on the most populated island of South Andaman.

REFERENCE: Ali and Ripley 1972.

COLLARED TREEPIE   Plate 18

Dendrocitta frontalis

Alternative names: Black-browed Treepie, Black-faced Treepie

A rare and little known forest treepie of Burma and adjacent regions, likely to be endangered through forest destruction.

IDENTIFICATION: A beautifully patterned small treepie of dense bamboo forest, recorded in the Himalayan foothills from north-east India to Tonkin. Black face and throat contrasts with clear pale grey (almost whitish) rear half of head and breast gives an appearance quite unlike that of Rufous, but like Rufous it lacks the white primary patch of Grey Treepie. The grey wing covert patch is less extensive than in Rufous, not extending to tertials and the tail is wholly black. The two do not overlap in habitat, Collared being a bird of humid forests, Rufous of lightly wooded country. Compare also Hooded Treepie.

DESCRIPTION: Length 38 cm (including tail). Bill short and stout, with strongly arched culmen. Legs short and weak. Wings short and broad. Tail long and graduated, central pair of feathers strongly elongated. Front half of head back to level of mid crown, mid ear-coverts and throat clear black, sharply contrasting with light grey of rest of head, mantle and breast, the grey being very pale

and forming a pale highlight where it borders black of head. Belly, flanks and undertail-coverts chestnut. Upperparts similar, but browner on back and scapulars. Wings black, with light grey greater coverts and darker grey lesser and median coverts. Tail wholly black. Bill and legs black. Irides dark red.

SEX/AGE: Sexes similar, although colour of males tends to be a little brighter and cleaner than females. Juvenile a little duller, with narrow brownish fringes to grey of head and breast. Presumably also differs in interior colour of mandibles, pinkish rather than black of adults.

MEASUREMENTS: Wing 120-126, tail 245-255, tarsus 30, bill c.28, weight not recorded.

GEOGRAPHICAL VARIATION: Monotypic. Birds from Tonkin have been separated as race *kurodae*, they are said to be duller and darker than western birds, but this form is not generally recognised.

VOICE: Virtually undocumented. Said to have a typical treepie range of calls.

HABITS: Little recorded. Said to be much as Grey Treepie in behaviour i.e. an arboreal treepie of dense forest, foraging in small parties. Also has been referred to as less noisy and less shy. Has been seen flycatching for flying termites from the tops of bamboo clumps in the manner of drongos. Food recorded includes the usual range of seeds, fruits, insects, small lizards, eggs and small birds.

BREEDING: Solitary nester. Nest smaller, neater and more compact than that of Grey Treepie, but similar. Constructed in bamboo thickets or in a small tree by the forest edge. Eggs three or four, resembling those of Grey Treepie, but smaller and more profusely marked. Breeding recorded April to July, more specifically eggs recorded in late May in Assam.

HABITAT: Dense mixed humid evergreen forests, with bamboo thickets in Himalayan foothills. Reported between 600 and 2100 m.

DISTRIBUTION: From Bhutan across the north-east frontier states of India, where recorded from the Dafla, Abor and Mishmi Hills, and around the head of the Brahmaputra valley in the north. Also the Cachar and Khasi Hills and in Nagaland and Manipur. Through the foothill valleys of western and northern Burma, into extreme western Yunnan (not known east of the Salween River) and in north-west Tonkin (Vietnam). Also recorded from further west, in both Nepal and Sikkim but not this century.

STATUS: Always considered a rare bird, the present situation is impossible to clarify as its distribution lies within politically sensitive areas, mostly in of forests that have not been ornithologically surveyed for decades. It is likely that this species is threatened as lowland forest has been widely cleared in at least some of these areas. During a three month survey of eastern Arunachal Pradesh, India in 1990 only one bird was observed. However parties of up to 20 birds were reported from the Namning area of east central Bhutan in 1991.

REFERENCES: Ali and Ripley 1972, Inskipp and Inskipp 1993, Katti *et al* 1992

RACQUET-TAILED and RATCHET-TAILED TREEPIES *Crypsirina and Temnurus*

Crypsirina is a small genus of two very small treepies of south-east Asian lowland forest; they differ from other treepies in having ten, not twelve, tail feathers, which are distinctly flared into a spoon-shaped tip on the central pair. Instead of the forwardly-projecting nasal bristles of other treepies, these species have a cushion of short, velvet-like feathers over the forehead and loral area. These are velvet black and can give a peculiar jet black fuzzy contrast to the oily gloss of the black of the head under exceptional viewing circumstances. The monotypic *Temnurus* is similar, and is sometimes combined with *Crypsirina*, but it is a larger bird with such a unique tail structure that it deserves its own genus.

RACQUET-TAILED TREEPIE   Plate 18

Crypsirina temia

Alternative name: Black Racket-tailed Treepie

One of the smallest of all corvids, an attractive little black treepie, with a remarkably long, flared tail.

IDENTIFICATION: Small black treepie, with very long tail, expanding at tip; feeds inside canopy of lowland secondary or open forest. Easily confused with rarer Ratchet-tailed Treepie, but tail longer and of different shape, but see that species for further discussion. Size and colour suggests a long-tailed drongo more than a treepie but has stouter bill, bluish (not red) eye and is more secretive.
DESCRIPTION: Length 31-33 cm (including tail). Bill stout, with strongly curved culmen. Legs short and weak. Wings short and broad. Tail very long and graduated, central pair of feathers gradually flaring to a spatulate tip. Forehead and loral feathering dense and velvety, jet black. Remainder of plumage oily blackish-green, with slight bronze sheen. Tail and flight feathers blacker, only slightly glossed. Bill and legs black. Irides blue, varying from turquoise to light blue.
SEX/AGE: Sexes similar. Juvenile dull greyish-black, lacking sheen, tail feathers narrower, not widening at tip, irides dark brown. After first moult much as adult in colour, but retained juvenile flight feathers greyer and tail also juvenile; irides remain dark brown until at least early in second year of life.
MEASUREMENTS: Wing 110-116, tail 175-200, tarsus 28, bill 23, weight not recorded.
GEOGRAPHICAL VARIATION: Monotypic.
VOICE: Typical calls uttered by foraging parties: a short, high-pitched, but gruff and somewhat ringing 'chu'; also a deep, rasping 'churg-churg' which can be uttered in a higher pitch as 'grasp-grasp' or even 'chrrrk-chrrrk', occasionally rising towards the end with an enquiring quality as 'churrrk ?'.
HABITS: Little documented for such widespread, unusual and comparatively common species. Usually encountered singly, in pairs or small family parties in the lower canopy level of forest edge or tall understorey by clearings, often in shrubby edges of forest by villages. Despite their drongo-like colouration they do not behave like drongos (which flycatch from the outside of mid and upper canopy). They forage in the shrubbery, hopping and climbing through with agility and much movement of their long tails, which they use to balance themselves. They rarely come down to the ground, but

have sometimes been observed bathing. In such circumstances their long tails and short legs make the bird seem very awkward; the tail is cocked high over its back as if to counteract its balance. They are primarily insectivorous, but also take berries.
BREEDING: Solitary nester. Nest of twigs, tendrils and creeper stems, lined with fine rootlets and tendrils. Built inside bushes and bamboo thickets, from 2 to 5 m above ground level. Site often in isolated thickets in open grassy areas. Eggs two to four, varying from white to greenish-buff, usually profusely marked with various shades of brown, sometimes marked with more sparse but larger blotching. Eggs recorded April to August in Burma and Thailand and April in Tonkin.
HABITAT: Lowland open forests of various types, including mixed deciduous woodland, secondary forest bamboo and mangroves. Recorded up to 1000 m.
DISTRIBUTION: From lowlands of southern and eastern Burma, extreme northern Malaysia, eastwards through Thailand (except extreme south and central areas), Cambodia, Laos and Vietnam, just extending into China in southern Yunnan. Strangely absent from Sumatra, but present again on Java and Bali.
STATUS: Relatively common over most of range.
REFERENCE: Goodwin 1986.

HOODED TREEPIE   Plate 18

Crypsirina cucullata

Alternative name: Hooded Racket-tailed Treepie

One of the least known of all Asian corvids, endemic to lowland Burma where its habitat has been decimated;;clearly it is a threatened species.

IDENTIFICATION: Rare little treepie, very similar to the last species in shape. Its plumage is quite different: grey with contrasting black hood, flight feathers and long, spoon-ended tail. Unlikely to be confused with other species.
DESCRIPTION: Length 30-31 cm (including tail). Bill stout, with strongly curved culmen. Legs short and weak. Wings short and broad. Tail very long and graduated, central pair of feathers gradually flaring to a spatulate tip. Forehead and loral feathering dense and velvety, jet black. Remainder of head black, with oily green gloss and a narrow whitish border to the black. Body pale grey with mauve-fawn tinge to underparts and bluish-grey wash to upperparts. Wing-coverts fawn-grey with whitish fringes to greater coverts; tertials

similar. Outer secondaries blackish with whitish outer web, forming narrow white stripe along folded wing. Primaries and primary coverts black. Central tail feathers black, remainder (usually concealed) light fawn-grey. Bill and legs black. Irides dark blue. Orbital ring dark grey or blackish.

SEX/AGE: Sexes similar. Juvenile duller and browner grey overall, with dark blackish-brown hood; irides presumably dark brown; elongated tail feathers narrower and not spoon-shaped; bill blackish with extensive orange gape and interior of bill (black in adult); orbital ring pale blue with orange edges. After first moult, first-year birds differ from adult in being darker grey, especially on nape and mantle, lacking narrow whitish border to hood and retaining narrow juvenile tail feathers; gape patch yellow rather than orange. After second moult as adult, but some pale might remain on gape area into second year.

MEASUREMENTS: Wing 102-108, tail 180-200, tarsus 26-27, bill 20, weight not recorded.

GEOGRAPHICAL VARIATION: Monotypic.

VOICE: Said to have harsh discordant calls, and a mewing call like the excitement cry of a Collared Dove.

HABITS: Little documented. Reported as found singly, in pairs or small family parties. Food items recorded include grasshoppers, locusts, mantises and winged termites. Wings reported to make a whirring sound in flight. General behaviour probably much as in the previous species.

BREEDING: Solitary nester. Nest of twigs, tendrils and rootlets, possibly with a partial dome of thorny twigs suggesting a miniature nest of the Black-billed Magpie. Built in a small tree or shrub. Clutch two to four. Eggs creamy or greenish-white, profusely marked with brown, coalescing at the broader end. Eggs recorded in May and July.

HABITAT: Lowland dry forest, including secondary growth and bamboo jungle, recorded up to 1000 m.

DISTRIBUTION: Endemic to the dry lowlands of central, northern and southern Burma.

STATUS: Formerly quite common, but the destruction of lowland forest in central Burma has been considerable in recent decades and it is almost certainly now very localised and possibly endangered.

REFERENCES: Goodwin 1986, Smythies 1953.

RATCHET-TAILED TREEPIE   Plate 15

Temnurus temnurus

Alternative name: Notch-tailed Treepie

A little known black treepie of the rainforests of Indochina, its remarkable tail structure is unique.

IDENTIFICATION: An unobtrusive black treepie, quite plump and sluggish in its habits, thus easily overlooked. Only likely confusion is with the commoner Racquet-tailed, which is relatively smaller, sleeker, much longer tailed and has quite a different tail shape. Ratchet-tailed has almost an oblong tail shape with inconspicuous points sticking out at either side, whereas Racquet-tailed has a very long narrow tail which gradually widens to a broad tip, but note that first year birds have a narrow tail of almost even width. Much more easily passed off as a drongo in a brief view, unless tail seen well.

DESCRIPTION: Length 32 cm (including tail). Rather larger than Racquet-tailed Treepie, and more heavily built. Bill stout, with strongly curved culmen. Legs short and weak. Wings short and broad. Tail long, but relatively short for a treepie; graduated, all feathers widely-forked at the tip, the points of the outer part of the fork projecting at either side of the closed tail. Forehead and loral feathering dense and velvety, jet black. Remainder of plumage dark greyish-black, with slight sheen on head, wings and tail. Bill and legs black. Irides dark red or dark brown.

SEX/AGE: Sexes similar. Juvenile not described, but first year birds with retained juvenile tail have narrower feathers, with slightly shorter and blunter tail projections; the shortest outer feathers have virtually no points and are quite blunt.

MEASUREMENTS: Wing 138-140, tail 160-180, tarsus 27-28, bill 30-31, weight not recorded.

GEOGRAPHICAL VARIATION: Monotypic.

VOICE: Has several calls, but some of these are probably variants of two or three vocalisations. Utters an inconspicuous sibilant, ringing call of obvious treepie quality, but probably individually variable. Two paired birds recorded calling in duet, one with an incisive start following by ringing squeaked terminal tone: 'clipeeee', the other bird with a rapid double hollow 'pupu' at the start: 'pupueeee'. Similar but more regularly repeated is a ringing double 'clee-clee'. Also a constantly repeated short two syllable call, ringing, squeaky and rising in inflection: 'eeup—eeup—eeup...' A short, rather high pitched rasping ripple 'rrrrrrrr', with or without ending in an abrupt hollow resonance. A harsh, grating, slow and rhythmic repeated 'graak-graak-graak....' of slightly varying pitch and intensity is probably an alarm chatter.

HABITS: Little information. An unobtrusive treepie, rather sluggish in its movements, generally revealing its presence by persistent calling. Typically found singly or in pairs sitting rather upright inside mid canopy of forest. Small parties, occasionally reported, are presumed to be family groups. Follows mixed feeding parties of other forest birds, particularly Greater Racket-tailed Drongos and various babblers.

BREEDING: The nest has recently been discovered in Thailand, but no details have as yet been published.

HABITAT: Lowland forests, especially with extensive bamboo.

DISTRIBUTION: Mostly Vietnam where quite widespread from Tonkin south to Central Annam; also extends into eastern central Laos. An isolated population in China on Hainan. In 1991 discovered breeding in Thailand, in forest to the south-west of Bangkok, well away from previous known range.

STATUS: Not uncommon in Vietnam, but little known elsewhere. Habitat destruction on Hainan now limits range to only a few patches of remaining forest. The remarkable recent discovery in Thailand indicates how easy it is to overlook this species.

REFERENCES: Goodwin 1986, Robson, C. (tape recordings)

PIED MAGPIES *Pica*

A small but nonetheless, rather complex genus, composed of two allopatric species. These magpies provide a link between the true crows and the jays and tropical magpies. They are terrestrial birds of open country, walking and hopping on the ground (jays only hop) and use tree cover primarily for roosting and nesting. With the exception of Stresemann's Bush-Crow of Ethiopia they are the only corvids to construct a domed nest.

BLACK-BILLED MAGPIE   Plate 13

Pica pica

Alternative names: Magpie, Common Magpie

One of the most widespread and familiar of all corvids, seldom found far from cultivation or human habitation

IDENTIFICATION: Widespread across the northern hemisphere. Like the true crows this species favours open habitats. The striking black and white plumage, very long graduated tail and rounded black and white wings render it almost unmistakable (the exception being in California, see Yellow-billed Magpie).
DESCRIPTION: Length 43-50 cm (including tail). Bill medium, with gently curved culmen. Nasal tuft prominent as in *Corvus*, with base of culmen bare to forehead. Tail graduated, with central pair of feathers projecting beyond next pair, tail feathers widest at about mid point, narrowing to a blunt tip. Outermost (first) primary narrow and curved. Nominate race: Head, neck, mantle and breast black, with weak purple and green sheen. Underparts below breast white, but black thighs and ventral region. Mantle, back and rump to uppertail-coverts black, with narrow greyish band across rump. Scapulars white. Wings black, highly glossed green or green-blue, especially on secondaries and tertials; inner webs of primaries white, with black bases and tips, showing as wide white band in flight, but concealed at rest. Tail black, highly glossed metallic green, turning to reddish-purple then dark purple over terminal third, to blackish at very tip of feathers. Bill and legs black. Irides dark brown.
SEX/AGE: Sexes similar. Juvenile has head and breast dull greyish-black with pale interior to mandibles, irides and small patches of bare skin about eye and gape bluish-grey greyish at fledging, the irides soon turning brown; moults tail as well as body plumage at first moult, but not flight feathers. Ageing not possible in first year except in hand.
MEASUREMENTS: Male averages larger than female. Wing 182-209, tail 217-273, tarsus 48-53, bill 41-49, weight 180-275.
GEOGRAPHICAL VARIATION: Complex, some 13 subspecies recognised, all but four (and these are all isolated forms) intergrade with another adjacent race. All acceptable races are briefly listed below, with fuller comment discussing features of the most different and isolated forms following on.
  P. p. pica: Northern and eastern Europe, described above.
  P. p. galliae: western Europe, but not the south-west, slightly smaller with a little less white on wings and rump.

P. p. melanotos: Spain and Portugal, like the last but rump black.
P. p. mauritanica: North-west Africa, differs from last in having relatively shorter wings and longer tail, a little less white in the wings and a patch of bare blue skin about the eye (comment below).
P. p. fennorum: Scandinavia to western Russia, slightly larger than nominate, with a little more white in the wing.
P. p. bactriana: central and eastern Russia, south to Middle East, more white in the wing and a large white rump patch.
P. p. hemileucoptera: west and central Siberia, south to Xinjiang Zizhiqu (Sinkiang), larger and with even more white in the wing than last.
P. p. leucoptera: southern Transbaicalia and eastern Mongolia, like last but larger and with even more white in the wing.
P. p. camtschatica: north-east Siberia, the most extensive white in the wing of all forms, showing as white tips to the primaries even on folded wing. Tail gloss very green (comment below).
P. p. sericea: eastern Asia, from Amurland south to Vietnam and Laos, much as nominate form, but with relatively longer wing and shorter tail, gloss on wings and tail gloss more purple blue.
P. p. bottanensis: north-east Qinghai, south to north east India and Bhutan, the largest form (wing 244-265) but with tail relatively the shortest, colour like the last.
P. p. hudsonia: North America, close to nominate race but has relatively longer wings and tail, irides seem to have blue in at least the first year (comment below).
P. p. asirensis: isolated in the Asir massif of western Saudi Arabia, is a very distinct form, rather dull black but with tail glossed purple, its bill and legs are large and it has the least amount of white on wings and scapulars of all forms (see comment).
Of all the Old World races, the one most worthy of possible specific status is the Arabian race *asirensis*. Long isolated from its nearest relatives in northern Iraq, it has evolved the most marked structural differences with a relatively larger bill and stronger feet than other forms as well as having reduced areas of white on the upperparts; however this form remains almost unstudied. Its presence in south-west Arabia is mirrored by the endemic Yemen Linnet and two endemic species of *Alectoris* partridges, the ancestors of which also came from the north probably during the Pleistocene era when Arabia had a temperate climate.

The North African race *mauritanica* is also a distinct form but is somewhat linked by birds of Spain and Portugal which approach it. Indeed a proportion of birds in southern Spain also show vestigial bluish bare skin about the eye typical of the North African race (but also typical of juvenile magpies in general). A similar situation arises with Levaillant's Woodpecker, a North African endemic but with some intermediate features approached by birds of the adjacent Spanish race of Green Woodpecker.

The beautifully marked north-east Siberian race *camtschatica* has the most extensive white in the wing of all forms. It is also isolated and brightly glossed by comparison to its nearest relatives in Amurland and is in need of further study.

Surprisingly the American race *hudsonia* differs little in outward appearance from the nominate race of Europe, yet its distribution reaches Alaska which is close to the very different *camtschatica* birds of Anadyr. This suggests that its distribution has spread from further south in North America rather than from Asia. Indeed all of the evidence so far collected indicates that *hudsonia* and the Yellow-billed Magpie are genetically close to each other and that both are quite distantly related to Old World forms. This is also borne out by vocal and behavioural studies and the fact that *hudsonia* varies little over its wide range in North America, which is unusual for a North American corvid.

VOICE: Usual calls include a staccato chattering 'Chack-chack-chack-chack-chack' of alarm, these calls are uttered in rapid, frantic bursts of eight to twelve or more notes. Also gives an enquiring 'ch'chack' and a more squealing 'keee-uck'. A full discussion on the variety of calls is given by Goodwin (1986). There does seem to be some geographic variation in the pitch of the calls, as well as in the calls themselves, which is not surprising considering the massive global range of the species. Chatter of American race is deeper, slower and gruffer, given in bursts of three or four notes: 'chug-chug-chug'. North African race seems to utter a more varied selection of calls than European races, the chatter being higher in pitch and uttered with a more undulating rhythm. Eastern race *sericea* has a somewhat softer chatter than the nominate.

HABITS: A very sociable and conspicuous bird, feeding in the open at field edges, scrubby habitats and the like. Although normally in pairs or family parties, regularly gathers into small loose flocks of 20 or more birds and forms communal roosts which may be used throughout the year. In Tibet, large roosting nests have been recorded with as many as ten birds using them; these seem to be specially built for roosting and have the appearance of several small nests being built around each other. This seems not to have been recorded elsewhere but huge magpie nests on electricity pylons are a familiar sight in the countryside around Khabarovsk in Amurland. Some pairs maintain a territory throughout the year, others forsake it at the end of the breeding season and re-occupy it the following early spring. Non-breeding birds also live in the territories of a breeding pair, presumably young birds of previous years but despite this semi-social lifestyle they do not contribute to nest construction or feeding the young. In areas where nesting sites are sparse, several pairs may nest quite close together and give the impression of colonial breeding. Black-billed Magpies are successful birds and

are omnivorous in their diet; they feed chiefly on the ground on various invertebrates, especially beetles, also various seeds, fruits and berries, small mammals and reptiles, small birds and their eggs and nestlings. They often ride on the backs of domestic animals, taking ectoparasites, and they also peck at sores and wounds of animals. Carrion is also readily taken, and pairs habitually investigate roadsides, especially in the early mornings, searching for animal casualties. Human food scraps of various kinds are eaten and, where unmolested, they scavenge around houses, picnic sites and in parks, where they can become quite bold, but always seem to remain wary. Strangely, few acorns are eaten. Surplus food items are freely hidden but usually retrieved within a few days. Frequently chases and mobs other birds carrying food, such as gulls or kites, and is often successful at making them drop what they are carrying. On the ground walks with a confident strutting gait, carrying the tail somewhat elevated, flicking wings and tail when excited, breaks into occasional side-stepping hops to inspect a potential food item. Readily sits on exposed perches such as tree tops, roofs and walls. Rises with rapid flapping wing beats often just high enough to lift over bushes before disappearing out of sight. Fight is a mixture of several flapping beats and a pause, or continually flapping, groups of birds flying in single file. Looks rather awkward in flight but remarkably agile in pursuit of large predators, i.e. when chasing them away from nesting area. Several birds may gather together to pester and dive-bomb predators such as cats or a roosting owl. There is an excellent monograph of this species Birkhead (1991).

BREEDING: Solitary nester, although often several nests in quite close proximity might indicate a loose colony. Nest a distinctive large domed construction of thorny twigs, with a side entrance, cup lined with soft plant materials, wool and other animal hair. Usually placed near crown of a tree or large shrub and quite conspicuous, also frequently constructed between struts of electricity pylons. In very open treeless country often virtually on ground by low stone wall, but more often in a bramble patch. Usually builds a new nest each year, but when nesting on pylons (as in Amurland) new nests may be built on top of old ones, thus creating massive constructions which exceed three metres in height. Both sexes build the nest. Clutch two to eight, average five to seven, but American race has larger clutches, typically eight or nine, with as many as 13 recorded. Eggs bluish-green, occasionally creamy, speckled and spotted brown. Incubation 14 to 23 days, average 17 or 18, by female, being fed at nest by male. Both sexes feed young for ten days, then fledglings leave nest but spend several days in close proximity. Black-billed Magpies are the favoured host of the Great Spotted Cuckoo. Disused nests are used by a wide variety of other birds, from ducks to Kestrels and Long-eared Owls as breeding sites.

HABITAT: Open country with scattered trees from farmland to mountain sides. Often in parks and large gardens, even in some city centres. Locally in areas devoid of trees, i.e. islands. Avoids large tracts of open country lacking in trees and extensive areas of dense forest.

DISTRIBUTION: Holarctic. Widespread throughout Europe, except Iceland, also in North Africa from Mauritania east to Tunisia. Eastwards throughout most of central and southern Siberia to the Pacific, with northern limit of main population being the lower Amur valley. An isolated population in north east Siberia on Kamchatka extending to Anadyrland. Absent Sakhalin and Japan apart from introduced population on Kyushu. Widespread southwards from Amurland in eastern Asia, through Korea, Taiwan and eastern China reaching southern limit in central Annam (Vietnam), northern Laos and north Burma. Eastern range extends westwards over eastern Tibet south to extreme north Bhutan and Sikkim. Absent from arid regions of western China and southern Mongolia but widespread further west over whole of central Asia south and east to Kashmir, Ladakh and the north-west frontier of Pakistan. Westwards may be found throughout Afghanistan, northern and western Iran, northern Iraq, eastern Syria, the whole of Turkey and adjacent Cyprus. An isolated population in the Asir of south-west Arabia. Also widespread in western North America from west-central Alaska east to western Ontario, south to north-eastern California and northern New Mexico. North American birds somewhat disperse in winter, with vagrants occasionally reaching eastern USA and Canada. In the Old World very much a sedentary bird.

STATUS: Common to abundant over most of range, has increased dramatically in parts of Europe since 1960s especially in Britain; isolated Arabian race described as rare. Present status in Mauritania and Tunisia needs confirmation; reported from Lebanon but perhaps only as a vagrant from Syria.

REFERENCES: Birkhead 1991, Goodwin 1986

YELLOW-BILLED MAGPIE   Plate 13

Pica nuttalli

The isolated Yellow-billed Magpie of California has been extensively studied and its specific distinctions are generally upheld, although it is very closely related to the American race of Black-billed Magpie.

IDENTIFICATION: Replaces Black-billed Magpie in the sheltered valleys of central California; the two species do not overlap although Black-billed is an occasional winter vagrant to the region and breeds further north and east in California. Easily identified by clear bright yellow bill and patches of bare skin about eye, it is also a somewhat smaller and slimmer bird.

DESCRIPTION: Length 38-45 cm. Structure as Black-billed Magpie, but smaller and sleeker, with slightly shorter bill and culmen a little more curved. Nasal bristles form more pointed patch at either side of base of upper mandible. Bare patches of skin both above and more conspicuously below eye. Orbital-ring a little more swollen. Plumage as Black-billed Magpie of race hudsonia colour and pattern. Bill, patches of skin about eye, orbital-ring and soles of feet bright yellow. Legs black. Irides dark brown.

SEX/AGE: Sexes similar, juvenile dull greyish black on head and breast until first moult.

MEASUREMENTS: A comparison between Yellow-billed Magpie and North American race (hudsonia) of Black-billed Magpie is given.

	Wing	Tail	Tarsus	Bill	Weight
Yellow-billed	182-196	224-254	44-50	30-32	156-189
Black-billed	182-211	232-302	43-50	31-39	135-209

GEOGRAPHICAL VARIATION: Monotypic.

VOICE: The chattering call is typically magpie-like but compared to European birds is somewhat softer, more nasal and higher in pitch, and uttered in slower bursts of three to five notes. Also freely given is a nasal, whining jay-like 'qwiieeee' which is quite unlike any call of European magpie. Calls are said to be identical to hudsonia race of Black-billed Magpie, which seems to be vocally different from European forms, but recordings indicate that the chatter is distinctly higher and less gruff than in hudsonia.

HABITS: Mainly as Black-billed Magpie, but more sociable, having communal feeding areas which may be shared by several colonies. Pairs have life-long bond; mated pairs holding territory throughout the year, averaging 1.2 ha per pair. Territorial size shrinks in breeding season to allow 'colonial' breeding activities, but increases once young leave nesting tree. Parties of non-breeders are more mobile and roam over quite extensive areas of the valley bottom and wooded slopes. Generally more bold and less fearful of man than Black-billed, many nesting areas being adjacent to houses.

BREEDING: Nests in loose colonies but not more than one nest per tree. Nests invariably in taller trees than Black-billed, at 15 to 20 m from ground, usually by water. Of similar construction, built by both sexes. Like Black-billed usually builds a new nest each year, sometimes on top of old one, or may re-use old one. Clutch five to eight. Eggs like those of Black-billed. Incubation about 18 days by female. Fed by both sexes. Young fed for about seven weeks after leaving nest. Typically a pair of American Kestrels breed in an old magpie nest in each 'colony.'

HABITAT: Farmland with stands of tall trees and orchards, also wooded slopes of hill valleys after breeding. Freely around habitation and closely associated with waterside trees. Intolerant of extremes of climate, thus confined to sheltered valleys which partly explains restricted range.

DISTRIBUTION: Endemic to California. Confined to an area approximately 250 km wide and 830 km long. The central valleys of California, west of the Sierra Nevada, chiefly in the Sacramento and San Joaquin valleys from Shasta county south to counties of Ventura and Kern; also in coastal valleys from Ventura northwest to San Francisco. Very sedentary but occasional birds have wandered up the Pacific coast as far as Oregon.

STATUS: Common to locally abundant over relatively small range.

REFERENCES: Birkhead 1991, Goodwin 1986.

STRESEMANN'S BUSH-CROW *Zavattariornis*

A monotypic genus. An extraordinary corvid: its overall shape and small size suggest an affinity to the ground-jays of central Asia although in plumage colouration it is surprisingly similar to Clark's Nutcracker of North America whilst its bulky tree-top stick nest indicates a distant relationship with the magpies. All of these factors, coupled with its very restricted range in southern Ethiopia, make it one of the most intriguing of all corvids - perhaps it is a surviving relict population of an ancient ancestor to several of these groups.

STRESEMANN'S BUSH-CROW   Plate 25

Zavattariornis stresemanni

Alternative names: Zavattariornis, Ethiopian or Abyssinian Bush-Crow

This peculiar starling-like corvid was not described until 1938 and it remains a mysterious crow of remote southern Ethiopia.

IDENTIFICATION: A medium-sized grey passerine of acacia savannah, recalling a starling rather than a crow. The overall grey head and body plumage contrasts strongly with the black wings and tail and superficially resembles the colouration of non-breeding Wattled Starling, but differs in being purer grey, the bill and legs are black (not fleshy, except in juveniles) and has bright blue (not yellow) bare skin about eye. Additionally the bush-crow is a little larger and relatively longer-tailed than Wattled Starling and does not form large flocks.

Wattled Starling *Creatophora cinerea*

DESCRIPTION: Length 28 cm. Bill relatively small, slightly decurved, sharply pointed. Tail medium, almost square at tip. Nasal tuft inconspicuous, whitish. Head, mantle, scapulars, back, rump and uppertail-coverts pale grey, more pale bluish-grey in fresh plumage, shading almost whitish on forecrown and uppertail-coverts. Face and throat creamy-white shading pale grey on breast and flanks and whitish again on belly and undertail-coverts. Lesser and median coverts pale grey, tail and remainder of wing slightly glossy, blue-black. When worn upperparts become slightly tinged brownish due to bleaching of feather tips. Bare loral skin, extending to surround eye, bright blue. Bill and legs black. Irides dark brown.
AGE/SEX: Plumages similar; juvenile duller, more brown-

ish grey, with creamy-fawn fringes to body feathers and forewing, uppertail-coverts brownish-grey with paler fringes; bare facial skin, bill and legs duller, possibly fleshy-grey.
MEASUREMENTS: Little data. Wing 137-150, tail 117-122, tarsus 33-37, bill 33-39, weight - no information.
GEOGRAPHICAL VARIATION: Monotypic.
VOICE: Poorly documented. The only call described is a high-pitched "chek".
HABITS: Little information. Normally encountered in pairs or small parties of six or so birds in areas of large acacias. Feeds both on ground and in trees, often mixed with parties of starlings, especially White-crowned Starlings. Little information on diet, although known to be insectivorous; J.S. Ash (*in litt*) recorded watching a party of six feeding on dead termites together with 20 Red-billed Hornbills, 20 Superb Starlings and ten Red-billed Buffalo Weavers.
BREEDING: Solitary nester. Benson (1946) recorded that there often seem to be three birds in attendance at the nest but the significance of this is unknown. Nest an untidy globular structure, tapering to a point on the roof which has an entrance tunnel to the internal chamber; it is some 30 cm in length and 60 cm in diameter, constructed of thorny twigs; the nest chamber is some 30 cm in diameter and is lined with dry grass and dried cattle dung; access is via a vertical tunnel in the roof. This peculiar nest is usually situated some 5 or 6 m high at the summit of an acacia. Clutches of six eggs have been recorded; they are creamy with pale lilac blotches, concentrated in a ring at the larger end. No details known on incubation period etc. Eggs recorded in March; large young in nest and recently fledged family groups recorded early June.
HABITAT: Acacia scrub in park-like country of short-grass savanna, below 2000 m.
DISTRIBUTION: Endemic to an area of some 2400 sq kms around Yabelo, Mega and Arero in Sidamo province, south-western Ethiopia.
STATUS: Extremely local but quite common in its restricted range. Absent from areas of virtually identical habitat nearby. In February 1989 recorded as quite plentiful to the north and east of Yabelo, but none seen to the north-west of the town. A major threat to this unique bird is clearance of acacia scrub for cultivation and further habitat degradation by over-grazing of domestic herds. The Ethiopian Wildlife Conservation Organisation is in the process of establishing a field station at Yabelo in conjunction with the University of Oslo; it is hoped that subsequent research will help in the conservation of the bush-crow and the White-tailed Swallow which is also endemic to this district.
REFERENCES: Ash and Gullick 1989, Benson 1946, Urban 1980.

GROUND-JAYS *Podoces and Pseudopodoces*

Ground-Jays (also known as 'Ground-Choughs') are terrestrial birds of central Asian desert scrub (*Podoces*) and Tibetan steppe (*Pseudopodoces*); they are a remarkably distinct group of birds, quite unlike other corvids in colouration or shape, perhaps most closely-related to nutcrackers (certainly in flight the shape is not dissimilar) and bearing no resemblance to either jays or choughs. Indeed in basic shape, behaviour and colouration *Podoces* species recall Hoopoe Lark, whereas the plain little Hume's is very suggestive of Isabelline Wheatear - a fine example of parallel evolution producing superficially similar species which are quite unrelated.

Ground-Jays feed principally by digging with their strong, curved bills for insects, especially beetles; they also pick seeds and grain from the ground or from amongst camel and horse droppings; small lizards are also a prey item but it is not known how these are taken; perhaps they drop on them from bush tops in the manner of shrikes as *Podoces* species spend a lot of time perched on bush tops.

The normal gait is a strutting, somewhat waddling walk, but if surprised they run remarkably quickly, holding their bodies in a horizontal posture, scuttling along dune slopes and hiding behind bushes. They run extremely well on their relatively long legs and can be very frustrating birds to follow in difficult terrain, e.g. dunes of soft sand. In flight the broad wings show extensive areas of white making them very conspicuous; the flight action is rather slow and slightly undulating, generally not over long distances, merely flapping along for a short distance at bush-top height before alighting and running-on; they are reluctant to take to the wing, preferring to escape from intruders by running but if young or nest are nearby they seem to show themselves by flying from bush to bush, calling excitedly to distract a potential predator or intruder.

Sexes are similar in plumage and juvenile plumages differ little from that of the adults in most species.

In the western China (Sinkiang)/Kazakhstan border region the ranges of four of the species come very close to each other but only Biddulph's and Henderson's actually overlap, and even then the two species occupy rather different habitats. Thus over most of central Asia only one species is to be found, limiting the chances of confusion between them.

HENDERSON'S GROUND-JAY Plate 19

Podoces hendersoni

The most northerly ground-jay, with a range centred on the flat deserts of Mongolia and Sinkiang.

IDENTIFICATION: Only likely confusion is with similar and overlapping Biddulph's, but Henderson's easily separated by wholly black (not chiefly white) tail and black on head restricted to crown (extensive black also on malar region in Biddulph's). Henderson's is also slightly stouter-billed than Biddulph's and is distinctly darker, less whitish and pinkish in overall colouration and has a little less white on the wing. Habitat also differs, Henderson's favouring flatter, more stony or gravel desert whereas Biddulph's prefers sandy deserts. In flight Henderson's shows black wings with strikingly (almost wholly) white primaries. Pander's differs in having a black patch on breast (lacking in juveniles), lacks black on crown, has shorter uppertail-coverts (thus exposed tail seems longer), has much more white (appearing almost white-winged) in flight, and favours sandier desert.

DESCRIPTION: Length 28 cm. Bill relatively slender and curved. Nasal tuft inconspicuous, sandy. Rear crown slightly loose-feathered. Uppertail-coverts long, extending over basal half of tail. Crown black, glossed bluish or purplish; remainder of head, to above eye, neck, underparts and upperparts rusty-buff, richest on scapulars, rump and uppertail-coverts, becoming whiter on throat and bleaching to a yellowish-buff. Wings glossy blue-black, except for white primaries which have black bases and tips and rusty-buff lesser wing-coverts; some birds have white extending onto inner webs of outermost three secondaries. Tail blue-black.

Bill and legs black. Irides dark brown.

AGE/SEX: Plumages similar. Juvenile has black of wings duller, not glossy, and greater coverts and crown feathers tipped buff, the buff tips soon wearing away.

MEASUREMENTS: Male averages slightly larger than female. Wing 130-142, tail 100-107, tarsus 41-46, bill 42-45, weight (one) 149.

GEOGRAPHICAL VARIATION: Monotypic.

VOICE: Poorly documented. Calls have been described as similar to the 'clack, clack, clack' of a wooden rattle and as a harsh whistle. Other documentation suggests calls are similar to those of Pander's.

HABITS: Usually met with in pairs or family parties. Generally shy and elusive. Often first noticed running at remarkable speed on ground, disappearing behind bushes. Only flies if hard pressed or to draw attention to itself if intruder near young, when it perches on bush tops and flies to next bush. Feeds by digging with strong curved bill for insects and also recorded picking grain from droppings of domesticated animals.

BREEDING: Data sparse. Nest a compact structure of twigs and roots, lined with camel hair; situated on the ground amongst boulders or at the base of a small bush. Clutch and eggs unrecorded. Small young found in nests in first half of May; nest with almost fledged young recorded in latter part of June in Kazakhstan; in Chinese Turkestan nest with well-fledged young recorded mid to late April.

HABITAT: Flat stony or gravel desert, with scattered bushes (especially Caragana and to a lesser extent Tamarisks) and small trees; possibly locally in more sandy deserts.

DISTRIBUTION: Deserts of southern Mongolia and north-western China (western Inner Mongolia, northern Sinkiang and northern Kansu), range just extending into Kazakhstan in region of Zaizan Nor.

STATUS: Certainly very rare in Kazakhstan and distinctly uncommon in southern Mongolia. In China probably relatively uncommon, but wide range and desolate habitat suggest, that it is not under threat. Over-grazing of desert scrub, especially by domestic herds of camels may pose local problems however.
REFERENCE: Dement'ev and Gladkov 1954.

BIDDULPH'S GROUND-JAY Plate 19

Podoces biddulphi

Alternative name: White-tailed Ground-Jay

Closely-related to Henderson's, sharing latter's long uppertail-coverts and black crown; this inhabitant of sandy deserts of western China seems to have become much rarer in recent decades.

IDENTIFICATION: Only Henderson's overlaps with this species, but Biddulph's has almost wholly white tail, although juveniles may show some dusky tail markings (Henderson's has wholly black tail); Biddulph's has black sides of throat and malar region and speckled throat centre so that in most views appears to have extensive black throat (Henderson's has black confined to crown). Biddulph's has a longer and slimmer, curved bill than Henderson's and is distinctly paler, more pinkish-sandy overall and shows white trailing edge to black secondaries (Henderson's lacks white trailing edge). Habitat also differs, Henderson's favouring flatter, more stony or gravel desert whereas Biddulph's prefers sandy deserts.
DESCRIPTION: Length 28 cm. Bill long, slender and curved. Nasal tuft inconspicuous, sandy. Rear crown slightly loose-feathered. Uppertail-coverts long, extending over basal half of tail. Crown black, glossed bluish or purplish. Throat dull black with white feather tips giving mottled effect, appearing blacker with wear. Sides of throat and malar area dull black with faint pale feather tips, extending to small patch behind eye. Remainder of head, to above eye, neck, underparts and upperparts pinkish-sandy buff, much paler below and bleaching to almost creamy-buff. Wings glossy blue-black, except for white primaries which have black bases and tips, white alula and broad white tips to secondaries; lesser wing coverts sandy-buff. Tail white with dark streaks by shafts, not extending to tips. Bill and legs black. Irides dark brown.
AGE/SEX: Plumages similar. Juvenile has black of crown and wings duller, not glossy, and greater coverts tipped buff-brown; tail feathers with more extensive, but diffuse, dusky markings. Bill and legs greyish-brown rather than black.
MEASUREMENTS: Male averages slightly larger than female. Wing 148-155, tail 103-108, tarsus 46-48, bill 54-58, weight - no information.
GEOGRAPHICAL VARIATION: Monotypic.
VOICE: Poorly documented. Two types of call have been described: 'a thrice repeated "chui-chui-chui", the last syllable on a higher note' and 'a succession of low whistles in rapidly descending scale'.
HABITS: See introduction to genus. Usually met with in pairs or family parties. Generally shy and elusive. Moves rapidly over ground with a fast corvid-like 'waddle'

rather than a direct run. Seems to take to the wing more readily than other ground-jays, even flying for considerable distances on rather weak, laboured wing-beats. Perches readily on bushes and small trees into which it will take cover when approached. Feeds by digging vigorously in sand with strong curved bill. Stomach contents include both insects and grain, the latter presumably picked from droppings of domesticated animals.
BREEDING: Nests within bushes and small trees, about a metre from ground but possibly also in holes in ground; a structure of twigs with a deep cup of wool, hair, dry grass, fluffy seeds and leaves. Clutch: 1-3. Eggs light bluish-green, profusely speckled and blotched with various shades of brown. Nests with eggs found in March.
HABITAT: Sandy desert with shrubs and small trees (particularly poplars).
DISTRIBUTION: Endemic to the Tarim Basin of Sinkiang (western China), from Tarim Azne east to Lop Nur.
STATUS: Almost certainly this species has seriously declined since 1930 when it was reported as being 'very plentiful' between Tarim Azne and the Yarkand River and between Kashgar and Aksu. A recent (1988) visit to the area failed to record any between Kashgar and Aksu but a family party was discovered near Korla. Degradation of the desert vegetation by over-grazing and by cutting for fire-wood, plus increasing irrigation is probably the reason for this apparent decline.
REFERENCES: Grimmett 1991, Ludlow and Kinnear 1933.

PANDER'S GROUND-JAY Plate 19

Podoces panderi

Alternative name: Grey Ground-Jay

Forms a species-pair with Pleske's of Iran, both having pale legs, short upper tailcoverts, chest patches and are pale-crowned unlike the previous two species. The most studied of the ground-jays.

IDENTIFICATION: The only ground-jay in its range, although the little known relict population by Lake Balkash comes close to the western limit of Henderson's. Differs from Henderson's in having plain sandy-grey (not black) crown, a black chest patch (absent in juveniles), whitish (not black) legs, short black (not long rusty-buff) upper tailcoverts, white (not black) secondaries and much greyer plumage overall. When perched, white bar at tips of greater coverts contrasts with black bar at bases of flight feathers, but bird is transformed in flight when virtually the whole of the wing appears white at any distance; Henderson's has black wings with most of primaries white. Habitat also differs, Henderson's favouring flatter, more stony or gravel desert whereas Pander's prefers sandy deserts. Only other bird in its habitat with undulating flight action and largely white wings is White-winged Woodpecker.
DESCRIPTION: Length 25 cm. Bill medium, slender, slightly curved. Nasal tuft inconspicuous, sandy-grey. Uppertail-coverts short. Loral patch black, widening towards eye. Large black patch on upper breast (absent in juveniles); underparts below breast patch rosy-grey

becoming whiter ventrally. Upper tail coverts glossy black. Remainder of head and upperparts sandy-grey, throat whiter. Primaries and secondaries almost wholly white, but with black tips to primaries and bases to primaries and secondaries; tertials black with white tips; lesser wing coverts grey, median coverts banded black and white, greater coverts black with white tips. Tail glossy blue-black. Bill black. Legs greyish-white. Irides dark brown.

AGE/SEX: Plumages similar. Juvenile buffer, less grey, above, lacks chest patch and has greyer loral patch; bill shorter and pink when first fledged, becoming greyer.

MEASUREMENTS: Male slightly larger than female. Wing 107-125 (male 113-125, female 107-115), tail 92-93, tarsus 43-45, bill 25-31, weight 87-95.

GEOGRAPHICAL VARIATION: Probably monotypic, birds from Transcaspia (*transcaspius*) and from Lake Balkash (*ilyensis*) have been separated on minor colour tone differences, but effects of wear and bleaching make this difficult to evaluate and neither were admitted by Vaurie (1954).

VOICE: Call a clear, ringing 'chweek-chweek-chweek-chweek', given from bush top especially in early morning or evening. Similar sound, but more emphatic, given by distressed adults when intruder in vicinity of nest or young.

HABITAT: Usually met with in pairs or family parties. Generally shy and elusive. Moves rapidly over ground when disturbed, running with horizontal body but head held up, sometimes with wings partially-opened and executing long, low bounds assisted by wings. Although perches readily and for long periods on bush tops, particularly in morning and evening, does not enter bushes or trees as does Biddulph's. Flies with great reluctance, but in flight the stunning white wings and slowly undulating flight action draw rapid attention to it; generally only flies for short distances before alighting and running-on. Prefers to run until out of sight of intruder, then hides behind base of shrub. Feeds along sandy tracks, digging at animal droppings with to-and-fro bill movements and rummaging at bases of bushes. In winter chiefly feeds on seeds and has habit of creating food storage spots by burying food in sand; sometimes scavenges through human rubbish along caravan trails, looking for grain, rice etc. Much more insectivorous in spring and summer when prey items include beetles, ants, woodlice, scorpions and spiders; also small lizards. Often said to have no need of water, but other reports suggest that they visit wells and cattle troughs to drink.

BREEDING: Nests within bushes and small trees amongst bushy dunes, up to a metre above ground, rarely as high as two metres; occasionally nests in disused huts and on ground, but reports of ground hole nesting have not been confirmed; nest a twiggy structure, often with a weak dome of twigs, rather wide (to prevent overheating) and with a deep cup lined with hair, wool, rags and leaves. Clutch four to five, rarely six. Eggs pale bluish-green to greyish, speckled and blotched with various shades of brown. Breeding season rather long, eggs have been found between late February and late May, but main laying period late March and early April. Incubation, 16-19 days begins with third or fourth egg, by female alone, being fed on nest by male; young fledge at some 17-18 days, young being fed chiefly on small invertebrates but with some grass seeds.

HABITAT: Sandy desert with dunes and good coverage of shrubs (particularly saxaul but avoids densest saxaul 'forest' thickets).

DISTRIBUTION: Deserts of central and northern Turkmenistan, northern and central Uzbekistan and very locally in Kazakhstan (south-east of Lake Balkash). Mainly resident but some dispersal outside breeding season to areas where not known to breed.

STATUS: In Turkmenistan earlier this century found to be numerous in Kara Kum (highest density: ten birds per 12 km transect in central part of this desert, thinning out considerably in southern and northern parts); said to be common in Kyzyl Kum desert (Uzbekistan) but isolated Balkash population very scarce, only five birds located in 1000 km transect in 1949. Remains relatively numerous in virgin desert (e.g. Repetek reserve in Turkmenistan) but has no doubt decreased considerably in other areas through intensive irrigation and destruction of desert vegetation for fuel and through over-grazing by domestic animals.

REFERENCES: Bardin 1988, Dement'ev and Gladkov 1954, Sopyev 1964.

PLESKE'S GROUND-JAY   Plate 19

Podoces pleskei

Alternative name: Persian Ground-Jay

The only endemic bird of Iran, very closely related to Pander's, which it replaces south of the Kopet Dag on the eastern Iranian plateau.

IDENTIFICATION: The only ground-jay in Iran, very similar to Pander's but sandy-buff overall, lacking grey in its plumage; has smaller breast patch, is slightly longer-billed and has much more black in wings - the black wings crossed by a wide white band, narrowing on outer primaries and inner secondaries (in flight wings chiefly white in Pander's). Most likely to be confused with Hoopoe Lark which, however, has dark grey breast streaks (not a solid black patch), grey-brown tail with white outer feathers (tail wholly black in the ground-jay), greyish (not black) bill, lacks black and white banding on wing-coverts and does not show such strikingly black and white wings in flight.

Hoopoe Lark *Alaemon alaudipes*

DESCRIPTION: Length 24 cm. Bill medium, slender, distinctly curved. Nasal tuft inconspicuous, streaked black and buff. Uppertail-coverts short. Loral stripe black, extending slightly behind eye. Black patch on upper breast (absent in juveniles). Remainder of head and body plumage of both upper and underparts sandy-buff, with pinkish tones, becoming whitish on throat and face. Primaries black with broad white band, narrowing on outermost feathers; secondaries black with broad white tips, which become broader on outermost feathers; greater coverts black with broad white tips forming a bar; median coverts banded black and white; lesser coverts buff. Tail glossy blue-black. Bill black. Legs greyish-white. Irides dark brown.

AGE/SEX: Plumages similar. Juvenile lacks breast patch and probably has a pinkish bill as in Pander's.

MEASUREMENTS: Male averages a little larger than female. Wing 120-121, tail 91-92, tarsus 45-47, bill 36-41, weight 85-90.

GEOGRAPHICAL VARIATION: Monotypic.

VOICE: Call has been described as a clear, rapid (ten notes per second) and high-pitched 'pee-pee-pee-pee-pee' given from bush top, especially in early morning or evening, recalling distant song of Rock Nuthatch.

HABITS: Little studied, probably very similar to Pander's. Generally shy and elusive and met with singly or in pairs. Runs rapidly over ground when disturbed. Perches readily on bush tops, particularly in cool of morning and evening, flaunting tail as it calls. Flies with great reluctance, only for short distances before alighting and running to hide behind shrubby cover.

BREEDING: Virtually undocumented. Zarudny (1911) stated that the nest is constructed in bushes, generally about a metre from the ground, higher if bushes are large, and resembles the nest of the Desert Finch (but is presumably rather larger). Clutches recorded are four and six eggs.

HABITAT: Sandy desert with with scattered shrubs.

DISTRIBUTION: Desert depressions of eastern Iran, chiefly in the Dasht i Lut of Khorasan and extreme eastern Kerman; northernmost record from northern Semnan (Sharud), recorded south to Iranian Baluchistan. Could possibly occur just over border into Pakistani Baluchistan and perhaps even extreme western Afghanistan but so far unrecorded outside Iran.

STATUS: No information, but seems to be sparsely distributed.

REFERENCES: Hollom et al 1988, Sharpe 1907, Zarudny 1911.

HUME'S GROUND-JAY   Plate 19

Pseudopodoces humilis

Alternative names: Little or Tibetan Ground-Jay, Hume's Ground-pecker

The world's smallest corvid, a mouse-brown terrestrial bird of the high Tibetan plateau, this peculiar crow bears a superficial resemblance to a wheatear.

IDENTIFICATION: A small dull brownish ground-jay of grassy and stony plateaux, plumage rather featureless apart from off-white outer tail feathers which are often

shown as bird bounds around or in weak, fluttering flight. The strong, curved bill and digging feeding action prevent confusion with Isabelline Wheatear with which it might be mistaken at longer ranges.

DESCRIPTION: Length 19 cm. Bill short, thin and distinctly curved. Body plumage soft and slightly fluffy. Nasal tuft inconspicuous whitish. Head and most of upperparts dull mouse-brown with whitish area on nape and dusky loral stripe. Wings slightly darker brown, with brown and white barred alula. Throat, lower sides of head and whole underparts off-white, washed buff on sides of head, throat and breast. Tail white with dark brown central feathers. Bill and legs black. Irides dark brown.

AGE/SEX: Plumages similar. Juvenile shows weak barring on throat and breast and has bill and legs greyer, the latter quite fleshy-grey.

MEASUREMENTS: Sexes virtually identical in size. Wing 84-99, tail 52-64, tarsus 27-34, bill 20-28, weight 42-48.

GEOGRAPHICAL VARIATION: Probably monotypic. Easternmost birds have been described as being smaller and darker and have been named *saxicola*, but Vaurie (1954) found that individual variation made these distinctions invalid.

VOICE: Call is a weak, somewhat prolonged 'cheep'. Also gives a short 'chip' followed by a prolonged, rapidly whistled 'cheep-cheep-cheep-cheep'.

HABITS: Generally encountered in pairs or family parties. Often remarkably confiding, especially around human settlements and isolated monasteries, but away from human contact often shy and timid. Feeds on ground, digging with its strong bill amongst yak droppings and in grassy turf for beetles and other invertebrates. Very energetic, flicking and bounding about on the plains like a wheatear, perching readily on walls, rocks and even roof tops of low buildings. Flicks wings and tail and bows and curtsies as it perches; on ground literally bounces along, pausing with head high before bending vigorously to dig in the ground. Flight low, very weak and fluttering, generally only over short distances, preferring to leap away in little bounds when closely approached and only flying as a last resort. Roosts in holes excavated by the bird, using old nest sites for non-breeding roosting.

BREEDING: Excavates its own nesting holes in low banks, stone walls and buildings, seemingly not using old rodent holes. Holes can be up to two metres in length, at the end of which is a small chamber in which the open nest of grasses and mosses is constructed on a base of wool or animal hair. The clutch of four to six unmarked white eggs are laid from late May and throughout June. Young are fed by both parents at the nest and for a considerable time after fledging.

HABITAT: Grassy plains and foothill slopes, with scattered boulders and very sparse scattered bushes, above the tree-line. Recorded in breeding season up to 5335 m. Favours yak-grazed pastures but also feeds in rough cultivation near monasteries and small settlements.

DISTRIBUTION: Western China, extreme northern India (north Sikkim) and extreme northern Nepal (Dolpo, Mustang) to the north of the Himalayas. In China range extends over the Tibetan plateau region to southern and western Sinkiang (few records in the west), southern Gansu and western Sichuan.

STATUS: Seems to be quite common over most of its range.

REFERENCES: Ali 1962, Ali and Ripley 1972.

NUTCRACKERS *Nucifraga*

A small genus of two, possibly three, species, with relatively short tails, broad wings and long, pointed, straight bills. They are forest birds, closely associated with montane coniferous forests. Nutcrackers are specialised feeders, on pine seeds and nuts, and they have a ridge on the inside of the lower mandible which enables the bird to crack nuts with relative ease; below the tongue is a well-developed pouch which allows them to carry quite large numbers of nuts and seeds either back to the nest or to their personal store. These food stores are scattered throughout the territory of each pair, each individual bird of a pair having numerous stores of its own. They are therefore probably the most important planters of northern forests, aiding the spread of young trees in more open areas where the nuts would otherwise be unlikely to fall. Their dependance on certain species of conifer does have some disadvantages; in years of high seed production their breeding successes are high, but in seasons of seed failure a percentage of the birds have to move out of their native forests in search of new food sources. It seems likely that few of these return and such movements are a natural control of high populations. They are the only known corvids in which the male shares incubation duties with the female.

SPOTTED NUTCRACKER   Plate 12

Nucifraga caryocatactes

Alternative names: Nutcracker, Eurasian Nutcracker

A beautifully marked crow, widespread in pine forests of Europe and Asia. Notable for its dependance on the Arolla Pine, although some populations feed principally on hazel-nuts.

IDENTIFICATION: Distinctive short-tailed, broad-winged corvid of coniferous forests. At long ranges appears all dark with white ventral region and tail corners, but closer views reveal profuse white spotting over entire body; populations of China and the Himalayas have small and indistinct spotting and even at moderate ranges appear merely brownish on body with blacker crown and wings, but show very striking white in tail and on vent like northern races. Relatively short tail and long bill give a distinctive silhouette when perched on tree top or in flight. Flight action, size and shape recalls a short-tailed Jay but white ventral region and most of tail underside gives an impression of a dark stocky bird with completely white rear end from below. On breeding grounds harsh calls attract attention, the bird usually calling from the top of a tall tree. See also Larger-spotted Nutcracker which is treated separately.
DESCRIPTION: Length 32-34 cm. Race *macrorhynchos*: Bill relatively long, pointed. Nasal tufts short and dense, whitish. Tail medium-short, slightly rounded at the corners. Crown and nape dark brown, darkest on forecrown. Lores white. Sides of head, neck and most of body plumage dark brown profusely marked with white, densest on sides of head where becomes almost whitish on face; spots largest on breast and most sparse on flanks and scapulars; rump and uppertail-coverts unmarked dark brown. Lower belly and undertail-coverts white. Wings glossy black, covert feathers tipped with white (chiefly lesser coverts). Underwing similar. Tail glossy black with broad white feather tips, increasing in extent towards outermost but only narrowly on central feathers; white most extensive from below with black visible only as narrow band at tail base when tail closed. Bill and legs black. Irides dark-brown.
AGE/SEX: Plumages similar; juvenile duller, with unglossed wings and tail and smaller body spotting. By

first autumn may be aged by some retained juvenile drab wing feathers, including white edge to tips of greater coverts (adults can have small white arrow-head marks here); ventral and lower nape plumage looser and softer in texture than adult. Much as adult by first spring.
MEASUREMENTS: Male averages slightly larger than female. Nominate race: wing 173-195, tail 115-136, tarsus 40-45, bill 39-52, weight 124-200.
GEOGRAPHICAL VARIATION: Eight subspecies, falling into two groups, are recognised here. However as might be expected from a largely sedentary, specialised, mountain forest bird a number of other races have been described which have involved local variations linked by clines. Some of the races listed here might be better linked in this way on a broader front e.g. *hemispila-macella-interdicta* (see Vaurie 1954). The well-marked form of the north-west Himalayas, *multipunctata*, is very distinct and does not fall into the pattern of clinal variation; as it virtually meets *hemispila* and retains its differences (although limited hybridisation is known) it is given separate treatment here as a potentially good species.
Northern group:-
Dark brown body plumage, profusely marked with white.
  N. c. caryocatactes: Europe east to the Urals. As *macrorhynchos*, but bill slightly thicker and shorter. Bill length 39-52, bill depth at widest point (distal of nasal tuft) 13-16.3. White tail tips narrower (12-23 mm on outermost).
  N. c. macrorhynchos: Siberia, from the Urals east to the Pacific, including Sakhalin. Bill length 42-53, bill depth at widest point (distal of nasal tuft) 11.5-13.8. White tail tips broader (19-32 mm on outermost).
  N. c. japonica: Japan and southern and central Kurile Islands. As *macrorhynchos* but bill shorter and stouter.
  N. c. rothschildi: Tien Shan mountains of western Sinkiang, Kirghizstan and extreme south of Kazakhstan. As *macrorhynchos* but a little larger and with a relatively stouter, shorter and more curved bill; darker, more blackish-brown ground colour to body plumage (wing 183-202).
Southern group:-
Medium brown body plumage, spotting smaller and less intense, chiefly confined to sides of head, breast and upper mantle. Tail relatively longer than in northern

races and with considerably more white in outermost feathers.

N. c. interdicta: northern Hopeh and Shansi (north China). Close to *macella* but ground colour of body plumage lighter brown and bill small.

N. c. macella: Yunnan and central China to Burma, Assam and Sikkim, intergrading into *hemispila* in eastern Nepal. Darker than *interdicta* and stronger-billed, Himalayan birds averaging lighter than those from Yunnan and with spotting extending onto central belly.

N. c. hemispila: Himalayas from Darjeeling westwards through Nepal to at least central Himachal Pradesh (its reputed occurrence in Pakistan needs confirmation). Intergrading into *macella* from central Nepal east-wards. Similar to *macella* but paler brown, spots on underparts averaging larger and more numerous; however, some are virtually unmarked below the breast. Juveniles lighter and warmer brown with buffish, rather than whitish markings.

N. c. owstoni: Taiwan. Ground colour of body sooty-brown; spotting similar in extent to other southern forms, i.e. small white spots confined to sides of head, breast and mantle.

VOICE: Usual call a dry, harsh 'kraaaak', rather prolonged and far-carrying; sometimes quickly repeated as a discordant rattle or shortened to a weaker 'zhree'. Somewhat softer and less frantically screeched than similar call of Eurasian Jay. Also has a quiet musical song of various piping, clicking, squeaking, whistling and whining notes, interspersed with some mimicry. Begging call of young a nasal goat-like bleat, often accompanied by a guttual 'kraak', given by fledged young following parents in forest.

HABITS: Usually solitary or in pairs; parties in summer of up to 200 have been recorded in Siberia but more typically groups of ten or so may be found outside the breeding season; these gatherings seem to allow birds nearing breeding age to select mates and can occur within established territories of a pair without attracting hostility. Experiments however have shown that if one of the visiting birds attempts to take food from the site, then the owners of the territory attack it. Nutcrackers pair for life and keep their territories throughout the year. Within these territories a pair builds up several stores of nuts and seeds to keep them going through the long, snow-covered northern winters, burying many thousands of food items each autumn, thus they are extremely important as distributors of new forest trees. The main food items are seeds of various species of conifers, especially pines, and hazel-nuts, but a variety of insects and other invertebrates are taken in summer and berries in autumn; in Siberia they are reported as taking fish or meat used as bait by fur-trappers and have been noted catching insects on the wing. During the massive invasion of Spotted Nutcrackers into Britain in 1968 a quite extraordinary variety of food items were taken, including a live rodent, house sparrows, cake, a Cornish pasty and bird table scraps! Clearly such birds must have been desperate for food. They feed both in trees and on the ground, where they move with jaunty hops as well as walking and running; nuts are wedged in a crevice or held by the feet and opened by hammering with the bill, whilst seeds are prised from cones and cracked in the bill. Vagrants which have reached western Europe are often remarkably confiding, showing no fear of humans whatsoever; perhaps these are mainly young birds as in their native ranges nutcrackers seem to be more wary of man although they are noisy and demonstrative if the nest is approached. The flight is generally low, swooping up to perch on a tree top, flicking wings and tail, but when flying over longer distances the flight action is quite direct, although with a rather hesitant flapping.

BREEDING: Solitary nester. The nest is a crow-like construction of twigs, interwoven with bramble shoots and lichen, the cup is lined with plant materials such as moss, grass and willow seeds. It is placed close to the trunk of a conifer, but on a base of smaller side-branches, typically at a height of about six m; the construction takes some twelve days. Clutch, two to five, usually three or four eggs, pale bluish, speckled and blotched light brown. Incubation 16-18 days by both sexes (nutcrackers are the only crows in which the male is known to share incubation). Young are fed at the nest by both parents for about 23 days and stay with the parents for three months or more after fledging. Breeding commences early: March in central Europe, Japan and the Himalayas, April in Finland and central Siberia, and early May in the Tien Shan.

HABITAT: Coniferous forests, but also in mixed forests where conifers dominate; prefers areas of open forest for prime foraging and equally at home both in flat taiga and montane alpine forests. In the Himalayas occurs up to 4000m. Vagrants during eruptive movements may turn up in almost any location with trees, including urban parks and gardens in coastal areas.

DISTRIBUTION: Northern races are mainly resident, from southern Norway, Sweden and Finland eastwards across the taiga zone to the Pacific, including Kamchatka, Korea, Sakhalin and Japan (south to Shikoku); southern limits are extreme northern Mongolia and north-eastern China, with an extension southwards through the Altai to the Tien Shan mountains. There are isolated populations in mountain forests of central and eastern Europe west to eastern France, south to northern Italy, Romania and Bulgaria. Southern races are widespread in montane forests of central and south-west China, south to Yunnan and extending westwards through northern Burma and the Himalayas to the borders of Kashmir; a very isolated population also occurs in the mountains of Taiwan.

INVASIONS: Although largely resident from time to time large numbers forsake their native forests and disperse in search of new food supplies. These invasions or eruptions are associated with failures in seed production of their dependant conifer species. This tends to happen after several seasons of good seed production which in turn builds up nutcracker population levels. Invasions have occurred in Europe some 25 times in the past 250 years, since the first reference to it in 1753. Some dispersed vagrancy is occasionally recorded from the European nominate form but large scale invasions are almost exclusively of the Siberian race; the most documented and perhaps the largest such eruption took place in 1968 (see Hollyer 1970), when many thousands invaded Europe from late July onwards; over 800 were reported from Belgium and 300 from Britain, with a few individuals getting as far as Portugal and North Africa. Further east there were reports of nut-crackers in the Gobi Desert of Mongolia at the same time but clearly the main movement was to the south-west as there were no reports of unusual numbers from south-east Europe in that year. Earlier movements have taken Siberian birds as far as the Crimea, Turkey, Iran, western Kazakhstan, the Caucasus and Japan.

STATUS: Clearly an abundant species over its wide distribution, although the localised Taiwan population might well be threatened by forest destruction.

REFERENCES: Coombs 1978, Goodwin 1986, Hollyer 1970, Swanberg 1951, Turcek and Kelso 1968.

LARGER-SPOTTED NUTCRACKER Plate 12

Nucifraga (caryocatactes) multipunctata

A distinct nutcracker of the western Himalayas, which is perhaps worthy of specific status.

IDENTIFICATION: Replaces Spotted Nutcracker in the western Himalayas, with a distribution to the north and west of race *hemispila* of that species, the two being separated in Kashmir by the Pir Panjal range. Some overlap undoubtedly occurs as birds with hybrid characters have been collected in the Kulu district of northern India. Larger-spotted is strikingly different in plumage: *hemispila* has only limited small white spotting and has the rump, uppertail-coverts and flanks unmarked brown; by contrast Larger-spotted has the entire body so heavily marked with white that it gives the appearance of being almost wholly greyish-white in the field, contrasting with black crown and wings; the rump and uppertail-coverts are spotted unlike all other forms and although the tail pattern is intermediate between northern and southern populations of Spotted Nutcracker it has wider white tips to the central feathers than any other form. In behaviour and calls however it is very similar.

DESCRIPTION: Length 35 cm. Slightly longer-tailed than adjacent *hemispila* race of Spotted Nutcracker. Crown and nape blackish. Sides of head and most of body blackish grey-brown, very heavily and broadly streaked, striped and spotted with white. Ventral region and undertail-coverts pure white. Rump and uppertail-coverts spotted and streaked white (unlike all races of Spotted Nutcracker which have these areas unmarked dark brown). Wings glossy black with white tips to coverts and secondaries (more extensive than in Spotted Nutcracker races). Tail glossy black with wide white tips, even to central feathers, white on outermost feathers extending some two-thirds towards base (*hemispila* has white reaching base but no or narrow white tips to central feathers). Bill and legs black. Irides dark brown.

AGE/SEX: Plumages similar. Juvenile has dull brown, not glossy black, wings and tail; spots on wing-coverts smaller and buffier. Entire body plumage more sandy-brown than adult with dull white feather centres and sandy-brown feather fringes; rump and uppertail-coverts darker brown and with smaller and duller spotting. By first autumn plumage similar to adult but may be aged by retained dull juvenile wing feathers and tail.

MEASUREMENTS: Male averages a little larger than female. Wing 195-212, tail 144-159, tarsus 43, bill 39-47, weight 155-177.

VOICE: Probably much as Spotted Nutcracker. Reported to have hoarse, grating calls but Bates and Lowther (1952) only heard repeated squealing cries, which they likened to the 'squealings of little pigs' but as their observations were made chiefly in May and June these could well refer to food-begging cries of the young.

HABITS: As Spotted Nutcracker, although not given to invasive wandering.

BREEDING: A notoriously difficult nest to find. Probably much as Spotted Nutcracker. Only empty nests presumed to be of this species have been described: a compact nest of twigs some 25 cm in diameter, with a large amount of lichens interwoven; the deep cup is lined with roots and pine-needles. It is placed against the main trunk of a large conifer, at least ten metres from the ground. Breeding seems to commence as early as late March or early April.

HABITAT: Oak and conifer forests, favouring a predominance of Blue Pine and spruce; chiefly between 2000 and 3000 m.

DISTRIBUTION: North-west Himalayas, from extreme eastern Afghanistan (Kunar valley and Safed Koh) through northern Pakistan (Safed Koh, Chitral, Gilgit, Baltistan) and Kashmir (north of the Pir Panjal range) to north-west India (Lahul region of Himachal Pradesh). Straggles lower in winter with records from Peshawar in the North West Frontier of Pakistan and nearby Fort Sandeman in northern Baluchistan.

STATUS: Seems to be rather patchily distributed but reported to be quite common in forests of Blue Pine above 2000 m.

TAXONOMY: This form does not fit into the pattern of clinal variation of either northern or southern races of Spotted Nutcracker. Perhaps like the Kashmir Red-breasted Flycatcher (which is usually regarded as a separate species from the Red-breasted Flycatcher of Siberia) it became isolated in the western Himalayas from northern origins. Its isolation might well have resulted in the exaggerated development of white spotting which renders it so different from the adjacent weakly-spotted *hemispila* race of Spotted Nutcracker which is presumed to have spread along the Himalayas from the east. The two forms may compete with each other, the established *multipunctata* perhaps pushing the invading *hemispila* along the southern Himalayan ranges. Such a situation suggests that *multipunctata* is reaching speciation level, but intermediate specimens from the Kulu region restrict its complete elevation to full species status until degree of hybridisation is better known.

REFERENCES: Ali and Ripley 1972, Bates and Lowther 1952, Paludan 1959, Vaurie 1954.

CLARK'S NUTCRACKER Plate 12

Nucifraga columbiana

A small grey nutcracker of western North America; despite the difference in colouration this bird is closely-related to the Spotted Nutcracker of the Old World and is presumed to have originated from the same ancestor.

IDENTIFICATION: A lovely dove-grey corvid with striking black eyes and bill, the grey head and body plumage contrasting with glossy black wings and tail. In flight shows stunning white outer tail feathers and white band on the secondaries; from below tail looks all white unless fanned. Unlikely to be mistaken for any other North American bird, although grey plumage and black and white wings might momentarily suggest Mockingbird; however, compare Grey Jay and Pinyon Jay which occur in the same habitat, neither of which shows black or white in wings and tail. Like the Grey Jay it is often extremely confiding and scavenges about campsites and settlements.

DESCRIPTION: Length 31 cm. Bill relatively long, slender, slightly decurved and pointed. Nasal tufts short and dense, whitish. Lores and face whitish, shading to dove grey over most of remainder of head and body plumage; rump slightly darker grey becoming blackish-grey on uppertail-coverts; lower belly and undertail-coverts white; with wear almost whole head may appear whitish. Wings glossy black with wide white tips to secondaries, except the tertials. Underwing similar. Tail white with glossy black central pair of feathers and some black markings on inner webs of next pair. Bill and legs black. Irides dark brown.

AGE/SEX: Plumages similar. Juvenile duller, more brownish-grey overall, with greyer legs and irides when recently fledged and duller wings and tail; much as adult by first autumn but may be aged by retained dull juvenile wing and tail feathers.

MEASUREMENTS: Male averages a little larger than female. Wing 188-194, tail 111-118, tarsus 33-38, bill 38-45, weight 106-161.

GEOGRAPHICAL VARIATION: Monotypic.

VOICE: Usual call a nasal, grating 'kraaaa', often repeated three or four times in succession; a sweeter, more musical version of this call is given in spring. When excited, e.g. mobbing predators, a high-pitched, penetrating metallic screech is freely and repeatedly uttered. Other calls more closely associated with breeding are are series of alternate cracking and whistling sounds, accompanied by bowing displays; young birds have a squealing food-begging call and a slow frog-like rattling is freely given by both sexes in their first year of life.

HABITS: Typically encountered in pairs or small parties, although larger gatherings of a hundred or more are frequent outside the breeding season (where attracted by rich food supplies) or during eruptive movements. Mated pairs hold their territories throughout the year, but may forage outside their area and are often remarkably tolerant of intruders visiting their own territories. Feeds mostly on the ground, chiefly walking as it forages for insects and fallen nuts; they also feed with remarkable agility in the trees, prising open cones with their specialised bills or flying with cones to a more substantial branch to break them open. Like the Spotted Nutcracker nuts may be wedged in a convenient crevice or held by the feet and hacked at until the shell is broken. They scavenge at campsites and farmsteads where they are quite fearless of humans, even entering tents and cabins in search of food scraps. Both small birds and their eggs, and small mammals are not infrequently taken and they have been noted digging into rotten logs for beetle larvae and turning over cow-pats for invertebrates. As in the Spotted Nutcracker much food is stored during the autumn; thousands of caches of nuts and seeds may be present over a hillside, each bird of a territorial pair having its own personal series of stores; these stores are the primary source of food given to the young in the nest in the following spring. In late winter males pursue the females over quite large distances, often carrying a twig. The flight action is low and undulating over short distances, reminiscent of a woodpecker, but when on longer flights is quite direct and rapid. They are very inquisitive birds and will follow animals such as a coyote or a deer for some time. They also enjoy swooping down over a canyon with closed wings, opening them to check their flight speed with a resultant loud rocket-swoosh. Despite their varied diet the major food items are the seeds of the Pinyon Pine and Whitebark Pine and as with the Spotted Nutcracker, if the crop fails swarms of Clark's Nutcrackers may leave the mountain forest and spread out all down the Pacific coastlands of North America; these eruptive movements take place roughly every 15 years. The longevity of corvids is well shown by a wild individual which was recovered 17 years after it had been ringed.

BREEDING: Solitary nester. The nest is a crow-like construction of twigs, interwoven with fibrous bark, especially around the edge of the nest cup; the cup is deep and thickly lined with fibrous bark and wood pulp. It is placed close to the end of a branch or near the crown of a juniper or pine at heights varying between three and 50 m. Clutch two to six, usually three, eggs pale green, spotted and flecked with varying shades of brown. Incubation 16-18 days. Young leave the nest between 22 and 28 days after hatching and follow the adults for several weeks before independence. Both sexes construct the nest and share in incubation and the feeding of the young. Egglaying begins in March.

HABITAT: Mountain conifer forests, especially juniper and pines, up to the upper limits of the treeline, between 1800 and 2500 m, but non-breeders down to 900 m. During eruptive movements birds may be encountered in a variety of habitats from urban gardens to coasts and even in the desert.

DISTRIBUTION: The Rocky Mountains and Sierras of south-west Canada and western United States, just entering extreme northern Mexico. Breeding range extends from northern limits in central British Columbia and south-west Alberta, south over western Montana, west and south-east Wyoming, eastern Washington, eastern Oregon, Idaho, Utah, western Colorado, Nevada, central and eastern California, eastern Arizona and western New Mexico; its range just enters Mexico in extreme northern Baja California. Eruptive dispersals have taken birds with varying degrees of frequency to central Alaska, Yukon, Saskatchewan, Manitoba, South Dakota, Nebraska, Kansas and west Texas but it is exceptionally rarely recorded in the Midwest states.

STATUS: Widespread and locally common over most of its main range.

REFERENCES: Bent 1946, Davis and Williams 1957 and 1961, Mewaldt 1956

CHOUGHS *Pyrrhocorax*

The two species of this genus differ from *Corvus* crows in having a smooth, not scaled, tarsus, very short, dense, nasal feathers and brightly-coloured bill and feet. Both are lovers of open rocky and grassy habitats, chiefly in mountainous regions although the Red-billed Chough also occurs on coastal cliffs in the extreme west of its range. Both species are highly gregarious and widely overlap in distribution: at times flocks occur together on the same mountain slopes, although the Alpine Chough has a preference for higher elevations than the Red-billed Chough, the latter favouring grassy slopes and plateaux with grazing animals. Both species feed primarily on invertebrates but the Alpine Chough also freely scavenges around human habitation.

ALPINE CHOUGH   Plate 20

Pyrrhocorax graculus

Alternative name: Yellow-billed Chough

With its more varied diet the Alpine Chough has become a familiar scavenger at ski resorts; in parts of Europe the development of the winter sports industry has greatly increased the population of this endearing crow.

IDENTIFICATION: The small clear yellow bill, often appearing whitish, is diagnostic when this crow is close but at longer ranges it can be easily confused with Red-billed Chough, which shares its habitat, red legs and gregarious habits. Alpine, even in silhouette, has a shorter bill and relatively smaller head and longer tail than Red-billed, the latter projecting well beyond wing tips when at rest (equalling wing tips in Red-billed). The flight shape also differs but can be difficult to judge accurately unless birds are directly overhead. However Alpine has a smaller head, less 'square' wings due to gradation of primary lengths and more curving trailing edge to wing, with more pinched appearance to wing base; the primaries are less strongly fingered and the tail a little longer and less square at the tip - the tail of Alpine being longer than width of base of wing, about equalling wing width on Red-billed. Calls are also quite diagnostic (see Voice). Beware recently-fledged Red-billed Chough which has shorter yellowish bill, but bill is dull, dingy orange or fleshy-yellow, not clear bright pale yellow of Alpine and such birds are invariably accompanied by adults. Usually found in flocks about boulder-strewn slopes and alpine pastures, wheeling about cliff faces and indulging in aerobatics; often quite tame at mountain resorts. Compare also Western Jackdaw, which has different calls, relatively larger head and stouter black bill, less bouyant flight, shorter wings and squarer-ended tail.

DESCRIPTION: Length 37-39cm. Bill, short small, slighty decurved. Nasal tufts very short, inconspicuous. Tail relatively long, slightly rounded towards tip. Entire plumage black, lightly glossed bluish-green on wings and tail. Bill yellow or orange-yellow, shading to slightly greenish towards base. Legs and feet red. Irides dark brown.

AGE/SEX: Plumages similar; juvenile dull, not glossy, black with horn-coloured bill, soon turning yellow; legs dull brownish or blackish, becoming red by first spring; first summer birds often remain duller than adults.

MEASUREMENTS: Male averages larger than female.

Race *digitatus*: wing 262-301 (male 274-301, female 262-273), tail 165-193, tarsus 41-48, bill 29-38, weight 191-244.

GEOGRAPHICAL VARIATION: Slight. Two races, differing only in size:-

P. g. graculus: Europe, North Africa, Turkey, Caucasus and northern Iran. Smaller and with weaker feet than the eastern race (wing 250-274; tail 150-167; bill 31-37).

P. g. digitatus: From the Lebanon, Syria and Iran (except north) eastwards over remainder of range. Differs from nominate only in having stronger feet and being larger (see measurements).

VOICE: Usual calls quite uncorvine: a sweet, rippling 'preeep' and a descending thin whistled 'sweeeoo', both calls varying somewhat in pitch and intensity, the latter recalling a squeaky version of the call of Red-billed Chough. A rolling 'churrr', possibly an alarm call, is often given and a succession of quiet warbling, chittering, squeaky and churring notes may be heard from birds feeding undisturbed or quietly resting together.

HABITS: Very sociable, travelling in flocks to and from roosting and feeding areas; parties break up into smaller groups when feeding and pairs seem to keep together within these groups. Flocks, often of well over 100 birds, soar and swoop over ridge-tops, then sweep down over mountainsides, with smaller groups breaking away to feed on slopes. In some places loosely associates with parties of Red-billed Choughs at good feeding spots, but typically replaces Red-billed at highest elevations. Works in small sub-groups over slopes, flitting a few metres between feeding patches, walking quite quickly, occasionally running and hop-stepping excitedly. Energetic, groups and pairs indulge in boisterous calling and displays, especially in winter and early spring. Natural food chiefly invertebrates, especially beetles and small snails, picked or dug from ground or rock crevices. Scavenges around human settlements taking all manner of scraps, but especially fond of sultanas and will take some carrion such as dead mice. Also feeds seasonally on berries and other fruit, perching awkwardly with much flapping on branches. Food-hiding not infrequent, but noted chiefly with human food scraps, which are pushed into rock crevices and covered over with rapid to-and-fro movements of the bill. Freely bathes and enjoys sunbathing. Descends to lower elevations in winter, reaching valley bottoms although does not go far down below treeline; indeed they will remain all winter at active ski-resorts. Very inquisitive and often remarkably confiding where unmolested, following mountain walkers and climbers and coming to windows for food. Wonderful flyers, adept at using air currents, swooping, gliding and tumbling with ease over rock faces and ridges. Roosts in caves or rock crevices, non-breeders forming large communal roosts.

BREEDING: Solitary nester; several pairs may breed in quite close proximity to each other, but there is no hard evidence for colonial nesting which has been suggested in some literature. Nest a bulky structure of twigs and roots, lined with grasses and fine roots, and situated in caves, rock chimneys and crevices or inside roof of building. Clutch three to six, average four. Eggs vary from cream to buff and pale greenish, clouded with greyish and speckled and blotched brown. Incubation 18-20 days, by female only who is fed at nest by male. Young fledge at about 30 days, being fed by both parents, and when fledged other adults may also feed young after family have joined flock. Breeding begins in late April or early May over most of its range.

HABITAT: High elevation mountain pasture, with rocky ravines and cliff faces; above treeline in summer, but in winter descends a little lower into high valleys. Locally around alpine villages and ski resorts. In Europe usually breeds between 1260 and 2880 m (but breeding recorded as low as 600 m in the Balkans), in North Africa from 2880 to 3900 m and in the Himalayas from 3500 to 5000 m; birds have been recorded following climbers as high as 8235 m in Nepal.

DISTRIBUTION: The mountains of central and southern Europe: from Spain (Pyrenees, Cantabric range, and Malaga), France (Pyrenees, Alps) through the Alps, Italy (Abruzzi range) and the mountains of south-eastern Europe, with more isolated populations in the Rif and Atlas of Morocco and on Corsica and Crete. In Asia it is found in the mountains of central and eastern Turkey, the Caucasus and the Zagros of western Iran; eastwards across the Elburz of northern Iran, central and northern Afghanistan, central Asia north through the Altai to the western Sayan mountains; throughout the Himalayan region, including southern Tibet to western Sinkiang and Sichuan. Its precise status in Syria, Israel and the Lebanon requires clarification; it possibly only visits Syria in winter and there have been no recent Lebanese records although there were reports of small numbers on Mt Hermon throughout the year in the 1970s. It has occurred as a vagrant to Czechoslovakia, Hungary, Gibraltar and Cyprus.

STATUS: Generally seems to be more abundant in Europe than in Asia but generally locally common throughout its range, with reports of increases in central Europe probably linked with easy pickings from ski-resort areas. Small numbers have been noted in the Malaga region of southern Spain since 1975, and are believed to be an offshoot of the Moroccan population.

REFERENCES: Blasco *et al* 1980, Buchel 1983, Goodwin 1981, Holyoak 1972.

RED-BILLED CHOUGH   Plate 20

Pyrrhocorax pyrrhocorax

Alternative names: Chough, Cornish Chough

Although largely a mountain bird, western populations inhabit coastal cliffs and inshore islands; a strange combination, but echoed by two other passerines, the Water/Rock Pipits and the Twite.

IDENTIFICATION: The slender, curved red bill and red legs are diagnostic. Confusion is only likely with Alpine Chough in high mountainous regions and the two species often occur together; but the flight silhouette of Red-billed, with broad markedly rectangular wings, strongly-fingered primaries and shorter, more square-ended tail are useful clues. Even in silhouette Alpine has a shorter bill and relatively smaller head and longer tail than Red-billed, the latter projecting well beyond wing tips when at rest (equalling wing tips in Red-billed). See also Alpine Chough for discussion. When bill colour is not discernible, the slender curved shape is often apparent at reasonable ranges. On the ground at long range, when bill and leg colour not obvious, Red-billed Choughs feed in a distinctive manner, digging strongly with their curved bills to displace surface vegetation and turning over small stones. Gregarious and very vocal by nature, most calls are diagnostic (see Voice). Flight is very buoyant with deep bounding progression and often indulges in aerobatics over cliff faces. Does not freely mix with other crows, although loosely associates with Alpine Chough and Western Jackdaw in places. The latter, although similar in size, has shorter, round-tipped wings, a longer tail and a chunkier head and bill.

DESCRIPTION: Length 36-40 cm. Bill, slender, decurved, upper mandible slightly overlapping lower. Nasal tufts very short, inconspicuous. Tail moderate, almost square-ended. Entire plumage velvet-black, slightly glossed bluish-purple or greenish on body, a little more glossy on wings and tail. Bill scarlet or crimson-red, sometimes pinkish-red. Legs and feet red. Irides dark brown.

AGE/SEX: Plumages similar; recently-fledged juvenile, dull, not glossy, black with shorter bill, darker and browner at very first but soon becoming orange, finally red by first autumn; legs pinkish brown or blackish at first, soon becoming red; invariably accompanied by adults at this stage which prevents confusion with Alpine Chough.

MEASUREMENTS: Male averages a little larger than female. See Geographical Variation for racial comparisons. Nominate race: wing 249-304, tail 126-145, tarsus 55-59, bill 41-56, weight 285-380.

GEOGRAPHICAL VARIATION: Slight: eight races were recognised by Vaurie (1959), differing in size and colour and intensity of plumage gloss.

P. p. pyrrhocorax: British Isles and possibly Brittany, although latter somewhat approach the next race. Smallest race (wing mean 273).

P. p. erythropthalmus: Europe (very fragmented), except Britain and Greece. Slightly larger (wing mean 293) and with greener plumage gloss than British birds.

P. p. barbarus: North Africa and the Canary Islands. Slightly larger than the last and gloss still greener; has longest and deepest bill of all races (bill 62-67, wing mean 303).

P. p. baileyi: Ethiopia. Dull, little gloss. The two Ethiopian populations are well isolated from each other and might be racially distinct (bill 60-66, wing 302-306).

P. p. docilis: Greece and Western Asia east to Afghanistan where it intergrades towards *himalayanus*.

Relatively larger but smaller billed than North African race; has a very green wash to plumage but gloss weak (bill 52-61, wing mean 315).

P. p. himalayanus: Himalayas and western and central China; birds from the western Himalayas are intermediate between this and *centralis*. The largest race and with tail proportionally longer than western forms; plumage gloss blue or bluish-purple (wing mean 318).

P. p. centralis: Central Asia (Pamirs and Turkestan). Resembles *himalayanus* but smaller and less intense blue, tail relatively even a little longer.

P. p. brachypus: Central and Northern China, Mongolia and southern Siberia. Very close to *centralis* but bill weaker.

VOICE: Usual call a high-pitched, almost hoarse 'chee-aw', uttered both in flight and on ground. Although distinctive, Western Jackdaw's vocabulary includes a similar call, but that of Red-billed Chough is clearer, more explosive and higher in pitch. Other calls are essentially variants of this call but more distinct is a harsh, scolding 'ker ker ker', seemingly given in alarm. Soft low warbling and chittering murmurs may also be heard from contented birds together.

HABITS: Gregarious at all times, with breeding birds freely joining parties of non-breeders when away from the nest. Paired birds stay together throughout the year and seem to keep in family groups within foraging flocks. Pairs defend a territory near the nest site, but often tolerate the presence of a third adult in the vicinity; the significance of this is unclear. Flocks roost communally in rock crevices and caves but paired birds roost together in caves at or near the nest site. In areas where Red-billed Choughs are still numerous flock numbers can be quite remarkable, especially in late summer when new families swell the numbers of non-breeders, and parties of over 200 are not unusual. They freely forage alongside Alpine Choughs and other corvids, although they prefer flatter, heavily-grazed plateaux to craggy slopes. Walking with a sauntering gait and jaunty hops they pause to dig and probe the surface of the ground; animal dung and small stones are turned over and small tufts of grass tugged-at and loosened as they methodically search for insects. Red-billed Choughs seem to have a number of favoured feeding spots which they investigate at various times of the day. Red-billed are more specialised feeders than Alpine Choughs, their diet consisting almost entirely of invertebrates chiefly ants, beetles and leatherjackets (crane-fly larvae), also earthworms and spiders; ants are probably the most important component of their diet, indeed they have even been reported hawking for flying ants. They are inquisitive but rarely become as confiding as the Alpine Chough, although in central Asia and Tibet they readily feed in close proximity to villages and settlements; in Mongolia they occur close to and within the capital Ulan Bator, breeding on modern buildings and foraging in fields near the city outskirts. They have occasionally been noted picking over picnic scraps left by hill-walkers. In the Himalayan region some damage to cereal crops has been documented, the birds breaking-off heads of ripening barley and thrashing them on the ground to extract the corn; in Britain they also feed on fallen grain in stubble fields in the autumn and winter. Red-billed Choughs are very vocal, calling excitedly upon taking wing and on the ground, with an upward flip of the wings; like the Alpine Chough they indulge in aerial acrobatics. Food-hiding has rarely been noted in the wild but is frequent with captive birds. Like the Alpine Chough they frequently sunbathe but unlike that species Red-billed has been observed to indulge in anting (rubbing ants over their feathers to extract formic acid which deters parasites from invading their plumage).

BREEDING: Solitary nester, although in the Tibetan region several nests have been reported in close proximity suggesting that some populations are semi-colonial. The nest of sticks, lined with wool (sometimes just wool) is quite large and is built in the dark recess of a cave or rock chimney; old buildings are freely used and in Tibet they have been reported nesting in the rooftops of monasteries and other buildings which are in use, exceptionally, as in Mongolia, including modern buildings within towns. Rarely a hole may be excavated in soft soils of a sandstone cliff, with tunnels up to a metre in depth being dug. Clutch three to five, rarely as many as nine but average four. Eggs vary from whitish to pinkish-buff or pale greenish, clouded with greyish and speckled and blotched brown. Incubation 17-21 days, by female only who is fed at nest by male. Young fledge at 36-41 days, being fed by both parents. Egg laying begins in late March in Britain, mid to late April in the Caucasus.

HABITAT: Craggy mountains with adjacent pastures, favouring areas where domestic animals create short-turfed grassland, e.g. yak and sheep pastures. In North Africa it is most numerous between 2000 and 2500 m, in the Himalayas chiefly between 2400 and 3000 m, but in summer ascends to 6000 m and has been recorded as high as 7950 m on Mt Everest. In winter moves to lower elevations but rarely below the treeline. The populations of Britain, Ireland and Brittany are virtually confined to rocky coasts and inshore islands, where they forage along the seashore as well as on adjacent grassland; coastal as well as inland areas are used on Palma in the Canary Islands and in north Wales.

DISTRIBUTION: Very fragmented in the west where it occurs in the British Isles (Ireland, Wales, Isle of Man and west Scotland), France (Brittany and the south), Spain and Portugal (widespread); further east in Europe relict populations are found in the Swiss and German Alps, the Italian Appenines and in Greece as well as on Sardinia and Crete. In Africa there are isolated populations on the Canary Islands (Las Palmas only), the mountains of Morocco and Algeria and two very isolated pockets in Ethiopia (Simien and Bale mountains). It is far more widespread in Asia, from central Turkey and the Caucasus eastwards across northern Iran and Afghanistan. It is found throughout the Himalayan and central Asian mountains north to the Sayan mountains, to the south of Lake Baikal. In China it is widespread in the northern and central mountain ranges, but absent from the intervening desert regions of Sinkiang and northern Tibet. In winter many birds descend to lower elevations and it has been recorded as a vagrant to the Lebanon, northern Israel and northern Egypt.

STATUS: Common, locally abundant over most of its Asian range but an isolated population in the southern Urals has long been extinct; an example of the abundance of this bird in parts of interior Asia is shown by

Mongolia, where in the city of Ulan Bator a population of between 50 and 100 pairs were considered breeding in 1977. It remains numerous in the Moroccan Atlas but there is no recent information from Algeria; in Tunisia it became extinct in the last century. The isolated Ethiopian population is quite numerous in its very limited range. Most European populations (apart from the British and Iberian) have long been in decline, hence present fragmented distribution. It has gradually disappeared from England over the last 175 years. The Brittany population decreased from 30-40 pairs in 1972 to 25 pairs in 1982, and is still declining. The 1982 census of British and Irish Red-billed Choughs produced some 850 non-breeding birds plus about 900 breeding pairs, 600 pairs occurred in Ireland; 140 in Wales; 65 in Scotland and 50 in the Isle of Man. The reasons for the European decline may be complex; in the Alps competition for breeding sites with Alpine Chough and Western Jackdaw has been suggested but in Britain it is considered that changes in land use are the major factor, with less rough grazing of coastal cliffs by sheep and cattle allowing taller, scrubby vegetation to take over and encroach upon what was formerly invertebrate-rich short maritime turf. This situation can be locally improved by the reversion to traditional cliff grazing techniques but recolonisation will take some time, although it is possible as juvenile dispersal is known to take place.

REFERENCES: Bignall and Curtis 1988, Bullock *et al* 1983, Darke 1971, Holyoak 1972, Kitson 1985, Roberts 1985, Ryves 1948.

PIAPIAC *Ptilostomus*

A monotypic genus. This long-tailed black African corvid recalls both magpies and *Corvus* crows in outward appearance but it is a unique form with a number of anatomical peculiarities, including the fact that it is one of the few passerines with merely 10, not 12, tail feathers. It might well be that like *Zavattariornis* of Ethiopia it is perhaps a surviving relic of a long extinct group of crows that have no close link with the present-day corvids; indeed both of these African aberrant crows share a remarkable superficial resemblance to quite different groups of starlings.

PIAPIAC   Plate 25

Ptilostomus afer

Alternative name: Black Magpie

An aberrant corvid of west and central Africa, which recalls Long-tailed Glossy Starling and has an association with *Borassus* palms.

IDENTIFICATION: A medium-sized long-tailed black bird of savannah woodland. Unlikely to be mistaken for other than one of the long-tailed glossy starlings, but head and bill quite different, having a bulky crow-like head, dark iris and a very stout dark or pinkish bill; all of the long-tailed glossy starlings have striking whitish or yellow irides, sleeker head and small, weak bill. Duller and browner primaries can give the appearance of having two-toned wings in flight, especially if seen from below and against the light. Moves through low scrub or palms in small parties, perching with a horizontal stance.

Long-tailed Glossy Starling *Lamprotornis caudatus*

DESCRIPTION: Length 35 cm. Bill stout, with arched culmen. Tail of ten relatively narrow and pointed feath-

ers, very long and strongly graduated. Nasal tuft very short and curved upwards, inconspicuous. Entire plumage black, lightly glossed with a purplish or bluish sheen. Rump and uppertail-coverts duller black. Primaries and adjacent secondaries very dark brown with blacker tips and lighter brown inner webs. Underwing coverts sooty, contrasting with greyish underside of primaries and secondaries. Tail dull blackish-brown, wearing browner. Bill and legs black. Irides purple, pinkish-purple or reddish.

AGE/SEX: Plumages similar, but females inclined to have redder irides than males; juvenile has brown irides and pinkish-red, dark-tipped bill which is apparent for about the first year of life although the irides become purplish soon after fledging.

MEASUREMENTS: Wing 152-172, tail 225-300, tarsus 44-47, bill 32-36, weight (one) 128.

GEOGRAPHICAL VARIATION: Monotypic.

VOICE: Parties are particularly noisy prior to going to roost. Shrill squeaking and deep piping contact calls are the most frequently heard vocalisations; these may be given by birds moving through the bush or when perched. Literature references mention a harsh chattering or croaking alarm call.

HABITS: Sociable. Small parties of a dozen or so birds forage low down in scrubby or lightly wooded dry grassland, following each other in babbler-like fashion across open spaces. They feed principally on the ground, moving with great agility as they run and hop about, picking and digging at the soil and leaf litter with their stout bills. Piapiacs also follow grazing animals, either feeding on the ground near their feet or following them to take insects which are disturbed by the moving animals. They also feed on and from the backs of animals, using them as perches from which they dive to pick up disturbed insects or to search for parasites (e.g. ticks); it has been remarked that elephants seem to tolerate the attentions of Piapiacs far more than oxpeckers which rely almost entirely on this form of feeding. In some parts of West Africa they have become quite bold and confiding and have little fear of man, foraging in and around villages and towns but in other parts of their range seem to be much more wary. Flocks appear to have one or more sentinels which keep watch whilst the group is feeding. In addition to insects they also feed on the seeds of the oil palm. Most active in the cooler parts of the day, resorting to the tree canopy where they rest when the weather is hot. In the evenings the various parties of an area gather together in noisy groups to form communal roosts, typically in stands of *Borassus* and other palms near villages. In general they fly low and direct on slow and heavy beats, with their long tails trailing out behind them.

BREEDING: Solitary nester. Nest a substantial structure of twigs, branches and grasses, the deep cup thickly lined with grasses and palm fibres, often almost entirely of palm fibres. Usually situated in the canopy of a palm. Clutch three to seven. Eggs pale blue, either unmarked or mottled and blotched with brown towards the larger end. No information on incubation. Eggs recorded mid March to late April.

HABITAT: Dry savannah with scattered trees, favouring grazing pastures of both domestic and wild herds of animals with stands of *Borassus* palms; also in areas of dry cultivation, villages and even locally in towns. Usually between 600 and 1500 m.

DISTRIBUTION: Widespread across the savannah belt of central Africa, ranging from Senegambia, Guinea and Sierra Leone eastwards through southern Mali, Burkina Faso, southern Niger, southern Chad, Central African Republic and south-west Sudan to south-west Ethiopia and most of Uganda; south to the Ivory Coast, northern Ghana, Benin, Nigeria, northern Cameroon and northern Zaire. Mackworth-Praed and Grant (1960) state that the species is subject to irregular dispersive migrations but there is little evidence for this in western parts of its range; it has occurred as a vagrant to Kenya.

STATUS: Locally common over most of its wide range, but rare and little known in Ethiopia where continued presence needs confirmation.

REFERENCES: Goodwin 1986, Mackworth-Praed and Grant 1960.

JACKDAWS sub-genus *Coloeus*

Despite the striking plumage differences between adults of the two jackdaws, they are clearly very closely related and form a species pair; both are seemingly identical in behaviour, calls, size and shape. There is a good case for lumping them as one polymorphic species but there is little evidence of hybridisation where the two forms marginally meet (in the region of Lake Baikal and Mongolia). The difference in eye colour might be an important factor in preventing other than very occasional mixed pairings between out of range individuals and nesting habits might also marginally differ.

WESTERN JACKDAW   Plate 20

Corvus monedula

Alternative names: Jackdaw, Eurasian Jackdaw, Common Jackdaw

One of the smallest and most familiar of European crows, equally at home nesting in chimneys of town houses or on rugged cliff faces.

IDENTIFICATION: Sociable small black crow, its small size and short, small bill readily distinguishing it from all other Palearctic crows except dark immature Daurian (which see). The grey nape and sides to head contrasts well with the blacker crown and throat and the pale iris may often be visible at close range, although these features are lacking in recently fledged juveniles which are more uniformly dark. Noisy and very gregarious, often forming mixed flocks with Rooks to feed in fields. In flight small neat head and bill distinctive, wing action quicker and flight faster than other crows. See also House Crow, choughs and Daurian Jackdaw.

DESCRIPTION: Length 34-39 cm. Race *spermologus*: Forecrown rather flat rising to small peak on rear crown. Bill short. Nasal tufts moderate. Tail relatively long, slightly rounded at tip. Forecrown black, glossed bluish. Rear crown, nape and sides of head dark grey becoming darker on ear coverts and dark greyish-black on lores and throat; grey palest at rear border of black cap. Breast and remainder of underparts greyish-black. Upperparts dark greyish-black, slightly glossed bluish. Wings and tail similar but blacker and gloss stronger. Irides greyish-white. Bill and legs black.

AGE/SEX: Plumages similar; juvenile has dark, not pale, iris and nape and neck sides darker, less contrasting than in adults; entire plumage duller, tinged brownish, virtually without gloss. By first winter body plumage closer to adult but juvenile wing and tail remain unmoulted and drab until first summer; pale iris usually attained during first winter but often still quite dark in first spring.

MEASUREMENTS: Males average a little larger than females. All races very similar in size. Wing 215-251, tail 124-140, tarsus 39-49, bill 30-36, weight 139-265.

GEOGRAPHICAL VARIATION: Marked differences between population extremes but variation clinal and complex. Algerian race most distinct. four races recognised by Vaurie (1959) (followed here), seven by Voous (1950); several others have been named but both individual and clinal variation makes demarcation of these unclear.

C. m. monedula: Scandinavia, paler than *spermologus*, especially nape, often with faint whitish collar at base of nape.

C. m. soemmeringii: Eastern Europe and Asia. Body

plumage slightly greyer than nominate, with very pale grey nape shading to a distinct whitish line at base of nape; in southern and eastern populations this line broadens to form whitish blotch at sides of neck (these forms sometimes separated as *collaris*). NB Stepanyan (1990) does not recognise this form merely treating it as part of a cline with, and under, the nominate.

C. m. spermologus: Europe (except north and east) and Morocco east to north-west Algeria. Described above, becomes progressively darker southwards (dark Iberian birds have been named *ibericus* and even darker Moroccan population as *nigerrimus*).

C. m. cirtensis: Constantine area of north-east Algeria. Very uniform slate-grey race, paler overall and less contrasting than the others and very isolated.

VOICE: Typical call an abrupt, high 'chjak' often repeated seven or eight times in excitement; other calls include a low, drawn 'chaairurr' which recalls call of Red-billed Chough but is usually accompanied by a 'chak' to prevent confusion and a slurred, high 'kyow'.

HABITS: Sociable, usually seen in flocks, often in very large numbers scattered and mixed with flocks of Rooks and Starlings in fields and open country; in flight keeps together in closely packed groups. Bold and inquisitive, striding about with a confident walk, picking and digging at the ground in search of food. Diet extremely varied, although not an ardent feeder of carrion; one study showed some 84% plant materials including grain, plant seeds and berries but during the nesting season is primarily insectivorous, mainly feeding on moth larvae taken from tree foliage. They are great opportunists, however, and readily take items as large as frogs, nestling birds and birds eggs and raid litter bins and bird tables for human food scraps. During flying ant swarms they will hawk high in the sky with gulls to take advantage of this rich feast and have even been recorded stealing fish from puffins and raiding wasp nests. Their association with animal pastures allows them to take advantage of animal parasites; sheep will allow jackdaws to ride on their backs as they graze, the birds searching ardently for ticks as well as plucking wool from them for nest contruction. Coastal populations forage along the tide-line and estuarine flats and it readily scavenges at rubbish dumps. Jackdaws roost communally together with Rooks and crows in tree plantations in the winter months, often in enormous numbers, but summer roosts are smaller. When assembling for the roost, flocks wheel about calling excitedly for some time before descending into the stands of trees. In mixed corvid roosts each species seems to be segregated into its own stands of trees within the wood and mated pairs keep close together. The flight action is the quickest of the northern crows, and next to the choughs they are the most agile on the wing; they often hang motionless on strong updraughts of wind over cliff faces, almost in the manner of a kestrel, swinging from side to side; they seem to delight in various swooping and diving antics in such situations but their relatively shorter wings do not allow them to soar high on thermals as the two choughs will do.

BREEDING: Semi-colonial. Builds a stick nest, lined with wool and rags. Nest situated in a variety of holes and crevices including tree holes, nest-boxes, quarry and cliff faces, church steeples, old buildings, old mineshafts and chimney pots (even of inhabited buildings); quite happily breeds in cliff crevices amongst nesting kittiwakes and guillemots. Rarely breeds in disused rook nests and sometimes builds a nest in the open, although this is usually in a dark situation amongst a mass of branches. Clutch three to eight, usually four. Eggs very pale bluish-green, speckled and blotched greyish and brown. Incubation 17-19 days but up to 23 days recorded, by female alone who is fed at nest by male. Young fledge at about 30 days. After fledging families congregate together in flocks. Eggs laid from early April, but chiefly last week of April or early May in Europe and Kashmir, later in northern Russia and interior Asia.

HABITAT: All forms of open country with scattered trees, from parkland to wooded steppe, towns and villages in agricultural country, coastal and inland cliff faces and woodland edges. Ascends as high as 2000 m in parts of Asia and Morocco.

DISTRIBUTION: Breeds throughout mainland Europe and the British Isles (although absent from Isles of Scilly, Corsica, south-west France and Atlantic coast of Spain), reaching northern limits in central Scandinavia. Range extends eastwards across Siberia reaching eastern limits at Lake Baikal and in extreme north-west Mongolia; southern European limit bounded by the northern shores of the Mediterranean with exception of isolated populations in north-west Africa east to Algeria. Widespread across Turkey, Cyprus and the Middle East south to central Israel and northern Iraq east to north-west Iran. East of the Caspian Sea it breeds south to the plains of the Amu Darya in northern Afghanistan, and north of the Tien Shan in Central Asia, reaching its eastern limit in western Sinkiang, with an extension south-eastwards into the vale of Kashmir. West European birds are resident, but over much of interior and northern Europe and Asia it is a summer visitor, birds moving out of breeding areas to winter over southern parts of the breeding range and south to central Iraq, central Iran, northern Pakistan and extreme north-west India. Vagrants have occurred in Iceland, the Faeroes, Canary Islands, Tunisia, northern Egypt, Jordan, Tibet and even as far afield as Japan; most extraordinary are sporadic appearances of vagrants along the eastern seaboard of North America, including a flock of 40 in Quebec and a breeding record from Pennsylvania.

STATUS: Over most of range abundant, slowly increasing and spreading its range but in Central Europe appears to be decreasing, e.g. in Switzerland a decrease from 1500 pairs in 1972-78 to less than 1000 pairs in 1989. Small numbers now breed on several Scottish islands, including Shetland; it has spread northwards in Scandinavia and eastwards in northern Siberia in the past 50 years. Algerian race endangered, a colony near Ben Harroun was not located in 1989 (possibly displaced by dam construction); 25 noted in the gorge at Constantine in 1982 (SJ Farnsworth). Breeding in both Syria and Lebanon remains unproven but in Israel there are several colonies in the north, south to Jerusalem. In Siberia the eastern limits of range are fragmented, perhaps only a recent colonist around new towns and cities e.g. Bratsk and northern Lake Baikal.

REFERENCES: Coombs 1978, Smith 1985, Vaurie 1954, 1959, Voous 1950

DAURIAN JACKDAW   Plate 20

Corvus dauuricus

Eastern counterpart of Western Jackdaw, with two colour phases, one pied and the other black. At times these phases have even been considered as different species, but it has recenty been shown that the black phase is merely an immature plumage stage.

IDENTIFICATION: Closely resembles Western Jackdaw in structure, behaviour and calls. Daurian however has a pied plumage which is quite distinctive: recalls a miniature Hooded Crow in basic pattern, with whitish underparts and collar contrasting with blackish head, breast, wings, upperparts and tail; compare Collared Crow in southern China and with suspected vagrants. Beware partial albino Western Jackdaw; look for dark iris and silver ear-covert streaking of Daurian. The black phase is an immature plumage stage: very similar to Western Jackdaw, differing in being blacker, overall less blackish-grey, with nape only a little paler, although offering some contrast with blackness of rest of body, and sometimes showing hint of pale collar at base of nape; at close range the iris is dark, not pale, and there is an area of fine silver streaks behind the eye; thus there is a risk of confusion with juvenile Western Jackdaw which has dark iris and darker nape than adult, but Daurian has silvery streaked ear-coverts visible under close viewing conditions.

DESCRIPTION: Length 32 cm. Structure as Western Jackdaw, but second primary usually shorter than fifth (equal in Western) and first primary shorter, but these differences are not consistent. Pied phase: crown, lores, throat and upper breast glossy black; sides of head behind eye black, streaked white; nape, lower sides of head, lower breast and flanks white, tinged pinkish-grey in fresh plumage. Belly, thighs, undertail-coverts and entire upperparts, including wings and tail coal black, dull and grey tinged on lower underparts; glossed with bluish-purple on crown, throat, wings and tail. Black phase: as pied phase but whitish parts of plumage blackish, less glossy and white streaking on sides of head less extensive. Bill and legs black, irides dark brown in both phases.

AGE/SEX: Sexes similar; adults always pied, juvenile is also pied but duller than adult with duller black parts of plumage and white areas tinged grey; most (perhaps all) moult into the black phase in first autumn and remain blackish until 2nd spring or summer, therefore moulting birds are seemingly intermediate.

MEASUREMENTS: Males average a little larger than females. Wing 213-243, tail 123-129, tarsus 38-45, bill 26-32, weight (one) 123.

GEOGRAPHICAL VARIATION: Probably monotypic but birds from Sinkiang have been named *khamensis* and separated by longer wing (230-249) but Vaurie (1954) refuted this distinction. Sometimes treated as a subspecies of Western Jackdaw but only one hybrid specimen known despite known overlap of ranges (Vaurie 1954).

VOICE: Usual flight call a short 'chak', indistinguishable from call of Western Jackdaw. No vocal differences between the two jackdaws have been described.

HABITS: Generally as Western Jackdaw, which it replaces in eastern Asia. Similarly sociable and typically encountered in small flocks in open steppe country. Roosts communally and often with rooks in stands of trees; also ruined buildings and isolated monasteries in open country where, in Tibet at least, it shares these roosts with Red-billed Choughs and Blue Hill Pigeons. Food and feeding habits also similar to Western Jackdaw; in summer chiefly invertebrates, including moth larvae gleaned from foliage of trees but in autumn and winter gathers to feed on stubble, taking chiefly fallen grain and weed seeds; recorded to peck at and turn over yak dung in search of food items. In open country usually not far from farmsteads and settlements, where they forage in adjacent fields, follow the plough and breed in buildings.

BREEDING: Semi-colonial, even colonial at times. Builds a similar stick nest to that of Western Jackdaw, but unlike that species is inclined to build open nests in tree canopy; in some areas this appears to be the norm and several pairs may nest in the same stand of trees. However, this might only be in areas where tree holes are scarce as they freely nest in tree holes, cliff crevices and old buildings when these are available. Clutch four to six, eggs very similar to those of Western Jackdaw. No information on incubation period etc. Eggs recorded late May in Tibet, early June in Tuva but as early as mid-February in China.

HABITAT: Grassy steppe, riverine plains and foothills; preferring open meadowland with grazing animals and stands of trees; often near habitation and even the outskirts of cities. Avoids heavily forested regions but locally occurs in valley forest with clearings. Outside breeding season flocks are encountered in open steppe well away from trees. Recorded up to 2000 m in the Altai.

DISTRIBUTION: Breeds over most of eastern Siberia to the south of the taiga forest belt, with western limit at extreme north-west and southern Lake Baikal (where it possibly meets Western Jackdaw). Range extends eastwards to Amurland and Ussuriland and south over Mongolia and northern and central China; in China breeds as far west as extreme north-east Sinkiang (Hami region), eastern Tsinghai and south-east Tibet, and south to Yunnan and Shantung. Summer visitor to northern and interior parts of range, dispersing southwards in winter, when it occurs in Korea, Japan and further south in China reaching Fukien, Kwangtung and rarely Taiwan and the Ryukyu Islands. To the west of the normal range it occasionally reaches Uzbekistan and vagrants have occurred near Krasnoyarsk in central Siberia and, incredibly, also Finland and Sweden.

STATUS: Locally quite common, but even in the heart of its range it does not seem to reach the level of abundance attained by its western counterpart.

REFERENCES: Dement'ev and Gladkov 1954, Jollie 1985

CROWS AND RAVENS sub-genus *Corvus*.

The largest group within the *Corvini*, it contains some of the world's most common corvids such as the Carrion Crow, the Northern Raven and the Rook as well as some of the most threatened species such as the Hawaiian Crow.

HOUSE CROW   Plate 22

Corvus splendens

Alternative name: Indian House Crow

One of the most conspicuous of all Indian birds, this crow abounds in towns and villages throughout the subcontinent. Its dependence on human habitation excels even that of the House Sparrow and like that species has become established in towns a long way from its native range.

IDENTIFICATION: A sleek, flat-crowned and relatively long-billed medium-sized crow with grey nape, sides of head and breast. Very much a bird of habitation, foraging in and around towns and villages with virtually no fear of man. Often alongside Jungle Crow but latter less dependant on habitation, needing proximity of more extensive stands of trees which House Crow can do without. Jungle Crow is slightly larger, wholly black, with deeper, but similar calls and has steeper forehead and slightly longer wings. Dark Burmese populations of House Crow most easily confused with Jungle Crow if not seen well. In Kashmir overlaps with smaller, small-billed, pale-eyed Jackdaw but confusion unlikely. Although basic plumage pattern can be approached by some hybrid Carrion x Hooded Crows and Pied Crow x Dwarf Raven, only latter encountered in range of House Crow (Ethiopia and Somalia) and head and bill shape quite different.

DESCRIPTION: Length 40 cm. Bill relatively long, with slightly arched culmen; forehead and crown almost flat. Wings relatively broad, especially primaries. Tail relatively long, almost square at tip. Nominate race: Forecrown, face, throat and upper breast glossy black. Nape, sides of head and neck, breast sides grey shading into dull blackish of lower underparts. Mantle greyish-black, becoming blacker from rump to tail; wings and tail glossy black. Bill and legs black. Irides blackish-brown.

AGE/SEX: Plumages similar; juveniles duller with grey areas dingier than those of adult and black of plumage dull, not glossy; lack of gloss persists into second calendar year. Inside of mouth redder when juvenile, darkening to greyish-black in older birds.

MEASUREMENTS: Male averages a little larger than female. Nominate race: wing 237-286, tail 154-175, tarsus 44-51, bill 42-56, weight 245-371.

GEOGRAPHICAL VARIATION: five subspecies recognised but perhaps only four warranted, differing chiefly in overall tones of grey in plumage, being palest grey and most contrastingly patterned in drier north-west of range.

C. s. *splendens*: India (including Laccadive Islands), Nepal, Bhutan and Bangladesh east to Burma. Described above.

C. s. *zugmayeri*: Pakistan, Kashmir and Jammu (India).

Much paler grey than nominate, grey areas becoming almost whitish-grey in worn plumage.

C. s. *protegatus*: Kerala (south-west India) and Sri Lanka. Grey areas of plumage markedly darker and less contrasting than nominate form. Intergrades with nominate race in southern India.

C. s. *maledivicus*: Maldive Islands. A poorly separated form that could be included with *protegatus*, but slightly larger and nape purer grey.

C. s. *insolens*: Burma and western Yunnan (China). Grey areas of plumage dark grey, offering less contrast than in other forms, bill also more strongly arched culmen.

Birds established in parts of the Middle East and East Africa probably originated from several populations and are difficult to allocate racially but those in Israel are considered to be the nominate form.

VOICE: Very vocal, typical call a flat, toneless, dry 'kaaa-kaaa', weaker than similar call of Jungle Crow, recalling caw of Rook but softer and flatter in tone. As may be expected from such a sociable corvid there is quite an extensive vocabulary, with a variety of shorter, less diagnostic calls.

HABITS: Wherever human settlements occur in the lowlands of the Indian subcontinent, so does the House Crow; from small villages to the heart of the largest cities this is one of India's most familiar birds. Highly gregarious they scavenge amongst street debris and hang about railway stations and rubbish dumps. In parts of the Middle East where they are self-introduced they are far too sociable, with populations reaching immense numbers in some cities (e.g. Aden) and are a potential human health hazard (see Status). Bold by nature House Crows ride on the backs of cattle, pigs and mules, not only picking off ticks but also pecking at sores which the hapless animals have developed. They are omnivorous, taking almost anything from grain, fruit and flower nectar to stealing kitchen scraps and fish; they raid birds nests and can be very destructive to heronries and weaver colonies; fish are also taken by picking them from the water surface in the shallows and even by awkward plunge-diving from the air; insects of all types are eaten and flying ants may be taken on the wing by awkward fly-catching techniques from exposed perches. They scavenge along lakesides, rivers and seashores for carrion, shell-fish and crabs. Seemingly unafraid of man, they seem to ignore human presence in the manner of feral pigeons but remain wary and alert of danger. Pre-roost gatherings form at the tops of tall buildings with much aerial gambolling and frolicking, dropping to twist and turn, loop-the-loop and shooting back to a high perch, often displacing another crow from its perch; as the sun goes down they fly off in straggling groups, converging with other flocks to form very large gatherings in favoured stands of trees. They may travel considerable distances to their roosts which often hold several thousand birds; as this species does not breed until its third calendar year, roost gatherings remain high throughout the year. Birds leave the roosts just before dawn. Birds of prey are harried quite mercilessly; they jump on and off the backs of vultures sitting gorged on the ground, or tease and worry vultures and other large birds of prey sitting tight on their nests. Almost any low-flying raptor is challenged and chased away. On the ground they move with a bold striding walk, accompanied by a jaunty sideways hop and wing-flick when anything of interest is spotted. The flight action is steady, direct and unhurried with the tail held tightly closed; generally flies high when moving to and from roosts. Despite their sociable nature they are monogamous and seemingly pair for life; even outside the breeding season pairs mutually preen each-other and keep in close contact. Despite this the copulatory activity of a pair excites much interest from other crows and there is some evidence of promiscuity generated by mating activities. Almost the only creature to get the better of a House Crow is a cuckoo, the Koel, which lays its eggs in the nest of the House Crow. There is some controversy over the technique employed by the Koel to get access to the nest, and it has been reported that the male Koel distracts the sitting House Crow away from the nest whilst the female slips in to lay its egg; another report describes a female Koel sitting on the nest with the incubating House Crow alongside, jockeying for position! In such cases, calls rather like that of a young House Crow were heard, suggesting that the Koel called like a young crow to appease the rightful owner of the nest. Scavenging around ports and docks has resulted in birds being unintentionally transported by ships to various ports in the Indian Ocean region, and even beyond; in several areas where they have been accidentally introduced and established they have become very abundant (e.g. Aden, Suez, Egypt and coastal ports of Kenya and Tanzania).

BREEDING: More or less a solitary nester, but often several nests in a single tree or building and colonial nesting has been reported in Egypt where population densities are very high and trees quite sparse. Nest an untidy structure of twigs and garbage, with a cup lined with animal hair and plant fibres, placed in a tree fork or ledge of a building, on electricity pylons etc. Clutch of four or five pale blue-green, speckled and streaked brown eggs. Incubation 16-17 days; probably by female alone, although some references state that both partners share incubation, both sexes feed young and take part in nest construction. In India the breeding season is principally from March/April to July/August, but some birds nest October-December; however, these could be younger birds reaching sexual maturity later in the season. Breeding has been recorded in February in the Sudan and from October to January in Zanzibar.

HABITAT: All forms of lowland human habitation from small villages to cities, locally ascending into foothills of the Himalayas reaching 2100m in Darjeeling and at several other hill stations; a vagrant pair reported at 2900 m in Sikkim.

DISTRIBUTION: Native range extends throughout Pakistan, Bangladesh, India and Sri Lanka, including the Maldive and Laccadive Islands, and the Himalayan foot-hills of Nepal and Bhutan, eastwards through Burma to extreme southern China (Yunnan). Formerly occurred Thailand (Phetchaburi) but no recent records. Vagrant to extreme southern Afghanistan (Khost 1964). Introduced (probably chiefly self-introduced by ship) and well established in Malaysia (Pelabohan Kelang and Penang), Singapore, Iran (Bushire), Kuwait, Oman, Saudi Arabia, Persian Gulf States, Yemen (Aden north to Hodeidah), Egypt (chiefly Suez), Sudan (Port Sudan), Eritrea (Mits'iwa), Djibouti, coastal Kenya (chiefly Mombasa), Mauritius, Zanzibar, Tanzania (Dar es Salaam), South Africa (chiefly Durban), and marginally established in Jordan (Aqaba), Israel (Eilat) and southern Mozambique (no recent information). Presumed ship-borne individuals have been reported from other parts of the world including Australia (several times), eastern USA (New Jersey 1971, South Carolina 1986), Japan (Osaka 1981) and Gibraltar (1991).

STATUS: Very abundant throughout native range and at alien sites. Fears that such a successful large bird in an alien environment would displace native species, or become an agricultural pest or even a human health hazard have resulted in it being destroyed in Australia. In Kenya, it has locally displaced the Pied Crow. In the Middle East, has become extremely abundant in some towns, e.g. Suez and Aden where large numbers have been destroyed.

REFERENCES: Ali and Ripley 1972, Ash 1988, Feare and Mungroo 1989, Gill 1985, Jennings 1992, Meininger et al 1980.

NEW CALEDONIAN CROW   Plate 24

Corvus moneduloides

This crow sometimes uses a twig to probe out insect larvae from tree bark; the use of tools as a feeding aid is well known in the Large Tree and Woodpecker Finches of Galapagos but is virtually undocumented in other birds.

IDENTIFICATION: Endemic to New Caledonia where it is the only crow. A medium sized black crow with a peculiarly shaped bill; confusion with other species unlikely.
DESCRIPTION: Length 40 cm. Bill stout, with culmen almost straight and lower mandible angled upwards at the gonys. Tail relatively long, slightly rounded at tip. Throat feathers fine, almost hair-like. Entire plumage deep black, glossed purple and dark blue, with a hint of green on the primaries. Bill and legs black. Irides dark brown.
AGE/SEX: Plumages similar.
MEASUREMENTS: Wing 241-267, tail 170-186, tarsus 42-48, bill 42-50, weight 230-330.
GEOGRAPHICAL VARIATION: Monotypic.
VOICE: A soft, hoarse, rather high-pitched 'waaaw'; also a louder, high-pitched 'wak-wak' and a more prolonged, high-pitched 'aaup' have been documented.
HABITS: A solitary crow; although often in family parties, seems not to form large gatherings. Apparently quite confiding, flying towards people at their approach. The chisel-shaped bill suggests specialised feeding techniques but its diet seems to be varied and omnivorous. Bill shape no doubt useful for hammering open snails and nuts but this needs confirmation; it certainly drops these onto rocks and tree buttresses to break them open, with piles of shells forming at favoured spots. Also feeds on seeds and invertebrates; noted to capture large insects on the

wing with great agility and one pair was watched repeatedly using a twig to probe into tree bark and hollows, presumably to 'winkle-out' invertebrates. Occasionally takes eggs and chicks of domestic chickens and, in former times, reported feeding on human corpses placed in trees !

BREEDING: Solitary nester. Nest a platform of twigs, lined with plant and root fibres, and placed quite high in a tree. Eggs two or three, light greenish or bluish-green profusely blotched and spotted olive, brown and grey. Eggs laid September to November.

HABITAT: Woodland and open country with scattered trees.

DISTRIBUTION: Endemic to New Caledonia in the south-west Pacific; also on nearby Loyalty Islands (on Mare) where introduced.

STATUS: Common, both about cultivation and in wooded habitats. Egg-stealing behaviour of the crows is considered to be detrimental to the pigeon population of the islands.

REFERENCES: Goodwin 1986, Hannecart and Letocart 1980, Layard 1882, Orenstein 1972

INDONESIAN and PHILIPPINE CROWS

Crows inhabiting the Indonesian and Philippine islands are a taxonomic nightmare, several of the island taxa having received various treatments by different authorities and it is really a matter of conjecture, on present knowledge, to decide how far some of these forms have travelled along their own evolutionary road. Sudden replacement of different forms on adjacent islands without overlap does not necessarily mean that they had the same direct ancestor and even in the interior of large land masses there is often a sudden change in the corvid species present, e.g. with Hooded Crow and Brown-necked Raven in the Middle East and Central Asia. In the Indonesian islands speciation is in itself particularly complex, some taxa having Australasian affinities whereas others have oriental ancestry.

Two extremes of bill shape exhibited by the complex on adjacent island groups in the Moluccas:

C. (e). violaceus of Ceram, Buru and Ambon (upper).

C. e. mangoli of Sula, Mangole and Sanana (lower) Note base of culmen ridge is bare of bristles in both.

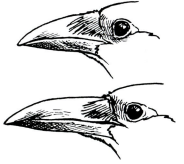

Extreme populations today normally classified under Slender-billed are quite different in bill shape, degree of plumage gloss and colour of the body feather bases but others, not necessarily on adjacent islands, appear somewhat intermediate. Birds inhabiting the island of Ceram and the Philippines differ in bill shape and plumage gloss from those of the remainder of the range of the Slender-billed complex and were given specific treatment by both Stresemann (1943) and Dorst (1947) as the Violaceous Crow *C. violaceus*. Vaurie (1958) reviewed the situation and considered it safer to treat them all as forms of one polymorphic species and this has been followed by other taxonomists since. He also considered the virtually unknown Banggai Crow as a form of Slender-billed but did highlight its close structural resemblance to the Piping Crow. Crows on several of the islands are considered to have rather different calls but this has been poorly documented and the degree of variation is very vague. An analysis of the range of calls given by each population is a daunting venture but coupled with a behaviourial study and taking into account structure and plumage variation, would no doubt eventually yield amazing results (cf studies of Australian corvids by Rowley 1970). To bring attention back to this problem the two groups of taxa have been given semi-separate treatment in this work in the hope that birders visiting the islands will take behavioural notes and record a range of calls given by the forms that they encounter.

SLENDER-BILLED CROW   Plate 22

Corvus enca

A medium-sized, long-billed black crow of Malaysia, Borneo and the Indonesian islands, overlapping quite widely with Large-billed Crow.

IDENTIFICATION: An all-black crow differing from similar Large-billed Crow in its smaller overall proportions, large but markedly slimmer bill with curved rather than strongly arched culmen, relatively shorter and almost square-ended tail (Large-billed has strongly arched

bill and slightly wedge-shaped tail) and duller, less glossy plumage. All of these features vary to a degree amongst the races (see Geographical Variation) but none show the markedly thick, arched bill of Large-billed. Calls are also rather different, those of Slender-billed being markedly higher in pitch than those of Large-billed. Largely a bird of interior forest edges, shunning human habitation, being replaced in coastal areas, open country and towns by Large-billed; however on islands where Large-billed is absent Slender-billed occupies a wider variety of habitats. In the hand the very base of the culmen is devoid of rictal bristles (densely clothed with short bristles in Large-billed). Compare also Violaceous and the virtually unknown Banggai Crows.

DESCRIPTION: Length 43-47 cm. Bill long, with gently curved culmen, appearing distinctly decurved in the field. Forehead slightly steepens onto bill base. Wing distinctly rounded with long outermost primary. Tail medium-short, almost square or slightly rounded at tip. Throat hackles short and inconspicuous. Nasal tufts conspicuous, absent at base of culmen where ridge is bare to forehead feathering. Small bare patch behind eye. Bases of body feathers white or whitish. Entire plumage blackish, with slight purplish gloss (depending on race). Bill and legs black. Irides dark-brown.

AGE/SEX: Plumages similar; juvenile duller and greyer, with blacker feather tipping, especially on upperparts.

MEASUREMENTS: Male averages a little larger than female. See Geographical Variation for measurements of all races.

GEOGRAPHICAL VARIATION: Eight subspecies recognised in the complex, which, for field purposes, are best considered under two groupings (see introduction to the Slender-billed complex. Four races are grouped under Violaceous Crow (which see) and four with Slender-billed, the latter are listed below:-

C. e. compilator: Malaysia, Sumatra, Borneo.
The largest form, with distinct sheen to its dull black plumage. Wing 316-343, tail 160-170, tarsus 56, bill 65-69.

C. e. enca: Java, Bali and Mentawi islands.
Markedly smaller than compilator, with slightly duller plumage. Wing 282-293, tail 139-151, bill 55-60.

C. e. celebensis: Sulawesi and adjacent islands.
Like nominate but with a slightly shorter, less slender, bill and blacker, more glossed, plumage. Wing 255-298, tail 114-147, bill 53-58.

C. e. mangoli: Sula islands. Bill relatively the longest of all, nearly as long as that of compilator despite being a much smaller bird overall. Plumage duller than celebensis. Wing 260 & 275, tail 133 & 134, bill 59 & 63.

VOICE: See also comments under introduction to the complex. On Borneo compilator has a dry, high-pitched 'ahk-ahk-ahk' (much higher in pitch than Large-billed); this caw is often quite short, but when excited becomes longer and prolonged into a series of cawing 'caaaw' or 'aaaaw' notes, varying in both pitch and length of each note; intermingled with this is a remarkable resonant, almost twanging, nasal 'pe-yong' or 'ne-awh', the latter usually given in flight (recordings by C. Robson, D. Showler in litt). Sulawesi race has similar cawing notes, but from recordings seems to lack the nasal twanging call.

HABITS: Much more of true forest bird than the Large-billed, particularly where the two species occur together, feeding more inside the foliage of trees and shunning human habitation, except on Sulawesi where common around habitation. However where Large-billed is absent and therefore offers no competition, Slender-billed is less specialised and readily forages in semi-open country and farmland. Usually in pairs or small parties. Seemingly shy and wary by nature. Flight action has been described as 'heavy' and 'pigeon-like'. Food items recorded include lizards, fruit and insects as well as maize.

BREEDING: Perhaps largely a solitary nester but Smythies (1981) states that a colony of nests has been found in one very large solitary jungle tree. Nest a structure of twigs, roots and large stems with cup lined with fine roots and plant fibres, distinctly smaller than that of Large-billed. Clutch of four eggs (nominate, Java) or merely one (compilator, Borneo), pale bluish-green to off-white with olive-brown to greyish and blackish spotting and speckling (nominate, Java). No information on sexual roles or length of incubation recorded. Eggs recorded June to July (compilator, Borneo).

HABITAT: Lowland forests and forest edges, especially along rivers, including secondary growth, up to 1000 m. Locally in coastal mangroves (compilator, Malaysia) and semi-open farmland, recorded as feeding about human habitation on Sulawesi (celebensis) but generally avoids human contact elsewhere.

DISTRIBUTION: Peninsular Malaysia north to Penang (but not recorded Thailand) southwards through Sumatra and Java to Bali; widespread on Borneo and Sulawesi (perhaps including Banggai) and over the Sula islands of Mangole, Sanana and Taliabu.

STATUS: Although widely distributed it is only really numerous in forest habitats. Common on Sulawesi and fairly common on Borneo. In Malaysia it is local and uncommon, but widespread.

REFERENCES: Smythies 1981, White and Bruce 1986.

VIOLACEOUS CROW   Plate 22

Corvus (enca) violaceus

A group of island crows closely allied to and probably conspecific with Slender-billed Crow. Taxonomically confusing, the whole of this group is in need of revision based on intensive field research.

IDENTIFICATION: Very similar to Slender-billed Crow but with markedly smaller and with relatively shorter, stouter bill. Overlaps only on the Philippines with distinctly larger, bigger-billed Large-billed which also differs in having a more wedge-shaped tail tip and favouring clearings and cultivation, whereas Violaceous is much more of a true forest bird.

DESCRIPTION: Length 40-42 cm. Bill medium, with curved culmen, appearing slightly decurved (varies somewhat with race in degree of stoutness). Forehead relatively flat. Tail medium-short, almost square or slightly rounded at tip. Throat hackles short and inconspicuous. Nasal tufts conspicuous, absent at base of culmen where ridge is bare to forehead feathering. Small bare patch behind eye. Entire plumage black, with slight gloss (depending on race). Base of neck feathers white or grey (depending on race). Bill and legs black. Irides dark-brown.

AGE/SEX: All plumages similar; juvenile duller.

MEASUREMENTS: Male averages a little larger than female. See Geographical Variation for measurements. Weights of Philippine forms: 222-225.

GEOGRAPHICAL VARIATION: See also introduction to the Slender-billed complex. 4 races form the group known as Violaceus Crow:-

C. (e.) v. violaceus: Ceram, Buru and Ambon. Bill short and stout; plumage with pronounced matt-looking mauvish sheen and irides varying from dark grey-brown to dark reddish-brown. Wing 236-253; tail 131-136; tarsus 42-45; bill 50-53.

C. (e.) v. pusillus: Philippines (Balabac, Palawan and

Mindoro). Like *violaceus* but slightly larger and with relatively more slender bill and plumage a shade blacker and more glossy. White bases to body feathers. Mindoro birds average blacker and more glossy and have slightly heavier bills than those of Palawan. Wing 245-248; tail 127-134; bill 50-53.

C. (e.) v. sierramadrensis: Philippines (northern Luzon). The smallest form, with a relatively short and slender bill and very black plumage. Grey bases to body feathers. 2 females: wing 216, 220; tail 112, 113; bill 48, 49.

C. (e.) v. samarensis: Philippines (Samar and Mindanao). Like *pusillus* but smaller and bill relatively thicker. Pale grey bases to body feathers. Plumage more intensely black, glossed purplish-blue. Wing 214-240; tail 103-120; bill 52-56.

VOICE: See also comments under introduction to the complex. In the Philippines they seem to vary between the races: those of Palawan (*pusillus*) are considered to be the highest in pitch, whereas those of Mindanao (*samarensis*) have the deepest; *sierramadrensis* of Luzon has rather slower calls which are less high in pitch than *pusillus* (T. Fisher in litt). On Ceram the calls of *violaceus* have been described as high in pitch.

HABITS: Little documented. On the Philippines considered a true forest bird but on Ceram readily forages in semi-open country and farmland. Usually in pairs or small parties but on Ceram recorded as flocking to feed on fields of ripening maize. On Mindanao and Luzon they associate with mixed feeding flocks of other larger passerines (cuckoo-shrikes, bluebirds, trillers etc), moving through the forest canopy with them. Seemingly shy and wary by nature.

BREEDING: Presumably much as for Slender-billed. No specific information other than that the eggs of *violaceus* (Ceram) have been described as white sparsely speckled with yellowish-brown. Eggs recorded in June on Mindoro for *pusillus*.

HABITAT: Lowland forests and forest edges, including secondary growth. On the Philippines both *samarensis* and *sierramadrensis* are associated with lowland primary forest but *pusillus* is more tolerant of secondary forest, forest edges and cleared areas.

DISTRIBUTION: The Philippine islands (specific islands are mentioned under Geographical Variation) and the island of Ceram in the Moluccas (Maluku).

STATUS: Although widely distributed through most of the Philippines it is only really common on Palawan and Samar; elsewhere it is distinctly uncommon or scarce. On Luzon *sierramadrensis* was considered rare but has recently been found to be more numerous in the extreme north of the island. On Mindoro and Mindanao because of forest destruction has become distinctly rare.

REFERENCES: Dickinson *et al* 1991, Rand and Rabor 1961, Vaurie 1958.

PIPING CROW   Plate 23

Corvus typicus

Alternative name: Celebes Pied Crow
A distinctive crow, endemic to Sulawesi, where it widely overlaps with the Slender-billed Crow.

IDENTIFICATION: Easily identified by combination of restricted range and conspicuous white nape and underparts, the pattern of which suggests the palest forms of House Crow. However range only overlaps with wholly blackish Slender-billed Crow.

DESCRIPTION: Length 39-40 cm. Bill medium in length, rather curved and tapered. Tail medium-short, almost square at tip. Throat lacks hackles, but feathers are distinctly hairy in texture. Nasal tufts conspicuous, absent at base of culmen where ridge is bare to forehead feathering. Small patch of bare skin behind eye. Head and upper nape black, with bluish-purple gloss; throat unglossed brownish-black. Nape, sides of neck, upper mantle and underparts from breast to belly, white. Bases of neck feathers dark grey. Mantle to tail, lower belly and undertail-coverts, 'thighs', and wings and tail black, glossed with blue and purple except on mantle and lower underparts which are unglossed greyish or brownish-black. Bill and legs black. Irides dark red-brown.

AGE/SEX: Plumages similar; female with duller and more diffuse demarcation of dusky throat with white of breast; juvenile duller and with white of nape and underparts sullied greyish-brown.

MEASUREMENTS: Male averages slightly larger than female. Wing 203-221, tail 108-117, tarsus 42-48, bill 40-47.

GEOGRAPHICAL VARIATION: Monotypic. Closely-related to Slender-billed and Banggai Crows.

VOICE: Remarkable for a crow. Utters a raucous, shrill screech, which may be repeated three or four times, reminiscent of the screech of one of the larger parakeets. Other descriptions refer to a series of three rising whistled notes, followed by a crowing sound, often uttered from the top of a tall tree; also reported are a variety of creaking and trilling notes.

HABITS: Little information. Often in small parties. Seems to be shy, wary and very nervous, flying off with noisy, swooshing wing-beats; flight action rapid recalling a large pigeon.

BREEDING: No information.

HABITAT: Forest edges and open woodland with clearings, up to 1400 m.

DISTRIBUTION: Endemic to central and southern Sulawesi, including the adjacent islands of Muna and Butung.

STATUS: Patchily distributed in central Sulawesi.

REFERENCES: Stresemann and Heinrich 1940, White and Bruce 1986.

BANGGAI CROW   Plate 23

Corvus unicolor

A mysterious crow, known from only two specimens collected from a small island off the coast of Sulawesi. Could well be extinct.

IDENTIFICATION: A small wholly black crow endemic to the island of Banggai; until recently it was thought to be the only crow to occur on the island but recent observations of black crows there suggest that perhaps Slender-billed Crows have recently arrived. The nearest populations of Slender-billed are on the Sula islands to the east; this form (*mangoli*) has a particularly long bill and is unlikely to be confused if seen well. Birds of the

Sulawesi race *celebensis* might however be involved; this too is long-billed and is a much bigger bird than Banggai Crow. Banggai Crow has an insignificant bill by comparison and more highly glossed plumage; additionally the bases of the neck feathers are grey, not whitish as in adjacent races of Slender-billed. Presumably it also differs vocally but nothing is known about this. It is possible that Banggai Crow is a shy forest bird still surviving in the forested hills of the islands, whereas Slender-billed is presumed to be a recent colonist in the cleared areas of the lowlands.

DESCRIPTION: Length 39 cm. Structurally very similar to Piping Crow. Bill medium in length, with gently curved culmen, slightly deeper and heavier than bill of Piping Crow. Tail medium-short, almost square at tip. Throat lacks hackles. Small patch of bare skin behind eye. Entire plumage black, glossed with bluish or greenish. Bases of neck feathers grey. Bill and legs black. Irides presumably dark-brown.

AGE/SEX: No information.

MEASUREMENTS: The only two specimens collected were unsexed. Wing 210 and 213, tail 105 and 111, tarsus 41 and 44, bill both 46.

VOICE: Undocumented. Perhaps close to that of Piping Crow.

HABITS: Undocumented. Suspected to be a shy forest bird.

BREEDING: Undocumented.

HABITAT: Presumed to be forest, possibly hill forest, which on the Banggai islands reaches 900 metres.

DISTRIBUTION: Endemic to the island of Banggai in the Banggai islands, which are situated some 20 km east of the eastern peninsula of Sulawesi.

STATUS: Known only from two specimens in the collection of the American Museum of Natural History in New York. There were sightings of black crows on Banggai in 1981 but these could just possibly have been Slender-billed rather than Banggai Crows.

TAXONOMY: This crow has at times been treated as a form of Slender-billed Crow but in structure it is very close to the Piping Crow and it could in fact be an isolated, wholly blackish form of this species. A review by Jollie (1978) continued to treat it as a form of Slender-billed Crow.

REFERENCES: Goodwin 1986, Vaurie 1958, White and Bruce 1986.

FLORES CROW
Plate 23

Corvus florensis

Confined to the Indonesian island of Flores, this black forest crow is threatened by habitat destruction.

IDENTIFICATION: A small, slim, relatively long tailed black crow confined to lowland forest. Large-billed also occurs on the island but Flores Crow is much smaller, has a small, stout bill and dark grey (not whitish-grey) bases to the neck feathers. Overall head and bill shape reminiscent of Jackdaw therefore unlikely to be confused with Large-billed which has a long, stout and arched bill and steep forehead. It is a true forest bird, being replaced by Large-billed in open and semi-open areas near habitation.

DESCRIPTION: Length 40 cm. Bill relatively short, with gently curved culmen. Nostrils long, twice as long as those of Slender-billed Crow. Nasal tufts conspicuous, covering base of bill for half its length, clothing base of culmen. Tail medium-long, almost square at tip. Small patch of bare skin behind eye. Entire plumage purplish-black, not highly glossed, softer in texture than plumage of Slender-billed. Bases of body feathers smoky-grey. Bill and legs black. Irides presumably dark brown.

AGE/SEX: No information.

MEASUREMENTS: Available data from one female specimen. Wing 226, tail 164, tarsus 46, bill 48.

VOICE: Recently tape recorded by Smith (1993). The sounds produced by this peculiar crow are quite remarkable. The calls were given from amongst a party of six birds, uttered with a head bobbing, tail dipping and wing raising display. The call which is regularly uttered is a grating, explosive sound which is very difficult to describe but recalls the advertising call of a European Grey Partridge heard at close quarters. Another sound given on the same recording is a liquid bubbling of an almost oriole-like quality.

HABITS: Undocumented. Probably a shy forest bird.

BREEDING: Undocumented.

HABITAT: Lowland forest, up to at least 700 m.

DISTRIBUTION: Endemic to the island of Flores in the Lesser Sundas of Indonesia.

STATUS: Known only from a few specimens. There have been recent observations of it in lowland forest at Kisol and coastal forest at Nanga Rawa. Destruction of lowland forest for agriculture is a serious threat to this specialised crow which seems unable to adapt to open habitats. Forest destruction has no doubt aided the spread of the larger and more successful Large-billed Crow. Only habitat protection will save the species from extinction.

TAXONOMY: This crow has at times been treated as a form of Slender-billed Crow but it is distinctly different in plumage texture and has base of culmen covered with nasal bristles and much longer nostrils than in any form of that species. Its true affinities remain obscure.

REFERENCES: Collar and Andrew 1988, White and Bruce 1986, Smith 1993.

MARIANA CROW
Plate 23

Corvus kubaryi

Alternative names: Micronesian Crow, Guam Crow

A unique crow of uncertain affinities, confined to two islands in the western Pacific.

IDENTIFICATION: Endemic to the Mariana Islands where it is the only crow. A relatively small wholly dull black forest crow with a relatively small bill. The only other black birds on the islands are the much smaller pale-eyed Micronesian Starling and the introduced Black Drongo which has a long and deeply forked tail.

DESCRIPTION: Length 40 cm. Bill relatively long, surprisingly narrow, but deep, with gently curving culmen and tapered tip. Nasal tufts relatively short, just concealing base of culmen. Wings relatively short and broad. Tail medium-long, slightly rounded at tip. Plumage quite soft, with almost hair-like texture. Base of neck feathers

white. Entire plumage dull black, with a dull bluish gloss on back, wings and tail. Bill and legs black. Irides dark brown.
AGE/SEX: All plumages similar, juveniles duller, lacking slight gloss of adults.
MEASUREMENTS: See Additional Information on page 192.
GEOGRAPHICAL VARIATION: Monotypic.
VOICE: See Additional Information on page 192.
HABITS: See Additional Information on page 192.
BREEDING: See Additional Information on page 192.
HABITAT: Forests.
DISTRIBUTION: Endemic to the Mariana Islands of Guam and Rota.
STATUS: Guam population decreasing, estimated at 350 birds in 1982 but known to have decreased since. On Rota the population is reasonably stable and was estimated at 1300 birds in 1982 but a decrease is suspected there too.
REFERENCES: Jenkins 1983, Michael 1987, Tomback 1986.

LONG-BILLED CROW   Plate 23

Corvus validus

A large, long-billed crow of the northern Moluccas, Indonesia where it overlaps with the Torresian Crow. Goodwin (1986) regards this crow as related to the Australian corvids whereas Vaurie (1958) allied it with Slender-billed. Whatever its ancient affinities were it is clearly a very distinctive bird.

IDENTIFICATION: Confined to the northern Moluccas, there is little chance of confusion with the sympatric Torresian Crow. Long-billed is a large, glossy black crow with a massive long and deep bill and whitish eyes, whereas the Torresian is even more glossy and whiter-eyed and has a smaller, insignificant bill; note that young Torresian (and possibly also Long-billed) has brownish eyes in its first year. Range does not overlap with either Large-billed or Slender-billed Crows although a form of the latter *mangoli* is found on the Sula group of islands of the adjacent western Moluccas; *mangoli* has a duller matt black plumage and is a smaller bird altogether.

Long-billed is far more of a true forest bird that Torresian, which is more typically found in open and semi-culti-vated country. In flight a much larger bird than Torresian Crow with a thicker neck and long bill, the wings are noticeably broad and long, all of these features contrib-uting to a distinctive shape.
DESCRIPTION: Length 46-48cm. Bill very long, gradu-ally tapering from a relatively deep base with curved culmen. Nasal tufts conspicuous, but hardly covering base of culmen. Tail medium-short, almost square tip. Wing relatively more pointed than in Slender-billed, with shorter first and longer second and third primaries. Bases of neck feathers pure white. Entire plumage black, blossed purple on upperparts and wings, steel-blue on head and greenish on throat; lower underparts duller black with very weak greyish feather fringes. Bill and legs black. Irides bluish-white.
AGE/SEX: Plumages similar. Juvenile duller black, irides said to be bluish-white in nestlings, but these probably darken after fledging as with Torresian Crow and its allies.
MEASUREMENTS: Male presumed to average a little larger than female. Wing 345-365, tail 170-183, tarsus 52-64, bill 80-85, weight - not recorded.
GEOGRAPHICAL VARIATION: Monotypic.
VOICE: A rather loud and distinctive short, dry croak, very abrupt and clippered delivery: 'cruk...cruk...cruk...cruk'. Quite different to Torresian Crow. In fact not unlike short, clipped croaks of Fan-tailed Raven.
HABITS: Poorly documented. A relatively shy crow, inhabiting forest where it keeps very much to the tree canopy, perching conspicuously on tree tops from where it utters its territorial calls. Seems to be solitary by nature, being usually encountered in pairs or family parties. Flight action strong and direct, often well above tree height.
HABITAT: Forest.
DISTRIBUTION: Endemic to the northern Moluccan islands of Morotai, Kayoa, Halmahera, Bacan and Obi.
STATUS: Little information, but on Halmahera at least it seems to be relatively numerous and widespread in forested country.
REFERENCES: Goodwin 1986, White and Bruce 1986, Smith 1993.

NEW GUINEA CROWS

In addition to the widespread Torresian Crow, the main island of New Guinea and adjacent islands are inhabited by a group of rather massive-billed crows. Three of these species have very restricted ranges and are possibly all quite closely related. The very variable Grey Crow is widespread throughout New Guinea and is remarkable for having a complex series of plumage stages which is unique amongst *Corvus* crows.

The two crows inhabiting the Solomon Islands are clearly closely related; they are usually treated as subspecies under *C. woodfordi*, but have a striking difference in bill and iris colour and the arrangement of the nasal bristles. Therefore it seems reasonable to consider them as having reached specific level, as was proposed by Mayr (1955).

WHITE-BILLED CROW   Plate 24

Corvus woodfordi

Alternative name: Solomon Islands Crow.

The southernmost of the two crows inhabiting the

Solomon Islands, the two often being considered conspecific under this form.

IDENTIFICATION: A heavily built, short-tailed crow with a massive pale bill. Replaced on the more northern islands by the Bougainville Crow which has a black bill.
DESCRIPTION: Length 40-41 cm. Head rather large but

VARIATION OF SIZES OF THE WHITE-BILLED CROW				
	Wing	Tail	Bill	Sample
Choiseul males:	280-293	131-145	64-66	8
females:	265-278	128-136	61-64	5
Santa Isabel males:	288-300	140-148	69-70	3
females:	285-290	130-140	66-69	5
Guadalcanal males:	268-282	124-136	59-67	9
females:	263-279	124-134	61-63	5

dominated by massive bill, with strongly arched culmen, tapering to a sharp tip. Tail short, almost square but slightly rounded at tip. Nasal bristles few but prominent against pale bill, separated at bill base to expose culmen ridge as bare to forehead. Small patches of bare skin in inter-ramal area (chin). Bases of neck feathering whitish. Plumage of head and neck fine and silky in texture. Head, neck and upper breast shiny black, with oily green gloss, remainder of underparts duller black. Upperparts shiny black with violet-purple sheen. Bill ivory, shading pale bluish towards blackish tip; towards base shading through light bluish to purplish-blue at very base. Irides grey or dull white. Legs black with orange soles to the feet. Bare patches of skin visible under the chin, purplish-red.

SEX/AGE: Sexes similar; juvenile, no information.

MEASUREMENTS: There seems to be some variation between the islands. Males from the islands of Choiseul and Santa Isabel apparently distinctly larger than females, whereas those from Guadalcanal are very similar in size (see table). Other measurements: tarsus 52-58.

GEOGRAPHICAL VARIATION: Monotypic as treated here. Birds from Santa Isabel have been separated as *vegetus* but Vaurie (1958) considered it invalid. Birds from Santa Isabel and Guadalcanal slightly duller in plumage gloss than those from Choiseul.

VOICE: Little information. Call described as like that of Torresian Crow but higher in pitch and faster. Another transcription refers to a loud, high-pitched 'Ao...Ao....Ao...'. These two descriptions are probably of the same call.

HABITS: Little information. Apparently forages in small parties in the forest canopy, where it feeds on insects, primarily beetles, and various fruits. Keeps high in the tree tops and flies above the canopy but normally keeps quite well hidden when feeding.

BREEDING: Unrecorded.

HABITAT: Recorded as misty, hill forest on Guadalcanal.

DISTRIBUTION: Endemic to the central Solomon Islands of Choiseul, Santa Isabel and Guadalcanal

STATUS: No information but presumed to be widespread in forests on the islands.

REFERENCES: Cain and Galbraith 1956, Goodwin 1986, Mayr 1955, Vaurie 1958.

BOUGAINVILLE CROW   Plate 24

Corvus meeki

Alternative name: Solomon Islands Crow.

Little is known about this strangely-shaped crow, which replaces the White-billed Crow in the northern Solomons.

IDENTIFICATION: Like the White-billed Crow this species has a remarkably long and highly arched bill which, in view of its short tail, makes it seem top-heavy. Despite similarity in shape this bird is readily separated from the White-billed Crow by its black bill and range.

DESCRIPTION: Length 41 cm. Shape and structure as White-billed Crow, except that the nasal bristles are not divided over the base of the bill as in that bird, but form a short tuft at the very base of the culmen. Plumage very similar to White-billed Crow but plumage brighter, more highly glossed overall. Bill wholly black. Irides dark brown. Legs black with orange soles to the feet. Bare patches of purplish-red skin visible under the chin.

SEX/AGE: Sexes similar; juvenile, no information.

MEASUREMENTS: Unlike the White-billed Crow, there seems to be little difference in size between the sexes or birds from different islands. Wing 278-311, tail 127-149, tarsus 53-55, bill 65-73.

GEOGRAPHICAL VARIATION: Monotypic as treated here.

VOICE: No information. Feeding parties said to be 'noisy' but no precise description of voice seems to have been published, presumably very similar to that of White-billed Crow.

HABITS: Little information. Apparently similar to that of the White-billed Crow, inhabiting forest where it feeds in the canopy in small parties. On Bougainville island they forage in noisy parties in trees in large gardens and are recorded as eating paw-paws.

BREEDING: Unrecorded.

HABITAT: Chiefly lowland forest on Bougainville, but recorded up to 1600m.

DISTRIBUTION: Endemic to the northern Solomon Islands of Bougainville and nearby small island of Shortland.

STATUS: No information but presumed to be widespread in forests on the islands.

REFERENCES: Goodwin 1986, Mayr 1945, 1955, Vaurie 1958.

BROWN-HEADED CROW   Plate 24

Corvus fuscicapillus

A rare and very local crow, with bill shape resembling that of the bills of the crows of the Solomons. It has similar fruit-eating habits but is remarkable for its sexually dimorphic bill colouration.

IDENTIFICATION: A scruffy-looking, top-heavy blackish crow with large, arched, bill (black or yellowish according to sex and age), brownish head and relatively short tail. Only possible confusion is with poorly seen

Grey Crow but latter is longer-tailed and has bare, pinkish facial skin and smaller bill. Torresian Crow has small bill and longer tail and is less of a forest bird.

DESCRIPTION: Length 45 cm. Bill large and long, with highly arched culmen. Nasal tuft prominent, divided at base of upper mandible, with culmen bare to forehead. Tail relatively short, slightly graduated but almost square-ended. Feathers of throat distinctly bristly, those of lower throat and breast rather loose, giving scruffy appearance, with visible white bases. Forehead, face and throat brownish-black becoming lighter drab brown on upper breast, neck and hindneck. Remainder of underparts blackish with distinct brown tone and slight sheen or gloss. Upperparts, wings and tail black, quite well glossed with purple and purplish-blue, most strongly on wings and tail. Irides blue. Legs blackish. Bill, black in males; yellow with black tip in females.

SEX/AGE: Sexes differ in bill colour, bill black in males, yellow with a black tip in females. Juvenile similar but plumage more scruffy and is paler and browner overall, with uniform pale yellowish bill and presumably has darker irides. Age process not known.

MEASUREMENTS: Nominate race: Wing 335, tail 171, tarsus 63, bill 74 (one specimen measured), weight unrecorded.

GEOGRAPHICAL VARIATION: Two very similar subspecies. It seems unclear as to which subspecies the mainland populations belong.

C. f. fuscicapillus: Aru islands, described above.

C. f. megarhynchus: Waigeu and the Gemien islands, similar but bill larger (bill 80).

VOICE: Described as a harsh 'gakock gakock' and a drawn-out 'er er er er'.

HABITS: A very localised and little known species, usually encountered singly or in pairs, but sometimes in small flocks of up to twelve birds. Feeds in canopy of lowland rainforest and in mangroves, primarily on fruits but probably also takes invertebrates. Apparently soars over forest on occassions.

BREEDING: Unrecorded.

HABITAT: Lowland and foothill rainforests and mangroves, up to 500 m.

DISTRIBUTION: Endemic to New Guinea, where only known from the Aru Islands, the West Papuan islands of Waigeo and Gemien and at two sites along the north coast of mainland New Guinea: the Lower Mamberamo River and to the west of Jayapura, the latter site being only very recently discovered.

STATUS: Rare, very local and poorly known.

REFERENCES: Beehler et al 1986, Rand and Gilliard 1967.

GREY CROW   Plate 24

Corvus tristis

Alternative name: Bare-faced Crow

A remarkably variable crow, with the most complex plumage sequences of the entire genus. Often looks scruffy, with bleached flight and tail feathers and white feather bases showing through thin plumage of head and breast.

IDENTIFICATION: Widespread forest crow of New Guinea. Plumage very variable but relatively long tail, stout bill and bare facial skin obvious at any age. Plumage generally appears rather scruffy. Full adults are extensively blackish-grey on head and upperparts with browner underparts. Immature plumages often very pale brownish-grey with very pale bill, but can be blackish above with pale brown head and underparts. Easily distinguished from very rare Brown-headed Crow by long, almost wedge-shaped tail, bare pink face and stout, but not massively arched bill. In flight long wings and tail and overall greyish colouration can easily suggest Channel-billed Cuckoo, but latter is a much longer, lankier bird with very long wings and tail, longer down-curved bill and has black and white barring on underside of tail.

DESCRIPTION: Length 42-45 cm. Bill quite long and stout, exaggerated by naked face, culmen almost straight at base, curving down to pointed tip, not strongly arched as in Brown-headed Crow. Nasal and ricital bristles few, hardly visible. Loral region, face and extensive surround to eye naked. Tail long (for *Corvus*), somewhat graduated at tip. Wings long. Plumage variable with age, prone to bleaching; feathers of head and breast rather short, showing whitish feather bases. Adult: Uniform greyish-sooty or brownish-black, with slight sheen on the wings and tail, most contour feathers with very narrow greyer edges and marks on inner webs of feathers contributing to a somewhat mottled, scruffy appearance, particularly on head and underparts. Lower underparts slightly paler. Bill dark lead-grey, with fleshy-pink areas along cutting edges and at base when not quite mature. Legs rose-pink, mottled with grey. Bare facial skin rose-pink. Irides clear blue.

SEX/AGE: Sexes similar. Age process complex. Takes some three years for very pale brown and whitish juvenile stage to attain fully sooty-grey adult plumage. The following summary is based on an analysis by Jollie (1978). Ageing is complicated by varied hatching dates, a seemingly prolonged moult which takes place irregularly throughout the year, feather bleaching and basic individual variation. Prior to Jollie's paper there was much confusion, e.g. Meinertzhagen (1926) was almost convinced that the palest birds were adults and that the darkest were juveniles (we now know that the reverse is true). Juvenile and first-year: head, neck and underparts whitish, washed grey-brown on lower underparts; whitish nape merges on mantle and lower hindneck with grey brown of upperparts, wings and tail similar, all feathers with narrow pale fringes; bill whitish, legs fleshy white, irides dark brown. Birds soon moult their head and body plumage into their first-year plumage, which differs in being washed brownish-grey on the crown; a dark tip may form on the bill in males. Second-year: head and neck grey-brown with pale feather fringes, throat paler due to white feather bases showing; upperparts darker grey-brown; underparts washed grey-brown; bill, facial skin and legs whitish-flesh, bill and facial skin with rose-pink flush, irides blue; males may have extensively dark upper mandibles, whereas females often wholly pale billed; tail feathers broad, not narrow or incompletely grown as first-year. Third year/adult: see Description.

MEASUREMENTS: Males average larger than females. Wing 315-352, tail 204-232, tarsus 58-60, bill 63-72, weight 635 (one).

GEOGRAPHICAL VARIATION: Monotypic.

VOICE: Typical call a frequently repeated, rather plaintive, almost startled, rising 'ahhh....ahhh....ahhh'. When a distant flock is calling the overall chorus gives the impression of yelping. Also said to give a whining caw and excited outbursts of hoarse cries.

HABITS: May be encountered in parties of five to eight birds feeding inside canopy of fruiting forest trees. Flocks are very noisy and excitable, the plaintive calls being quite far carrying, therefore in general this crow is far more often heard than seen. When glimpsed flying between the tops of forest trees the pale immatures look quite strange and might not suggest a crow at first. Flocks are of mixed age stages, the paler birds outnumbering the older dark adults. They feed primarily on fruits and have a fondness for those of a climbing arum. Although chiefly canopy feeders they will come lower and may be found feeding on the ground. Likewise they have a habit of coming down onto sandbars in rivers where they scavenge for fallen fruits and presumably some animal life to supplement their diet. Feeding groups tend to be rather scattered through the trees, but keep in vocal contact with each other.

BREEDING: Poorly documented. Nest undescribed. A clutch of two eggs are very pale greenish-cream with a sparse scattering of dark brown and grey flecks and spots forming a cap at the larger end. Breeding probably takes place between late August and late September, as recently fledged young have been taken in late October.

HABITAT: Forest canopy and forest borders, including large trees by villages in clearings and secondary forest. Found in both the lowlands and hills up to 1400m.

DISTRIBUTION: Endemic to New Guinea, where found throughout the island, except at the higher elevations; also on the islands of Salawati, Batanta, Yapen and the D'Entrecasteaux Archipelago.

STATUS: Relatively common over most of the island.

REFERENCES: Beehler et al 1986, Goodwin 1986, Jollie 1978, Meinertzhagen 1926, Rand and Gilliard 1967.

BLACK CROW and ROOK

Two widespread and distinctive corvids, the Black Crow is also widely known as the Cape Rook.

BLACK CROW   Plate 25

Corvus capensis

Alternative name: Cape Rook

The only wholly black crow over most of Africa. Despite its superficial similarity to the Carrion Crow, the structure of the nasal bristles and throat feathers indicate ancestral relations with the African ravens; it is one of the few crows to lay pink eggs.

IDENTIFICATION: Overlaps with Dwarf Raven in northeast Africa. However Black Crow prefers lush upland farmland to the semi-arid plains inhabited by Dwarf Raven. It is further distinguished by its slender bill, more square-ended tail and highly glossed black plumage, which worn becomes duller and browner.

DESCRIPTION: Length 48-50 cm. Forecrown rounded, giving domed appearance to head when feathers relaxed. Bill very slender and pointed, culmen gently decurved. Nasal bristles short, not covering nostrils. Throat hackles developed and slightly forked. Tail moderate, slightly rounded at tip. Wing relatively long, equalling tail tip when perched. Legs relatively long. Plumage glossy black, being glossed bluish and purplish, more bronze on head and neck. Plumage becomes browner with wear and bleaching. Bill and legs black. Irides dark browm.

AGE/SEX: All plumages similar; juvenile is dull black, not glossy and feather texture is softer and more woolly than adults.

MEASUREMENTS: Male averages larger than female. Nominate race: wing 293-350, tail 163-200, tarsus 62-70, bill 54-63, weight mean 697.

GEOGRAPHICAL VARIATION: Two ill-defined subspecies, which are probably not worthy of separation owing to individual variation within both populations.

C. c. capensis: southern Africa.

C. c. kordofanensis: north-east Africa. Averages smaller.

VOICE: Quite a wide vocabulary. Most frequent is a harsh cawing 'kraa-kraa-kraa' increasing in tempo and volume if danger suspected. Also gives a soft, bubbling, but far-carrying 'ker-lollop' or 'kwollop' with variations. A variety of other growls, croaks and gurgles may also be uttered.

HABITS: Territory-holding birds remain in pairs but non-breeders form small flocks of up to 50 birds in southern Africa, although larger flocks even in excess of 1000 birds are recorded from Kenya; even in southern Africa communal roosts have attracted as many as 600 birds. These roosts are usually in favoured stands of trees, but sometimes on telegraph wires in open plains. Established pairs are strongly territorial, driving away intruding crows; territories in southern Africa average some 60 ha in extent. Utters advertising call from tree or telegraph pole with horizontal stance and erected throat feathers. Walks easily on ground, its long legs giving quite a striding gait. Flies with deep, regular wingbeats but seldom soars as other corvids will; in display flight, and when chasing intruders from territory, often flies with stiffly-bowed wings and quivering opened primaries whilst uttering bubbling call. Forages almost entirely on the ground, especially in ploughed fields, feeding chiefly on grain, seeds, roots, bulbs, berries, fruits and insects, which it probes and digs for with its slender bill. Carrion sometimes taken; freely breaks open birds' eggs and takes frogs and young birds; reported occasionally to take young domestic poultry.

BREEDING: Solitary nester. Nest a bulky mass of twigs and sticks, sometimes wire, thickly lined with wool, dry dung and rags; possibly constructed only by female. It is situated in the upper branches of large tree or bush, or often on a telegraph pole. Clutch, three to six, average four. Eggs pale pinkish, speckled with darker pink, reddish-brown and grey. Incubation 18-19 days by female, but male might also help incubate. Both sexes feed and tend young which fledge at 36-39 days and remain with the parents for some six months after leaving the nest. Eggs recorded chiefly September-November in southern Africa and February-April in Ethiopia.

HABITAT: Various types of open country with scattered trees, from open cultivation to moorland and alpine meadows, acacia savanna and riverine trees in semi-desert situations. Apart from feeding in farmland it has little direct contact with man and tends to avoid towns. Prefers upland areas to lowland plains; in East Africa most numerous between 1200-2500 m and in Ethiopia chiefly above 1800 m.

DISTRIBUTION: Africa in two disjunct populations. Northern populations in the Ethiopian highlands, extreme western Somalia and south-eastern Sudan, extending south over western and central Kenya and marginally into south-east Uganda and northern Tanzania. It is also widespread over southern Africa, reaching its northern limits in central Angola in the west and north-west Mozambique in the east; however it is very local in Botswana (chiefly in the south and south-east).

STATUS: Common or abundant over much of its range, but often very localised; it is considered to have increased dramatically in Kenya with the spread of cultivation, which is no doubt the reason why it has colonised northern Tanzania in recent years.

REFERENCES: Maclean 1985, Skead 1952.

ROOK   Plate 21

Corvus frugilegus

A unique crow, its strongly sociable lifestyle and naked face setting it well apart from all other northern corvids.

IDENTIFICATION: Bare whitish face and basal portion of bill distinctive of adults, making the bill appear relatively long and giving the forehead a distinctly stepped appearance. In eastern race *pastinator*, however, face is almost fully feathered but extensive whitish over basal area of bill is still very striking. Juveniles and immatures have fully feathered face and are difficult to separate from Carrion Crow, but have less flat crown, more conical (straighter culmen) and sharply pointed bill and rather looser plumage, especially about 'thighs' and wing coverts; calls are also different, but juveniles tend to be more silent than adults. In flight overall silhouette similar to Carrion Crow, but Rook has distinct wedge-shape to tail tip, rather longer, narrower and more prominently-fingered wing-tip; primaries are held slightly flexed back during beats and the bill and head project further than in Carrion Crow; the wing action is rather quicker, less laboured than that of Carrion Crow and the pale face of adults is usually visible. Rooks are very gregarious, gathering in large flocks and nesting in tree-top colonies. Flocks freely mix with jackdaws. Carrion Crow is typically a solitary nester but can be sociable at other times as non-breeders form quite large congregations at roosting and favoured feeding sites. Slightly wedge-shaped tail and fingered primaries can

suggest Northern Raven.

DESCRIPTION: Length 47 cm. Nominate race: Forecrown slightly peaked, an effect created by the bare bill base (lacking nasal bristles) and bare chin and loral region. Bill relatively long, culmen gradually tapering to a sharp tip, almost conical in profile. Tail slightly graduated. Second primary longer than sixth, sixth primary not emarginated (cf Carrion Crow). Plumage especially dense and silky in texture on head and neck. Bases of neck feathers grey. Entire plumage black and highly glossed with metallic blue, green and purple (varying with angle of light). Bill whitish at base, becoming dusky over terminal half. Legs black. Irides dark brown.

AGE/SEX: Sexes similar; juvenile has shorter bill than adult, fully feathered face and prominent nasal tuft covering basal half of upper mandible; these areas become bare in latter part of first winter but not fully bare until first spring (April to June) by which time bill has attained full length; entire plumage dull and unglossed; by first spring flight and tail feathers abraded and quite brown-toned (glossy black in adults).

MEASUREMENTS: Male averages slightly larger than female. Wing 290-330, tail 157-175, tarsus 52-58, bill 53-57, weight 337-531.

GEOGRAPHICAL VARIATION: Two well differentiated subspecies recognised:-

C. f. frugilegus: Europe and western Asia, including Central Asia, east to the Altai. Described above.

C. f. pastinator: Eastern Asia, west to northern Mongolia. Adults have less extensive or no bare skin on lores and throat than the nominate and average a little smaller.

VOICE: Calls are distinctly different in pitch to those of Carrion Crow, notably a relatively drier and flatter 'kaah', uttered with increasing intensity and excitement when alarmed; also has a high-pitched, almost plaintive 'kraa-a'. Various other calls are given, its vocabulary being quite varied. 'Sings' from exposed perch, uttering various cawing sounds, accompanied by chuckling, gurgling and clicking noises and by backward and forward head movements.

HABITS: Highly gregarious, flocks forage in fields in open country often in company with jackdaws and starlings. Despite highly social flocking behaviour, pair bonds are very strong and last for several years, perhaps for life; pairs keep together within the flock and roost together even when joining massive communal roosts. Winter roosts may attain very large numbers; although the precise location may change during a season they tend to be generally centred on a rookery. These winter roosts also attract crows, jackdaws, magpies and ravens. Most rookeries are forsaken in winter but may be used as pre-roost gatherings where flocks assemble before moving off to their main roost site. At the onset of the breeding season birds return to their own rookeries to roost, although usually not until egg-laying has begun. Feeds by probing and digging with relatively long, pointed bill, walking confidently between bouts of probing, chiefly in grassland but also freely along seashores and tidal flats; scavenges at rubbish dumps, picnic sites and in town streets. Diet quite varied although far less of a carrion feeder than other northern corvids. Main food items are earthworms and fallen grain but a variety of other invertebrates are taken, especially leatherjackets (crane-fly larvae) and some molluscs and crustaceans (rarely recorded dropping mussels onto rocks to break them open). Vegetable matter an important component of its intake, especially fallen grain in stubble-fields, potatoes, acorns and some fallen fruits; will also take small rodents and eggs and young of ground-nesting small birds. In general, although some damage to crops is done, this is partly outweighed by the amount of insect pests that Rooks destroy; however, in Britain recent changes in farming methods have provided germinating cereal crops at times when other food sources are scarce, and this has resulted in local but quite heavy crop damage. Pecks at and turns over animal droppings in search of beetles and grain and locally has taken to visiting garden bird tables in search of human food scraps. Stores food items, especially acorns, which are carried to the birds' favoured food storing spot and buried in the ground, sometimes carrying such items as far as three kms. In some urban areas and at picnic sites individual birds may become remarkably confiding and approachable but generally flocks wary and alert when humans are around. The flight action is steady, direct and unhurried but in late winter displaying birds perform a peculiar stiff-winged, deeply-flapping flight over the rookery, often joined by other birds in pursuit of each other. Rooks have fairly complex display postures, which are well described and illustrated in Coombs (1978). On migration and when flying to and from winter roosts generally flies quite high. Readily soars, often in company with jackdaws, and indulges in brief aerial bouts of tumbling and diving on updraughts of air over hillsides and even when flying high over open country, especially in windy conditions. A mass of noisy birds will rise and harry an approaching large raptor if in vicinity of rookery but less persistent in chasing birds of prey than Carrion Crow. Remarkably tolerant of falcons nesting within rookery; both Kestrel and Lesser Kestrels sometimes breed within active rookeries but Red-footed and Amur Falcons are almost dependant on them, their breeding distribution being closely linked to the presence of rookeries. These falcons form small colonies within rookeries; they do not arrive until the Rook breeding season is well advanced and take-over disused nests, but when nest-site space is limited they will evict both eggs and young Rooks from nests and take them over. Long-eared Owls will also nest in old Rook nests within active rookeries and there is a record of a pair Ospreys doing so in Siberia. In the Volga delta mixed colonies of Rooks, cormorants, herons and Glossy Ibises are formed.

BREEDING: Highly colonial, forming colonies in stands of tall, chiefly deciduous, trees. Exceptional nests in bushes and even on the ground are on record. Nest a bulky construction of sticks and branches, with a deep cup lined with roots, grasses and dead leaves situated close to top of tall trees, usually several nests in each tree. Clutch two -seven, (average four). Eggs, pale blue-green, densely marked with brown and grey shading and mottling. Incubation 16-18 days by female, although male sometimes briefly covers eggs when female leaves nest. For first 10 days young rely on food brought to nest by male, but female joins in foraging for food as young become larger. Young fledge at 32-33 days, not returning to nest but roost in trees near the rookery. Young remain with the parents for several weeks until they become independent. Egg-laying commences as early as late February in Britain but in central Europe not until early April, mid April in Moscow region and not until early May in Kazakhstan.

HABITAT: Prefers agricultural land, wooded steppe and riverine plains with fragmented woodland or stands of trees; also fringes of cities, towns and villages with large trees and in winter often along the seashore, with preference for lowland districts. Breeding colonies recorded up to 2000 m in central Asia.

DISTRIBUTION: Continental Europe and Asia. From Britain and Ireland south to central France, eastwards over the low countries to the north of the Alps; absent from the Mediterranean basin and Iberia with exception of isolated population in northern Spain (Leon), also very sparingly in Switzerland and Austria. Widespread over eastern Europe (except along Adriatic watershed), south to Bulgaria and Thrace and north to Denmark but in Scandinavia uncommon and localised in extreme southern Norway, southern Sweden and southern Finland. Range extends eastwards over Anatolian plateau of Turkey into western Iran and further north across Russia to the Altai mountains, northern limit being about 60 N. Range extends southwards along steppe bordering Altai and Tien Shan south to Uzbekistan and eastern Turkmenia. Eastern race *pastinator* much less common but extends across northern Mongolia and eastern Siberia, reaching northern limits in Yakutia and southern limits in eastern China along the Yangtze valley. Absent from mountainous and desert regions of western China. Northern populations forsake breeding grounds in winter, dispersing south to the shores of the Mediterranean, Egypt, Israel, Iraq, southern Afghanistan and Pakistan, a few penetrating into extreme north-west India. Such movements also occasionally take flocks to areas where normally absent, e.g. Iceland and northern Sweden. Eastern birds move further south in China and also winter in Korea and Japan (in small numbers). Vagrants recorded eastern Greenland, Iceland, the Faeroes, the Azores, Madeira, North Africa, Novaya Zemlaya and elsewhere in Arctic Russia, Hong Kong, Hainan, Taiwan and the Ryu Kyu Islands (Okinawa). It has been introduced and become quite well-established in New Zealand.

STATUS: Nominate race locally very abundant. Considered to be increasing in Britain following decline since the 1940s, censuses in 1975 and 1980 produced an estimate of 1.5 million pairs in Britain and Ireland. Similarly common in France, Germany (2,250 pairs in Bavaria in 1986) and the low countries, including Denmark. At the edges of its European range it remains very localised. Spain: the very isolated population in Leon province was discovered in 1953, the 23 rookeries were studied between 1976 and 1979 but a worrying decrease was recorded; from a total of 984 nests in 1976 to 800 nests in 1979. Norway: the few pockets along the southern coastal belt totalled a meagre 350 pairs in 1986. Switzerland: only two colonies of any size, totalled some 250 pairs in 1981. Austria: 13 rookeries totaled some 300 pairs in 1980. Turkey: some 60-65 rookeries are known, but clearly many more remain unrecorded. In eastern Europe and southern European Russia it is an abundant, but relatively local' bird but in Romania extensive use of pesticides is known to have severely depleted the population; further east in Central Asia it is even more localised in the steppe regions to the north of the Tien Shan and western foothills of the Altai. Eastern race *pastinator* rare by comparison and sparsely distributed in China and Eastern Siberia, marginally more numerous in the northern Mongolia and Transbaikal steppe but specific references are vague. Clearly there has been a considerable decrease in the eastern Asian populations which is echoed by the very few observations of Rooks made during studies in north-east China at Beidaihe in 1985. In the same area in the 1940s it was recorded as a common breeding species in the area and very large numbers were noted passing through. Introduced New Zealand population estimated at 30,000 birds in 1978, chiefly on North Island.

REFERENCE: Coombs 1978, Ena 1984, Goodwin 1986, Kasparek 1989, Williams 1985, Yeates 1934.

AMERICAN CROWS

The North American crows form an interesting group of closely-related species. Basically there is one widespread crow, the American Crow, which meets or overlaps in range with three other smaller, but otherwise allopatric, smaller species. Therefore for field purposes the observer need only worry about distinguishing between two species of crows at any one location. However this seemingly straightforward situation is complicated by racial variation of the widespread American Crow. In areas of known or potential overlap with both the smaller Fish and Northwestern, Crows the smaller forms of American Crow occur. This situation is very vexed in areas along the Pacific coast of extreme northern USA where small crows with strange calls are difficult to allocate to either species. This has called into question the specific validity of the Northwestern Crow, but after decades of controversy the AOU continues to recognise it as a distinct species. The precise identity of the crows along the Oregon coast has still to be resolved; they appear to be intermediate. Physical appearance however seems to be of little importance in crow speciation, an excellent example of which is the Tamaulipas and Sinaloa Crows of Mexico. These are totally different vocally, yet in the hand would be impossible to separate with accuracy unless the location was known. The American Crow clearly replaces the Carrion Crow complex of the Old Word, being similar in size and habits, but despite superficial similarity, vocally it is rather different and it might well be only distantly related to it. The Palm Crow of the West Indies is related to these crows, whereas the other West Indian species may have originated from a much older form of crow.

NORTHWESTERN CROW Plate 27

Corvus caurinus

One of North America's most controversial bird species, a small crow of the coastal Pacific northwest.

IDENTIFICATION: Typically a very sociable and relatively small, rather short-billed and leggy crow, feeding along seashores, river mouths and islands. Over almost the whole of its range it is the only black crow apart from more massive Northern Raven. Problems arise at the very southern limits of its range, especially in coastal Oregon and northern California where birds occur which seem to be intermediate between the smaller race *hesperis* of American Crow and this species. Typical *hesperis* is however distinctly bulkier and relatively shorter legged than Northwestern Crow and has a slightly different voice, but the voice of *hesperis* is rather different to eastern populations of American Crow. Northwestern Crows are highly sociable but this would hardly be the case with wandering birds south of their normal range. The western race *hesperis* of the American Crow is more highly glossed on the upperparts than Northwestern but this is also of very limited value in the field. Voice seems to be the most useful field feature. See Voice and Measurements for further comparisons.

DESCRIPTION: Length 33-41 cm. Compared to nominate American Crow, markedly smaller, with shorter and more stubby bill, the nasal tuft on average seems to be denser, covering more of the upper mandible (however, these features do not hold true in a range of skins). Legs relatively longer than in American Crow. Plumage completely black, lightly glossed purplish. Bases of body feathers dark grey. Irides dark brown. Bill and legs black.
SEX/AGE: Sexes similar. Juvenile dusky black on head and underparts, with glossier, blacker wings and tail. First-summer birds duller than adults, becoming glossy black in their second year.
MEASUREMENTS: Males average larger than females. Measurements are compared with those of the western race of American Crow (*hesperis*). Weight 315-486, mean weights, male 415, female 368.
GEOGRAPHICAL VARIATION: Monotypic.
VOICE: Call a raucous, 'kraah', often repeated, lower and hoarser than call of western race American Crow and markedly more so than in eastern forms of that species. Also has a yelping 'yo-yo-yo-yo'. Gives a popping sound with head bobbing movements. Flocks are very noisy and excitable. Usual corvine rattles and low, bubbling sounds and even mimicry also reported. Essentially very close to calls of western race of American Crow.
HABITS: Very sociable marine crow, foraging along

COMPARATIVE MEASUREMENTS BETWEEN NORTHWESTERN AND AMERICAN CROW					
	Length	Wing	Tail	Bill	Tarsus
Northwestern	33-41 cm	259-292	145-171	42-49	45-53
American	39-44 cm	278-325	159-190	46-50	53-59

COMPARATIVE MEASUREMENTS BETWEEN AMERICAN CROW SUB-SPECIES					
	Length	Wing	Tail	Bill	Tarsus
C. b. brachyrhynchus:	39-49 cm	282-333	155-198	46-53	55-65
C. b. hesperis:	39-44 cm	278-325	159-190	46-50	53-59
C. b. pascuus:	43-48 cm	280-324	153-185	48-55	59-66

seashores and inshore islands. Noisy and very active they scavenge across tidal flats and rivers, attending salmon runs and quite freely associate with gulls, ravens and magpies. They are territorial in the breeding season, but breeding pairs tolerate the presence of non-breeding individuals, which are young birds from that pair of the previous year. Such birds often become 'helpers' either at the nest of the pair or merely by mobbing or warning of potential predators. Helpers are actually fed several times a day by the male of the pair, even if the helper takes no part in sharing the chores of feeding the young. Helpers will also store food items on the territory, a habit freely indulged in by the adults. They walk with a strutting gait as they forage. Their diet is completely omnivorous, feeding on offal, carrion, stranded fish, shellfish, crabs, sandhoppers, grasshoppers, beetles; also scavenges around fishing villages for human food scraps, raids seabird colonies for eggs and takes nuts and berries. Habitually drops mussels onto rocks from a height. Also forages in fields, especially in spring, flying a few miles inland to areas rich in invertebrate life. Mobs and chases large raptors with noisy twisting pursuits, chasing away birds as large as Bald Eagles. Flight action rather quicker than that of American Crow.

BREEDING: Solitary nester, but concentrations of nests in certain favoured areas. Nest of sticks, strips of bark, mud, and plant fibres, with cup lined with grasses, rootlets and animal hair. Typically in fork of a tree or shrubs, sometimes on ground under shelter of large boulder on treeless islands. Built by both sexes. Clutch four to five. Eggs very much as those of Fish and American Crows. Incubation about 18 days by female. Both sexes feed the young, often with their attendant helper. Nests with helpers tend to have a higher success rate than those without. Eggs laid May and June.

HABITAT: River mouths, wooded bays and open shorelines, inshore islands and coastal villages.

DISTRIBUTION: Pacific north western North America. Range extends from southern Alaska (Kodiak island), south along coastal Canada to southern Washington. Presence possible a little further south in winter, but situation confused by identification problems.

STATUS: Common.

REFERENCES: Bayer 1989, Davis 1958, Paulsen 1989, Paulson 1989, Roberts 1990, Verbeek and Butler 1991.

AMERICAN CROW   Plate 27

Corvus brachyrhynchos

Alternative name: Common Crow

The most widespread American crow, one of the few birds with a range encompassing the whole width of North America.

IDENTIFICATION: Over most of North America it is the only crow, but overlaps with Fish Crow in eastern USA and is replaced by probably conspecific Northwestern Crow along the Pacific coast north of Washington. American Crow however, occurs in inland regions north to British Columbia and the status of at least some populations along the Pacific coast is open to doubt (see introduction to American crows). Smaller, and with distinctly shorter, broader wings, shorter and more round-tipped tail, lack of throat bulge and with less projecting head than Northern Raven. Chihuahuan Raven has bill intermediate between Northern Raven and American Crow but is closer in size to the latter, it is a longer-winged and longer-necked bird than the crow and has a more croaking voice. Chihuahuan Raven is very much a bird of desert and arid, scrubby grassland, generally replacing the crow in its more southerly range. See also Tamaulipas Crow.

DESCRIPTION: Length 39-49 cm. Compared to Carrion Crow is relatively smaller, and has rather softer and less glossy plumage, especially on upperparts and wings. The bill is slightly stouter and the wings are blunter, appearing relatively broader in flight. Nasal bristles, prominent, covering at least basal third of upper mandible. Plumage wholly black, lightly glossed violet-blue, gloss more greenish-blue on wings. Bases of body feathers dark grey. Irides dark brown. Bill and legs black.

SEX/AGE: Sexes similar. Juvenile has grey-blue irides at first, soon turning brown, dusky black on head and underparts, with glossier, blacker wings and tail. First summer birds duller than adults, becoming glossy black in their second year. Inside of mouth red in first-year birds.

MEASUREMENTS: Males average larger than females. Measurements of three races are compared below. Weight (mean): male 458, female 438.

GEOGRAPHICAL VARIATION: Four subspecies are recognised. Differences are minor, but are important influences on identifying the more localised smaller crow species.

C. b. brachyrhynchus: Most of northern and interior part of range, described above.

C. b. hesperis: western USA, distinctly smaller and with weaker bill than nominate race, voice has tendency to be lower in pitch.

C. b. pascuus: Florida, smaller than nominate, with relatively larger bill.

C. p. paulus: southern USA, small like *pascuus*, but bill relatively smaller.

VOICE: Call a short hoarse 'ahhh', repeated with variations in emphasis and pitch, including a rhythmic panting 'ahh ahh ahh ahh ahh' when excited. These calls are quite different to those of Carrion Crow, being shorter and markedly higher in pitch. A variety of other calls are given, including the yelping 'yo-yo-yo' and various rattles and low murmurings and bubblings which have been mentioned for Northwestern. West-

	Length	Wing	Tail	Bill	Tarsus
Tamaulipas	34-38 cm	236-253	145-153	39-42	38-41
Fish	36-41 cm	265-300	138-177	39-45	45-50

ern populations of American Crow locally have very hoarse voices and are impossible to separate from Northwestern. The range of sounds produced by this crow are very varied.

HABITS: Usually found in pairs or family parties but large gatherings form at good food sources, sometimes exceeding a few hundred birds. Their communal roosts however are often immense in autumn and winter, birds travelling as far as 80km to reach them. Exceptional roosts have been estimated at 200,000 birds. Such huge gatherings have led to calls for their control, some roosts having even been bombed. Sadly this crow receives much bad 'press' simply through its overfamiliarity with man and his agricultural activities. It is actually a very beneficial bird and takes relatively little grain, apart from fallen grain in autumn stubbles. It does however, take young birds and their eggs when the opportunity arises, and clears up carrion and animal carcases alongside Turkey and Black Vultures. More important is that the greater part of its diet at certain seasons is insectivorous, feeding on the larvae of many pest insects. It is on the whole quite omnivorous, in coastal areas feeding along the shoreline and indulging in mussel-dropping in much the same way as Northwestern Crows and Carrion Crows do. Food hiding reported. Like the Northwestern Crow pairs on territory sometimes allow an extra non-breeding bird to live with them; this 'helper' may not feed young but helps in chasing-off or warning of potential predators. Always wary of man and his activities, a by-product of the persecution that it has long received. Northern populations are migratory, moving in very large flocks along quite narrow flyways, hence the massive autumn and winter roost concentrations mentioned above.

BREEDING: Solitary nester. Some western populations form small colonies, with as many as three occupied nests in one tree recorded. Nest of sticks, strips of bark, mud, and plant fibres, with a cup lining of grasses, rootlets and animal hair. Typically in fork of a tree, often in bushy thickets or telegraph pole, but only rarely on ground. Built by both sexes. Clutch three to seven, usually four to five. Eggs bluish-green to pale olive, mottled, speckled and blotched brown and grey. Incubation some 18 days by female, possibly aided by male. Both sexes feed the young, often with their attendant helper. Eggs recorded February to June. Nests are exceptionally parasitised by the Brown-headed Cowbird.

HABITAT: Extremely varied, only avoiding areas of dense forest or aridity. Favours lush agricultural country with scattered trees.

DISTRIBUTION: Widespread across North America, from the interior of British Columbia in the extreme north-west to Newfoundland in the north-east, with southern limits lying in northern Baja California, Colorado and central Texas. Absent most of west Texas and along the Mexican border of the Rio Grande valley. Canadian populations highly migratory, moving out of the interior to winter in central USA and along Atlantic seaboard. Sporadic in winter to coastal Sonora, northwest Mexico.

STATUS: Common to abundant.

REFERENCE: Davis 1958, Goodwin 1986.

TAMAULIPAS CROW   Plate 28

Corvus imparatus

Alternative name: Mexican Crow.

A small crow of the Gulf coastal lowlands of Mexico, vocally very different to Sinaloa Crow, its counterpart on the Pacific slope. The two are often treated as conspecific, together being known as Mexican Crow.

IDENTIFICATION: A small and very glossy crow with a short, small bill and remarkable frog-like nasal calls. Recalls a small Fish Crow but latter not recorded in range of Tamaulipas except in winter in south Texas. Fish would be best distinguished by slightly larger size, relatively longer wings and different call. American Crow absent from south Texas. Only black corvid in range of Tamaulipas Crow is Chihuahuan Raven which is hardly likely to be confused. Virtually identical Sinaloa Crow does not occur away from Pacific slope, again voice is all-important.

DESCRIPTION: Length 34-38 cm. Smaller than Fish Crow, with smaller, shorter, neater bill and head proportions, relatively slightly longer tail and wings, also has shorter legs, with unremarkable 'thighs'. Nasal tuft relatively short. Its plumage is quite soft and a lovely silky black, with a heavy gloss of blue, blue-green and purple. Bases of body feathers light grey. Irides dark brown. Bill and legs black.

SEX/AGE: Sexes similar. Juvenile duller than adult, but has much more of a sheen to its plumage than many other juvenile crows.

MEASUREMENTS: Males average larger than females. Measurements are listed below in comparison with those of the Fish Crow. Weight unrecorded.

GEOGRAPHICAL VARIATION: Monotypic. Forms a superspecies with Sinaloa and Fish Crows.

VOICE: Call distinctive. Typical call a low-pitched, and very reedy but nasal, frog-like sound, very difficult to transcribe accurately; may be rendered as 'nark' but has been transcribed as 'gar' or 'nar-ur'. Juvenile food-begging call rather different, in fact very close to call of Fish Crow; youngsters leaving nest in late May were still not calling like adults in November.

HABITS: Poorly documented. Very sociable little crow, foraging in semi-arid brushland and dry cultivation in small parties which gather together into quite large flocks when flying to communal roosts. At Brownsville in Texas they fly across the Rio Grande from Mexico to

MEASUREMENTS BETWEEN TAMAULIPAS AND SINALOA CROWS					
	Length	Wing	Tail	Bill	Tarsus
Tamaulipas	34-38 cm	236-253	145-153	39-42	38-41
Sinaloa	34-38 cm	235-250	148-157	39-41	39-41

spend the day feeding on the town's large garbage dump, associating with large numbers of gulls and Chihuahuan Ravens. They apparently return to Mexico to roost in the evenings.

BREEDING: Apparently nests in loose colonies in the wild. Typical crow nest, built by both sexes. Clutch four. Eggs pale blue, delicately streaked with pale olive-buff. Incubation 17 or 18 days by female. Eggs laid early April.

HABITAT: Lowland scrubby farmland and open woodland, including villages and ranch yards even in semi-desert conditions; avoids lush vegetation, coasts and mountains. Chiefly between 30 and 300 m, but reported 0 to 475 m.

DISTRIBUTION: Almost endemic to Tamaulipas in north-east Mexico. Range extends over an area roughly 150 km in width and 400 km in length, from the lower Rio Grande valley of extreme south-east Texas west to China in Nuevo Leon, southwards through Linares (Nuevo Leon) to a spot some 25 km south of Valles in San Luis Potosi and about Tampico on the southern Tamaulipas/Veracruz border.

STATUS: Common over most of its range. First noticed in Texas in 1968, now tolerably common along lower Rio Grande but most breed in Mexico, merely feeding in Texas.

REFERENCES: Davis 1958, Hardy 1990, Webber and Hardy 1985

SINALOA CROW   Plate 28

Corvus sinaloae

Alternative name: Mexican Crow.

A small and shiny blue-black crow, almost identical to Tamaulipas Crow, but with totally different calls and replacing it on the Pacific slope of northern Mexico.

IDENTIFICATION: Virtually identical to Tamaulipas Crow (with which it was formerly lumped as Mexican Crow) but voice totally different and tail slightly longer. The ranges of these two lowland crows are separated by the central highlands of Mexico. It is quite remarkable how different the calls of these otherwise almost identical cows are: Sinaloa has a short thin, high 'ceeaw'; Tamaulipas a short nasal, deep 'nark'. In winter some American Crows are possible in northern Sonora, but small size, small bill and peculiar call renders this bird unlikely to be confused.

DESCRIPTION: Length 34-38 cm. Essentially as Tamaualipas Crow, although tail relatively slightly longer.

SEX/AGE: As Tamaulipas Crow.

MEASUREMENTS: Males average larger than females. Measurements are shown in comparison with those of Tamaulipas Crow. Weight 229 and 258.

GEOGRAPHICAL VARIATION: Monotypic. Forms a superspecies with Tamaulipas and Fish Crows.

VOICE: Call distinctive. Typical call a short, plaintive, high-pitched cawing note 'seeaw'. Quite different to call of Tamaulipas Crow. Juvenile apparently has a slightly different note, quite likely this is the juvenile begging call which is typical of North American corvids and sounds very much like the call of the Fish Crow.

HABITS: Poorly documented. Very much as Tamaulipas Crow and in general found in similar habitats, but favours the seashore and tidal estuaries, both of which are shunned by Tamaulipas Crow. However like that species it is quite at home foraging around towns and villages.

BREEDING: No precise information. Said to have eggs in early June, rather than April as in Tamaulipas Crow.

HABITAT: Semi-arid brushland and scanty woodland, towns and villages, intertidal beaches and river mouths. Recorded up to 325m.

DISTRIBUTION: Endemic to coastal plain of north-west Mexico. Range extends over an area roughly 80 km in width and 800 km in length, from southern Sonora through Sinaloa, Nayarit and Jalisco to Colima.

STATUS: Common over most of its range.

REFERENCES: Davis 1958, Hardy 1990.

FISH CROW   Plate 27

Corvus ossifragus

A small, gregarious crow of low-lying wetland habitats in eastern USA, closely related to the two Mexican crows.

IDENTIFICATION: In flocks by marshes and lowland rivers of eastern USA, a very sociable small crow, with peculiar nasal barked call, often mixes with feeding American Crows from which it may be distinguished by smaller size, relatively longer legs, with long and prominent tibia, relatively flatter forehead which slopes into smaller, weaker bill and more rounded tail tip. Although the call is quite distinctive at most seasons, caution should be exercised in late summer as the begging call of young American Crows is virtually identical to the call of the Fish Crow. Compare Tamaulipas Crow which it could potentially meet in extreme south-east Texas.

DESCRIPTION: Length 36-41 cm. Compared to American Crow is relatively smaller, and has rather more dense, silky and highly glossed plumage, the bill is slimmer and the legs relatively longer. Nasal bristles form a rather pointed tuft. In flight the wings seem a little more pointed and the tail more rounded at the tip. Plumage wholly black, glossed lightly with bluish-green. Bases of body feathers light grey. Irides dark brown. Bill and legs black.

SEX/AGE: Sexes similar. Juvenile has grey-blue irides at first, soon turning brown, dusky black on head and underparts, with glossier, blacker wings and tail. First-

MEASUREMENTS BETWEEN AMERICAN AND FISH CROW					
	Length	Wing	Tail	Bill	Tarsus
American	43-48 cm	280-324	153-185	48-55	59-66
Fish	36-41 cm	265-300	138-177	39-45	45-50

summer birds much as adults, except for inside of mouth which is red in first-year birds.

MEASUREMENTS: Males average larger than females. Measurements are listed below in comparison with the Florida race of American Crow *pascuus*. Weight 195-332.

GEOGRAPHICAL VARIATION: Monotypic. Forms a superspecies with the two 'Mexican' Crows.

VOICE: Call distinctive, especially when uttered by rising flock, a short, nasal, falsetto, hoarse and dry bark 'ark, ark, ark' or 'arruk'. Distinctive when known although in late summer the begging call of recently-fledged young American Crows is very similar but not quite so abrupt as the call of the Fish Crow. Interestingly the calls of young Tamaulipas Crows and probably also Sinaloa Crows are similar, suggesting that they may be descended from Fish Crows. Vocabulary seems limited.

HABITS: Very much a bird of the coastal lowlands and riverine plains. Always extremely gregarious even in the height of the breeding season; although breeding concentrations not dense, they have favoured feeding areas where non-breeders may be joined by foraging adults. In winter, gatherings of very large numbers form roosts, often mixed with thousands of American Crows. Fish Crows feed along the seashore and in marshes, often wading in the shallows. They feed primarily on animals, especially amphibians, crabs and shrimps, they also rob seabirds and shorebirds of their eggs and chicks. Unlike most crows they have not been recorded taking human food scraps, but presumably do so if the opportunity arises. Will patrol low over the surface to pick items from the water, such as a floating dead fish or even small live ones which are grabbed in their claws as the birds hover and plunge dive. Flight action is faster than that of American Crow.

BREEDING: Forms small colonies, but not normally more than one nest in each tree. Will also nest as single pairs. Nest typical of other crows, built in a tree fork by both sexes. Clutch usually four to five. Eggs bluish-green to greenish-buff, mottled, speckled and blotched with various shades of brown and grey. Incubation some 18 days by female. Both sexes feed the young. Eggs, April to June.

HABITAT: Marshes, both fresh and brackish, low-lying riverine plains with scattered trees and coastal seashores.

DISTRIBUTION: The coastal lowlands of the Atlantic coast of the USA from New England to Florida, widespread over Florida. Range extends south-west around the lowlands of the Gulf of Mexico as far as Galveston in Texas. Inland it penetrates the Mississippi valleys to southern Illinois, but it is generally only a summer visitor away from the coast.

STATUS: Common to abundant. Seems to be increasing and spreading inland along the riverine complex of the Mississippi, where overwintering by riverside rubbish dumps is becoming more frequent.

REFERENCES: Davis 1958, Hardy 1990.

WEST INDIAN CROWS

Strangely, despite the abundance of species in adjacent Central America, no jays occur in the West Indies. On the other hand there are no crows south of Nicaragua in the Neotropics, therefore it is interesting that no less than four endemic crow species have evolved on the larger islands of the West Indies - nearly as many as in the whole of North America.

All four share affinities with each other and three of them share several structural features: upcurving and relatively short nasal bristles which leave the nostrils more or less exposed, a small bare patch of skin below the eye and on the lores, strong sharply-pointed bills and remarkably varied, quite musical chuckling voices.

Palm Crow is the oddity of the group as it is the only one to occur on islands inhabited by other crows; it also has better developed nasal bristles and a more typically corvine voice.

Distribution summary of West Indian crows.

Caicos (Bahamas)	Cuba	Hispaniola	Puerto Rico	Jamaica
Cuban	Cuban Palm	White-necked Palm	White-necked (extinct ?)	Jamaican

PALM CROW   Plate 28

Corvus palmarum

The only West Indian crow to overlap with two other crow species, and with the most developed nasal bristles typically concealing the nostrils.

IDENTIFICATION: Overlaps with both White-necked and Cuban, but is very rare on Cuba (now perhaps only Camaguey province), differing from both by being distinctly smaller, relatively stockier and broader-winged and in having a somewhat shorter bill. Close examination reveals that nostrils are covered by a tuft of prominent spreading nasal bristles, extending nearly a third of the way along culmen ridge; by comparison Cuban has exposed nostrils with a short tuft of velvet-like feathers at base of upper mandible and White-necked has upswept nasal tufts which extend over base of the culmen ridge rather than spreading in a fan-like fashion as in Palm. Palm has a distinctive habit of slowly raising tail and flicking it suddenly downwards, such movements are unrecorded for either Cuban or White-necked. Flight action of Palm is more rapidly flapping on relatively broader wings than the other two. Vocally quite different to either, lacking remarkable squawking and jabbering sounds which are typical of the other three West Indian species.

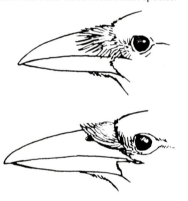

Palm (upper) and Cuban (lower) Crows, to show difference in bill shape and nasal bristles (swept upwards and only partially concealing nostrils in Cuban).

DESCRIPTION: Length 34-38 cm. Nominate race: Bill relatively stout and deep-based, tapering suddenly to a sharp tip. Nasal tufts conspicuous, spreading, concealing nostrils. Tail moderate, square-ended. Bases of neck feathers grey. Entire plumage coarse in texture, black, with purplish or bluish sheen; becoming duller and slightly brownish-black when worn. Bill and legs black. Irides dark brown.
AGE/SEX: All plumages similar; juvenile duller, not glossy, black.
MEASUREMENTS: Male averages larger than female. Nominate race: wing 227-264, tail 135-150, tarsus 49-51, bill 44-55, weight not recorded.
GEOGRAPHICAL VARIATION: Two races, differing in size.
    C. p. palmarum: Hispaniola (Haiti and the Dominican Republic). See above.

C. p. minutus: Cuba. Smaller than nominate, and slightly duller, less glossed. Wing 232-249, tail 127-148, tarsus 48-53, bill 45-51, weight (2) 263 and 315.
VOICE: Recalls that of both American and Fish Crows. A series of up to six sharp, high-pitched, nasal and quickly repeated loud 'craa' or 'aagh' notes, with some variation in pitch and speed of delivery; an excited flock calling together produces quite a babble of loud cawing. It seems to lack the accompanying squawking and fruity whistles, gobbles and bubbling sounds uttered by Cuban and White-necked Crows.
HABITS: Usually encountered in pairs or small parties of four to six birds in hill forest; small flocks of 20 or so have also been noted which are presumed to be parties of non-breeders. Reported to be relatively approachable, allowing observers to get within within 20 m of feeding birds; indeed seems also to be distinctly inquisitive, recorded to actually approach intruding observer to within three or four m whilst calling noisily, with drooped wings and flicking tail movements. Mobs larger birds, seen to chase a Yellow-crowned Night Heron persistently until it took to dense cover. Also recorded accompanying foraging White-necked and Cuban Crows. Feeds both in tree canopy and on the ground, chiefly on invertebrates and seems not to feed on carrion; food items recorded include beetles, caterpillars, cicadas, lizards, snails and fruits. Pairs and groups indulge in boisterous calling, with distinctive tail flicking movements; tail flicking is given by both calling and silent birds. Flight low, normally between trees, seldom above tree-top level; has rapid, flapping beats on relatively broad wings.
BREEDING: Presumed to be a solitary nester. Nests found in tall trees, especially in stands of palms and pines, at some 10 m from the ground. Clutch four. Eggs pale greenish or yellow-green, speckled and blotched with varying shades of brown and grey. Eggs recorded late April.
HABITAT: Forests and woodland both in lowlands and mountains, also in quite dry scrubby country and swampy woodland. In Cuba in open lowland cultivation with small groups of palm trees. On Hispaniola favours pine forests above 1300 m but also found in lowland forest, both in swampy country and quite dry plains with wooded ravines. Seems to be tolerant of hillsides with surviving areas of patchy forest interspersed with cultivation.
DISTRIBUTION: Endemic to Haiti and the Dominican Republic (Hispaniola) and west and central Cuba.
STATUS: Seemingly not uncommon but localised, both in lowland and in hill forest in the Dominican Republic, where quite easily seen at the Valle Nuevo Scientific Reserve and Lake Enriquillo; formerly widespread with older reports from between Bani and Azua, San Jose de Ocoa, Bahoruco Mountains (Polo), Constanza, Lake Enriquillo, Samana Bay, Las Matas and between Monti Cristi and Navarrete. Little recent information from Haiti but formerly widespread with older references to its presence at Mirebalais, Las Cahobes, Gantier, Thomazeau, Glore, Trou Caiman, Petit Goave, Port-au-Prince, base of Morne a Cabritis, Bombardopolis, the Etang Saumatre, Hinche, Caracol, St Marc, mouth of the Antbonite, east of Gonaives, Hatte Lathan, St Michel, L'Atalaye, Dondon, Cerca-la-Source and at the summit of La Salle. The only published recent observations have

been from the Massif de la Selle (south of Port-au-Prince); it has clearly declined through forest destruction but is presumed to be locally quite numerous, although its flesh is said to be quite palatable and no doubt this will have contributed to its apparent decrease. Cuban race has always been rare and extremely local, it has not been recorded from Pinar del Rio Province (where it formerly occurred between Guane and La Esperanza) for some time but is locally quite frequent in cultivation with scattered palms near Camaguey city.

REFERENCES: Bond 1971, Garrido and Montana 1975, Hardy 1990, Holyoak 1983, Wetmore and Swales 1931.

JAMAICAN CROW   Plate 28

Corvus jamaicensis

The only crow of Jamaica: a small, grey version of the Cuban and White-necked Crows.

IDENTIFICATION: Very similar in structure to both Cuban and White-necked Crows but smaller and markedly duller, with virtually no gloss in its sooty-grey plumage.
DESCRIPTION: Length 35-38 cm. Bill stout, deep-based and relatively long, culmen suddenly curving to a sharp tip. Nasal bristles short and sparse, nostrils more or less exposed. Patch of bare skin behind eye and at base of bill. Tail moderate, square at tip. Bases of neck feathers grey. Plumage relatively loose and soft in texture. Entire plumage dark brownish-grey, dull and unglossed, becoming blacker on face, throat and forecrown; wings and tail darker grey, with a slight gloss. Bill slate grey. Legs black. Irides grey-brown or reddish-brown (possibly an age or sex difference).
AGE/SEX: Plumages similar; no information on juvenile, but presumably has duller wings and tail than adult.
MEASUREMENTS: Male averages a little larger than female. Wing 224-237, tail 136-145, tarsus 48-50, bill 51-52, weight - no information.
GEOGRAPHICAL VARIATION: Monotypic.
VOICE: A remarkable variety of bubbling, turkey-gobbling, jabbering and chuckling sounds uttered together in a series of varied garbled outbursts. A harsh 'craa-craa', a more typical crow sound, is also given but the normal vocalisation is the garbled jabbering. The calls seem to vary with the season, the crow-like cawing possibly being a territorial call uttered during the breeding season, whereas the melodious 'jabbering' seems more typical of social gatherings.
HABITS: Little information. Typically encountered in pairs or small parties in forests and woodland, spending most of their time feeding quite high in trees, perching and calling from topmost bare branches. Larger numbers gather for communal roosts in the evenings. Works the tree canopy, its pointed, large bill being a useful tool for probing the bases of clumps of epyphitic plants, under loose bark and for digging in rotten wood for insects and other invertebrates. Primarily a fruit-eater, taking a variety of fruits and berries, including figs and bananas. Also reported to take eggs and young of small birds and birds which have been trapped by snares. Harries birds of prey, chasing them through the trees in typical corvine manner. Flight action distinctly slow and heavy, with deliberate wing-beats, pairs following each

other and calling when flying off after being disturbed.
BREEDING: Little information. Presumed to be a solitary nester. Nests in tall trees, possibly also in tree holes. Eggs pale greenish to greenish-white, speckled and blotched with varying shades of brown and grey.
HABITAT: Forests and woodland, including open forest mixed with cultivation and large gardens; favours hill and mountain forest but descends to lower levels in dry seasons.
DISTRIBUTION: Endemic to Jamaica.
STATUS: Locally common and possibly increasing its range in Westmoreland and Manchester, easily seen in Cockpit Country, about Moneague, near Good Hope, Wortly Park and in the John Crow Mountains but apparently absent from the Blue Mountains. Its dependence on forest habitats, however, makes it vulnerable to excessive forest clearance.
REFERENCES: Bond 1971, Cruz 1972, Downer and Sutton 1990, Goodwin 1986, Gosse 1847, Hardy 1990, Jeffrey-Smith 1956.

CUBAN CROW   Plate 28

Corvus nasicus

The widespread crow of Cuba. Very closely related to the White-necked Crow of neighbouring Hispaniola.

IDENTIFICATION: Cuba. The most likely crow to be seen on Cuba (sympatric Palm Crow perhaps now confined to Camaguey province). Compared to Palm Crow, Cuban is larger, with a longer, more tapering, pointed bill, is distinctly longer winged in flight, which is slower and has heavier beats; it also lacks Palm Crow's habit of flicking tail downwards. Under exceptional viewing conditions the nostrils may be visible, not covered by the nasal tuft as in Palm Crow. Voice is also quite different (see below). Compared to White-necked, Cuban is smaller and has grey, not white, bases to body feathers but the two species do not occur on the same islands.
DESCRIPTION: Length 40-42 cm. Bill relatively long, deep-based and pointed, with gently curving culmen. Nasal bristles short, stiff and velvet-black, reaching base of nostrils, which are exposed. Patch of bare skin behind eye and at base of bill. Tail moderate, square at tip. Bases of neck feathers grey. Entire plumage deep black, glossed bluish-purple. Bill and legs black. Irides dark reddish-brown.
AGE/SEX: All plumages similar; no information on juvenile, but presumably has duller wings and tail than adult.
MEASUREMENTS: Male averages a little larger than female. Wing 255-295, tail 142-174, tarsus 48-62, bill 48-60, weight 345-510.
GEOGRAPHICAL VARIATION: Monotypic.
VOICE: A ringing, high-pitched, thin screeched 'aaaauh', rising in inflection, less nasal and abrupt than that of Palm Crow, usually uttered with a variety of other sounds. Various liquid, bubbling trills and ringing high-pitched notes are given, but seemingly less varied and rich in delivery than either White-necked or Jamaican Crows.
HABITS: Little information. Quite sociable and conspicuous, usually in small and noisy parties flying be-

tween trees where they forage for fruits, berries and insects. Freely descends to the ground to feed on grains and other seeds. Often quite approachable where unmolested. In the Camarguey region freely mixes with smaller Palm Crow in the same trees and on the ground. Flies with languid, deep wing-beats in comparison to Palm Crow.

BREEDING: No information, other than nests in trees.

HABITAT: Forests and woodland, including areas of semi-cleared forest and sparsely wooded cultivation; often about woodland edge, villages and farmsteads with trees and with large gardens. On the Caicos islands is found in large gardens and areas of crops and wild fruiting trees.

DISTRIBUTION: Cuba and adjacent Isla de Pinos, also Caicos Islands in the southern Bahamas. A party of ten recorded in December 1984 on nearby Grand Turk were no doubt wanderers from the Caicos as there is no habitat to sustain a population there.

STATUS: Widespread and locally quite common, its range extending over the provinces of Pinar del Rio, southern Las Villas, northern Camarguey, southern Oriente and the Island of Youth (Isla de Pinos). Its dependence on wooded habitats makes it vulnerable to excessive forest clearance but it seems to be remarkably tolerant of clearance and has adapted well to living in areas of mixed woodland and cultivation. In the southern Bahamas it is still common, and is found on the islands of Caicos, North Caicos, Middle Caicos, Pine Cay, Parrot Cay and Providenciales.

REFERENCES: Bond 1971, Buden 1987, Garrido and Montana 1975, Goodwin 1986, Hardy 1990.

WHITE-NECKED CROW   Plate 28

Corvus leucognaphalus

The largest, and now the rarest, West Indian crow; like the closely related Cuban Crow it also occurs alongside Palm Crow.

IDENTIFICATION: Hispaniola. Very similar to Cuban Crow but larger and with white, not grey, bases to body feathers. On Puerto Rico it was the only crow but may no longer exist there; on Hispaniola it occurs alongside Palm Crow, differing in being much larger and having a relatively larger, longer and more tapering bill, more upcurving nasal bristles which sweep up from bill base over culmen ridge (Palm has thicker and more fan-shaped tuft) and bare skin about bill base and below eye. White-necked seems to lack the tail flicking movement which is characteristic of Palm and has a remarkable parrot-like squawking voice (Palm utters harsh caws). Its flight action is stronger, steadier and less rapidly flapping than Palm, and it readily soars high for long periods on its relatively long wings - unlike Palm Crow which keeps below or near canopy level.

DESCRIPTION: Length 42-46 cm. Bill long, heavy and deep-based, culmen gently curving to a tapering sharp tip. Nasal tufts fairly conspicuous, upcurving over sides of base of bill, partially obscuring nostrils. Loral region of short, stiff, very black velvet-like feathers. Area of bare skin below eye and at base of lower mandible. Tail moderate, square-ended. Bases of body feathers white. Entire plumage black, glossed purplish or bluish. Bill and

legs black. Irides red-brown (yellow also reported, possibly an age difference as both reddish and yellow-eyed birds were females).

AGE/SEX: All plumages similar; juvenile presumably duller, not glossy, black.

MEASUREMENTS: Male distinctly larger than female. Wing male 299-321 (female 285-292), tail male 192-203 (female 178-186), tarsus 52-53, bill male 56-60 (female 53-56), weight - not recorded.

GEOGRAPHICAL VARIATION: Monotypic. The population formerly inhabiting Puerto Rico were separated as *erythropthalmus* on the basis of supposedly slightly smaller size (male wing 300-312, female wing 288-298), but a wider selection of specimens has proved this invalid.

VOICE: An extraordinary mixed babbling, bubbling and squawking, very varied in content, some notes rich and sweet, others raucous and squawked. Recalls a chattering parrot rather than a crow. Wetmore and Swales (1931) also reported "high-pitched notes that are rather like those of the raven".

HABITS: Little information. Pairs or small parties in hill forest; larger gatherings of "hundreds" also recorded (in the last century) as gathering to feed in fruiting trees and bushes, with Palm Crows. Very large roost gatherings also formed, with immense flocks reported flying very high to and from communal roosts in the mountains in the evenings and mornings, often calling loudly; descending to lowland forests to forage for the day. Feeds chiefly in tree canopy on various fruits and berries and takes animal food to a certain extent, e.g. small toads and nestlings recorded in stomachs of collected birds; presumably insects make up a small proportion of its diet. Unlike Palm Crow often flies high over tree canopy, and also soars and glides high over forest. Flight action described as leisurely and graceful with deliberate sweeping wing strokes (contra Palm Crow).

BREEDING: Little information. Seemingly a solitary nester. Nests high in large trees; one nest described was in the crotch of a large pine. Eggs undescribed but nests with both eggs and well-grown young recorded from Puerto Rico in March.

HABITAT: Forests and woodland both in lowlands and mountains, favouring hill forest, especially pines, on Hispaniola. Only recorded in hill forest on Puerto Rico. Probably favours old, mature forest and is intolerant of areas which have been opened-up by forest clearance.

DISTRIBUTION: Endemic to Haiti and the Dominican Republic (Hispaniola); also recorded Ile de la Gonave and Isla Saona; and formerly Puerto Rico where probably extinct.

STATUS: Now only on Hispaniola where rare, being most regularly seen in hill forest in the south of the island in the Haiti-Dominican Republic border regions. It was formerly widespread and abundant over both Haiti and the Dominican Republic, but scarcer in the drier country of the north of the island. Even by the early part of this century it was evident that a considerable decrease had taken place and this decline seems to have continued. The bird was readily eaten by the local people, its flesh being considered "excellent". Considerable forest destruction also took place over the island around the turn of the century. However good forest areas remain. On Puerto Rico it is almost certainly extinct. Although formerly widespread it has suffered considerable persecution by man through forest clearance and by the gun;

the last confirmed record came from Luquillo in 1963. There have been sightings of single crows at El Yunque in recent years which raises hope for its survival, but escaped pet crows, brought over to the island from elsewhere, might be responsible for these sightings.

REFERENCES: Bond 1971, Goodwin 1986, Hardy 1990, Wetmore and Swales 1931.

CARRION and HOODED CROWS

Despite its striking plumage pattern the Hooded Crow is considered to be conspecific with the Carrion Crow. Most taxonomists seem to agree that this is the most sensible conclusion as the two forms are almost identical in structure and vocalisations, freely hybridise at zones of contact, producing fertile offspring, and geographically replace each other; in short they only really differ in plumage colour. Hybrids are common in Scotland and are now frequent in northern Ireland and the Isle of Man as Carrion Crow spreads slowly northwards through Britain; in Europe, hybrids are common in Austria, Switzerland, western Hungary and Germany. Eastern zone of hybridisation extends across Central Asia; hybrids are numerous across northern Afghanistan and north to the Aral Sea, steppes of Kazakhstan, northern Altai and the Yenisei valley. Despite this, Stepanyan (1990), in his the recent review of Soviet birds, has once more separated the two forms as species. The two wholly black races (Carrion Crow) are well separated at opposite ends of the species range by three Hooded Crow races over the interior of the Palearctic landmass. The situation is complicated by a third, possibly even more defined form, the Mesopotamian Crow of the lowlands of Iraq (an area which has two other endemic passerine species: Iraq Babbler and Basra Reed Warbler) which is very close to the Hooded group of races in plumage pattern, but differs in structure, whiteness of body plumage and possibly vocally; this little-studied taxon might well have already reached specific level through long isolation. The fact that all three of these forms are easily separable in the field is good enough reason for the semi-separate treatments given below.

CARRION CROW   Plate 21

Corvus corone

Alternative name: Eurasian Crow

The two black races of this crow are well separated, and they probably evolved independently in the wetter, maritime regions at opposite ends of the Eurasian continent.

IDENTIFICATION: Widespread black crow of western Europe and eastern Asia. In Europe it is only likely to be confused with Rook or Northern Raven. Sleeker and less intensely glossy black than Rook, lacking latter's bare, whitish face and bill base when adult, but immature Rook is very similar, best identified by proximity of adults and young Rook's almost straight, not curved, culmen which gives bill a more conical, pointed appearance (see also Rook for discussion). In flight, wings slightly shorter and less strongly fingered than Rook and tail more evenly rounded (when spread) or square (when closed) at tip. Northern Raven is considerably larger, with longer, more fingered wing tip, longer neck, stouter bill, longer, wedge-shaped tail and has different call. Asian populations widely overlap with Rook and Large-billed Crow; the latter has much more massive, strongly arched bill and steep, not flat, forehead, relatively broader wings and longer tail and rather different call. In central Asia range virtually meets Brown-necked Raven but the latter is a bird of the desert, rather than the lush cultivation and wooded hillsides favoured by Carrion Crow; although Brown-necked Raven is vocally quite close to Carrion Crow its shape and proportions are much as Northern Raven and it differs in the same structural features. Less gregarious by nature than Rook, Carrion Crow is a solitary nester; however large congregations gather at communal roosts and on favoured feeding grounds, e.g. estuaries or rubbish dumps; therefore degree of sociability should not be taken too literally. Where range overlaps with Hooded Crow, the two forms freely interbreed, hybrids showing variable intermediate plumage features.

DESCRIPTION: Length 48-56 cm. Nominate race: Crown relatively flat. Bill moderately short, with gently curved culmen to blunt tip. Nasal tufts conspicuous, covering base of culmen (bristles cross each other from sides, unlike Large-billed in which they are parallel) and extending over basal third of upper mandible. Throat hackles slightly developed. Bases of body feathers grey. Tail medium, slightly rounded at tip. Second primary shorter than sixth, emarginated sixth primary (cf. Rook). Entire plumage black, with bluish to purplish sheen, dullest on mantle and underparts. Bill and legs black. Irides dark brown.

AGE/SEX: Plumages similar; juvenile duller, lacking sheen, but much as adult by autumn although flight feathers abraded by first winter (fresh in adults), inside of upper mandible pink, blackish in adults. Second-autumn birds only ageable in hand by grey base to inside of upper mandible (wholly blackish in adults).

MEASUREMENTS: Male averages larger than female. Nominate race: wing 290-345, tail 156-195, tarsus 55-64, bill 54-62, weight 396-602.

GEOGRAPHICAL VARIATION: Two well separated subspecies in the black group of this complex (see introduction to Carrion and Hooded Crows for hybrid distribution):-

C. c. corone: western Europe.

C. c. orientalis: central and eastern Asia. Larger than western race; in the field gives impression that it is also relatively broader winged and longer tailed. Wing 310-375, tail 197-218, bill 48-69, weights recorded up to 690.

VOICE: Calls more rolling and resonant than those of Rook, slightly higher in pitch and a little less 'dry'. Usual call a vibrant 'kraaa', often repeated in a rather harsher, but similar, form. Has several other calls; sometimes gives an almost raven-like hollow 'konk-konk' but normally more typical calls are uttered soon afterwards. There is minor variation in pitch over its range, and to my ears the voice of the eastern race is a little 'drier' than western birds.

HABITS: Less gregarious than Rook, generally found in pairs or family parties. Breeding territories vary from 14 to 49 ha, the defended territory area retracting during the actual nesting period when the birds have to be more persistent in defending the actual nest site against potential predators. Some holders can be remarkably tolerant of allowing other individual crows into their territories, whereas others will even chase away crows visiting neighbouring territories; persistent intruders are not tolerated and members from adjoining territories will get together and destroy nests being constructed by an intruder attempting to squeeze into the margins of their territories. Most birds do not breed until they are three or four years old, although they reach maturity at the end of their second calendar year. Outside the breeding season territory holding birds forsake their territories and join communal roosts, often mixed with other corvids in winter, especially Rooks and jackdaws. During the breeding season they roost near the nest. Non-breeders are more sociable, forming quite large gatherings at good feeding sites, especially on tidal flats and rubbish dumps, often mixed with Rooks and jackdaws. Essentially a scavenger, foraging along seashores and lakeshores, rocky coasts as well as in fields and about towns, visiting gardens and parks where unmolested but always wary of man. Feeds by picking and probing, turning over stones and weed in search of invertebrates, molluscs, frogs, small birds and mammals, eggs, nestling birds, human food scraps and carrion, chiefly dead fish or road casualty animals, but also dead sheep; recorded snatching live fish and frogs from water surface in shallows and commonly carries shellfish into air and drops them onto rocks. Diet also includes a certain amount of vegetable matter which becomes seasonally important, including fallen grain, plant seeds, potatoes, fruits and nuts but largely carnivorous by nature. Freely steals food from other birds and will chase gulls and other corvids; occasionally small birds are chased and captured and there is even a record of a bat being caught in flight. When on territory chases raptors and other large birds well out of their territories, often joined by a pair from an adjoining territory. Normal flight action is steady and deliberate, a little slower and with bolder beats than Rook; soars less than either Rook or ravens and generally only flies high when on migration or when moving to and from roosts. In display flight this slow wing action is exaggerated with a deliberate down-beat, followed by an upward flick and wings held above the horizontal; flies towards an intruding crow and will circle intruder whilst executing this peculiar flight; Coombs (1978) summarises and illustrates other various social display postures particularly well. Crows seem to 'play' with objects, carrying things into the air and dropping them and enjoy swinging upside down from telegraph wires. They also readily bathe and indulge in anting.

BREEDING: Solitary breeder, strongly territorial. Exceptionally rarely two and even three active nests recorded in the same tree. Nest a bulky construction of sticks and branches, with a deep cup lined with roots, mosses, wool and hair; constructed by both sexes. Usually built on crown of a tall tree, but readily uses electricity pylons and, in more open country, cliff ledges, shrubby bushes, disused buildings and even occasionally the ground.

Clutch two to seven, average four or five. Eggs greenish-blue or pale greenish, speckled, blotched and shaded with olive, grey and brown. Incubation 17-19 days by female alone, who is fed at nest by male. For eight to ten days young rely on food brought to nest by male, but female joins in foraging for food as young become larger. Young fledge at 32-36 days, and are fed by parents for four to five weeks after fledging but remain with parents for several weeks afterwards. Egg laying commences as early as late March but generally in Europe peak is mid April. Eastern race more variable over wide range; recorded late April and early May in central Asia, early April in Ussuriland and late May and early June on Kamchatka. Nest occasionally parasitized by Great Spotted Cuckoo in Spain.

HABITAT: Great variety of habitats from open farmland, parks, large gardens, open woodland and forest clearings to coastal cliffs and upland moorland; forages along estuarine mud-flats, lakeshores and river sides, offshore islands and the sea-shore. Eastern race breeds as high as 3600 m in parts of Central Asia.

DISTRIBUTION: Nominate race widespread in western Europe from north-central Scotland, southwards over British Isles (Ireland, Isle of Man and northern Scotland inhabited by Hooded Crow), France, Spain and Portugal; eastwards to include Denmark and western Germany, south to Czechoslovakia, Austria, Switzerland and northern Italy. Winter dispersal takes birds south to Corsica, Sicily and the Balkans, occasional in Norway and Sweden and vagrants have reached Arctic Russia, Madeira, the Azores, Morocco and Turkey. Eastern race widespread over eastern Siberia, east of the Yenisei River, north to the limit of the forested taiga zone, southwards through Kamchatka and the Kurile islands to the main islands of Japan; on the mainland it breeds in Korea, northern China and Mongolia, with a southwards extension over the central mountains to Yunnan. Absent from the arid regions of western China, but extends south along western slopes of the Altai south to the Tien Shan and Pamirs, reaching southern limits in eastern Afghanistan and extreme northern and western Pakistan, Ladakh and possibly northern Kashmir. Northern populations highly migratory, wintering south to south-eastern China; some winter at river mouths even as far north as Anadyr and Kamchatka; occasionally reaches northern Iran in winter and vagrants recorded in northern Vietnam (Tonkin) and Hong Kong.

STATUS: Both races common throughout the main parts of their ranges, but distinctly localised in Afghanistan and North West Frontier districts.

REFERENCES: Coombs 1978, Dement'ev and Gladkov 1954, Goodwin 1986.

HOODED CROW   Plate 21

Corvus (corone) cornix

'The crow' of most of eastern and southern Europe, western Asia and the Middle East.

IDENTIFICATION: Essentially a grey and black Carrion Crow, which it resembles in everything apart from plumage which is grey on body and mantle, contrasting with black head, breast, wings and tail. In poor light the difference in colouration may not always be apparent, especially with rather darker European form. Hybridises freely with Carrion Crow over narrow overlap zones of the two forms; the hybrids variably show features of both parent forms. Range almost meets House Crow but no precise overlap known; the latter is less contrastingly patterned, with grey on nape and sides of breast (rest of underparts blackish) and slimmer bill and head. Compare Pied Crow which has occurred as a vagrant in Libya and is therefore a potential vagrant to the Middle East and see Mesopotamian Crow which replaces Hooded in lowland Iraq.

DESCRIPTION: Length 48-52 cm. Structural features as Carrion Crow. Crown, upper nape, sides of head, throat and upper breast glossy black, the lower border of the breast with black blotching. Nape, sides of neck, mantle, rump, axillaries and remainder of underparts grey, with an ashy tone, the feathers with having fine dark shaft streaks. Tibia black. Tail, uppertail-coverts and wings glossy black. Irides dark brown. Bill and legs black.

AGE/SEX: Plumages similar; juvenile has black plumage parts dull, not glossy; for ageing process see Carrion Crow.

MEASUREMENTS: Male averages larger than female. Race *cornix*: wing 302-330, tail 170-185, tarsus 51-61, bill 51-61.

GEOGRAPHICAL VARIATION: Three subspecies within the strict Hooded Crow group as recognised here (*capellanus* treated separately); these forms all seem to intergrade and *sardonius* is ill-defined.

C. c. *cornix*: northern and eastern Europe, south to the Danube and east to the Urals. Darker grey than others.

C. c. *sardonius*: south-eastern Europe, Italy, Mediterranean islands, the Middle East and Egypt. North to the Danube and east to eastern Turkey. Paler grey in worn plumage, but little difference when feathers fresh; averages slightly smaller and weaker-billed.

C. c. *sharpii*: Siberia from the Urals to the Yenisei, the Caucasus region, Iran and central Asia. Grey of body paler, less ashy than *cornix*.

VOICE: Largely as Carrion Crow, but differences in tones detectable (as with Carrion Crow), almost in the form of local dialects.

HABITS: Very much as Carrion Crow but in much of the Asian and Middle Eastern part of the range more closely-linked with human habitation, being common in the centres of towns and cities. It is also far more sociable by nature than Carrion Crow, becoming almost colonial; in Israel and central Asia this is particularly noticeable with nests as close as 100-120 m in areas where particularly abundant. In Europe and western Siberia however no such semi-colonial breeding seems to have been recorded, nests in Siberia being normally at least one km apart. This crow is widely used as a host by the parasitic Great Spotted Cuckoo in Israel, where Black-billed Magpie is absent.

BREEDING: As Carrion Crow but see comments under Habits. Egg dates also vary over wide range, recorded from mid January in Egypt, February in Israel, but later further north: late March in the Volga delta, mid April in the Moscow region and mid May in the Faeroes and Scandinavia.

HABITAT: See comment under Habits.

DISTRIBUTION: The Faeroes, Ireland and north-west Scotland, Scandinavia, eastern Czechoslovakia, Italy (except north), Corsica, Sardinia, Sicily. Eastwards across eastern Europe and Siberia to the Yenisei River south to Aral Sea and Lake Balkash. Widespread through Turkey and the Middle East, including northern Syria, northern Iraq and most of Iran (except south-east) to Turkmenistan and western Uzbekistan, marginally in extreme north-west Afghanistan but in this region most seem to be hybrids with Carrion Crow. In Near East extends south to central Israel and along Mediterranean coast to the Nile delta of Egypt and south along the Nile valley to Aswan. Northern populations migratory, dispersing south to southern Iran, lowland Iraq and southern Afghanistan, some reaching western Pakistan and western China (Sinkiang). Vagrants recorded Greenland, Iceland, Bear Island, Svalbard, Novaya Zemlya, Tunisia and Libya.

STATUS: Common or abundant over main range.

REFERENCES: Dement'ev and Gladkov 1954, Goodwin 1986, Shirihai (in prep).

MESOPOTAMIAN CROW   Plate 21

Corvus (corone) capellanus

Alternative name: Iraq Pied Crow

An isolated crow in lowland Iraq, strikingly different to adjoining populations of Hooded Crow and possibly a good species, but little studied.

IDENTIFICATION: Resembles Hooded Crow but generally appears black and white in the field rather than black and grey. In fresh plumage whitish parts of plumage slightly greyer. Overlaps with Hooded Crow in winter when Hooded descends into Iraq lowlands but observers who have seen it stress its very different piebald appearance and more massive bill. Compare Pied Crow of Africa which has occurred as a vagrant in Libya and is therefore a potential vagrant to the Middle East; the latter is easily distinguished by black lower underparts and mantle.

DESCRIPTION: Length 50-54 cm. Structural features similar to Hooded Crow, but bill stouter and with more strongly curved culmen, throat feathers more elongated and lanceolate in shape and tail more strongly graduated. Plumage as Hooded Crow but grey of plumage much paler, almost whitish; silvery-grey with faint rosy flush when fresh, bleaching to almost off-white when worn.

AGE/SEX: Presumably as Hooded and Carrion Crows.

MEASUREMENTS: Male averages larger than female. Wing 304-328, tail 178-197, tarsus 61-62, bill 60-64, weight - not recorded.

VOICE: Ticehurst (1922) stated that its call was harsher, deeper and gruffer than that of other forms of Hooded Crow. Moore and Boswell (1956) commented that it utters a peculiar rattling call, resembling a speeded-up version of the bill rattle of White Stork. This rattle lasts about a second and is repeated three times in ten seconds. Whether this is the typical call or not is difficult to say as very little has been published. It could be the rattling call which is occasionally given by other crows, including Hooded Crow, but if it is the typical call then the specific validity of this crow is strengthened.

HABITS: Very much as Carrion and Hooded Crows as far as is known, strongly territorial when breeding but non-breeders form flocks. Seems to be quite aggressive by nature, raiding nests of small birds and noted to chase other birds and even a hare. On the Euphrates they assemble in parties on sand-bars together with birds of prey and feral dogs.

BREEDING: Little information. One nest described was a "comparatively small" construction of sticks and palm fibres and was placed at a height of five m in an apple tree in a riverside orchard. Clutch four to five. Eggs are said to be distinctly larger than those of Hooded Crow, in fact very much like those of the Brown-necked Raven. Eggs recorded mid March to late April.

HABITAT: Lowland riverine agricultural country, with groves of palms and orchards; forages around slaughter-houses, gardens and river banks.

DISTRIBUTION: Southern Iraq, based on the Euphra-

tes delta, extending northwards to Ramadi and Samarra and to Kirkuk and Khanaqin in Kurdistan; range extends just over the border into extreme south-west Iran along the coastal lowlands towards Bushire. Replaced further north in the hills of Kurdistan and in the Zagros of southern Iran by the typical Hooded Crow.

STATUS: Described as very common in lower Iraq in the 1950s.

TAXONOMY: Despite marked differences in build and plumage colouration, a very few birds seem to show intermediate characters. Some Hooded Crows collected to the north of Baghdad and others from the southern Zagros of Iran are typical Hooded in build but are distinctly paler than normal. Until detailed field studies of breeding birds are undertaken it is safer to regard this form as a very distinctive taxon within the Carrion-Hooded complex.

REFERENCES: Goodwin 1986, Moore and Boswell 1956, Ticehurst et al 1922, Vaurie 1959.

LARGE-BILLED AND JUNGLE CROWS

An interesting situation has occurred in the evolution of this group which is widespread over eastern Asia. Generally southern populations are smaller and have rather weaker voices than those further north. In India they behave as two species, with large, deep-voiced birds throughout the Himalayas and smaller, squarer-tailed birds with weaker voices in peninsular India. Sibley and Monroe (1991) elevated the Indian forms *culminatus* and *levaillantii* to specific status as Jungle Crow (*C. levaillantii*) but more detailed study is required in south-east Asia where the two 'allo species' meet before a definitive view on the situation can be reached. Strictly speaking, it could be argued that *levaillantii* approaches *macrorhynchos* more so than it does *culminatus* and that it is only *culminatus* that warrants this split. For the sake of convenience and to highlight the problem, the solution given by Sibley and Monroe is followed here and the two groups are given separate treatment below. The Philippine population has at times also been given specific status, but here as with most other reviews, it is considered merely a form of Large-billed.

LARGE-BILLED CROW   Plate 22

Corvus macrorhynchos

The larger northern and eastern counterpart of the Jungle Crow, occupying a wide range of climes from the cold coasts of Siberia to the tropics of south-eastern Asia.

IDENTIFICATION: Range overlaps with Northern Raven, Carrion Crow, Slender-billed Crow and marginally with probably conspecific Jungle Crow (see Jungle Crow for comparisons). In all races head and bill structure make distinction easy from Carrion Crow, Large-billed having a relatively long bill with distinctly arching culmen and a sudden step where bill joins forehead; quite different to the smooth contour of the smaller-billed, flat-crowned, squarer-tailed Carrion Crow. Most likely confusion is with Northern Raven; in the Himalayas Northern Raven is a bird of the Tibetan steppe and northern faces of the main range. Confusion arises when observers are more familiar with the smaller, squarer tailed populations of India (here treated as Jungle Crow); the Himalayan Large-billed Crows are bigger and have a distinctly wedge-shaped tail and deeper call-notes, thus they suggest Northern Raven when soaring overhead on thermals (which true Jungle Crows do not normally indulge in). However the wings

of Large-billed are shorter and broader than those of Northern Raven, less fingered at the tips and the head projection is unremarkable. By comparison Northern Raven has the well-known 'Maltese cross' silhouette, with relatively long neck, relatively longer and more strongly fingered primaries and more strongly wedge-shaped tail. On the ground Northern Raven is bigger and flatter crowned, bulkier overall and of course utters the well-known deep croaks which Large-billed does not. The smaller populations of south-east Asia and the Philippines need to be separated from the similar Slender-billed Crow (which see for discussion).

DESCRIPTION: Length 48-59 cm (northernmost birds largest). Bill relatively long, with markedly arched culmen (stoutness of bill varying with race); forehead suddenly steepens onto bill base. Wings relatively broad, especially primaries. Tail relatively long, slightly wedge-shaped at tip (only obvious when spread in soaring flight). Throat hackles inconspicuous except on upper throat where often forms lump under chin. Nasal tufts conspicuous; although tufts meet at base of culmen the plumes are short and parallel with bill (cf Carrion and Slender-billed). Entire plumage black, highly glossed in some races, duller black in others, bases of neck feathers vary from dusky-grey to whitish according to race (see Geographical Variation for comparisons). Bill and legs black. Irides dark-brown.

AGE/SEX: Plumages similar; juvenile dull, not glossy,

almost brownish black. First year birds retain drab, unglossed wings and tail of juvenile plumage. Inside of mouth pink when juvenile, darkening to greyish-black in older birds.

MEASUREMENTS: Male averages a little larger than female. See Geographical Variation for racial comparisons. Race *tibetosinensis*: wing 320-380, tail 186-260, tarsus 57-62, bill 60-73, weight 450-650.

GEOGRAPHICAL VARIATION: nine subspecies recognised; another three have been described but are not worthy of separation (*mengtszensis* of Yunnan, *hainanus* of Hainan and *timoriensis* of Timor). Races differ in intensity of plumage gloss, colour of neck feather bases, stoutness of bill and overall size. The two forms of Jungle Crow no doubt also belong here but no intergrades are known, despite known overlap in the eastern Himalayas, therefore they have been given separate treatment.

    C. m. japonensis: Sakhalin and the Kurile Islands and Japan.The largest race, with very glossy plumage, dusky-grey bases to neck feathers and most strongly ridged bill (wing 355-390, bill 70-80).

    C. m. connectens: Ryu Kyu Islands of Japan (except southernmost). Similar to *japonensis* but smaller (wing 315-342, bill 62-69).

    C. m. osai: Southernmost Ryu Kyu Islands (Ishigaki, Iriomote, Kobama, Kuru and Aragusuku). Similar but even smaller (wing 270-295, bill 55-59).

    C. m. mandshuricus: Far East of Siberia (Amurland and Ussuriland), Korea and Manchuria. Similar to japonensis but less glossy overall and smaller, bill shorter but relatively deeper and more highly ridged (wing 320-376, bill 60-68).

    C. m. colonorum: Remainder of China and Indochina, including Taiwan and Hainan. Similar to japonensis but smaller and almost unglossed on neck and underparts, gloss of wing and upperparts less purplish (wing 310-350, bill 57-61).

    C. m. tibetosinensis: Eastern Himalayas (west to Bhutan), south-east Tibet, northern Burma and Southwest China. Large; the blackest and most glossy race, between *colonorum* and *japonensis* in size, with bases of neck feathers varying from dark grey to whitish (wing 320-380, bill 60-73).

    C. m. intermedius: Western Himalayas, from northeast Afghanistan east across northern Pakistan and north-west India to east Nepal, grading into previous race in eastern Nepal. Large but dull, greyish-toned, black with whitish bases to neck feathers and slimmer bill than *tibetosinensis* (wing 292-378, bill 54-73).

    C. m. macrorhynchos: Malaysia and Indonesia. Very black with slight purplish gloss lacking dull grey tones, bases to neck feathers whitish-grey (wing 300-335, bill 60-69).

    C. m. philippinus: Philippines. Much as nominate race, but with relatively longer tail, whiter bases to neck feathers and shorter, less strongly arched bill. This form was elevated to specific status by Stresemann (1943) but such a move has not been followed by other taxonomists; the latest review of Philippine birds (Dickinson et al 1991) also considers it as a form of *C. macrorhynchos* and this treatment is followed here.

VOICE: Typical call a rather loud, dry 'kaaa-kaaa', stronger and lower in pitch than *culminatus* Jungle Crow; also utters a variety of single, hoarse and musical notes, including a single, weak gruff note which could suggest Raven, but this lacks the far-carrying resonance or hollowness of the deep croaking 'prruuk-prruuk' of Raven.

HABITS: Although Large-billed Crows are usually found in pairs or small parties they assemble into large congregations where a good food source permits and forms large communal roosts. Young birds roost near the nest when fledged, joining communal roosts about 19 days after fledging, but seemingly do not return to nest area once communal roost joined, although they stay with their parents until about 94 days from fledging. In the Himalayas parties gather over ridge tops and play and soar on thermals and wind-currents, tumbling, swirling and diving in the manner of choughs, which they often accompany during these acrobatics; but northern populations seem not to indulge in aerial acrobatics like the Himalayan birds. Northern and Himalayan races freely forage well away from trees, the latter following herds of goats, sheep and yaks and even mountaineering expeditions high into the mountains. Like many other crows this is a true scavenger and is quite omnivorous in its feeding habits. In Japan a breeding bird has been observed to store and hide food items during early morning foraging, returning later in the day to retrieve them to feed both mate and young in the nest. In the Indian Himalayas, I observed a bird repeatedly hammering at a presumed, but unseen, food item with a stone held in its bill; such tool using behaviour is rarely recorded for any bird species. Has very strong pairbonds, probably for life, pairs keeping together outside breeding season.

BREEDING: Solitary nester. Nest a bulky and untidy platform of twigs, cup lined with wool and animal hair, placed in a fork of a large tree. Clutch of four to six eggs, similar in colour to those of House Crow but larger. Their incubation is wholly by the female for about 18 days; both sexes feed young and take part in nest contruction. Breeding season varies slightly over wide range, eggs recorded chiefly April and May in Afghanistan and Kashmir, May in eastern Siberia, March to June in the Philippines and February to April in Malaysia.

HABITAT: Woodland and forest edges of various types, chiefly riverine valleys in the far north but in the Himalayan region on mountainsides up to limit of the tree-line and beyond. Throughout its range it freely associates with human habitation, especially villages; in Japan and Siberia breeds in parks in the heart of large cities. It has been found as high as 5000 m in Tibet and birds have followed climbers to as high as 6400 m on the route up Everest. Northern populations forsake frozen interior in winter and congregate along coasts and river mouths. In Malaya chiefly in coastal regions, especially mangroves and around fishing ports, where range overlaps with Carrion Crow and Northern Raven, which replace Large-billed in more open countryside; conversely, in south-east Asia where it overlaps with Slender-billed Crow, the latter is the true forest species, and is replaced by Large-billed in more open habitats.

DISTRIBUTION: The northern limits are the southern Kurile Islands, Sakhalin and adjacent mainland of Siberia, southwards throughout Korea, Japan and China, west to Kansu and south-east Tibet, westwards through the Himalayas to north-eastern Afghanistan, southwards throughout tropics of south-east Asia, including the Philippines and Indonesian islands (Lesser Sundas east to Timor, but not Sulawesi or Moluccas and probably not Borneo). Its reputed former occurrence in south-east Iran and southern Tadjikhistan has never been confirmed (perhaps due to confusion with Brown-necked Raven and Carrion Crow) and its status in Borneo needs clarification (known from only four specimens).

STATUS: Everywhere a common, if not abundant, bird but status on some of the islands of south-east Asia is clouded by presence of other similar species (i.e. Borneo).

REFERENCE: Ali & Ripley 1972, Dement'iev and Gladkov 1954, Kuroda 1976, 1977.

JUNGLE CROW   Plate 22

Corvus (macrorhynchos) levaillantii

The only wholly black crow over most of its range, replacing the House Crow in the wooded countryside of India and Burma.

IDENTIFICATION: An all-black crow with a long, prominently arched bill, short, steep forehead and usually distinct chin bulge. It is replaced by the very similar Large-billed Crow (with which it is probably conspecific) throughout the Himalayas and by Northern Raven in the desert regions of north-west India. Therefore over its natural range in the more wooded areas of peninsular India and Sri Lanka it is the only all-black corvid. The situation in the Himalayan forests is complex and separation from the Himalayan forms of the Large-billed Crow is very difficult. In the western Himalayas true Jungle is absent, although in winter some Large-billed descend to the foothills. From Kumaon eastwards, Jungle Crows occur in the lowlands of the terai but the eastern form *levaillantii* ascends high in the eastern Himalayan valley forests, having been collected at 1850 m in Sikkim where it seems to be replaced by Large-billed only at very high elevations (above 3000 m). Differences from Large-billed are most obvious with the western race *culminatus*; the voice of this form is less powerful than that of Himalayan Large-billed, having a relatively softer 'kaak-kaak-kaak', deeper however than the call of the House Crow. In flight it is less raven-like, recalling House Crow with its virtually square-ended tail, whereas Large-billed has a definite wedge-shape to the tail when spread, or more rounded at the corners when closed. The eastern *levaillantii* is rather larger than *culminatus* but vocal differences still hold good, although the voice of *levaillantii* is considered to be rather different to *culminatus* (see Voice below). In the hand, or with close observation of a preening bird, the bases of the neck feathers of Jungle are dusky grey, almost whitish in *intermedius* Large-billed (western Himalayas through Nepal) but dusky in the very large *tibetosinensis* Large-billed (Bhutan eastwards). The latter however has the most wedge-shaped tail and is much larger and most raven-like than *levaillantii* Jungle which it replaces in the eastern Himalayas.

DESCRIPTION: Length 46-48 cm. Bill relatively long, with slightly arched culmen; forehead suddenly steepens onto bill base. Wings relatively broad, especially primaries. Tail relatively long, almost square at tip. Throat hackles inconspicuous except on upper throat where often forms lump under chin. Nasal tufts conspicuous, shorter but meeting at base of culmen. Both races: Entire plumage glossy black, bases of neck feathers dusky-grey. Bill and legs black. Irides dark-brown.

AGE/SEX: All plumages similar; juvenile dull, not glossy, blackish. First year birds retain drab, unglossed wings and tail of juvenile plumage. Inside of mouth pink when juvenile, darkening to greyish-black in older birds. Iris pale greyish in fledglings.

MEASUREMENTS: Male averages a little larger than female. Race *culminatus*: wing 260-319, tail 147-189, tarsus 49-59, bill 52-67, weight 320-410.

GEOGRAPHICAL VARIATION: Two subspecies recognised, but intergrades occur in Bengal.

C. *(m)l. culminatus*: Smaller than *levaillantii*, with shorter and less arched bill. Peninsular India and Sri Lanka, north to the lowlands of Nepal.

C. *(m)l. levaillantii*: Larger than *culminatus*. From extreme south-east Nepal eastwards through north-east India to Burma and northern Thailand, also Andaman Islands (wing 280-335, bill 55-69).

VOICE: Typical call a dry, 'kaaa-kaaa-kaak', harsher and deeper than call of House Crow. Also several short croaks and even some quite musical notes may be given at other times. Race *levaillantii* has a more nasal, 'quank, quank, quank' in comparison to Indian peninsular birds.

HABITS: Usually met with in pairs or small parties, often loosely consorting with feeding House Crows near habitation, but always near extensive stands of trees; larger congregations may form at favoured feeding spots. In general replaces House Crow in rural and wooded country and is less bold and fearless, but like House Crow is inquisitive and will relentlessly harry birds of prey, mobbing and aggravating both incubating birds on the nest and any low-flying large raptor which is persistently chased. Equally as omnivorous as House Crow, foraging in similar wide variety of methods, but less directly in town streets; forages along coasts and lakesides and like House Crow will clumsily hawk for flying termites. It will steal food from vulture nest sites, even from under the protesting gaze of the parent vulture which has regurgitated food for its chicks. Forms roost gatherings and flies considerable distances to roost as does House Crow, with which forms mixed roost congregations and flight-paths. Flight action and gait much as House Crow, but does not indulge in high-flying soaring and tumbling on thermals like the Himalayan races of Large-billed Crow. Like the House Crow, is parasitised by the Koel but to a lesser extent.

BREEDING: Solitary nester. Nest an untidy structure of twigs, cup lined with animal hair and plant fibres, placed in a tree fork, often near human habitation. Clutch of three to five eggs, similar in colour to those of House Crow but slightly larger. Incubation chiefly by female, but male thought to take some share in these duties, for 17-19 (usually 18) days; both sexes feed young and take part in nest construction; young fledge at about 3-4 weeks. Breeding season is principally March/April in northern India, January to March in Bangladesh and Assam, May-July in Sri Lanka, but breeding recorded at anytime over its range as a whole.

HABITAT: Wooded plains and hills, especially on the outskirts of towns and villages; locally also in town and city parks and gardens. Recorded breeding up to 2000 m in Sri Lanka, 2300 m in the Nilgiris and 1850 m in Sikkim. **DISTRIBUTION**: Peninsular India from central Rajasthan and Kumaon, south and east across the subcontinent to include Sri Lanka; north to the Nepal terai and higher in the eastern Himalayas through Bhutan, Bangladesh and Burma to northern Thailand.

STATUS: Numerous or abundant over most of its range, but distinctly sparse and uncommon in the dry country of Rajasthan.

REFERENCE: Ali & Ripley 1972.

AUSTRALIAN CROWS

Australian crows and ravens provide the birdwatcher with the ultimate challenge to his field skills; prolonged familiarity with the behaviour and calls of these birds is imperative before an observer can be confident of tentative specific identifications. Australia is unique in having five, possibly six, species most of which are sympatric with three others which are almost identical to the untrained ear and eye. They may even form mixed gatherings outside the breeding season; therefore distribution is only of limited help but will narrow the choice of species a little.

All adult Australian corvids are glossy black and have whitish eyes (immatures are dark-eyed), only one (Torresian Crow) occurs outside Australia. Following many years of taxonomic confusion Rowley (1970) produced a thorough and masterly review of the entire complex based on both intensive field-work and skin study. His descriptions of two new taxa, the Little Raven in 1967 and the New England Raven in 1970 helping to clarify part of the confusion, plus confirming that the Forest Raven was present on the Australian mainland as well as on Tasmania.

For field purposes, voice is the most useful aid to identifying Australian corvids but care and experience is needed correctly to interpret the sounds heard as most species utter a wide range of calls. The territorial or 'advertising' call is the one to listen for and posture and associated wing movements produced whilst calling are also important.

Basically the differences between Australian crows and ravens as separate groups are minimal for field purposes, but the following pointers might be helpful under certain conditions:-

'Ravens'
Grey bases to body feathers. Throat hackles pointed or forked, fanned (or erected) into a distinct bulge on throat when calling (obvious in Australian but hardly visible in Little Raven). Wings relatively longer than in the two crows (except in Forest and New England Ravens). Some bare skin on upper chin (inter-ramal region), most apparent on juveniles as the skin is pinkish rather than black of adults, but Little Raven has these areas feathered. When giving territorial call in flight, wings do not 'miss a beat'. Mostly southern in distribution.

'Crows'
White bases to body feathers. Throat hackles blunt, not forming conspicuous bulge when calling. When giving territorial call in flight, wings miss a beat. Mostly northern in distribution.

More detailed comparisons are given under the species accounts.
References: Rowley 1970, 1973.

TORRESIAN CROW   Plate 29

Corvus orru

Alternative name: Australian Crow.

Widespread over most of Australia (except the very south); the only Australian corvid not entirely confined to Australia.

IDENTIFICATION: Range overlaps with Long-billed Crow in the Moluccas from which it may be distinguished by its obviously smaller and shorter bill and preference for open habitats. In New Guinea it is the only wholly black corvid. In Australia it is widespread over most of the northern half of the country but is absent south of 30°S (except locally in the south-west). It is the only corvid over most of northern Western Australia, northern Northern Territory and the Cape York peninsula of Queensland. Elsewhere there is considerable overlap with other species: New England Raven and Little Raven in northern New South Wales (which see for discussion) and more widely with Australian Raven and Little Crow:-

Australian Raven: Marginal overlap in interior of southern Western Australia, extensive overlap over eastern half of the range of Torresian except Cape York peninsula where Australian Raven absent. Torresian separable by white (not grey) bases to body feathers and has slight, not prominent, bulge on lower throat (not the obvious fanned bulge of the raven) when calling. In flight wings and tail tip slightly more rounded in Torresian. Posture of Torresian when uttering territorial call is more upright than in Australian Raven, only lowering head and slightly flapping wings when calling; posture more crouching and horizontal in Australian Raven; some calls are slightly prolonged (see Voice) but does not really approach the mournful moan which is characteristic of Australian Raven. When uttering territorial call in flight, utters a single nasal 'akh' and misses a wing-beat whilst calling (this habit not done by the 'ravens'). Torresian has a distinctive habit of repeatedly lifting and shuffling wings when settling on perch, much more marked than in other Australian corvids (see also Habits).

Little Crow: Extensive sympatry over most of range, except coastal Queensland and upland Northern Australia where Little Crow absent. Torresian invariably

SUMMARY OF IDENTIFICATION FEATURES OF AUSTRALIAN CROWS

	Torresian Crow C. orru	Little Crow C. bennetti	Australian Raven C. coronoides	Little Raven C. mellori	Forest Raven C. tasmanicus
Unique Features	Shuffles wings obviously when alighting, two to three or more times. Only corvid over most of the north-west.	Flight feathers a little greyer than underwing coverts when overhead. Flocks often fly very high and indulge in aerobatics.	Call posture (below) Huge throat fan (below) Wailing call (below)	In courtship male struts around female, with tail raised and wings drooped.	The only corvid in Tasmania and vicinity of Wilson Prom.
Territorial Call	Short, amost frog-like barked calls, with final note often lengthened to a low growl.	Quicker, more buzzing, nasal call notes of more even length.	Strong 'aah-aah-aah', final note prolonged into a wailing mournful moan	Guttural, 'arkark-ark' of even notes.	Very deep, relatively slow, 'korr-korr-korr-korr' with final note often prolonged.
Territorial Perched Calling	Upright posture, slightly flicking wing-tips, from high perch, sometimes on ground.	Upright posture, with no wing-flicking, from low perch or ground.	Horizontal, with head down and huge throat fan, usually from high perch with no wing flipping.	Upright posture from perch or ground, flips wings with each call. No or very slight throat bulge.	Upright posture, from high perch. No wing flipping.
Territorial Flight Calling	Misses wing-beat with each single call-note.	Utters double call whilst missing a beat, but cals less in flight.	Utters wailing cries with continuous wing-beat.	Utters guttural calls with continuous wing-beat.	Calls in flight with continuous wing-beat.
Head Shape	Relatively flat, bill = or longer than head.	Slightly domed, bill shorter than head.	Crown slopes to peak at rear, bill large and longer than head.	Crown flat, bill longer than head.	Crown flat, bill very large and heavy, longer than head.
Throat Bulge	Slight when calling.	None.	Obvious, especially when calling.	Slight, but small bulge under chin when carrying food.	Slight.
Flight Shape	Wings relatively blunter than Australian and Little Ravens.		Wings relatively longer than the crows.	Wings relatively longer than the two crows.	Wings relativel broader and blunter and tail relatively shorter than other ravens, except in New England race.
Body Feather Bases	White in adults but grey in juveniles of both crows.	Sociable at all times. Flocks often very large.	Dark grey at all ages.	Dark grey at all ages in all three ravens.	
Flocking	Non-breeders form small flocks. Pairs strongly territorial.	Flocks and small parties favour arid and country. Feeds chiefly on the ground.	Non-breeders form small flocks. Pairs strongly territorial.	Non-breeders form large flocks. Often breeds in loose colonies.	Non-breeders form small flocks. Pairs strongly territorial.
Habitat	Varied, but prefers lush areas with trees, in arid country sparse by trees al;ong watercourses. Feeds in trees and on the ground.	Flocks and small parties in arid country. Feeds chiefly on the ground.	Varied, but prefers lush areas with trees, in arid country sparse by trees along water-courses. Feeds on the ground.	Flocks and small parties in more open country than Australian Raven. Feeds in trees as well as on the ground.	Forest edges and clearings, preferring more enclosed woodland than other two ravens where ranges meet. Feeds chiefly on the ground.

associated with trees along watercourses whereas Little Crow replaces it in more arid areas, especially in the interior where Torresian is sparse and local (flocks in arid country are Little Crows). Little Crow is a slightly smaller, sleeker, fuller-crowned, smaller-billed bird and often appears relatively longer-legged (perhaps exaggerated by sleeker plumage in hotter habitats) and the calls are less varied, and have a distinctly more nasal, buzzing quality. Little Crow has slightly greyer undersides to flight feathers offering slight contrast with blacker coverts and primary tips - underwing uniformly black in all other Australian corvids. Torresian does not perform tumbling aerobatics of Little Crow and generally does not fly so high; wing-beats of Little are also a little quicker. Calling postures resemble Torresian but does not flick wings, and calls more habitually from ground, not from high exposed perches; when uttering territorial call in flight, utters a double, not single, call and misses a wing-beat like Torresian. See also Habits.

DESCRIPTION: Length 50-55 cm. Race *ceciliae*: Bill moderately long with gently curving culmen. Nasal tufts moderate. Inter-ramal area fully feathered. Throat feathers slightly elongated, blunt or very slightly forked at tip. Tail medium-long, slightly graduated at tip. Entire plumage black, strongly glossed purple and purplish-blue. Bases of body feathers pure white. Bill and legs black. Irides bluish-white or white with bluish inner ring.

AGE/SEX: Plumages similar; juvenile dull, not glossy, black; irides bluish in nestlings, but darken to brownish at fledging, becoming mottled when just under a year old and finally white at end of second year.

MEASUREMENTS: Male averages a little larger than female. *C. o. ceciliae*: wing, 315-382; tail 166-216; tarsus 57-67; bill 47-60; weight 430-670.

GEOGRAPHICAL VARIATION: Four races recognised, differing in colour of gloss and slightly in overall size, bill shape and iris colour. The form *latirostris* is in need of a taxonomic review; its placement within this species might not be correct.

C. o. *ceciliae*: Australia. Described above.

C. o. *orru*: New Guinea and the Moluccas. Plumage gloss more violet and tail slightly shorter than *ceciliae*; wing 307-348; tail 162-187; bill 53-60.

C. o. *insularis*: Bismarck Archipelago. Slightly smaller than *ceciliae*, with bluish irides at all ages, even as a juvenile.

C. o. *latirostris*: Tanimbar and Babar Islands (Lesser Sundas). Differs from nominate in having slightly stouter bill, narrower and more pointed throat feathers (more or less forked at tip); purple gloss only obvious on wings and mantle; bluish-white irides; wing 305-325; tail 180-190; bill 55-60.

VOICE: Based on personal observations of *ceciliae*: Territorial call is a rather dry and quickly repeated "akh-akh-akh" (deeper, less nasal and without buzzing quality of Little Crow); more conversational is a slower, enquiring "qwak-qwak-qwark-qwaark ?" uttered with a frog-like croaking or small dog-like barking quality; often ending in a descending slow growl "qwaaaarg-aaaaarg". Latter notes suggest Australian Raven but are less prolonged, less mournful and retain croaking tone. Other calls in general are shorter and higher in pitch than those of Australian Raven. Birds inhabiting the more arid interior of Western Australia apparently utter a more stuttering falsetto call than those of the tropical north.

The voice of *C. o. insularis* seems to be similar; it has been described as 'krah, krah, kroaaa' with a comical emphasis on the drawn-out final syllable. This is perhaps akin to the enquiring croaked sequence described above for *ceciliae*. However the same author (Heinroth, 1903) says that the typical call resembled the native name for this bird "kottkott" which is difficult to assign to the above summary.

HABITS: Moderately sociable, forming flocks (presumably of non-breeders) of 60-100 birds in areas where abundant, together with flocks of Little Crows at good feeding sites such as rubbish dumps, slaughter-houses, towns, farmsteads and aboriginal encampments. At camp sites and picnic areas in northern Australia small gatherings are usually in attendance, where they often become quite bold and fearless. They are omnivorous, taking almost anything from grain, fruit and peanuts to beetles, grasshoppers and caterpillars; they also scavenge along seashores and mudflats, feeding on stranded fish etc. In general its food intake has been diagnosed as 31% plant material, 26% carrion and 43% insects. They are able to perch on standing cereals and pick grain from the growing crops and may do some local damage to cereal, fruit and peanut crops. Hiding of surplus food items is also recorded. The territorial call is uttered from a tree top or exposed branch, slightly flicking wing tips whilst calling; when calling from ground does so with tail slightly depressed, also flicking 'shoulders' as well as wing tips. When uttering territorial call in flight habitually misses a beat (a characteristic of Torresian, but also sometimes done by Little Crow, but not by the 'ravens'). Another useful behavioural trait is Torresian's habit of lifting and shuffling wings two or three times when settling on perch, much more marked than in other Australian corvids; this is even more marked when greeting mate at perch, with exaggerated wing-quivering, again apparently not done in other Australian corvids. Does not fly very high, usually not far above tree-tops, and never seems to indulge in high-flying aerobatics of Little Crow.

BREEDING: Solitary nester. Nest a bulky structure of twigs (but a smaller and rather weaker structure than nest of Australian Raven), with a cup lined with animal hair and plant fibres, placed high in the outer branches or fork of a tall tree. Clutch of two to five pale blue-green or whitish eggs, sometimes almost unmarked but usually weakly spotted and blotched with dark brown and olive-brown. Incubation by female only but both parents feed young at nest. Breeding season June to September in north-western Australia, October to February in Queensland, eggs reported in January in New Guinea, and February and March in the Bismarck Archipelago.

HABITAT: Open forest and riverine woodlands, coastal scrub and associated tidal beaches and mudflats; cultivation and wooded savannah with human settlements. Town parks and gardens, rubbish-dumps etc. In the more arid interior of Australia only along tree-lined watercourses, avoiding very arid regions where replaced by Little Crow.

DISTRIBUTION: Australia and New Guinea. In Indonesia it is found in the northern Moluccas (Morotai, Halmahera, Obi and adjacent smaller islands) - a specimen reported collected in northern Sulawesi is not formally accepted. It is also found in the eastern Lesser Sundas (Tanimbar and Babar) and throughout New Guinea, including islands off the east coast, east to the Louisades and the inner Bismarck Archipelago (including New Britain, New Ireland and New Hanover). In Australia it is widespread over the humid north and east of Queensland but is scarce in the very dry areas of the interior south and south-west; its range extends into north-eastern New South Wales; it is widespread over coastal Northern Territory and sparsely distributed across the interior; in South Australia it only occurs in the more vegetated parts of the Central Ranges in the extreme north-west; in Western Australia it is widespread in the humid north, extending southwards over Pilbara and the Goldfields region, being absent from the cooler south and south-west. More sedentary than the nomadic Little Crow.

STATUS: Abundant over the humid subtropical regions of northern and north-eastern Australia, having increased with the spread of cultivation. In the drier regions of the interior it is much scarcer, with scattered pairs along tree-lined watercourses; a population study in Queensland has given an average territory size of 131 hectares per pair.

REFERENCES: Blakers et al 1984, Curry 1978, Heinroth 1903, Rowley 1970, 1973, White and Bruce 1986.

LITTLE CROW   Plate 29

Corvus bennetti

A semi-nomadic, arid-country counterpart of the Torresian Crow, with which it widely overlaps in range.

IDENTIFICATION: Overlaps with the very similar Torresian Crow and Little and Australian Ravens although it is the most numerous corvid of desert and semi-desert regions of southern and central Australia. The smallest of the Australian crows, with the smoothest throat curve, most domed crown shape and smallest bill (it is the only one to have the bill shorter than the head) and is possibly the only Australian corvid to show a two-toned underwing when overhead. However size and structural features are relatively minimal in all of these species. Comparisons with the two major overlapping species are discussed below, but see also Little Raven and Habits section.

Torresian Crow: Extensive sympatry over most of range, except South Australia (Torresian only in extreme north-west) and New South Wales where Torresian absent in range of Little. Torresian invariably associated with trees along watercourses whereas Little Crow replaces it in more arid areas, especially in the interior where Torresian is sparse and local (flocks in arid country are Little Crows). Little Crow has slightly greyer undersides to flight feathers offering slight contrast with blacker coverts and primary tips (Torresian has uniformly black underwing, even in bright light but it seldom flies high enough to make this certain). Little Crow performs tumbling aerobatics, often in flocks (not so with Torresian). Little Crow is a sleeker, fuller-crowned, smaller-billed bird and often appears relatively longer-legged (perhaps exaggerated by sleeked plumage in hotter habitats) and the calls are less varied, and have a

distinctly more nasal, buzzing quality. Calling postures resemble Torresian but does not flick wings, and calls more habitually from ground, not from high exposed perches; when uttering territorial call in flight, utters a double, not single, call and misses a wing-beat like Torresian. See also Habits.

Australian Raven: Overlaps in southern Western Australia, southern South Australia and most of eastern part of range of Little Crow. Little Crow is distinctly smaller, sleeker and small-billed (bill shorter than head) and has no throat bulge; in flight overhead appears relatively small headed and short-necked and has broader-tipped wings and shows two-toned underwing. Small bill of Little Crow makes forehead appear slightly rounded, with flat crown centre, whereas in Australian Raven forehead and crown slope gently upwards to peak on rear crown; additionally Little Crow has white (not grey) bases to body feathers. Calls are quite different. Calling postures of Little Crow more upright, than in Australian Raven, and calls more habitually from ground; when uttering territorial call in flight, utters a double call and misses a wing-beat whilst calling (this habit not done by the 'ravens').

DESCRIPTION: Length 42-48 cm. Bill moderately short and small (shorter than head), with gently curving culmen. Nasal tufts moderate. Inter-ramal area fully feathered. Throat feathers not elongated, pointed at tip. Tail medium-long, graduated at tip. Entire plumage black, strongly glossed purple and purplish-blue. Bases of body feathers pure white. Bill and legs black. Irides bluish-white or white with bluish inner ring.

AGE/SEX: Plumages similar; juvenile dull, not glossy, black; irides bluish in nestlings, but darken to brownish at fledging, becoming mottled when just under a year old and finally white at end of second year.

MEASUREMENTS: Male averages slightly larger than female. Wing 299-346; tail 163-200; tarsus 49-61; bill 42-51; weight 290-500.

GEOGRAPHICAL VARIATION: No races recognised.

VOICE: Territorial call is a rather dry, nasal and quickly repeated " aak aak aak"; higher pitched, rather 'tighter', less croaky and with a distinct buzzing quality in comparison to similar call of Torresian. Said occasionally to utter longer, individual 'aak' notes and occasionally a bubbling conversational warble and croak.

HABITS: Very sociable, forming very large flocks which can number thousands outside the breeding season when food sources permit e.g. grasshopper swarms; often gathers with Torresian Crows (although neither very abundant within range of each other due to habitat preferences) and Little Ravens; sociable even when nesting (like Little Raven but unlike solitary-nesting Torresian Crow and Australian Raven). Little Crows are often remarkably bold and confiding, both when scavenging in streets of outback towns and when encountered in the bush, even allowing humans to walk up to tree in which they are perched and reported entering shop doorways in some Western Australian towns. This fearless nature is emphasised in the breeding season when they will boldly fly around human intruders, calling loudly and even pressing home an attack if the young are handled. They are omnivorous, although less of a scavenger than Torresian Crow, feeding principally on insects and other invertebrates, grain and seeds; when attending carcases with bigger-billed relatives takes advantage of the larger corvid opening up carcase, coming in to pick at the flesh when the larger bird has departed, but it has been suggested that Little Crows might be more interested in the attending insects rather than the carcase itself; its food has been analysed as being 26% carrion, 48% invertebrates and 26% plant material. Although primarily insectivorous they readily feed on rubbish dumps with other corvids and in coastal areas they scavenge along town waterfronts. The territorial call is uttered from the ground or low branch, less from a high branch or in flight as preferred by Torresian; when calling there is no wing-flicking and the posture is relatively erect even when on ground. When uttering territorial call in flight habitually misses a beat (a characteristic more frequently employed by Torresian, but not by the 'ravens') and utters two calls (only one by Torresian). Flocks readily fly high, direct and steadily when moving between feeding and roosting areas (a habit shared by Little Raven but not by the others) and are prone to soaring on thermals and indulge in swooping and tumbling aerobatics (unlike Torresian). Wing-beats are relatively quicker but shallower than those of Torresian Crow. This species is somewhat nomadic and does leave areas which have become unsuitable and visit others where normally absent, but identification problems hamper knowledge of the full extent of these wanderings. Ringing data supports its greater mobility compared to Torresian Crow: most distant recovery 691 km (compared with a meagre 22 km for Torresian Crow).

BREEDING: Sociable nester, usually in small, loose colonies with nests at least 45 metres apart. Nest a bulky structure of twigs (but smaller than those of other Australian corvids), with a cup lined with animal hair and soft plant materials; between the stick base and soft cup lining is a lining of mud or clay (it is the only Australian crow to use mud in nest construction). The nests are built in trees and shrubs, but in very barren habitats it will use telegraph poles or artesian windmills, and sometimes even nests on the ground. Clutch of four to six pale blue-green eggs, spotted and blotched with dark brown. Breeding season varies widely according to extent of local rains, and can be either in spring or autumn even at the same localities.

HABITAT: Open scrubby country, especially mulga, riverine woodlands, open grassland and farmland and coastal woodland; to a lesser extent even in open desert, including gibber desert but in these situations not far from water even if only artesian wells. In many areas closely associated with human settlements, including large towns where it has locally become a garden bird.

DISTRIBUTION: Throughout the interior and southern and western Australia, but absent from the subtropical north and east. In Western Australia it is widespread but absent from the far north (the Kimberleys) and scarce in the extreme south-west coastal areas; it occurs almost throughout South Australia except the extreme south-east where it overlaps with, but is largely replaced, by Little Raven; in Victoria it is only found in the extreme north-west; it is widespread over western New South Wales to the west of the Great Dividing Range; in Queensland it is widespread over the interior Rolling Downs region but absent east of the Great Dividing Range and from the Cape York peninsula; over interior

Northern Territory it is also widespread but absent from Top End. Being semi-nomadic it seems that it sporadically appears as far north as the Kimberleys and the Gulf of Carpentaria.

STATUS: Abundant over the dry interior of central, southern and western Australia, with populations thinning out northwards. In some areas of the south-east the clearance of mulga scrub for agriculture has seemingly allowed Little Ravens to locally increase to the detriment of Little Crows. A population study in western New South Wales gave an average territory of 0.45 hectares per nest, but as might be expected from such a sociable species the birds foraged over a much larger area.

REFERENCES: Blakers et al 1984, Curry 1978, Rowley 1973.

AUSTRALIAN RAVEN   Plate 29

Corvus coronoides

Marginally the largest, and certainly one of the most familiar of the Australian crows, favouring the lusher countryside of the south and east of Australia.

IDENTIFICATION: Overlaps with all other Australian corvids. Only a little larger than Torresian Crow, and smaller western birds are particularly confusing. Typically, however, it is a rather bulkier bird, with a relatively longer tail and heavier bill than Torresian Crow. The crown is very flat, sloping from bill base to a peak at rear crown, and the throat typically shows a bulge above the upper breast created by the elongated throat hackles. The feather line indents under the chin as this area is rather bare of feathering (only apparent in the hand however); at times, especially when calling, this bulge fans out into a baggy lump and is conspicuous even in flight. Territorial call with prolonged wailing terminal note, and calling posture (body, tail and head virtually horizontal) distinctive, but see comment under Torresian Crow. See all other species for discussion on distinctions.

The throat hackles are very prominent in this species, especially when calling (lower figure).

DESCRIPTION: Length 46-56 cm. Bill moderately stout and relatively long, with straight culmen, becoming more curved towards tip. Nasal tufts moderate. Inter-ramal area feathered only in centre, leaving visible bare skin at sides. Throat feathers elongated, long and pointed. Tail medium-long, graduated at tip. Entire plumage black, strongly glossed greenish-blue or purplish-blue, becoming more purplish or bluish-purple on back and mantle. Bases of body feathers brownish-grey to pale grey. Bill and legs black. Irides white with narrow bluish inner ring.

AGE/SEX: Plumages similar; juvenile dull, not glossy, black; bare skin of upper chin distinctly pink, not blackish of adults. Irides bluish-grey in nestlings, but darken to brownish at fledging, becoming mottled when just under a year old and finally white in third year.

MEASUREMENTS: Male averages a little larger than female. Wing 328-397; tail 182-238; tarsus 57-69; bill 47-66; weight 500-820.

GEOGRAPHICAL VARIATION: There is a cline from the largest birds in the east towards smaller birds in Western Australia; western birds have been named *perplexus* but clinal and individual variation inhibits its recognition.

VOICE: The territorial call has a distinctive prolonged, terminal cry which is not uttered by other Australian corvids, although Torresian Crow often draws-out the final note to a certain extent (see Torresian Crow for discussion). The usual call of the raven is a loud, guttural "ahhaar, ahhaar, aaar, aaaaaaaaaarrrrurrrarr" the pro-longed final note gradually becoming lower in pitch, very mournful and dying away in a gargled splutter; at dawn this call is often shortened to two notes - a rising "ahh" followed by a sad, fading wail: "ahh-owwwwwwwwwwwww". A number of other calls have been described from this well-studied corvid, including hoarse creaking, clicking and rattling/gargling notes and single or repeated caws.

HABITS: Usually in pairs or family parties; however non-breeding (chiefly immature) birds form flocks of up to 30 loosely-associated birds which become semi-no-madic - leaving the dry interior in summer and moving back in winter; these flocks sometimes join gatherings of Little Ravens but in general mix less with other corvids than Little Raven. Breeding pairs are strongly territorial throughout the year and are quite bold and aggressive in chasing other corvids from their territory; however, occupied territories which support a rich food source are sometimes invaded by non-breeding flocks. Usually rather wary of man but has moved into some cities (e.g. Perth, Canberra and Sydney) where it becomes quite bold, scavenging in gardens, parks and along roadsides and shorelines. Feeds chiefly on the ground on a varied diet which includes insects and other invertebrates, lizards, grain, fruit, carrion and birds eggs and nestlings; they often attend picnic and camp sites, keeping at a safe distance until humans have vacated the sites before flying in to pick over the spoils. They have been recorded taking eggs from a coastal colony of Pied Cormorants and to kill new-born lambs (probably only sickly ones). However, even in areas where dead lambs are a basic component of their diet, it has been esti-mated that ravens are responsible for less than 5% of lamb mortality. A study has shown that the Australian Raven's diet is composed of 34% carrion, 42% inverte-brates and 24% plant material. Food is readily carried in its throat, aided by the expansive inter-ramal pouch, and food-hiding and storing has been noted in the wild as well as in captive birds. Drinks frequently in hot weather and after feeding on carrion but has not been noted to bathe; in hot weather spends most of day sheltering in tree cover, being most active in the cooler parts of the day. Flight action is strong, direct and powerful, the wing-beats producing an audible sound when close. Shy and wary near nest preferring to slip away, flying low from intruder, unlike aggressive defence of Little Crow. Territorial call uttered from ground or high perch with head low, the head, body and tail being almost horizontal during calling, without or with only occa-sional wing-flapping; the small chin pouch and the lower throat bag are distended and the feathers above the eyes may be erected to form tiny 'horns'. When calling in flight do so with fluttering wing-action, uttering wailing cries.

BREEDING: Solitary nester. Nest a large, flattish struc-ture of twigs with a cup lined with animal hair, fibrous bark and wool. Typically placed at least 12 metres up in a large secondary tree fork or occasionally on telegraph poles, windmills, pylons or, in more open habitats, atop a large shrub. Very rarely on ground, if so usually against an object such as a fence post. Clutch of three to five, average four, green, bluish-green or greenish-white eggs, variably spotted, blotched or clouded with darker blackish, olive-brown and violet-grey markings. Incuba-tion by female only, for some 20 days, with the young fledging at about 43 days. Both sexes feed young which remain with their parents for up to four months after leaving the nest. Breeding season starts in mid July in southern New South Wales, earlier than that of Little Raven; older data, which did not distinguish the two species, is somewhat confusing.

HABITAT: Varied, but avoids both arid treeless areas and dense forest. Favours open lightly-wooded country, especially farmland with scattered trees, riverine wood-lands and coastal trees; ascends to 1500 metres in mountainous areas and is widespread along coasts, foraging by seashores and on inshore islands. Locally in town and city parks and large gardens.

DISTRIBUTION: Throughout the eastern third of Aus-tralia (except Cape York peninsula), the south-west and the intervening southern coast. In Western Australia it is widespread in the lusher south-west north to the Murchison River, its range extends thinly along coastal areas of south-east Western Australia and South Aus-tralia, becoming more widespread throughout the inte-rior of eastern South Australia. It is common throughout Victoria, New South Wales and most of Queensland, but in general it is scarce in north-east New South Wales and along the lush Queensland coast to the east of the Great Divide except around some towns; it becomes more sparse in the interior of northern Queensland, some reaching the Gulf of Carpentaria but avoiding the Cape York peninsula. In Northern Territory it is scarce, being sparsely distributed in the extreme east and south.

STATUS: Common over the lush farmland of the east and south-west but thinning out in the more arid interior and scarce along the sub-tropical east coast. Increasing agricultural development, particularly the provision of stock-pools in the interior, has encouraged a range expansion; exposed garbage tips and an adaption to living in urban situations has created local population increases. Studies have indicated that an average pair requires a territory of 112 hectares.

REFERENCES: Blakers *et al* 1984, Pizzey 1980, Rowley 1973.

LITTLE RAVEN   Plate 29

Corvus mellori

Long confused with the Australian Raven, this sociable corvid was not recognised until 1967, but it is in fact widespread over south-eastern Australia within the range of its more familiar cousin.

IDENTIFICATION: Although only found in south-eastern Australia the Little Raven overlaps in range with all other Australian corvids, albeit only marginally with Torresian Crow (in New South Wales). See also Forest and New England Ravens for distinctions. Other species are discussed below:-

Australian Raven: Throughout range of Little Raven, but latter by comparison is slightly smaller with a slightly weaker bill; the throat feathers are not strongly elongated and do not form a conspicuous fan whilst calling but like the Australian Raven has a small pouch under bill base which can expand to carry food. Little Ravens are quite gregarious, even breeding in loose colonies like Little Crow; therefore in social behaviour they are very different from Australian Raven. They do not have a special calling posture (unlike horizontal pose of Australian Raven) and may call from any position, flicking wings upwards with each call (usually no wing flicking in Australian Raven). The call too is quite different (see Voice). Like Little Crow, and again unlike Australian Raven, flocks are semi-nomadic and readily fly high when moving long distances. Little Ravens feed avidly in trees as well as on the ground whereas Australian Ravens feed almost entirely on the ground.

Torresian Crow: Range meets Little Raven only at Barrington Tops (north-east New South Wales). Torresian is typically a sleeker, slightly slimmer-billed bird, lacking small pouch under bill base often shown by Little Raven. Flies in lower airspace than Little Raven. Wings are relatively broader at tips than those of Little Raven. Torresian Crow has wing-shuffling habit as soon as it settles on perch; when calling in territorial flight, wings miss a beat (neither habit shared by Little Raven). Calls are higher in pitch and more croaked in quality, with less obvious or no wing-flicking whilst calling. Bases of body feathers are white, not the grey of the ravens.

Little Crow: Overlaps over northern part of range of Little Raven, the two species often gathering together at rich food sources. Little Crow is smaller, sleeker, much weaker-billed (bill shorter than head), has a more domed crown shape and lacks small pouch under bill base often shown by Little Raven. The call notes are more nasal and shorter and it does not wing-flip whilst calling. When uttering territorial call in flight, utters a double call and misses a wing-beat (like Torresian). In flight overhead Little Crow is relatively small-headed and short-necked, has broader-tipped wings, and underside of flight feathers is slightly greyer than blacker

wing-coverts (uniform black in Little Raven); additionally Little Crow has white (not grey) bases to body feathers.

DESCRIPTION: Length 48-50 cm. Bill moderately stout and relatively long, with straight culmen, becoming more curved towards tip. Nasal tufts moderate. Inter-ramal area almost completely feathered. Throat feathers hardly elongated, pointed or forked at tip. Tail medium-long, graduated at tip. Entire plumage black, strongly glossed greenish-blue or purplish-blue, becoming more purplish or bluish-purple on back and mantle. Bases of body feathers brownish-grey to pale grey. Bill and legs black. Irides white with narrow bluish inner ring.

AGE/SEX: Plumages similar; juvenile dull, not glossy, black; inter-ramal skin pink, not blackish as in adults. Irides bluish-grey in nestlings, but darken to brownish at fledging, becoming mottled when just under a year old and finally white in second year.

MEASUREMENTS: Male averages slightly larger than female. Wing 303-370; tail 178-216; tarsus 52-65; bill 42-56; weight 365-660.

GEOGRAPHICAL VARIATION: Montane birds average slightly longer-winged than others, but differences not sufficient to warrant subspecific separation.

VOICE: The territorial call notes are harder, more clipped and more quickly uttered in comparison to those of the Australian Raven; the call sequences lack the distinctive prolonged, terminal cry of Australian Raven and are accompanied by two or three wing flips (Australian Raven does not wing flip). The territorial call has been transcribed as a very guttural, almost barking, "kar-kar-kar-kar" or "ark-ark-ark-ark". Other harsh calls may be given at times.

HABITS: Sociable, forming flocks of up to 300 birds, often gathering with flocks of Little Crows and some non-breeding Australian and Forest Ravens at good feeding sites. These flocks are semi-nomadic, with northern birds moving south-east during the dry summer, returning again in autumn. Such movements suggest fluctuations in abundance which in reality are linked to the search for better feeding areas by non-breeding flocks. Unlike Australian Raven (a solitary breeder and strongly territorial) the Little Raven is often semi-colonial when nesting, with the highest recorded density of 15 nests in a small plantation of 270 x 45 m; other 'colonies' are more widely spaced, and there can be several nesting pairs within a single territory of the Australian Raven. Breeding pairs hold small territories but feed in communal feeding areas with other pairs and join up with non-breeding flocks outside the breeding season and wander with them. In some cities (e.g. Melbourne and Adelaide) has adapted to an urban existence but is less bold and confiding than the Little Crow. Feeds largely on the ground, especially on open grassland, but also forages in trees (unlike Australian Raven in that respect) and is less of a scavenger on carrion than its larger relative. Although omnivorous it feeds largely on insects (especially moth larvae) and will search tree foliage for stick-insects; one study showed its diet to be 61% insects, 25% plant materials and only 14% carrion. Flies with slightly faster wing-beats; when moving long distances usually flies at a height of 70-100 m on a direct path. The territorial call is given from the ground or a low perch, but the neck is typically stretched and each call note is accompanied by an upward flip of the closed wings (a very useful feature). When calling in flight does so with fluttering wing-action, not pausing as in the two crows. Has a distinctive courtship display which is not exhibited by Australian Raven; one bird strutting slowly before another with tail raised and wings drooped. Like the Little Crow its seasonal wanderings are quite strong, most ringing recoveries being up to 300 kms, the most distant being 352 km.

BREEDING: Solitary, semi-colonial or colonial nester (see Habits). Nest a structure of twigs (smaller than that of Australian Raven) with a deep cup lined with animal hair, fibrous bark and wool. Usually placed below 10 metres in a subsidiary fork of a large branch of a small tree or shrub; in more open country often on ground, if so usually against an object such as fence post. Clutch of three to five, average four, much as those of Australian Raven in colour (but slightly smaller). Young fledge at 37 days, i.e. some six days earlier than those of Australian Raven, joining flocks of adults soon after leaving the nest. Breeding season starts in early August in southern New South Wales, a little later than that of Australian Raven.

HABITAT: Similar to that of the Australian Raven in avoiding both arid treeless areas and dense forest. Favours open lightly-wooded, scrubby country, especially eucalypt woodland and acacia scrub; also in open farmland with scattered trees, including coastal lowlands. In the Australian Alps of Victoria and New South Wales reaches over 1600 m. Locally in town and city parks.

DISTRIBUTION: South-eastern Australia. It is common throughout Victoria and most of New South Wales (north to Barrier Highway-Narrabri and east to the western foothills of the Great Divide). It is widespread over southern South Australia, including Kangaroo Island, north to Port Augusta and west to the Gawler Range and Eyre Peninsula. It does not breed in extreme southern Victoria in the Otway Range or Wilson's Promontory but is a non-breeding visitor here, as it is to King Island in the Bass Strait; in these areas it then occurs alongside Forest Raven.

STATUS: Common, locally abundant, over most of its range. Studies have indicated that an average pair requires a territory of 2.6 hectares.

REFERENCES: Blakers et al 1984, Rowley 1967, 1970.

FOREST RAVEN   Plate 29

Corvus tasmanicus

Alternative name: Tasmanian Raven

This close relative of the Australian and Little Ravens is the only Tasmanian corvid, but it also largely replaces these species on the extreme south-eastern mainland of Australia.

IDENTIFICATION: The only corvid of Tasmania and at Cape Otway and the Wilson's Promontory area along the extreme southern coast of Victoria; further west its range just extends into the extreme south-east of South Australia where it gathers with Little and Australian Ravens. It has recently been proven to occur on King Island where the Little Raven is a non-breeding visitor. A markedly stocky corvid by Australian standards, differing from both Australian and Little Ravens in its relatively shorter, broader wings and shorter tail; the tail is often stated to be shorter than the wings but typically the wing and tail tips appear more or less equal when perched. The relatively short tail seems to give it a distinctly 'leggy' appearance on the ground and the plumage of the lower underparts seems 'looser' than in other Australian corvids, contributing to a slightly 'shaggy' rather than sleek appearance behind the legs. Like the Little Raven its throat hackles are short but the bill is distinctly stouter than that species, and even more massive than in Australian Raven. Call is also deeper in comparison to these two species. In Tasmania the identification is straightforward; the only other large, blackish passerine there being the endemic Black Currawong, which is a sleeker, longer-bodied and longer-tailed bird, with a longer bill and showing a white tail tip in flight.

DESCRIPTION: Length 50-52 cm. Bill stout and relatively long, with straight culmen, becoming more curved towards tip. Nasal tufts moderate. Inter-ramal area feathered but less completely than in Little Raven. Throat feathers slightly elongated, pointed or forked at tip. Tail medium-short, slightly graduated at tip. Entire plumage black, glossed greenish-blue or purplish-blue. Bases of body feathers grey. Bill and legs black. Irides white with narrow bluish inner ring.

AGE/SEX: Plumages similar; juvenile dull, not glossy, black; gape and inter-ramal skin (mostly concealed by feathering) pinkish instead of black as in adult. Irides bluish-grey in nestlings, but darken to brownish at fledging, becoming mottled when just under a year old and finally white in third year.

MEASUREMENTS: Male averages a little larger than female. Nominate race: Wing 333-377, tail 180-211, tarsus 61-69, bill 55-63, weight 500-800.

GEOGRAPHICAL VARIATION: Two races recognised, the nominate of Tasmania and extreme southern coastal Victoria and the isolated *C. (t.) boreus* of New South Wales. It has recently been proposed that the two forms are worthy of specific separation, therefore *boreus* is given semi-separate treatment in this work.

VOICE: The territorial call is relatively loud, deep in pitch and slow in delivery, with the final note often somewhat prolonged and 'rolling': "korr-korr-korr-korrrrr". Single call notes are readily given in flight and when perched. In general these notes are louder and more far-carrying than in other Australian corvids.

HABITS: Generally in pairs or family parties, with breeding pairs remaining in their territories throughout the year. Gatherings of non-breeding and immature birds may be found throughout the year, forming flocks of 30-40 birds on the mainland; larger gatherings of 100 or more regular in Tasmania in winter, with 250+ also recorded. On the mainland they often assemble with parties of Little and Australian Ravens at good food sources, e.g. rubbish dumps. Like Australian Raven this crow is a solitary breeder, but breeding densities are higher. It feeds chiefly on the ground, in Tasmania favouring paddocks and fields with good tree cover nearby but with the lack of competition from other corvids forages in a wide range of habitats, from the edges of villages and small towns to seashores, inshore islands and even well above the tree-line on mountain ridges. It scavenges about picnic sites and has been recorded taking eggs and chicks from seabird colonies and is locally regarded as an agricultural pest, damaging seedlings, potatoes and maize crops. Its diet is varied and similar to that of the Australian Raven in content; one study showed it be 31% carrion, 41% invertebrates and 28% plant material, but it is possible that it might be more specialised in areas of overlap with Australian Raven where it out-competes that species in open forest (i.e. south-east South Australia). Birds on territory spend much time perched on tree tops in ones and twos, and when weather conditions permit readily soar on thermals over ridges and hills; when flushed at close range the wings produce a swishing sound as in Australian Raven. The territorial call is usually given from a high tree top with throat hackles expanded, but no special posture is employed unlike Australian Raven.

BREEDING: Solitary nester. Nest a bulky structure of twigs (similar to that of Australian Raven) with a deep cup lined with animal hair, fibrous bark and wool. Usually placed high in the fork of a large tree. Clutch of three to six, average four, much as those of Australian Raven in colour and size. Breeding begins in August or September in Tasmania.

HABITAT: On the Australian mainland is confined to wooded coastal districts, chiefly eucalypt forest and conifer plantations, with associated farmland. In Tasmania it occupies a wide spectrum of habitats from inshore islands to open mountain plateaux, but is most abundant in wooded farmland and hill forests, including both dry and wet forests. Locally at the edges of villages and towns.

DISTRIBUTION: Tasmania and adjacent Australian mainland. In South Australia it is confined to the extreme south-east coast in the region of Naracoorte, extending eastwards along the coast of Victoria to just east of Wilson's Promontory. It has recently been found to be present on King Island. It is widespread on the Furneaux Island group, especially Flinders Island, and is common throughout Tasmania.

STATUS: Common, locally abundant, over Tasmania and on Flinders Island. On the mainland of Australia it is uncommon and localised but common on Wilson's Promontory, at Cape Otway and near Naracoorte. Studies have indicated that an average pair requires a territory of about 40 hectares.

REFERENCES: Blakers et al 1984, Rowley 1967, 1970.

NEW ENGLAND RAVEN   Plate 29

Corvus (tasmanicus) boreus

Alternative name: Relict Raven

The most isolated of all Australian corvids, confined to forests and woodland in north-eastern New South Wales. Described as a race of Forest Raven as recently as 1970 this interesting raven might be worthy of specific recognition, despite ecological and physical similarities.

IDENTIFICATION: Overlaps with Torresian Crow and Australian and Little Ravens. A distinctly bulky corvid, differing from Forest Raven of Tasmania in its slightly slimmer bill and relatively longer wings and tail; thus in proportions it is closer to Australian and Little Ravens. It is basically a forest bird, but along the New England coastal lowlands occurs in more open habitats. Differences from overlapping species are discussed below:-
Torresian Crow: Overlaps near Glen Innes, Barrington Tops and Armidale, but breeding territories are mutually exclusive. Torresian Crow is smaller billed, has a less 'full' tail, is sleeker and shows white (not grey) bases to body feathers; it has higher-pitched, more barking or frog-like croaking quality to its calls and when giving territorial calls in flight habitually misses a beat whilst giving single call note (ravens do not miss a wing-beat whilst calling). The crow readily and repeatedly shuffles its wings when alighting on a perch (unlike ravens).
Australian Raven: Overlaps throughout range of New England, but breeding territories are mutually exclusive. New England is a slightly larger, bulkier bird with a relatively larger bill than Australian; Australian Raven is relatively longer-winged in flight and shows a larger throat bulge, especially when calling as throat forms fanned bag (only ruffled bulge in New England). When giving full call Australian Raven adopts a very horizontal posture (more upright in New England) and call sequence terminates in prolonged mournful moan (calls louder and deeper, more gravelly in New England, with rolling slightly longer terminal note).
Little Raven: Overlaps with New England near Barrington Tops. Little is less bulky and a little smaller overall than New England and has a smaller bill; it is also relatively longer-winged in flight and when calling flips wings with the effort of each call note, a habit not shared by New England which also has a louder and deeper voice.

DESCRIPTION: Length 50-52 cm. Bill stout and relatively long, with straight culmen, becoming more curved towards tip. Nasal tufts moderate. Inter-ramal area almost completely feathered as in Forest Raven. Throat feathers slightly elongated, pointed or forked at tip. Tail medium, slightly graduated at tip. Entire plumage black, glossed greenish-blue or purplish-blue. Bases of body feathers grey. Bill and legs black. Irides white with narrow bluish inner ring.

AGE/SEX: Plumages similar; juvenile dull, not glossy, black; gape and underside of base of bill pinkish in juvenile. Irides bluish-grey in nestlings, but darken to brownish at fledging, becoming mottled when just under a year old and finally white in third year.

MEASUREMENTS: Male averages a little larger than female. *C. (t). boreus*: wing 336-394, tail 199-227, tarsus 63-70, bill 53-59, weight 550-740.

VOICE, HABITS AND BREEDING: As Forest Raven.

HABITAT: Two habitat types are utilised. Inland populations are confined to wet sclerophyll forest of the New England tablelands and feed in adjacent farmland. Coastal populations are found in paperbark swamps and eucalypt forest along duneland heaths.

DISTRIBUTION: Endemic to forested eastern slope of New England tablelands and coastal woodland of New South Wales. Range limits are Glen Innes and Coff's Harbour in the north and Mt. Barrington and Port Stephen in the south.

STATUS: Very local but not uncommon over very restricted range; clearance of forest and subsequent colonisation of more open habitats by the more successful and competitive Australian Raven and human control of crows and ravens in general are potential threats to this rare corvid.

TAXONOMY: *Boreus* and nominate *tasmanicus* are geographically isolated from each other. Clearly, however, they are closely related and are usually considered conspecific. McAllan and Bruce (1988), have proposed specific separation and this was followed by Sibley and Monroe (1991). However, the proposal to split them is controversial and seemingly will not be followed by the RAOU in the forthcoming revised check-list of Australian birds. To highlight this interesting situation the two forms have been given semi-separate treatment here but perhaps only DNA analysis will finally resolve this issue.

REFERENCES: Blakers *et al* 1984, Debus 1980, McAllan and Bruce 1988, Rowley 1967, 1970.

OTHER CROWS and RAVENS

COLLARED CROW   Plate 21

Corvus torquatus

Replaces the Carrion Crow in lowland southern China, with which it might be closely-allied but no hybridisation reported from areas of potential contact.

IDENTIFICATION: A distinctive crow of lowland China, resembling Carrion Crow in proportions but with conspicuous white nape and band across lower breast. Unlikely to be confused with any other corvid in range. Similarly piebald Daurian Jackdaw is much smaller and smaller-billed and has whitish underparts extending to legs, whereas Collared has narrow white band on lower breast, with remainder of underparts black. Widely overlaps with Large-billed Crow and marginally with Carrion Crow. Compare House Crow, with which it is not known to overlap but latter prone to turning up in coastal towns and cities away from normal range. Smaller House Crow differs in head shape and in having much greyer nape and underparts.

DESCRIPTION: Length 52-55 cm. Crown relatively flat. Bill moderate with almost straight culmen, curving towards blunt tip. Nasal tuft conspicuous, covering base of culmen. Throat hackles slightly developed, pointed at tips. Bases of body feathers grey. Tail medium, slightly rounded at tip. Hood, throat and upper breast glossy black, gloss purplish or greenish. Upper mantle, nape, sides of neck and band across lower breast white, with some weak grey shaft marks towards borders of black areas of plumage. Remainder of plumage black, glossed purplish or bluish, becoming greenish on primaries. Bill and legs black. Irides dark brown.

AGE/SEX: Plumages similar; juvenile duller, lacking sheen, with white areas sullied light greyish; much as adult by autumn although flight feathers abraded by first winter (fresh in adults), inside of upper mandible pale, (blackish in adults).

MEASUREMENTS: Male averages larger than female. Wing 316-344, tail 190, tarsus 58, bill 55, weight no data.

GEOGRAPHICAL VARIATION: Monotypic.

VOICE: Calls less rolling and slightly hoarser than those of Carrion Crow, but variable vocabulary of both species renders this of marginal value in the field. Usual call a loud 'kaaarr', which is often repeated. A variety of other calls may be given, including a Carrion Crow-like 'kaar-kaar' and several cawing, creaking and clicking sounds. In general, most calls higher in pitch and less harsh than those of Large-billed and like Carrion Crow, lacking Large-billed Crow's almost mocking quality.

HABITS: Little studied but thought to be basically similar to those of Carrion Crow, although in general seems to be less of a scavenger. Generally in pairs or family parties, favouring lowland cultivation near water, foraging along lakeshores, paddyfields and canal banks. Food items recorded include molluscs, insects, crustaceans and some vegetable matter (i.e. rice grains) and some human food waste but seems not to take carrion. Not as bold and pugnacious as Large-billed Crow; although freely forages around villages and the edges of towns.

BREEDING: Solitary breeder. Nest a bulky construction of sticks and branches, with cup lined with soft vegetation and animal hair; placed fairly high in a tree. Clutch two to six, average three or four. Eggs greenish-blue, speckled and blotched with olive-brown. No information on incubation or fledging seems to have been published.

HABITAT: Favours open lowland cultivation with scattered trees, usually below 60m and in riverine plains. Open farmland, parks, large gardens, edges of towns and villages especially near water.

DISTRIBUTION: Widespread over lowland eastern and southern China, from Liaoning, Hebei and Shandong to Zhejiang, Fujian, Guangdong, Hong Kong and Hainan. West to south Shaanxi (Tsinling Shan) and southern Gansu to Sichuan (Chengdu and Yachow), Hunan and Yunnan. Range extends into Vietnam over lowland Tonkin south to central Annam. Vagrant to Taiwan.

STATUS: Locally common over most of main part of range but its present status in Vietnam requires confirmation (there has only been one recent record).

REFERENCES: Cheng 1976, Goodwin 1986, La Touche 1952

HAWAIIAN CROW   Plate 23

Corvus hawaiiensis

Alternative name: Alala

The most endangered of all corvids, despite conservation action, the wild population had dwindled to only ten birds by 1987.

IDENTIFICATION: The only crow of the Hawaiian islands, now on the verge of extinction. A large, dull sooty forest crow with slightly browner primaries. The

only other large blackish bird of the islands, the dark phase of the Hawaiian Hawk, is unlikely to be confused.
DESCRIPTION: Length 48-50 cm. Crown relatively flat. Bill very stout, with slightly upturned shape created by strong curve to lower mandible and almost straight culmen. Nasal tuft conspicuous, covering base of culmen; rictal bristles well developed. Plumage relatively soft, slightly hairy in texture. Throat feathers fine and bristle-like. Bases of body feathers dull light grey. Tail medium, almost square at tip. Entire plumage sooty brownish-black, without gloss, outer webs of primaries lighter brown. Bill and legs black. Irides dark brown.
AGE/SEX: Plumages similar; no information on juvenile.
MEASUREMENTS: Male averages a little larger than female. Wing 292-325, tail 174-211, bill 51-61, tarsus 52-66, weight no data.
GEOGRAPHICAL VARIATION: Monotypic.
VOICE: Has quite a varied vocabulary. Usual call a loud, repeated, raucous squawking 'kerruk, kerrruk, kerrruk...'. In flight a loud, but more musical 'kraa-a-ik', somewhat upslurred and more modulated than other calls is given. Also gives a variety of shorter notes, including a quiet 'kwahk'.
HABITS: Pairs or family parties in forested country, especially montane forest clearings. When more abundant recorded as quite tame and confiding in presence of man. Feeds primarily on fruits and berries of forest trees but diet quite omnivorous, with references to it taking eggs and young of introduced bird species and even carrion (recorded feeding on a dead horse); it has been observed tearing away pieces of tree bark, presumably in search of invertebrates. Feeds both on the ground and in the forest canopy. Flight action strong, often flies high over the forested ridges, where they tumble and 'play' in the manner of ravens but apparently does not soar.
BREEDING: Solitary breeder. Nest a bulky construction of sticks and branches, with cup lined with soft grasses and plant stems, although one nest studied had no cup lining. The nest is often in somewhat isolated stands of large trees adjacent to a more open area; one nest was found at only 3 m from the ground in a large dead shrub. Clutch of five eggs recorded. Incubation by both sexes (as with Mariana Crow, but exceptional amongst other corvids). Eggs laid in latter part of April.
HABITAT: Forest and open woodland of various types, from wet hill forest to drier scrubby woodland and more open grazing country with scattered trees; now more or less confined to high mountain forest at some 3500 m.
DISTRIBUTION: Endemic to the main island of Hawaii.
STATUS: Formerly quite widespread over the island of Hawaii but has declined considerably in recent decades and now at the verge of extinction; cause of the decline is considered to be persecution by man (illegal shooting) and forest destruction. Population had declined to some 70 birds by the mid 1970s and a captive breeding programme was instigated, but by 1987 the four pairs in captivity had failed to breed and the wild population, now virtually confined to highest slopes of Mauna Loa above Kealakekua Bay, was down to some ten individuals.
REFERENCES: Pratt 1987, Sakai and Ralph 1980.

CHIHUAHUAN RAVEN   Plate 27
Corvus cryptoleucos

Alternative name: White-necked Raven (American)

A small raven of Mexican desert country, the ecological counterpart of the Brown-necked Raven of the Old World.

IDENTIFICATION: A small, crow-sized raven of Mexico and the arid interior of southern USA, overlaps marginally with American Crow but latter only in well vegetated valleys within range of Chihuahuan. Habitat is as good an indicator as any when in overlapping zones. However this species is a little larger, has longer and more fingered primaries and a longer and deeper bill with more extensive nasal bristles and more wedge-shaped tail. It is markedly smaller, slighter overall has less wedge-shaped tail than Northern Raven replacing it in arid, flatter country; call different to either but closer to Northern Raven.
DESCRIPTION: Length 44-51 cm. Bill medium long and deep, larger than American Crow, culmen almost straight until nearing tip. Nasal bristles very extensive, covering basal two-thirds of bill. Primaries quite long and more pointed than in American Crow. Tail distinctly graduated or rather wedge-shaped towards tip. Plumage wholly black, glossed with purplish or purplish-blue. Feathers of neck often with brownish tone. Bases of neck feathers snowy-white. Irides dark brown. Bill and legs black.
SEX/AGE: Sexes similar. Juvenile has grey-blue irides at first, soon turning brown; dusky black on head and underparts, with glossier, blacker wings and tail. First-summer birds much as adults, except for inside of mouth which is partially reddish-pink.
MEASUREMENTS: Males average slightly larger than females. Wing 328-379, tail 182-214, tarsus 56-68, bill 50-59, weight 378-607.
GEOGRAPHICAL VARIATION: Monotypic.
VOICE: Typical call be matched by range of those of Northern Raven, but is less variable and not as deep or as penetrating in pitch, a dry croaked 'craaak-craaak' or even 'kwaak-kwaak'. Vocabulary seems limited.
HABITS: Very much a bird of the desert scrub, generally in pairs perched on roadside poles or flying across the dry bushy landscape. Larger gatherings of non-breeders form which sometimes number a few hundred birds, even larger congregations form for communal winter roosts which gather in trees in isolated canyons. Pairs patrol and wait by roadsides for carrion, which is an important element of their diet, also takes a wide variety of invertebrates, small rodents, birds eggs and nestlings, fruit and even human food scraps. Food hiding also reported. Flight action steady and languid, interspersed with short glides. Displaying birds perform quite spectacular aerobatic tumbling, swooping and soaring, often at great heights. As they twist in the air, the parted neck feathers may show as a white ruff around the neck, but under normal circumstances the white is not visible. Tumbling display often triggered off by formation of a small 'dust-devel' which the bird will 'ride'. Much dispersal in autumn, with northern and interior populations moving into southern part of range for the winter.
BREEDING: Usually a solitary breeder, but where tree cover sparse, several nests might be quite close to-

gether. Nest a bulky structure of twigs and sticks, even wire, the cup lined with wool, rags and animal hair. Placed in large cottonwood, hackberry, sycamore or in mesquite thicket at varying heights. Often on an old building, windmill, telegraph pole or similar. Built by female. Clutch three to eight, usually five to seven. Eggs very pale blue to greyish-blue, marked with brown and grey blotches and very fine brown lines and squiggles which are almost like scratch marks. Incubation for about 21 days. Eggs generally in the first half of May to June.

HABITAT: Open country with scattered trees and shrubs, especially desert plains with mesquite scrub. Also in foothills and grassy plains and the edges of cultivation in such situations.

DISTRIBUTION: South-central USA and northern Mexico. From south-eastern Arizona, southern (and locally central) New Mexico, north-eastern Colorado, west and southern Texas north to extreme south-east Nebraska. Over most of the northern part of interior Mexico southwards to Mexico and Guanajuato. Northern populations move south in winter.

STATUS: Locally common, but scarce over northern limits of its range.

REFERENCES: Goodwin 1986, Terres 1980.

PIED CROW   Plate 25

Corvus albus

One of Africa's most widespread birds, the African representative of the ravens, which apparently hybridises with the Dwarf Raven over a narrow belt of the Horn of Africa. Despite this intriguing link with the ravens, several aspects of its social behaviour and display indicate a closer affinity to the Carrion Crows of Eurasia.

IDENTIFICATION: Conspicuous white collar and breast contrasts with otherwise black plumage and prevents confusion with all other African crows, although White-necked Raven often shows some whitish on breast as well as white nape but confusion unlikely as White-necked has a massive bill, broad wings and a short tail whereas Pied Crow has unremarkable proportions. With suspected vagrants in North Africa, beware possibility of partial albino corvids which could suggest this species, i.e. Brown-necked Raven. Differs from palest Hooded Crow in having black belly and upperparts and white, not merely pale grey, breast and collar. In Ethiopia and Somalia birds with white areas of plumage broken up by blackish markings are considered to be the result of not infrequent hybridisation with the Dwarf Raven (see discussion under Dwarf Raven).

DESCRIPTION: Length 46-50 cm. Bill moderately stout with curved culmen, stouter than Hooded Crow. Nasal bristles prominent. Throat hackles developed and pointed, but not long. Tail moderately long, somewhat graduated at tip. Wing relatively long, almost equalling tail tip when perched. Plumage glossy black, being glossed bluish and purplish, dullest on mantle and lower underparts; upper mantle, lower nape, lower sides of neck, breast and upper belly white, the white extending slightly onto axillaries on the underwing. Bill and legs black. Irides dark brown.

AGE/SEX: Plumages similar; juvenile has black, dull, not

glossy and white areas of plumage slightly mottled with narrow black feather tips.

MEASUREMENTS: Male averages larger than female. Wing 328-388, tail 175-200, tarsus 55-61, bill 51-58, weight 491-612.

GEOGRAPHICAL VARIATION: Monotypic. See Dwarf Raven for discussion on hybridisation.

VOICE: Typical call a harsh cawing 'karrh-karrh-karrh'. Also gives a deep, knocking 'kla-kla-kla' with variants.

HABITS: Found in pairs or small parties, but much larger numbers gather at good feeding sites and communal roosts, flocks of up to 300 birds recorded not infrequently and occasionally as many as 1000 or more at rubbish dumps and slaughter houses. Communal roosts similarly large, gathering in favoured stands of trees, where they will gather to shelter from the heat of the day as well as for nocturnal roosting. Walks easily on ground, frequently breaking into a rapid hopping. Flies with deep, regular wing-beats and often soars high in flocks on thermals but less given to soaring than White-necked Raven; when alighting habitually flicks wings, unlike ravens. Basically a scavenger, foraging amongst human habitation and cultivation, where may become remarkably fearless or wary depending on the tolerance level of the inhabitants. Feeds in trees as well as on the ground, and recorded taking and killing roosting fruit bats from inside tree canopy. Will catch flying insects and even chase and catch small birds on the wing; forages inside rubbish bins; picks ticks from backs of domestic and game animals and does some injury to sickly newborn animals. Food chiefly carrion and grain, also insects, small reptiles, frogs, rodents, young birds, fruits and seeds. Has a higher percentage of vegetable matter in its diet than the ravens and does some local damage to maize and other crops, chiefly by perching on stalks or by digging up sown grain. Habitually chases and harries large birds of prey.

BREEDING: Solitary nester. Nest a bulky structure of twigs and branches, or even wire, thickly lined with wool, dry dung and rags; constructed by both sexes. Placed in fork of large tree, telegraph pole or similar tall and relatively isolated structure. Clutch of one to seven, average four or five. Eggs pale greenish, blotched and spotted with brown, olive and grey, but less strongly patterned than others of genus, except Brown-necked Raven. Incubation 18-19 days by female, but male recorded to cover eggs when female leaves nest. Both sexes feed and tend young which fledge at 35-45 days. Eggs recorded chiefly September-October in southern Africa, October-November in Madagascar, September in Uganda and the Sudan and late February and March in Ethiopia; breeding usually associated with onset of local rains. Nest often parasitised by Great Spotted Cuckoo.

HABITAT: Various types of open country with scattered trees, from open hillside forest to cultivated plains, including environs of towns and cities. Locally also about oases in quite arid semi-desert and in dense rain forest only about cleared riverine areas with settlements. Most abundant at lower elevations, i.e. below 2000 m in East Africa but in Ethiopia chiefly between 1000 and 2500 m, occasionally as high as 3500 m.

DISTRIBUTION: Widespread over sub-Saharan Africa, but scarce or absent in very arid or densely forested areas. Northern limits of range fragmented by presence of desert oases, but occurs from southern Mauretania, northern Niger, northern Chad and central Sudan southwards throughout Africa to the Cape. Also Fernando Po, Madagascar, Aldabra and the Comoro Islands. Some dispersal and movement occurs within Africa, presumably dependant on local rainfall. Vagrants have wandered north to northern Libya (1931) and southern Algeria (1961, 1964).

STATUS: Common or abundant over much of its range, but closely associated with habitation; therefore very localised in arid or heavily forested areas. Perhaps competes with Black Crow and Dwarf Raven, as Pied seems to be less numerous where these birds are common.

REFERENCES: Ash 1983, Brooke and Grobler 1973, Gwahaba 1975, Maclean 1985, Smalley 1984, Wilson and Balcha 1989.

DWARF RAVEN   Plate 30

Corvus (ruficollis) edithae

Alternative names: Somali Raven, Lesser Brown-necked Raven

A crow-sized raven of north-east Africa, isolated from the nominate form and possibly worthy of specific status; in view of frequent hybridisation suggested by some to be conspecific with Pied Crow.

IDENTIFICATION: A miniature Brown-necked Raven, which it resembles closely in overall colouration and preference for rather arid open country, but differs in being much smaller, the size of a crow, and in having a relatively shorter and weaker bill and slightly less graduated tail. Size is difficult to evaluate in the field, therefore best identified by ranges which are not known to overlap; surprisingly ravens of the island of Socotra are true Brown-necked rather than Dwarf. Range overlaps with Black Crow, but latter has a markedly thinner bill and more highly glossed black plumage; it also favours lusher habitats than Dwarf Raven which it replaces in the forested highlands of Ethiopia. In some towns along the Red Sea coast the introduced House Crow is becoming established but is unlikely to be confused if reasonable views are obtained but beware hybrids with Pied Crow showing paler patches on neck and breast.

DESCRIPTION: Length 44-46 cm. Bill moderately stout, shorter and less slender than in Brown-necked Raven; nasal bristles prominent as in Brown-necked Raven. Throat feathers not obviously elongated. Tail moderately long, graduated. Bases of neck feathers white to pale grey. Plumage otherwise as in Brown-necked, including affects of bleaching and abrasion on feathers i.e. blackest when fresh, brownest when abraded. Irides dark brown. Bill and legs black.

AGE/SEX: As in Brown-necked Raven.

MEASUREMENTS: Male averages larger than female. Race edithae: wing 311-367, tail 168-180, tarsus 51-57, bill 50-57, weight not recorded.

VOICE: The call has been described as a harsh caw, rather like that of a Rook. Presumably therefore it is similar to that of Brown-necked Raven; but it might be less powerful and higher in pitch.

HABITS: Differs little from those of Brown-necked Raven.

BREEDING: Solitary nester, implications of social breed-

ing seem not to have been verified. Nest a typical bulky raven-like structure of twigs and branches, usually placed in trees, also on telegraph poles and locally on cliffs, especially in coastal situations. Clutch of three to five blue eggs, spotted and blotched with brown. No information on incubation. Eggs recorded April and early May in Somalia.

HABITAT: Desert and semi-desert plains and dry savanna, including coastal desert and islands; recorded up to 2000 m in the Ethiopian highlands.

DISTRIBUTION: North-east Africa. From the arid regions of northern Kenya northwards over Somalia, Djibouti and eastern Ethiopia, here chiefly in the lowlands but sparsely west to the western highlands.

STATUS: Locally quite common, but scarce or rare in the Ethiopian highlands.

TAXONOMY: It is on present knowledge best regarded as an isolated race of Brown-necked with which it is identical in colouration; however no other population of that widespread species differs strongly enough to warrant subspecific recognition. Within Brown-necked there is much individual variation in overall size, but even here there is a tendency towards larger birds in the south (as on the island of Socotra). The fact that edithae is so small implies that it has been long isolated and that speciation level might well have been reached although a similar parallel exists with the small tingitanus race of Northern Raven in Morocco.

HYDRIDISATION WITH PIED CROW: Over most of Africa the Pied Crow has no close counterpart, the similar-sized Black Crow being very different in feeding and social habits, and in several physiological aspects is closer to that of the Fan-tailed and White-necked Ravens. In Somalia and Ethiopia, Pied Crow comes into contact with the Dwarf Raven, although the latter predominates in arid situations where Pied Crow is sparse or absent. In these areas Pied Crow and Dwarf Raven frequently seem to hybridise, and show a whole range of intermediate plumage features (Ash 1983); the situation is similar to that of Carrion and Hooded Crows in Europe and Asia. It is too much of a coincidence that such birds have only been recorded where these two species meet and the theory that such birds are merely a dark phase of Pied Crow (Jollie 1978) seems therefore unlikely. At least some of these hybrids appear to be fertile, e.g. a hybrid paired with a Dwarf Raven reared young from a nest for three consecutive breeding seasons (Blair 1961, Alamargot 1987). Dwarf Raven and Pied Crow are very similar in size and structure, but whether or not they should be treated as conspecifc (or for that matter, considering a similar situation in Eurasia, Hooded and Carrion Crows be treated as separate species) is a matter of conjecture until detailed field studies reveal more positive conclusions. Interestingly no such hybrids have been recorded between Pied Crow and the nominate form of Brown-necked Raven where they meet further west in northern central Africa.

REFERENCES: Alamargot 1987, Ash 1983, Blair 1961, Goodwin 1986, Jollie 1978, Wilson and Balcha 1989.

BROWN-NECKED RAVEN   Plate 30

Corvus ruficollis

Alternative name: Desert Raven

Desert counterpart of Northern Raven, which it largely replaces across North Africa and the Middle East.

IDENTIFICATION: A raven of arid desert regions of North Africa and the Middle East. Smaller than Northern Raven but in structure, very similar, although bill less stout and throat less shaggy which gives a sleeker look to the head and neck; although the tail is less strongly wedge-shaped the central tail feathers project slightly more than in Northern Raven (in fresh plumage, not in abraded birds). When perched the tail is distinctly longer than the wing-tip, (virtually equal to wing-tip in Northern Raven). In flight head and neck often appear slimmer than in Northern Raven and the wing shape is slightly narrower and more pointed (basically the primaries). All of these points are difficult to evaluate in the field, the easiest distinction being voice: Brown-necked utters cawing, almost Rook-like calls, quite unlike the very deep croaks of Northern Raven. Over most of their ranges the two species are mutually-exclusive but occur alongside each other in foothill regions where ranges meet and Northern is common in some desert areas where Brown-necked might be expected, e.g. Iran and Afghanistan. Despite the implication of its common name it is not only Brown-necked that is brown on the head and neck and some populations of Northern Raven appear distinctly brownish on head and neck in worn plumage. Unfortunately these features are shown by Northern Ravens in the Middle East and North Africa. In general, however, in these regions Northern Raven is the only one of the mountains, whereas either might be expected in flat desert. The North African race of Northern, *tingitanus,* is smaller and shorter-billed than the European form and becomes dull dark brown in worn plumage but the bill is very stout and strongly arched on the culmen and the call is a little higher in pitch; it is best distinguished from Brown-necked by habitat (Brown-necked prefers *Artemesia* steppe in North Africa), much stouter bill, relatively shorter tail (primary tips equal tail tip at rest) and gruffer, croaked calls. See also discussion under Dwarf Raven and compare Fan-tailed.

DESCRIPTION: Length 52-56 cm. Bill relatively long and heavy, but less massive than in Northern Raven; nasal bristles prominent but relatively shorter than in Northern Raven (especially in comparison to *tingitanus*). Throat feathers slightly elongated and pointed. Tail relatively long, very strongly graduated but less strongly than Northern Raven. 3rd primary longer than 5th, creating more tapered look to primaries in flight; 3rd and 5th more equal in Northern in North Africa and Middle East but varies elsewhere over its wide range. Bases of neck feathers pale grey to dusky grey, rarely whitish. Fresh plumage: Head, throat and breast brownish black, glossed purple but crown, sides of head, nape and sides of neck browner, less glossy or glossed copper; remainder of plumage black, glossed purple and bluish. Worn plumage: Plumage prone to bleaching, with wear head and body plumage becomes dull dark brown, even rusty-brown at times, contrasting with blacker, more glossed, wings and tail. Bill, legs and feet black. Irides dark brown.

AGE/SEX: Plumages similar; for effect of wear see description. Juveniles show similar extent of wear, but fresh birds are a dull black, not glossy, including wings and tail.

MEASUREMENTS: Male averages larger than female but much individual variation. Nominate race: wing 360-432, tail 195-214, bill 60-73, weight 500-647. See also Dwarf Raven which is usually regarded as conspecific.

GEOGRAPHICAL VARIATION: Two races generally recognised, the nominate over most of its range and the isolated *edithae* of the horn of Africa; the latter however approaches specific status and is here treated separately. Over its wide range the nominate form shows marked individual variation in overall size, especially in bill size; this variation precludes other racial separations but the population of Socotra island (Yemen) is consistently large and might form a distinct subspecies. On Cape Verde Islands persistent partial albinism recorded, aggravated by island isolation.

VOICE: Usual call a dry, rising 'aarg-aarg-aarg' of varying intensity, at times recalling caw of Rook, several other calls are given however, including an abrupt croak, but the latter is distinctly softer and less resonant than the deep, dry croak of Northern Raven.

HABITS: Generally met with in pairs or small parties in open desert. Small gatherings occur at feeding stations such as rubbish dumps or at animal carcases; gatherings of non-breeding birds often considerable, forming large communal roosts in stands of trees or along cliff faces. Roosts exceeding 1000 birds recorded from central Israel and Sinai. Foraging parties however are much smaller, rarely exceeding 20 birds. Birds with established territories maintain territory throughout the year and are considered to pair for life; in central Israel the average distance between nests was 3.3. km, but nests as close as 1.2 km were also recorded. Breeding probably does not take place until birds are at least three years old. In open desert most frequently encountered near human settlements where food supplies likely to be more abundant. Walks with waddling action, occasionally hopping, but progression slow and methodical as it searches for prey items on ground. Flies with relatively slow, languid wing-beats, often quite low as it quarters feeding territory; also soars at great height on flat wings, spiralling on thermals in raptor-like fashion. Readily perches on cliffs and telegraph poles and where available, on trees. Mixes little with other corvids although at food sources mixes freely with Fan-tailed Raven; however harsh environment allows little contact with other species. Generally shy and wary like Northern Raven, but in areas where unmolested recorded as scavenging about desert encampments with remarkable boldness. Feeds on variety of items including carrion, grain, rice, dates, insects, reptiles and birds eggs and nestlings; picks grain from animal droppings and recorded tearing open sacks to obtain grain and rice and to perch on backs of domestic animals in search of ticks. During locust swarms in Saudi Arabia even recorded as catching locusts in mid-air with their feet and eating them whilst on the wing. Food-hiding is recorded from captive birds and is presumed to take place in the wild. Although largely resident, in Israel there is marked evidence of dispersal of young birds during July to September, when recorded rarely even on Mediterranean coast.

BREEDING: Solitary nester. Nest a bulky structure of

twigs and branches, lined with wool and rags; placed on cliff faces, telegraph poles, old buildings and isolated trees and bushes, even on oil drums in open desert. Clutch two to seven, average four. Eggs bright or pale blue, weakly spotted or streaked with brown. Incubation 18-23 days, by female only but fed at nest by male. Young fledge at about 35-42 days, being fed by both parents, and stay with their parents for several weeks after fledging. Breeding season varies little over wide range, egg-laying generally January to March, although recorded as early as mid November in Cape Verde Islands and December in the Sudan; eggs most frequent mid February and early March in Israel and average later in northern part of range in Kazakhstan where eggs laid late March and April.

HABITAT: Arid desert and semi-desert plains and foot-hills, especially about desert oases and human settle-ments and cultivation, including outskirts of towns and villages. In Morocco largely confined to *Artemesia* steppe. Noted as high as 3000 m in south Arabian mountains.

DISTRIBUTION: North Africa, Arabia and south-west and central Asia. From the Cape Verde Islands across the Saharan region of North Africa: southern Morocco, Mauritania, northern Senegal, Mali, Niger, Algeria (ex-cept north), Chad, southern Tunisia, Libya, the Sudan and Egypt. Its range continues over Sinai and into Asia where it is widespread throughout the Arabian penin-sula, including the island of Socotra, north to central Israel and Jordan; eastwards across southern and cen-tral Iraq, south-east Syria, central and southern Iran to south-west Afghanistan (Seistan depression) and south-ern Pakistan (Baluchistan and western Sind). The Cen-tral Asian population is isolated in the desert and desert-steppe of north-western Afghanistan, northwards over Turkmenistan, southern and central Kazakhstan and western Uzbekistan. Vagrants have been recorded in extreme south-eastern Turkey and central Syria.

STATUS: Common to locally abundant throughout its range, in many areas having increased as a conse-quence of human settlements with resultant easy forag-ing about rubbish dumps and slaughter-houses. Some decreases of a local nature have been reported, as in Bahrain where it died out in the 1960s. It is perhaps unsuccessful in competition with other corvids, as on Cape Verdes, where it is the only crow, it inhabits a wide variety of habitats; in Israel it is suddenly replaced by the Hooded Crow in cultivated and lusher situations; in the plains of eastern Iran and southern Afghanistan it seems to be entirely replaced by Northern Raven. With the increasing abundance of the House Crow in parts of the Middle East it could well be pushed out by this species in the vicinity of towns and villages.

REFERENCES: Bannerman 1968, Goodwin 1986, Symens 1990, Shirihai (in prep), Vaurie 1954.

NORTHERN RAVEN   Plate 30

Corvus corax

Alternative names: Raven, Common Raven

The most widespread of all corvids; the largest crow of the Northern Hemisphere.

IDENTIFICATION: An impressive crow, considerably larger than all other overlapping species; deep croaking calls are freely given and are diagnostic. Flight silhouette shows relatively long wedge-shaped tail, long promi-nently fingered wings and more prominently projecting head and neck than other crows. These structural points, as well as voice, are the most useful distinctions from Large-billed Crow with which it overlaps in eastern Asia but not from very similar Brown-necked Raven which see for discussion. Large and arched bill and shaggy throat feathers give markedly bulky appearance to head and neck both in flight and when perched. Soars on slightly depressed wings and performs rolling display flight at onset of breeding season. Other likely species with which it could be confused: Carrion Crow, which occasionally utters deep call-notes but has square or round-tipped tail, and relatively shorter wings, tail and neck and smaller bill; Rook approaches Raven in having fairly obviously-fingered primaries and slightly wedge-shaped tail, but Rook has more slender bill, whitish face when adult and very different call. See also Chihuahuan Raven for discussion on distinctions in North America.

DESCRIPTION: Length 58-69 cm. Nominate race. Bill relatively long and heavy, with strongly decurved distal part of culmen. Nasal bristles prominent, covering basal third to half of upper mandible. Throat feathers elon-gated and pointed. Tail relatively long, very strongly graduated. Bases of neck feathers pale brownish-grey. Entire plumage glossy black, gloss quite greenish on head, underparts, tail and primaries, more bluish-purple on upperparts, secondaries and wing-coverts. With wear, plumage becomes duller and less obviously glossed, with flight feathers and tail distinctly browner. Bill, legs and feet black. Irides dark brown.

AGE/SEX: Plumages similar; juvenile dull, not glossy, black; irides bluish-white, darkening soon after fledging. Immature birds separable by dull blackish-brown unglossed wing and tail feathers until 2nd summer.

MEASUREMENTS: Male averages larger than female, but much individual and regional variation. Nominate race: wing 380-473, tail 210-250, tarsus 64-73, bill 70-80, weight 920-1560.

GEOGRAPHICAL VARIATION: Chiefly clinal, a num-bers of localised races have been described but Vaurie (1959) allows eight. The tendency is towards largest and most glossy birds with longest throat hackles in the far north and in the Himalayas and smaller, duller birds with shorter throat hackles in the south. Measurements cited follow sample given in Vaurie (1959).

C. c. corax: Europe eastwards to Lake Baikal region, south to Caucasus and northern Iran. See descrip-tion. Possibly an isolate of this form on Cyprus. Iberian birds tend to be a little smaller and with shorter and more arched bill. Wing mean 414, bill mean 76.

C. c. varius: Iceland and the Faeroes. Less glossy than *principalis* or nominate and intermediate in size, bases of neck feathers whitish. Wing mean 425, bill mean 80.

C. c. subcorax: From Greece eastwards to north-west India, Central Asia and western China (except Himalayan region). Larger than nominate, but throat hackles relatively shorter. Neck and breast distinctly brownish in tone suggesting Brown-necked Raven with which it overlaps, but brown tone obscured by glossy black when plumage very fresh. Bases of neck feathers variable, often almost whitish. Wing mean 445, bill mean 78.

C. c. tingitanus: North Africa and the Canary Islands. Smallest race, with shortest throat hackles and distinctly 'oily' plumage gloss. Bill short but markedly stout and culmen very strongly arched. Plumage bleaches dark brown on head and body. Canary Island birds have slighter bill than mainland birds. Wing mean 388, bill mean 73.

C. c. tibetanus: Mountains of Western China and the Himalayas. Largest and most glossy race, with longest throat hackles; bill large but less imposing than on otherwise similar *principalis*. Bases of neck feathers grey. Wing mean 479, bill mean 82.

C. c. kamtschaticus: North-eastern Asia, intergrading into nominate in Baikal region. Intermediate in size between *principalis* and nominate, with a distinctly larger and thicker bill than the latter. Wing mean 430, bill mean 80.

C. c. principalis: Northern North America and Greenland. Large race, with the largest bill; plumage strongly glossed and throat hackles very well developed. Wing mean 455, bill mean 90.

C. c. sinuatus: south-central USA and Central America. Smaller and with smaller and narrower bill than *principalis*. Wing mean 431, bill mean 75.

VOICE: Usual call a distinctive, deep, hollow, croaking honk 'pruk-pruk-pruk', quite unlike any other corvid call when known. Has a very wide and complex vocabulary, which includes a high, knocking 'toc-toc-toc', a dry, grating 'kraa', a low guttural rattle and some calls almost of a musical nature. For a full discussion on vocabulary see Gwinner (1964).

HABITS: Usually met with in pairs or family parties, but non-breeders from quite large gatherings at favoured feeding sites and for communal roosting. Established pairs remain on territory throughout the year. Territories are quite large; in Britain studies have revealed territories of between 17 and 44 sq. km, with the closest distance between nests to be between 2.7 and 4.6 km. However territorial disputes are uncommon and pairs seem to be remarkably tolerant of other birds. Non-breeding flocks seldom reach large numbers, generally, tens rather than hundreds, except when gathering for communal roost but I have seen flocks of 100 or more feeding in the desert plains of north-eastern Iran in July and there is an old account of 800 gathering to feed on whale carcases in the Shetlands. Unspecified large flocks have been recorded in North Africa. Roost gatherings in Britain generally number about ten but as many as 150 recorded in Cornwall in mid-winter at a large mixed corvid tree roost. These roosts are not joined by pairs with established territory which roost within their own territory. Has complex and varied social display postures which have been summarised by Gwinner (1964) and Coombs (1978). Flight action powerful, rising with swooshing wing-beats, enjoys using air-currents and thermals on which to soar and 'play'; in early spring especially pairs and small parties indulge in tumbling and rolling acrobatics. Often pauses and rolls with closed wings whilst in direct flight over territory. Long wings allow for greater agility in flight than crows; soars effortlessly on flat, slightly depressed wings and glides over long distances. When searching for food quarters hillsides on slow, effortless beats in raptor-like fashion. On ground walks with a deliberate waddling gait and the occasional hop; readily perches on cliffs, telegraph poles and trees. At abundant food sources, e.g. slaughter houses and rubbish dumps, mixes readily with other crows but otherwise keeps very much to itself. Feeds principally on carrion especially dead sheep, cattle, rabbits and fish but takes a variety of food items, including nestling birds and eggs, rodents, shellfish, insects and various seeds, berries and grain. Seen occasionally to hawk for flying ants on the wing and to chase and kill other birds; in Greenland said to chase and catch ptarmigan in flight and to kill puffins emerging from their burrows; equally large Tibetan race recorded catching and killing an adult Tibetan Partridge in flight. They also indulge in food-hiding and storing. Generally shy and wary of man, but in areas where unmolested scavenges about camps and settlements and can become remarkably bold and fearless.

BREEDING: Solitary nester. Nest often a massive, bulky structure of twigs and branches, lined with roots, moss, wool and rags on a base of mud and dung; placed on cliff faces and large trees, less frequently in old buildings or even on low bushes or on the ground in undisturbed open country. Very occasionally on trees within a rookery or heronry. Clutch three to seven, average five. Eggs various shades of blue, from light blue to greenish blue, variably spotted or blotched olive, grey and brown. Incubation 18-21 days, by female only but fed at nest by male. Young fledge at 35-42 days, being fed by both parents and stay with their parents for some 6 months after fledging. Egg laying begins in late February over most of its range, later in higher altitude or northern areas (e.g. April in Greenland, northern Siberia and Tibet) or even earlier in the south of the range (as early as December in Pakistan).

HABITAT: Very varied but principally in 'wild' country from rugged coastlines and inshore islands to hill forest and mountains; also in forested lowland riverine plains, steppe and semi-desert. In Tibet up to 5000 m and recorded as high as 6350 m on Mt Everest.

DISTRIBUTION: Throughout the Holarctic region. In North America from the Aleutians and Alaska eastwards across Canada to both western and eastern coastal districts of Greenland, southwards over western USA west of the Great Plains east to central Texas, south through Mexico to northern Nicaragua. In eastern USA there is an isolated population along the Appalachian mountain chain. In the Old World is present throughout most of Europe (absent or very scarce in lowland eastern England and mainland Europe) including Iceland and the Faeroes and most Mediterranean islands. Widespread along coastal North Africa, including the Canary Islands, east to extreme north-west Egypt. It is widespread throughout Palearctic Asia, south to central Israel, northern Iraq, central Iran, northern Baluchistan (Pakistan) and western Rajasthan (India). It is absent from the true desert regions of western China but widespread over the Tibetan plateau. In China, it extends south to northern Heilungkiang and Inner Mongolia as well as Tibet. In Siberia, it is absent from the massive Taimyr peninsula but is otherwise widespread north to the Arctic circle. Northern birds disperse southwards in winter; it is a scarce winter visitor to northern Japan and vagrants have occurred on Svalbard and Novaya Zemlaya.

STATUS: Everywhere somewhat sparsely distributed but most numerous in mountainous and rugged coastal regions where locally quite common; for example Iceland has a breeding density of 1.5 to 6.8 pairs per 100 sq. km. Scarcest on lowland wooded plains and open forest. Has been heavily persecuted by man in the past and remains so over many parts of its range. In most parts of central and eastern Europe the species has become very scarce or disappeared during the present century. In Iceland a control programme instigated in 1976 had destroyed an estimated 4000 birds per year. Various population estimates have been made for certain countries: Iceland, 2000 pairs in 1990; Britain and Ireland, 5000 pairs in 1976 but decline through heavy afforestation of uplands since; Netherlands, extinct since 1927 but reintroduction programme instigated 1969, three pairs bred 1976 increasing to 64 by 1991; Belgium, extinct since 1919 but reintroduction programme in late 1970s resulted in breeding pair 1979; Israel, 25 pairs 1990 after decline through use of pesticides, (population in 1950s had been estimated as 'a few hundred' pairs); Egypt, one or two pairs in extreme north-west.

REFERENCES: Coombs 1978, Gwinner 1964, Heinrich (1989), Skarphedinsson 1990, Shirihai (in prep), Vaurie 1954, 1959.

FAN-TAILED RAVEN   Plate 26

Corvus rhipidurus

A remarkable raven, in flight recalling an enormous bat in shape. Despite the unremarkable head and bill proportions, the structure of the nasal bristles, tail shape and voice indicate an affinity with the African, rather than northern, ravens.

IDENTIFICATION: Quite unmistakable; with its remarkably short tail and broad-based wings this crow-sized raven usually appears tail-less at any distance. On the ground the primaries project well beyond the tail and this, coupled with its relatively long legs, contributes to a front-heavy appearance. Distinctive shape makes confusion unlikely but beware other species which may have accidentally lost their tails. However, Fan-tailed has much broader-based wings and a stubbier bill than either Brown-necked or Dwarf Ravens, with which it overlaps.

DESCRIPTION: Length 47 cm. Crown flat. Bill relatively short and stubby, with strongly curved culmen. Nasal bristles prominent, upcurved and somewhat fan-shaped, covering basal third of upper mandible. Tail extremely short, strongly wedge-shaped. Throat hackles slightly elongated and forked. Wing relatively broad at base; primaries relatively long and strongly fingered. Bases of upperneck feathers white, those of lowerneck and body grey. Entire plumage black, with an oily bluish-purple sheen; underwing coverts blacker than underside of flight feathers. With wear, becomes slightly brown-toned on head and neck. Bill and legs black. Irides dark brown.

AGE/SEX: Plumages similar; juveniles lack slight gloss of adults and worn plumaged birds of all ages may become slightly brownish.

MEASUREMENTS: Male averages slightly larger than female. Nominate race: wing 373-424, tail 154-172, tarsus 59-74, bill 55-62, weight (1) 745.

GEOGRAPHICAL VARIATION: See Additional Information on page 192.

VOICE: Most frequently uttered calls are a high-pitched, somewhat falsetto 'craah-craah' less harsh and shorter than calls of Brown-necked Raven. Others calls include short, guttural croaks and a quietly-uttered mixture of high-pitched croaks, squeals, trills and clucks which form the basis of a song.

HABITS: Generally met with in pairs or small parties sailing over barren desert cliffs, often in company with Brown-necked Ravens. Quite sociable, often forming small colonies with nests as close as 50-200 m apart but also a solitary nester with pairs holding more defined territories. Small parties gather at regular feeding sites such as garbage dumps and oases with fruiting trees. Birds with established territories remain on territory throughout the year but it is unsure whether or not they join communal roosts. Non-breeders form small flocks, with up to 70 being the largest feeding group noted in Israel, but feeding gatherings of 500 or more recorded in the Yemen at rubbish dumps. Large communal roosts seem to break up at onset of breeding season but non-breeders continue to use them; roosts are usually plantations of palm trees, where they freely mix with roosting Brown-necked Ravens; largest roost recorded in Israel was of 370 at a Dead Sea oasis from September to November but up to 800 recorded in the Yemen. Although associated with barren desert cliffs and canyons they are normally not far from oases and human settlements where food supplies are most abundant. Walks with relatively upright carriage, often with bill open as though panting in the heat. Feeds on variety of food items, including invertebrates, especially beetles, grain picked from animal droppings and stubble fields, carrion, fruits and berries and human food scraps; recorded perching on domestic animals searching for ectoparasites and even catching locusts in mid-air with their feet and eating them on the wing. Freely scavenges around human settlements and encampments; often bold and confiding where unmolested, otherwise wary like other large corvids. Broad wings and short tail excellent for soaring and wheeling on thermals, which it seems to spend more time doing than Brown-necked Raven. Perches on cliffs and telegraph poles and wires as well as trees, but usually seen either in flight or on the ground, seeming to spend little time perched. Although mainly resident, in autumn and winter small groups of non-breeders wander considerable distances, presumably in search of fresh feeding areas.

BREEDING: Solitary and social nester, often forming small colonies (see Habits). Nest a structure of twigs and branches, lined with animal hair, rags etc.; situated in cave or cliff crevice, exceptionally in trees and disused buildings. Clutch 2 to 6, average 5. Eggs greenish-blue, variously marked and shaded with brown and grey. Incubation 18-20 days, presumably by female only. Young fledge at about 35-40 days, being fed by both parents and stay with their parents for several weeks after fledging. Breeding season varies a little over range, egg-laying generally March and April in Israel, early May in Somalia and the Sudan, June in northern Kenya and more varied dates in Ethiopia where eggs recorded February, March, May and June. Nest has been exceptionally recorded as parasitised by Great Spotted Cuckoo.

HABITAT: Arid desert cliffs, canyons and ravines with nearby oases, descending to adjacent plains outside breeding season. In Ethiopia chiefly between 900 and 2400 m, but occurs up to 4000 m. In Israel and Jordan most numerous in vicinity of the Dead Sea, which is well below sea-level.

DISTRIBUTION: North-east Africa and the Middle East. Locally in the Air Massif of northern Mali and northern Niger, Chad and northern Central African Republic. More widespread over mountains of the Sudan and Ethiopia, extending into Djibouti and western Somalia, southwards into Uganda and northern and western Kenya and northwards to Gebel Elba on the Egypt-Sudan border. In the Middle East in southern Israel and Jordan (centred on the rift valley) and in the Hejaz and Asir mountains of western Saudi Arabia and the Yemen, east to extreme western Oman; locally also in the interior of Saudi Arabia in the Tuwaiq escarpment and Gebel Aja and Bebel Sama. Until recently also in southern Sinai. Outside breeding season some dispersal out of higher interior and recorded as a vagrant to Syria and Upper Egypt.

STATUS: Locally common over most of range and locally abundant western Arabia and Ethiopia. Decrease suspected in Israel, possibly due to competition with Brown-necked Raven; Israeli population estimated at 300 pairs in 1989. No other population estimates available. No recent breeding records from Sinai (Egypt) where now only rare winter visitor.

REFERENCES: Jennings 1986, Lewis 1989, Roselaar 1993, Shirihai (in prep).

WHITE-NECKED RAVEN   Plate 26

Corvus albicollis

Alternative name: Cape Raven

Large African raven, its short tail and broad wings suggesting Fan-tailed Raven but the enormous bill and white nape patch are shared only by the even larger Thick-billed Raven of Ethiopia.

IDENTIFICATION: Eastern and Southern Africa. The largest crow in its range, the short tail and broad-based wings are shared only by the smaller Fan-tailed Raven, with which it overlaps in the highlands of Kenya and Uganda, but the massive, arched bill and large white nape patch provide easy distinctions, although the latter is difficult to see in overhead views. Pied Crow is smaller and has a relatively longer tail, white breast and upper belly as well as nape and much smaller bill; some White-necked Ravens show inconspicuous whitish feathering on breast. Range does not overlap with similar but even larger Thick-billed Raven which is also separated by having a much longer, fuller tail. When soaring over mountain ridges broad wings and short tail suggest a raptor, but head and bill shape are normally evident at reasonable ranges to prevent confusion.

DESCRIPTION: Length 50-54 cm. Crown flat. Bill mas-

sive, with very strongly arched culmen. Nasal bristles prominent, upcurved and somewhat fan-shaped, almost covering basal third of upper mandible. Tail extremely short, wedge-shaped. Throat hackles slightly elongated, forked. Wing relatively broad at base; primaries relatively long and strongly fingered. Head, neck and underparts blackish-brown with slight purplish sheen, loral region blacker. Large white patch on lower nape extends slightly onto sides at base of neck; sometimes feathers of foreneck and breast fringed with whitish scaling forming indistinct breast band. Remainder of plumage, including wings and tail coal black with slight greenish sheen. With wear becomes slightly brown-toned overall and loses plumage sheen. Bill black with white or horn tip. Legs black. Irides dark brown.

AGE/SEX: Plumages similar; juvenile duller and browner-black overall, with more extensive whitish feathering on breast, and some black flecking in white nape patch; body plumage texture softer and more woolly.

MEASUREMENTS: Male averages slightly larger than female. Wing 376-430, tail 180-184, tarsus 72-79, bill 61-66, weight (1) 900.

GEOGRAPHICAL VARIATION: Monotypic.

VOICE: Usual call a high-pitched, somewhat falsetto 'kroorh-kroorh' or 'kraak-kraak-kraak'; higher in pitch than call of Northern Raven. Several other sounds may be given including a deeper and more throaty, rasping version of the croak.

HABITS: Usually found in pairs but at good feeding locations quite large gatherings form; as many as 150 have been reported assembling to feed on animal carcases, alongside Pied Crows, vultures and kites in South Africa and locust swarms have attracted even larger gatherings. Up to 800 have been recorded at a gathering in East Africa which indicates extensive wandering by birds in search of food. Pairs with established territories remain on territory throughout the year but forage over considerable distances in search of food. Non-breeders form small flocks and are possibly more nomadic. Walks with relatively upright carriage, but gait swaggering; also hops. Diet varied as with other large corvids, chiefly carrion, but will take small birds, nestlings, eggs, lizards, snakes, tortoises, large insects, rodents, grain, human food waste, fruit and berries. Although closely attached to mountainous areas and hills, they descend to the foothills and plains in search of food. Where not persecuted often becomes quite bold, scavenging about villages and settlements, even entering courtyards and tolerating presence of people to a remarkable degree. Can also be as wary as any other large corvid. Feeds chiefly on the ground, holding large items in its foot and tearing at them with its bill. Recorded as occasionally feeding in trees, taking insects from amongst the foliage, picking ectoparasites from the backs of large mammals and to drop tortoises onto rocky ground. Also patrols roads searching for roadside animal corpses and is often the first bird to arrive at a animal carcase, before either vultures or kites. Soars and glides well on broad wings, pairs spend a good part of the day soaring over mountainsides and cliffs where they readily indulge in aerial acrobatics, tumbling and rolling in manner of Northern Raven, the wings producing quite loud swishing sounds. Normal flight has relatively slow and shallow wing-beats.

BREEDING: Solitary nester. Nest a structure of twigs

and branches, lined with animal hair, rags etc.; situated on inaccessible cliff ledge or crevice, exceptionally in a tree. Clutch one to six, average four. Eggs light green, bluish-green or off-white, streaked and spotted olive, brown and grey. Incubation 19-21 days, presumably by female only. No information on fledging period available. Breeding season varies a little over range, generally earlier in south of range; egg-laying chiefly September and October throughout southern Africa and October to December in Kenya.

HABITAT: Mountain gorges and cliffs and escarpments in open country, including open mountain forest, descending to lower elevations to feed. Breeds chiefly between 1000 and 3000 m in East Africa but recorded as high as 5800 m and down to 400 m in lowlands. In southern Africa also in coastal hills.

DISTRIBUTION: Southern, central and eastern Africa. Northern limit of range is western Kenya and Uganda, extending southwards over eastern Zaire, Rwanda, Burundi, Tanzania, Zambia, Malawi, north and west Mozambique, Zimbabwe (except arid west) and southern and eastern South Africa to Cape Town. Wandering birds have reached extreme south-west Namibia and could conceivably occur occasionally in Botswana. There is one record of a vagrant from south-east Sudan.

STATUS: Generally uncommon or locally common over most of range, somewhat sparsely distributed (apparently declining in Kenya) but large numbers assembling at good food sources indicate greater level of abundance than is usually realised.

REFERENCES: Goodwin 1986, Maclean 1985, Uys 1966.

THICK-BILLED RAVEN   Plate 26

Corvus crassirostris

The largest of all corvids, closely-related to the White-necked Raven but isolated from it in the Ethiopian highlands and with an even more massive bill and much longer tail.

IDENTIFICATION: Easily identified by restricted range and overall appearance of White-necked Raven, with which it does not overlap. Differs from White-necked in having a considerably longer, wedge-shaped tail, an even larger, swollen-arched bill and the large white nape patch on upper nape, rather than lower nape as in White-necked, although Thick-billed also has some white on lower nape. Range overlaps with Fan-tailed Raven and Pied Crow but neither likely to be confused. In flight the massive bill seems to 'pull' the neck forward creating almost a hornbill-like impression.

DESCRIPTION: Length 60-64 cm. Crown flat. Bill massive, with very strongly arched and ridged culmen and deep nasal grooves. Nasal bristles relatively shorter than in White-necked, upcurved but not reaching culmen ridge. Tail moderate, strongly wedge-shaped. Throat hackles hardly elongated, and feathers of head extremely short. Wing relatively broad at base; primaries relatively long and strongly fingered. Plumage black with an oily sheen, most glossy on wings and tail; throat, sides of neck and breast browner and less glossy. Large white patch on upper hindneck and smaller patch at

base of nape connected by narrow white central stripe. With wear becomes slightly brown-toned overall and loses plumage sheen. Bill black with whitish-horn tip. Legs black. Irides dark brown.

AGE/SEX: Plumages similar; juvenile duller and browner black; body plumage texture softer and more woolly.

MEASUREMENTS: Male averages slightly larger than female. Wing 427-472, tail 232-237, tarsus 74-80, bill 80-85, weight not recorded.

GEOGRAPHICAL VARIATION: Monotypic.

VOICE: A low, guttural, somewhat wheezy croak 'phlurk-phlurk'; during courtship hoarse gurgling and choking sounds are produced. These seem to be the only described vocalisations.

HABITS: Normally encountered singly or in pairs but at rubbish dumps and slaughtering places parties of up to a dozen or more congregate. Breeding pairs seem to remain on territory throughout the year but like White-necked Ravens probably roam over considerable distances in search of food. Walks and hops with relatively upright carriage and waddling gait; perches freely in trees even well inside canopy. Forages readily about towns and villages and even cities; it is a familiar bird of the outskirts and in large gardens within Addis Ababa. Feeds on a variety of carrion, human food scraps, rodents, reptiles, grain and large insects; reported to do some damage to crops by tearing at the ears of growing wheat; on upland plateaux, digs for mole-rats with massive bill and breaks up animal dung by scattering it with bill held almost upside-down to pick out grains and beetle larvae; also reported stealing bones which have been dropped and smashed by Lammergeiers before rightful owner can retrieve fragments. Often bold and fearless when living near habitation, attends fishing boats off-loading catches by lakeshores, accompanying scavenging Hammerkops and Marabou Storks. Over cliffs and escarpments soars and glides on thermals, often with raptors, and enjoys tumbling aerobatics, the pair sometimes locking feet together and twisting down into deep ravines before breaking apart. When taking to the air the wings produce a loud swishing sound, but when airborne the beats are relatively slow and shallow.

BREEDING: Little documentation. Solitary nester. Nest a large structure of branches, constructed on a cliff face or in a tree. Clutch four. Eggs turquoise, marked with pale and reddish brown, chiefly towards the large end. Eggs recorded December to February, chiefly January.

HABITAT: Mountain ravines and escarpments are the most favoured haunts, but found over wide variety of habitats from open moorland to subtropical humid forests, including cultivation and large gardens in towns. Chiefly between 1500 and 2500 m, recorded up to 4000 m, rarely below 1200 m.

DISTRIBUTION: Endemic to Ethiopia where it is widespread throughout the highlands from Eritrea in the north to Sidamo province in the south. Recorded as an exceptional wanderer to extreme eastern Sudan (once) and north-western Somalia (once), also recorded south to border of extreme northern Kenya where vagrancy therefore possible but so far unrecorded.

STATUS: Relatively common over its limited range.

REFERENCES: Goodwin 1986, Hoy 1976, Urban 1980, Wilson and Balcha 1989.

BIBLIOGRAPHY

Alamargot, J. (1987). Pied Crows *Corvus albus* with atypical plumage. *Walia* 10: 7-12.
Ali, S. (1949). *Indian Hill Birds*. Bombay. Oxford University Press.
Ali, S. (1962). *The Birds of Sikkim*. Delhi. Oxford University Press.
Ali, S. and S.D. Ripley. (1972). *Handbook of the Birds of India and Pakistan*. Vol. 5. Bombay. Oxford University Press.
Alvarez, H. (1975). The social system of the Green Jay in Colombia. *The Living Bird* 14: 5-43.
Ash, J.S. (1983). Over fifty additions of birds to the Somalia list including two hybrids, together with notes from Ethiopia and Kenya. *Scopus* 7: 54-79.
Ash, J.S. (1988). Some observations in South Yemen in 1984 and a selected bibliography of the region. *Sandgrouse* 10: 85-90.
Ash, J.S. and T.M. Gullick. (1989). The present situation regarding the breeding endemic birds of Ethiopia. *Scopus* 13: 90-96.
Ash, J.S. and J.E. Miskell.(1983). Birds of Somalia: their habitat, status and distribution. *Scopus Special Supplement No. 1*. EANHS.

Baker, R.H. (1951) *The avifauna of Micronesia, its origin, evolution, and distribution*. University of Kansas Museum of Natural History Publications 3: 1-359.
Bannerman, D.A. and W.M. (1968). *History of the Birds of the Cape Verde Islands*. Oliver and Boyd. Edinburgh.
Bardin, A.V. in Ilyichev, V.D. (ed). (1988). Bird ecology and behaviour. Trans. *Vsesoyuz. Ornithol. Obschch*. 2: 132-134 (in Russian).
Bates, J.M., Parker, T.A., Capparella, A.P. and T.J. Davis. (1992). Observations on the campo, cerrado and forest avifauna of eastern Dpto. Santa Cruz, Bolivia, including 21 species new to the country. *Bull. Brit. Orn. Club* 112: 86-98.
Bates, R.S.P.B and Lowther, E.H.N. (1952). *Breeding Birds of Kashmir*. Delhi. Oxford University Press.
Bayer, R. (1989). Are "small" crows along the Oregon coast necessarily Northwestern Crows ? *Oregon Birds* 15: 277-279.
Beehler, B.M., Pratt, T.K. and D.A. Zimmerman. (1986). *Birds of New Guinea*. Princeton University Press. New Jersey.
Benson, C.W. (1946). Notes on the birds of Southern Abyssinia. *Ibis* 88: 448-450.
Bent, A.C. (1946). Life histories of North American jays, crows and titmice. *U.S. Nat. Mus. Bull*. 191: 310-322.
Bignall, E. and D.J. Curtis (eds). (1988). *Choughs and land-use in Europe*. Scottish Chough Study Group. Tarbert.
Birkhead, T. (1991). *The Magpies: the ecology and behaviour of Black-billed and Yellow-billed Magpies*. Poyser. London.
Blair, C.M.G. (1961). Hybridization of *Corvus albus* and *Corvus edithae* in Ethiopia. *Ibis* 103: 499-502.
Blakers, M., Davies, S.J.J.F. and P.N. Reilley. (1984). *The Atlas of Australian Birds*. Melbourne University Press. Carlton.
Blasco, M., Escudero, J.C. and J.M. Vargas. (1980). Presence of the Alpine Chough in Malaga (Spain). *Bird Study* 27: 56-57.
Blomgren, A. (1964). *Lavskrikan*. Stockholm.
Blomgren, A. (1971). Studies of less familiar birds 162. Siberian Jay. *Brit. Birds* 64: 25-28.
Bond, J. (1971). *Birds of the West Indies*. 2nd edn. Collins, London.
Brazil, M.A. (1991). *The Birds of Japan*. Christopher Helm. London.
Brazil, M.A. (1992). Finding birds in Taiwan. *Bull. Oriental Bird Club* 16: 40-44.
British Birds (editorial). (1985). Plumage, age and moult terminology. *Brit. Birds* 78: 419-427.
Britton, P.L. (ed). (1980). *Birds of East Africa*. Nairobi. EANHS.
Brooke, R.K. and J.H. Grodler. (1973). Notes on the foraging, food and relationships of *Corvus albus* (*Aves, Corvidae*). *Arnoldia* 6 (10): 1-13.
Brooks, D.J., Evans, M.I., Martins, R.P. and R.F. Porter. (1987). The Status of Birds in North Yemen and the Records of the OSME expedition in autumn1985. *Sandgrouse* 9: 4-66.
Brown, J.L. (1963). Aggressiveness, dominance, and social organisation in the Steller Jay. *Condor* 65: 460-484.
Brown, J.L. (1963). Social organisation and behaviour of the Mexican Jay. *Condor* 65: 125-153.
Brown, J.L. (1970). Cooperative breeding and altruistic behaviour in the Mexican Jay *Aphelocoma ultramarina*. *Anim. Behav*. 18: 366-378.
Brown, J.L. and E.G. Horvath. (1989). Geographic variation of group size, ontogeny, rattle calls and body size in *Aphelocoma ultramarina*. *Auk* 106: 124-128.
Brown, L.H. (1967). The occurrence of the chough *Pyrrhocorax pyrrhocorax* in the Mandebo-Araenna Mountains of the Bale Province, Ethiopia. *Ibis* 109: 275.
Browning, M.D. (1993). Taxonomy of the blue-crested group of *Cyanocitta stelleri* (Steller's Jay) with a description of a new subspecies. *Bull. Brit. Orn. Club* 113: 34-41.
Bruce, M.D. (1979). Notes on status, vocalizations and behaviour of Lidth's Jay *Garrulus lidthi*. *Le Gerfaut* 69: 353-356.
Buchel, H.P. (1983). Beitrage Zum Sozialverhalten der Alpendohle *Pyrrhocorax graculus*. *Orn. Beobachter* 80: 1-28.
Buden, D.W. (1987). *The Birds of the Southern Bahamas*. BOU. London.
Bullock, I.D., Drewett, R.R. and Mickelburgh, S.P. (1983). The Chough in Britain and Ireland. *Brit. Birds* 76: 377-401.
Bundy, G. (1976). *The Birds of Libya*. BOU. London.

Cain, A.J. and I.C.J. Galbraith. (1956). Field notes on Birds of the Eastern Solomon Islands. *Ibis* 98: 262-295.
Cheng, T-H. (1976). *Distributional List of Chinese Birds*. Beijing.
Collar, N.J. and P. Andrew. (1988). *Birds to Watch*. ICBP. Cambridge.
Coombs, F. (1978). *The Crows*. Batsford. London.
Crossin, R.S. (1967). The breeding biology of the Tufted Jay. *Proc. Western Foundation Vert. Zool*. vol. 1, no. 5.
Cruz, A. (1972). Food and Feeding beahviour of the Jamaican Crow, *Corvus jamaicensis*. *Auk* 89: 445-446.
Curry, P.J. (1978). On the field characters of Little and Torresian Crows in Central Western Australia. *Aust. Birdwatcher* 7: 265-269
Cyrus, D. and N. Robson. (1980). *Bird Atlas of Natal*. University of Natal Press. Pietermaritzburg.

Darke, T.O. (1971). *The Cornish Chough*. Bradford Barton. Truro.
Davis, J. and L. Williams. (1957). Irruptions of the Clark Nutcracker in California. *Condor* 59: 229-234.
Davis, J. and L. Williams. (1964). The 1961 irruption of Clark's Nutcracker in California. *Wilson Bulletin* 76: 10-18.
Davis, L.I. (1958). Acoustic evidence of relationship in North American crows. *Wilson Bull*. 70: 151-167.
Dean, W.R.J. and I.A.W. MacDonald. (1981). A review of African birds feeding in association with mammals. *Ostrich* 52: 135-155.
Debus, S.J.S. (1980). Little and Forest Ravens in New South Wales. *Aust. Birds* 15: 7-12.
Delacour, J. (1927). New birds from Indo-China. *Bull. Brit. Orn. Club* 47: 151-170.
Delacour, J. (1929). Revision du Genre Cissa. *L'Oiseau* 10: 1-12.
Delacour, J. and P. Jabouille. (1931). *Les Oiseau de l'Indochine Francasis*. vol. 4. Paris.
Dement'ev, G.P. and N.A. Gladkov (eds). (1954). *Birds of the Soviet Union*. Vol.5. 1970 translation. Israel Program for Scientific Translations. Jerusalem.
Dickinson, E.C., Kennedy, R.S. and K.C. Parkes. (1991). *The Birds of the Philippines*. BOU. Tring.
Dorst, J. (1947). Revision systematique du genre *Corvus*. *L'Oiseau* 17: 44-87.
Dos Santos, J.R. (1968). The colony of Azure-winged Magpies in the Barca d'Alava region. *Cyanopica* 1: 1-28.
Dow, D.D. (1965). The Role of Saliva in Food Storage by the Grey Jay. *Auk* 82: 139-154.
Downer, A. and R. Sutton. (1990). *Birds of Jamaica*. Cambridge University Press. Cambridge.
Dunning, J.B. (1993). *CRC Handbook of Avian Body Mass*. CRC Press. Boca Raton.

Ena, V. (1984). A population study of the Rook *Corvus frugilegus* in Leon Province, northwest Spain. *Ibis* 126: 240-249.

Feare, C.J. and Y. Mungroo. (1989). Notes on the House Crow *Corvus splendens* in Mauritius. *Bull. Br. Orn. Club* 109: 199-201.
Fleming, R.L., Heming, R.L. and L.S. Bangdel. (1976). *Birds of Nepal*. Fleming. Kathmandu.
Flint, V.E., Boehme, R.L., Kostin, Y.V. and A.A. Kuznetsov. (1984). *A Field Guide to the Birds of the USSR*. Princeton University Press, New Jersey.

Garrido, O.H. and F.G. Montana. (1975). *Catalogo de los Aves de Cuba*. Academia de Ciencias de Cuba. Havana.
Gayou, D.C. (1986). The social system of the Texas Green Jay. *Auk* 103: 540-547
Gill, F.B. (1985). Mystery crow in New Jersey. *Birding* 17: 188-190.
Goodwin, D. (1986). *Crows of the World*. British Museum (Natural History).
Grimmett, R. (1991). Little-known Oriental Bird: Biddulph's Ground-Jay. *Oriental Bird Club Bulletin* 13: 26-29.
Gwahaba, J.J. (1975). A contribution to the biology of the Pied Crow *Corvus albus* Muller in Uganda. *J. E. Afr. Nat. Hist. Soc. Nat. Mus*. No.153.
Gwinner, E. (1964). Untersuchungen uber das Ausdrucks und Sozialverhalten des Kolkraben (*Corvus corax corax* L.) *Z. Tierpsychol*. 21: 657-748.

Hall, B.P. and R.E. Moreau. (1970). *An Atlas of Speciation in African Passerine Birds*. British Museum (Natural History). London.
Hannecart, F. and Y. Letocart. (1980). Oiseaux de N'le Caledonie et des Loyautes. *Les Editions Cardinalis*. Noumea.
Hardy, J.W. (1969). A Taxonomic revision of the New World jays. *Condor* 71: 360-375.
Hardy, J.W. (1969). Habits and Habitats of certain South American jays. *Contributions in Science* no 165.
Hardy, J.W. (1971). Habitat and habits of the Dwarf Jay, *Aphelocoma nana*. *Wilson Bull*., 83: 5-30.
Hardy, J.W. (1973). Age and Sex differences in the black-and-blue jays of Middle America. *Bird Banding* 44: 81-90.
Hardy, J.W. (1974). Behavior and its evolution in Neotropical jays (*Cissilopha*). *Bird Banding* 45: 253-268.
Hardy, J.W. (1990). *Voices of the New World jays, crows and their allies*. Tape Cassette. ARA records. Gainesville.
Hardy, J.W. (1990). The Fish Crow (*Corvus ossifragus*) and its Mexican relatives: vocal clues to evolutionary relationships ? *Florida Field Naturalist* 18: 74-80.
Hardy, J.W. and R.J. Raitt. (1977). Relationships between the two races of San Blas Jay *Cyanocorax sanblasiana*. *Bull. Brit. Orn. Club* 97: 27-31.
Hardy, J.W., Webber, T.A. and R.J. Raitt. (1981). Communal Social Biology of the Southern San Blas Jay. *Bull. Florida State Mus*., 26: 203-264.
Heinrich, B. (1989). *Ravens in Winter*. Summit Books. New York.
Heinroth, O. (1903). Ornithologische Ergebnisse der "1 Deutschen Suddsee-Expedition von Br. Mencke". *J. Orn*. 51: 69-71.
Henry, G.M. (1971). *A Guide to the Birds of Ceylon*. Oxford University Press. London.
Hilty, S.L. and W.L. Brown. (1986). *A Guide to the Birds of Colombia*. Princeton University Press, New Jersey.
Holyoak, D.T. (1972). Behaviour and Ecology of the Chough and Alpine Chough. *Bird Study* 19: 215-227.
Holyoak, D.T. (1983). Notes on the Palm Crow *Corvus palmarum* in Haiti. *Bull. Brit. Orn. Club* 103: 81-82.
Holyoak, D.T. and M.B. Seddon. (1989). Distributional notes on the birds of Burkhina Faso. *Bull. Brit. Orn. Club* 109: 205-216.
Hollom, P.A.D., Porter, R.F., Christensen, S. and Willis, I. (1988). *Birds of the Middle East and North Africa*. Poyser. Calton.
Hollyer, J.N. (1970). The Invasion of Nutcrackers in Autumn 1968. *Brit. Birds* 63: 353-373.
Honsono, T. (1966-1983). A Study of the Life History of the Blue Magpie. Published in various parts in: *Misc. Rep. of the Yamashina Inst. for Ornithol.*

Inskipp, C and Inskipp, T.P. (1985). *A Guide to the Birds of Nepal*. Croom Helm. Beckenham.
Inskipp, C and Inskipp, T.P. (1993). Birds recorded during a visit to Bhutan in autumn 1991. *Forktail* 8: 97-112.
Irwin, M.P.S. (1981). *The Birds of Zimbabwe*. Quest Publishing. Harare.

Jeffrey-Smith, M. (1956). *Bird-Watching in Jamaica*.
Jenkins, J.M. (1983). The native forest birds of Guam. AOU *Orn. Monograph* No. 31. Washington DC.
Jennings, M.C. (1981). *The Birds of Saudi Arabia: a checklist*. Jennings. Cambridge.
Jennings, M.C. (1986). Fan-tailed Raven. *The Phoenix* 3: 8-9.
Jennings, M.C. (1992). The House Crow *Corvus splendens* in Aden (Yemen) and an attempt at its control. *Sandgrouse* 14: 27-33.
John, A.W.G. and J. Roskell. Jay movements in autumn 1983. *Brit. Birds* 78: 611-637.
Jollie, M. (1978). Phylogeny of the species of *Corvus*. *Biologist* 60: 73-108.
Jollie, M. (1978). The plumages of the Grey Crow *Corvus tristis* of New Guinea. *Emu* 78: 160-162.
Jollie, M. (1985). The dimorphism of *Coloeus dauuricus*, the Asian Jackdaw. *Journ. f. Orn*. 126: 303-305.

Kasparek, M. (1989). Breeding distribution of the Rook *Corvus frugilegus* in Turkey. *Sandgrouse* 11: 89-95.
Katti, M., Singh, P., Manjrekar, N., Sharma, S. and S. Mukherjee. (1992). An ornithological survey of eastern Arunchal Pradesh, India. *Forktail* 7: 75-89.
King, B.F., Dickinson, E.C. and M.W. Woodcock. (1975). *A Field Guide to the Birds of South-East Asia*. Collins. London.
King, W.B. (1981). *Endangered Birds of the World: The ICBP Bird Red Data Book*. Smithsonian Institution Press, Washington.
Kitson, A.R. (1985). Choughs and Jackdaws. *Brit. Birds* 78: 247.
Kuroda, N.H. (1976). Observations of territorial life in breeding season of a pair of Jungle Crows in City Tokyo. *Misc. Rep. Yamashina Inst. Orn*. 8, 2 and 3.

La Touche, J.D.D. (1952). *A Handbook of the Birds of Eastern China*. Vol. 1. London.
Lack, P. (1986). *The Atlas of Wintering Birds in Britain and Ireland*. Poyser. Calton.
Langrand, O. (1990). *Guide to the Birds of Madagascar*. Yale University Press. New Haven and London.
Layard, E.L. and E.L.C. Layard. (1882). Notes on the avifauna of New Caledonia. *Ibis* 6, 4th series: 520-522.
Lekagul, B. and P.D. Round. (1991). *A Guide to the Birds of Thailand*. Saha Karn Bhaet. Bangkok.
Lewis, A.D. (1989). Notes on two ravens *Corvus spp*. in Kenya. *Scopus* 13: 129-131.
Lewis, A.D. and D.E. Pomeroy. (1989). *A Bird Atlas of Kenya*. Balkema. Rotterdam.
Ligon, J.D. and L. Sandra. (1974). Notes on the behavioural ecology of Couch's

Mexican Jay. *Auk* 91: 841-843.

Ludlow, F & Kinnear, N.B (1933) A contribution to the ornithology of Chinese Turkestan. *Ibis* 13: 240-259, 440-473.

Mackworth-Praed, C.W. and C.H.B. Grant. (1960). *African Handbook of Birds*. Series 1, vol 2. Longmans. London.

Maclean, G.L. (1985). *Robert's Birds of Southern Africa*. John Voelcker Bird Book Fund. Cape Town.

McAllan, I.A.W. and Bruce, M.D. (1988). *The Birds of New South Wales. A Working List*. Biocon Research Group. Turramurra.

McNair, D.B. (1989). Status and the distribution of the Fish Crow in the Carolinas and Georgia. *Oriole* 52: 28-45.

Marzluff, J. and R. Balda. (1992). *The Pinyon Jay*. Poyser. London.

Mayr, E. (1945). *The birds of the southwest Pacific*. New York.

Mayr, E. (1955). Notes on the birds of northern Melanesia, 3, Passeres. *Amer. Mus. Novitates*, no 1707: 1-46.

Meinertzhagen, R. (1926). Introduction to a review of the genus *Corvus*. *Nov. zool.* 33: 89-111.

Meininger, P.L., Muillie, W.C. and B. Buruun. (1980). The spread of the House Crow, with special reference to the occurrence in Egypt. *Gerfaut* 70: 245-250.

Mewaldt, L.R. (1956). Nesting behaviour of the Clark Nutcracker. *Condor* 58: 3-23.

Michael, G.A. (1987). Notes on the breeding biology and ecology of the Mariana or Guam Crow. *Avicult. Mag.* 93: 73-82.

Moore, H.J. and C. Boswell. (1956). Field observations on the birds of Iraq. *Iraq Nat. Hist. Mus. Publication* No.10

Moore, R.T. (1938). Discovery of the nest and eggs of the Tufted Jay. *Condor* 40: 233-241.

Nikolaus, G. (1987). Distributional atlas of Sudan's birds with notes on habitat and status. *Bonner zoologische Monographien* no. 25.

Olsson, S.L. (1990). Review of McAllan and Bruce, The Birds of New South Wales, in *Auk* 107: 458-459.

Orenstein, R. (1972). Tool-use by the Caledonian Crow (*Corvus moneduloides*). *Auk* 89: 674.

Paludan, K. (1959). On the Birds of Afghanistan. *Dansk Natur. Foreng.* Copenhagen.

Parker, T.A., Parker, S.A. and Plenge, M.A. (1982). *An annotated checklist of Peruvian Birds*. Buteo Books. Vermillion.

Paulsen, I. (1989). Northwestern Crow distinction ? *Oregon Birds* 15: 279-280.

Paulson, D. (1989). Northwestern Crow distinction ? Maybe not. *Oregon Birds* 15: 285.

Pearman, M. (1993). Some range extensions and five species new to Colombia, with notes on some scarce or little known species. *Bull. Brit. Orn. Club* 113: 66-75.

Peters, J.L. (1962). Check-list of birds of the world 15. *Mus. Comp. Zool.*, Cambridge, Mass.

Petersen, A.T. (1991). New distributional information on *Aphelocoma* jays. *Bull. Brit. Orn. Club* 111: 28-33.

Peterson, R.T. and E.L. Chalif. (1973). *A Field Guide to Mexican Birds*. Houghton Mifflin. Boston.

Phillips, A.R. (1950). The San Blas Jay in Arizona. *Condor* 52: 86.

Pilcher, C.W.T. (1986). A Breeding Record of the House Crow in Kuwait with Comments on the Species' Status in the Arabian Gulf. *Sandgrouse* 8: 102-106.

Pitelka, F.A. (1951). Speciation and ecologic distribution in American Jays of the genus *Aphelocoma*. *Univ. Calif. Publs Zool.* 50: 195-464.

Pitelka, F.A. (1961). Comments on types and taxonomy in the jay genus *Aphelocoma*. *Condor* 63: 234-245.

Pizzey, G. and R. Doyle. (1980). *A Field Guide to the Birds of Australia*.

Collins. Sydney.

Pratt, H.D., Bruner, P.L. and D.G. Berrett. (1987). *A Field Guide to the Birds of Hawaii and the Tropical Pacific*. Princeton University Press. New Jersey.

Pratt, T.K. (1987). Recent observations March through May 1987. *Elepaio* 47: 93-95.

Raitt, R.J. and J.W. Hardy. (1976). Behavioral Ecology of the Yucatan Jay. *Wilson Bull.* 88: 529-554.

Raitt, R.J. and J.W. Hardy. (1979). Social Behavior, Habitat and Food of the Beechey Jay. *Wilson Bull.* 91: 1-15.

Rand, A. and E.T. Gilliard. (1967). *Handbook of New Guinea Birds*. Weidenfeld and Nicolson. London.

Rand, A.L. and D.S. Rabor. (1961). A new race of crow, *Corvus enca*, from the Philippines. *Fieldiana Zool.* 39: 577-579.

Rensch, B. (1931). Die Vogelwelt von Lombok, Sumbawa und Flores. *Mitt. Zool. Mus. Berlin* 17.

Ridgely, R.S. (1981). *A Guide to the Birds of Panama*. Princeton University Press. New Jersey.

Ridgely, R.S. and G. Tudor. (1989). *The Birds of South America*. Vol. 1. Oxford University Press. Oxford.

Ridgway, R. (1904). The Birds of North and Middle America. *Bull. U.S. Nat. Mus.*, 50, pt 3.

Roberts, C. (1990). More on the Northwestern Crow. *Oregon Birds* 16: 223-224.

Roberts, P.J. (1985). The Choughs of Bardsey. *Brit. Birds* 78: 217-232.

Robson, C.R., Eames, J.C., Wolstencroft, J.A., Nguyen Cu and Truong Van La. (1989). Recent records of birds from Vietnam. *Forktail* 5: 71-97.

Robson, C.R., Eames, J.C., Nguyen Cu and Truong Van La. (1993). Further records of birds from Vietnam. *Forktail* 8: 25-52.

Roselaar, C. S. (1993). New subspecies of Fan-tailed Raven and Greenfinch. *Dutch Birding* 15: 258-262.

Rowley, I. (1967). A fourth species of Australian corvid. *Emu* 66: 191-210.

Rowley, I. (1967). Sympatry in Australian Ravens. *Proc. ecol. Soc. Aus.* 2: 107-115.

Rowley, I. 1970. The genus Corvus in Australia. C.S.I.R.O. *Wildlife Research* 15: 27-71.

Rowley, I. (1973). The comparative ecology of Australian corvids. C.S.I.R.O. *Wildlife Research* 18: 25-650.

Ryves, B.H. (1948). *Bird Life in Cornwall*. Collins. London.

Sakai, H.F. and C.J. Ralph. (1980). Observations on the Hawaiian Crow in south Kona, Hawaii. *Elepaio* 40: 133-138.

de Schauensee, R.M. (1966). *The Species of Birds of South America*. Livingstone, Narberth.

de Schauensee, R.M. (1984). *The Birds of China*. Oxford University Press, Oxford.

de Schauensee, R.M. and Phelps, W.H. (1978). *A Guide to the Birds of Venezuela*. Princeton University Press. New Jersey.

Seel, D.C. (1976). Moult in five species of Corvidae in Britain. *Ibis* 118: 491-536.

Selander, R.K. (1959). Polymorphism in Mexican Brown Jays. *Auk* 76: 385-417.

Severinghaus, L.L. (1987). Flocking and cooperative breeding of Formosan Blue Magpie. *Bull. Inst. Zool. Academia Sinica* 26: 27-37.

Sharpe, R.B. (1907). A note on *Podoces pleskei* Zarudny. *Journal Bombay Nat. Hist. Soc.* 17: 554-557.

Shirihai, H. (in preparation). *The Birds of Israel*.

Sibley, C.G. and J.E. Ahlquist. (1990). *Phylogeny and Classification of Birds*. Yale University Press. New Haven and London.

Sibley, C.G. and B.L. Monroe, Jr. (1990). *Distribution and Taxonomy of Birds of the World*. Yale University Press. New Haven and London.

Skarphedinsson, K.H. et al. (1990). Breeding biology, movements and persecution of Ravens in Iceland. *Acta Nat. Islandica* 33.

Skead, C.J. (1952). A study of the Black Crow Corvus capensis. *Ibis* 94: 434-451.

Slater, P., Slater, P. and R. Slater. (1986). *The Slater Field Guide to Australian Birds*. Rigby. Dee Why West.

Smalley, M.E. (1984). Predation by Pied Crows Corvus albus on Gambian

Epauletted Fruit Bats *Epomphorus gambianus*. *Bull. Brit. Orn. Club* 104: 77-79.

Smith, P.W. (1985). *American Birds* 39: 255-258.

Smith, S.W. (1992). *Bird Recordings from Irian Jaya*. Tape Cassette. Smith. Lymington.

Smith, S.W. (1993). *Bird Recordings from the Moluccas*. Tape Cassette. Smith. Lymington.

Smith, S.W. (1993). *Bird Recordings from the Lesser Sundas*. Tape Cassette. Smith. Lymington.

Smythies, B.E. (1953). *The Birds of Burma*. Oliver and Boyd. London.

Smythies, B.E. (1981). *The Birds of Borneo*. 3rd edn. The Sabah Society and the Malayan Nature Society. Sabah and Kuala Lumpur.

Sopyev, O. (1964). On the breeding biology of Pander's Ground-Jay. *Invest. Akad. Nauk. Turkmeji. S.S.R., Ser. biol.* 4: 56-62.

Stepanyan, L.S. (1990). *Conspectus of the Ornithological Fauna of the USSR*. Nauka. Moscow (in Russian).

Stiles, F.G. and Skutch, A.F. (1989). *A Guide to the Birds of Costa Rica*. Christopher Helm. London.

Stresemann, E. (1940). Discussion and review of A. Kleiner's Systematic Studien uber die Corviden. *Ornith. Monatsber.* 48: 102-104.

Stresemann, E. (1943). Die Gattung *Corvus* in Australien and Neuguinea. *J. Orn* 91: 121-135.

Stresemann, E. and G. Heinrich. (1940). Die Vogel von Celebes. *J. Orn.* 88: 16-18.

Svensson, L. (1992). *Identification Guide to European Passerines*. Svensson. Stockholm.

Swanberg, P.O. (1951). Food storage, territory and song in the Thick-billed Nutcracker. *Proc. 10th Int. Orn. Congress* 1950: 497-501.

Symens, P. (1990). Effects of the mass migration of desert locusts *Schistocerca gregaria* on the birds of the Taif area, Saudi Arabia. *Sandgrouse* 12: 3-7.

Terres, J.K. (1980). *The Audubon Society Encyclopedia of North American Birds*. Alfred A. Knopf. New York.

Ticehurst, C.B., Buxton, P.A. and R.E. Cheeseman. (1922). The Birds of Mesopotamia. *J. Bombay Nat. Hist. Soc.* 28: 210-250, 381-447 and 937-956.

Tomback, D.F. (1986). Observations on the behaviour and ecology of the Mariana Crow. *Condor* 88: 398-401.

Turcek, F.J. and Kelso, L. (1968). Ecological aspects of food transportation and storage in the Corvidae. *Comm. Behav. Biol.* 1: 277-297.

Urban, E.K. (1980). *Ethiopia's Endemic Birds*. Ethiopian Tourist Commission. Addis Ababa.

Urban, E.K. and L.H. Brown (1971). *A Checklist of the Birds of Ethiopia*. Haile Sellassie 1 University Press. Addis Ababa.

van Marle, J.G. and K.H. Voous. (1988). *The Birds of Sumatra*. BOU. London.

Vaurie, C. (1954). Systematic notes on Palearctic birds. No.5. Corvidae. *American Museum Novitates* no. 1668.

Vaurie, C. (1958). Remarks on some Corvidae of Indo-Malaya and the Australian Region. *American Museum Novitates* no. 1915.

Vaurie, C. (1959). *The Birds of the Palearctic Fauna*. vol. 1. Witherby. London.

Vaurie, C. (1964). A survey of the Birds of Mongolia. *Bull. Amer. Mus. Nat. Hist.* 127: 103-144.

Vaurie, C. (1972). *Tibet and its Birds*. Witherby. London.

Verbeek, N.A.M. and R.W.W. Butler. (1991). Cooperative breeding of the Northwestern Crow Corvus caurinus in British Columbia. *Ibis* 123: 183-189.

Vinicombe, K., Harris, A. and Tucker, L. (1989). *The Macmillan Field Guide to Bird Identification*. Macmillan. London and Basingstoke.

Voous, K.H. (1950). The post-glacial distribution of Corvus monedula in Europe. *Limosa* 23: 281-292.

Voous, K.H. (1960). *Atlas of European Birds*. Nelson. London.

Voous, K.H. (1977). *List of Recent Holarctic Bird Species*. BOU. London.

Webber, T. and J.L. Brown. (In press). *Natural History of the Unicolored Jay in Chiapas,*

Mexico. *Proceedings of the Western Foundation of Vertebrate Zoology*.

Webber, T. and J.W. Hardy. (1985). Breeding and behaviour of Tamaulipas Crows Corvus imparatus in captivity. *Avicultural Mag.* 91: 191-198.

Welch, G.R. and H.J. Welch. (1984). Birds seen on an expedition to Djibouti. *Sandgrouse* 6: 1-23.

Wetmore, A. and B.H. Swales. (1931). The Birds of Haiti and the Dominican Republic. *U.S. Nat. Mus. Bull.* No. 155.

White, C.M.N. and M.D. Bruce. (1986). *The Birds of Wallacea*. BOU. London.

Williams, M.D. (ed). (1986). *Report on the Cambridge Ornithological Expedition to China 1985*. Scarborough.

Willis, E.O. and Y. Oniki. (1993). New and reconfirmed birds from the state of Sao Paulo, Brazil, with notes on disappearing species. *Bull. Brit. Orn. Club* 113: 23-34.

Wilmore, S.B. (1977). *Crows, Jays and Ravens*. David and Charles. Newton Abbot.

Wilson, T. and G. Balcha. (1989). Temporal and spatial ecology of the Birds of Ethiopia: Order, Passeriformes; Family, Corvidae. *Walia* 12: 30-34.

Witherby, H.F., Jourdain, F.C.R., Ticehurst, N.F. and B.W. Tucker. (1938). *The Handbook of British Birds*. vol. 1. Witherby. London.

Yeates, G.K. (1934). *The Life of the Rook*. London.

Yeatman, L. (1976). *Atlas des Oiseaux Nicheurs de France*. Societe Ornithologique de France. Paris.

Zarudny, N.A. (1911). Verzeichnis der Vogel Persiens. *J.f.O* 1911 : 185-240.

INDEX

INDEX OF ENGLISH AND SCIENTIFIC NAMES

Plate references are given in bold. Alternative vernacular names have only a text page entry. Subspecific names are not included in the index but the most frequently encountered synonyms are.

ADDITIONAL INFORMATION

MARIANA CROW   Plate 23   Text page 144

VOICE: Two call types have been documented. A series of harsh, high-pitched squawks, described as higher-pitched and more nasal than that of American Crow, given by birds in flight through forest or when greeting returning partner. A softer, squeakier call is uttered from foraging parties on the forest floor.

HABITS: An unobtrusive and relatively quiet foest crow, typically in small parties of 4 or 5, rarely up to 14, birds feeding in tree canopy or foraging on the forest floor. Mated pairs seem to keep in close contact, perching together and preening each other; foraging groups are presumed to be family parties which seem to keep together for some time after fledging. These crows search noisily through leaf-litter on the forest floor for various invertebrates and small reptiles, especially grasshoppers and lizards. Various plant materials, including flowers and buds, are also taken; they have a habit of spending much time hammering pieces of bark from tree trunks and broken branches, which are then eaten. Eggs from nests of other birds are readily taken, the crows sometimes being chased by other small birds, especially Micronesian Starlings and Black Drongos; conversely, they will also chase other birds themselves, chiefly Mariana Fruit Doves. Although generally wary of man, where unmolested can be quite confiding, allowing approach to within a few metres.

BREEDING: Solitary nester. Nest an untidy structure of branches, laid in criss-cross manner, at a height of at least 13m from the ground in a large fig tree. Clutch and eggs undescribed but adults with two and one recently fledged young suggest that the clutch sizes are small. Interestingly both adults take part in nest construction and both sexes are believed to share incubation (Jenkins 1983) but this needs further investigation, as shared incubation is exceptional in corvids. Breeding season seems to be protracted; possibly capable of breeding at almost anytime of the year: adults with fledglings have been noted in May, June, September and October: nest construction recorded in November and December.

FAN-TAILED RAVEN   Plate 26   Text page 181

GEOGRAPHICAL VARIATION: Two races differing in size.
C. r. rhipidurus: African range of the species.
C. r. stanleyi: Middle East and Sinai, smaller than African race. Wing 349-373, bill 50-58.